Constitutional Modernism

Constitutional Modernism

ARCHITECTURE AND CIVIL SOCIETY IN CUBA, 1933–1959

Timothy Hyde

UNIVERSITY OF MINNESOTA PRESS
MINNEAPOLIS • LONDON

This book is supported by a grant from the Graham Foundation for Advanced Studies in the Fine Arts.

The University of Minnesota Press gratefully acknowledges the work of Edward Dimendberg, editorial consultant, on this project.

Portions of the text have been published in Timothy Hyde, "Planos, planes y planificación: Josep Lluís Sert and the Idea of Planning," in *Josep Lluís Sert: The Architect of Urban Design,* ed. Eric Mumford and Hashim Sarkis (New Haven: Yale University Press, 2008), 55–75; and in Timothy Hyde, "Mejores ciudades, ciudadanos mejores: Law and Architecture in the Cuban Republic," in *Governing by Design: Architecture, Economy, and Politics in the Twentieth Century,* Aggregate (Pittsburgh: University of Pittsburgh Press, 2012).

Published by the University of Minnesota Press
111 Third Avenue South, Suite 290
Minneapolis, MN 55401-2520
http://www.upress.umn.edu

Library of Congress Cataloging-in-Publication Data

Hyde, Timothy.
Constitutional modernism : architecture and civil society in Cuba, 1933–1959 / Timothy Hyde.
Includes bibliographical references and index.
ISBN 978-0-8166-7810-5 (hardback) — ISBN 978-0-8166-7811-2 (pb)
1. Architecture and society—Cuba—History—20th century. 2. City planning—Cuba—History—20th century. 3. Modern movement (Architecture)—Cuba. I. Title.
NA2543.S6H93 2013
720.1′1309729109044—dc23
2012043823

Printed in the United States of America on acid-free paper

The University of Minnesota is an equal-opportunity educator and employer.

20 19 18 17 16 15 14 13 12 10 9 8 7 6 5 4 3 2 1

Contents

Abbreviations

AIA	American Institute of Architects
ATEC	Agrupación Tectónica de Expresión Contemporánea (Tectonic Group of Contemporary Expression)
BANDES	Banco de Desarrollo Económico y Social (Economic and Social Development Bank)
BANFAIC	Banco de Fomento Agrícola e Industrial de Cuba (Cuban Agricultural and Industrial Development Bank)
CIAM	Congrès Internationaux d'Architecture Moderne (International Congresses of Modern Architecture)
FC	Félix Candela Papers
GATEPAC	Grup d'Arquitectes i Tècnics Españoles per al Progrés de l'Arquitectura Contemporània (Group of Spanish Architects and Technicians for the Progress of Contemporary Architecture)
GSD	Graduate School of Design
JL	Jean Labatut Papers
JLS	José Luis Sert Collection
JNE	Junta Nacional de Economía (National Economy Board)
JNP	Junta Nacional de Planificación (National Planning Board)

MARS	Modern Architectural Research Group
MIT	Massachusetts Institute of Technology
OPRH	Oficina del Plan Regulador de la Habana (Office of the Master Plan of Havana)
PLW	Paul Lester Wiener Collection
SOM	Skidmore, Owings, and Merrill
TPA	Town Planning Associates

Introduction

Constitutionalism and Civil Society

> Before their appearance as material entities, cities had to be constructed as symbolic representations. Therefore, the permanence of the whole depended on the immutability of the signs themselves—on the words that transmitted the will to build the city in accordance with the stipulated norms—and also on the diagrams that translated the will into graphic terms. Without drawn plans the mental image created by the written directives was more likely to suffer permutations owing to local conditions or inexpert execution. Thinking the city was the function of these symbolic systems, and their growing autonomy suited them increasingly to the manipulations of absolute authority.
>
> —Ángel Rama, *The Lettered City*

Three photographs on the cover of the March 1955 issue of *Arquitectura* present a trinity of monumental public buildings: the Catedral de la Habana, the Capitolio Nacional, and, superimposed upon the other two, the new Tribunal de Cuentas (Figure I.1). This grouping of images portrays the seeming inevitability of a progressive development of Cuban architecture from the baroque style of the early colonial period, to the neoclassicism of the late nineteenth and early twentieth century, to the modernism of the postwar decades. The images evoke also a lineage for the progressive development of the Cuban nation, from its colonial past to its modern present, but it is a lineage charted in the latent terms of the persistent sway of hegemonic powers in Cuba. The Catedral was a symbol and reminder of the island's long existence as a Spanish colony, and though idiosyncrasies in its baroque form could be claimed as uniquely Cuban, it remained in 1955 an embodiment of the universalizing intention and the institutional reach of the former imperial enterprise. As for the

Capitolio Nacional, its quite faithful mimicry of the forms of the Capitol of the United States testified unmistakably to the political subordination of Cuba to its northern neighbor that persisted for decades after its independence from Spain. The newest building, which housed the government comptroller, demonstrated the internationalization of influence, with the modernist tropes of an international regionalism suggesting Cuba's dependence on the economic and cultural products circulating through international markets. More broadly, each building vividly recorded the presence of architecture within the social and political structure of Cuba at a given historical moment, and it is with the emphatic depiction of these presences that this trinity of images prompts the initial question of this book—how does architecture make its appearance in civil society?

This book explores the reciprocations of architecture and political circumstance in order to examine how architecture is incorporated within the developing course of civil society—the formal and informal mechanisms that organize exchanges among citizens and between citizens and the state, and that are themselves perpetuated through institutions and customs in order to manage the frictions and the desires of a body politic. By 1955, Cuba's historical progression as indexed by the three photographs had arrived at the autocratic rule of Fulgencio Batista. With civil society the venue for architecture's appearance, the modern architecture of the newly established Tribunal de Cuentas could no more be separated from the pervasive financial speculation and the sweeping financial corruption that were woven into Batista's regime than the cathedral building could have been separated from the prior encompassing philosophical and institutional organization of the Catholic church. Although bound up with the repressions of Batista's rule in the late 1950s, the architectural appearance of the Tribunal de Cuentas was framed by a longer period bracketed by two revolutions in 1933 and 1959, a period during which modern architecture participated in a singular convergence of influences. In the first half of the twentieth century, Cuba maintained many aspects of the cultural and social formations developed in the Spanish colonial period that had ended only a few decades earlier. As Cuba came increasingly under the political and the cultural influence of North America, European culture still remained a strong orientation for Cuban intellectuals and professionals. The result was a mix of colonial anachronisms, self-conscious traditions, and imported innovations that were through various mediums synthesized into modern tendencies.

FIGURE I.1 Cover of the March 1955 issue of *Arquitectura*, the journal of the Colegio Nacional de Arquitectos.

From 1933 to 1959, through periods of democracy and periods of dictatorship, and through optimistic moments of economic prosperity and uncertain moments of economic constraint, this convergence produced a cosmopolitan sphere of cultural activity whose intensity was all the more remarkable given the relative smallness of the island. Concentrated in Havana, this activity drew upon a sense of the uniqueness of Cuba's path into modernity, with the colonial legacy, Afro-Cuban traditions, and international modernism providing the spur for the imaginings of the novelist Alejo Carpentier or the poet Nicolás Guillén, for the paintings of Wilfredo Lam and Amelia Peláez, and for the music of Armando Romeu Jr. Over the three decades, architects in Cuba also absorbed the effects of this convergence, with successive groups of young architects utterly transforming the physical appearance of Havana and its suburbs. Civic buildings such as the Escuela de Ciencias designed by Pedro Martínez Inclán, or the Teatro Nacional designed by Nicolás Arroyo and Gabriela Menéndez, demonstrated the percipient transformation of the public realm as much as houses and apartment buildings by Eugenio Batista, Max Borges, or Mario Romañach did that of the private sphere of domestic life. Across developing tendencies of Cuban architecture ran also the strong influence of international architectural practices. Large firms such as Harrison & Abramovitz and Skidmore, Owings, and Merrill had commissions in Cuba, as did well-known architects such as José Luis Sert, Paul Lester Wiener, Jean Labatut, and Félix Candela.[1] With the design of a national monument (in the case of Labatut) or the design of a future Havana (in the case of Sert and Wiener), these architects with their Cuban counterparts placed architecture centrally within the compass of an emerging construction of civil society.

Like the Tropicana nightclub with its stage lined with showgirls, or a Mafia-owned casino filled with disinhibited tourists, or other iconic images of Batista's final years in power, the Tribunal de Cuentas marks only the concluding stage of a longer period and cannot be taken as a summary for the preceding decades. It is the constellation of the three photographs on the *Arquitectura* cover that offers the more definite synecdoche for the years between 1933 and 1959. The Catedral evokes the narrowed streets and stone *palacios* of Habana Vieja, the colonial quarter of the city, and seems to evoke also the delayed procession of the nation into independence. The Capitolio testifies to that independence but also corresponds to impressions of a tropical city now laced with wide boulevards and the defining arc of the Malecón. Modern Havana, with its expanding suburbs of Vedado and Miramar and streets lined with the latest automobiles from Detroit, followed from these earlier cities. In terms of physical fabric and the persistence of buildings, the modern city coexisted with its predecessors, and in terms of cultural imagination, the three cities were blended together in the currents of nationalism after 1933. Yet in terms of the manifestations of civil society, a distinction should be drawn between the three historical cities. Of the three exemplary buildings, the two earlier historical embodiments, the Catedral and the Capitolio, were both embedded within paradigmatic conceptions of law, the authority of the church as a manifestation of natural law in the former, and the legacy of Enlightenment theories of positive law in the latter. The third building, the Tribunal de Cuentas, was embedded within a conceptualization of civil society in Cuba that had commenced with the formulation of a paradigm of law defined with the drafting and promulgation of a new Cuban constitution in 1940, which provoked the elaboration of a larger concept of constitutionalism to underlie and encompass the actualization of the civic sphere.

This book argues that constitutionalism produced a potent and decisive confluence of law and architecture and is the crucial theoretical framework to elucidate the acts of design undertaken during this period of Cuba's history. The account that follows defines constitutionalism as mode of projection, a means to shape or plan the future of Cuba that employed conceptual strategies such as normalization and historical schemata such as prefiguration in order to achieve the transformational identification of a priori conditions as the foundation and the legitimation of a not yet accomplished future. This translation of the past into a deferred future was the central act of the drafting of the Cuban Constitution of 1940, which aimed to fulfill what was regarded as Cuba's incomplete historical transition from colony to nation by the establishment of a stable and durable civil society. With the motives of social and cultural activities thus oriented and conjoined, constitutionalism also sustained the purposiveness of those activities by drawing them toward a condensed aim, the construction of civil society. Constitutionalism functioned as a conceptual mode extending across several discourses, architecture prominently among them, through which such constitutional mechanisms and motivations were produced and reproduced by other disciplinary practices and intentions. For these discourses, constitutionalism offered principles of exchange, circulation, and transmission necessary for their disciplinary constructions of elements and processes in civil society. For example, the didactic programs of public education and the didactic intentions of modern architecture shared an obligation to define the uniqueness of Cuban experience within a common narrative of human endeavor, an obligation that derived its corresponding contours from the constitutional mandate to reconcile individual action and collective purpose. Here constitutionalism supplemented general motives such as nationalism or regionalism with the more definite aims of civil society, such as the self-identification of citizens or the classification of effective historical customs and forms. And to architecture—understood as a civic building by Martínez Inclán or a monument by Labatut; as housing designed by Mario Romañach or Nicolás Quintana; or as urban plans devised by Sert and Wiener—to this architecture particularly, constitutionalism presented the decisive ground of representation.

Conceptual abstractions such as the "nation" or the "people" conventionally have their representational correlatives contained in categories such as regionalism or identity. Because these categories are construed from the expressed characteristics of objects and behaviors, the diffuse abstraction of nation, for example, is understood to be revealed through concrete manifestations of legible form and materiality. The examination of constitutionalism proposed here enables a different inquiry into representation, a different understanding of the performance of architecture (and other aesthetic productions) as a conjunction of culture and politics. Architecture represents, and so assumes simultaneously a passive subordinance to and an active command over that which it represents. Any evaluation of architecture as a representation should therefore open a complex confluence of disciplinary practices, social conventions, and, finally, political possibilities and impossibilities. A representation, understood not simply as a consequential image but as a constitutive process of representing, incorporates the construal of the history that surrounds it and in so doing incorporates also specific presumptions about the actualization of the future. This book undertakes to discern these incorporations, in order to render not only the performance of a constellation of architectural projects in and through civil society in Cuba, but also the occasion and circumstance of that architecture making its appearance. The account of the Cuban republic that follows examines constitutionalism precisely because the engagement of architecture with constitutionalism in this period of Cuba's history enabled architecture to contribute, as a process of representation, to the formulation of civil society. Quite simply, constitutionalism was the medium through which architecture made its appearance.

Modernism and the Project of Reform

In the former colonies of Spanish America, the relationship between the law and the city—between legal and urban forms—was deeply embedded. Its origin lay in the ordinances drafted by Spanish kings in the sixteenth century to authorize and regulate the exploration and colonization of the New World.[2] Compiled together, the resulting 148 ordinances comprised a comprehensive plan for the settlement of the new territories and the subordination of their inhabitants to the Spanish Crown. Las Leyes de Indias (The Laws of the Indies), as they came to be known, granted license of discovery, stipulated principles to be followed in encounters with the inhabitants of the territories, specified where and how new towns and cities were to be founded, detailed the formal character and configuration of these towns as well as their distribution of land as property and their structure of government. Some of the articles supplied broad directives, advising, for example, that new towns should be located near available water and in sites with beneficial orientation to the sun and prevailing winds. Others issued narrow requirements, such as the exact dimensions of the two permissible types of urban lots. The typical form of colonial cities in the New World—with a Plaza de Armas fronted by the edifices of church and state placed at the center of a gridded plan of *cuadras* (blocks) that extended outward with ordinal regularity—resulted from the principles delineated in the Laws of the Indies.

In his posthumously published *La ciudad letrada (The Lettered City),* Ángel Rama proposed an interpretive examination of the significance of the Laws of the Indies in the cultural formation of Latin American cities.[3] Rama pointed out that it was the requisite order (a word, he noted, that recurred with great frequency in the very earliest instructions) of the desired social structure that compelled the physical order of the urban grid, projected through the intermediate rational language of geometry. "More important than the much-discussed grid design," Rama wrote, "are the general principles behind it, directing a whole series of transmitted directives . . . so that the distribution of urban space would reproduce and confirm the desired social order. But even more important is the principle postulated in the quoted directives of the king: before anything may be built, the city must be *imagined* in order to avoid circumstances that might interfere with its ordained norms."[4] The ordinances were not passive translations, but active ones that produced a necessary mediation between the abstract conception of order and the realities of physical form; they were in themselves substantive, functional symbolic representations, constructed first, in order to then enable the subsequent construction of the actual city. As a consequence, Rama realized, the Latin American city sustained itself as two parallel existences, as a real, material site of accident and invention, and also as symbolic configuration, always already complete and enduring. This latter city, moreover, was not merely a diagram or description. Recognizing the historical importance of *los letrados*—the notaries, scribes, and lawyers whose literacy gave them a privileged status in the textual machine of Spanish colonial administration, and whose cultural role was subsequently inherited by the writers and journalists of modern Latin America—Rama proposed the image of *la ciudad letrada,* a figurative city populated, controlled, and directed by the *letrados* who, through their institutions and structures of communication and exchange, circulated the documents that stipulated, interpreted, and enforced the norms to be enacted in the visible city. This lettered city, Rama insisted, had accompanied the urban environments of Latin America since its scale and intentions had first emerged from the royal instructions of the sixteenth century; it was present still in the twentieth century in the institutions and individuals whose activities continued to confirm the reciprocity of urban forms, social organizations, and legal norms. In the twentieth century, *la ciudad letrada* was a symbolic yet comprehensive system of laws and individual and institutional agents, an order that was distinct from, yet also inextricably linked to, the facts of the real city. "*Thinking the city,*" in Rama's pointed phrasing, was the purpose of these manipulable symbolic systems, which were as susceptible as the real city to the caprice or conversely the resolution of the agents of civil society who attempted to achieve and to defend the correspondence between the two.[5]

In Cuba, beginning in the late 1930s, the establishment of an enduring civil society was seen to entail the production of just such a correspondence, and in consequence constitutionalism prompted an attention toward the city, as an object, a concept, and a discourse; not only the physical city (with Havana serving always as the privileged specimen) but also the abstract city of regulations and institutions, equally susceptible to transformation and from many perspectives in similarly urgent need of reform. For, in its first three decades as an independent nation, Cuba had endured a turbulent political environment. When the other colonies of Spanish America gained independence in the early nineteenth century, Cuba remained as a vestige of the Spanish empire. Although the first war of independence, begun in 1868 and continued for ten years, ended in the defeat of the first generation of revolutionaries, the independence movement persisted into the final decade of that century. Under the leadership of José Martí, who would come to be regarded as the founding figure of the Cuban nation, a new revolt began in 1895. The United States, motivated by the opportunity to consolidate its hemispheric influence, declared war on Spain and assumed the guise of liberator. A defeated Spain relinquished the colony in 1898 and political independence was formally gained through a new Cuban constitution drafted in 1901 and promulgated in 1902; but that charter was deeply compromised by the appendage of the Platt Amendment, which reserved for the United States the right to intervene in Cuba at any time either to deter a threat to the new nation's independence or to maintain the stability of its government. In the following years, the U.S. government invoked the Platt Amendment both as a cautionary threat and as sanction for actual interventions, and the persistence of this extranational authority prevented the attainment of real national sovereignty. The consequent influence over Cuban political and economic affairs caused recurrent disruptions in both of those spheres, which, along with the persistence of pervasive government corruption, spurred the steady increase of civil protest.[6]

These dissensions crested in 1922 and 1923, in opposition to the government of President Alfredo Zayas, as a number of groups pressed for the reform of various aspects of Cuban civil society. Students led a successful revolt to purge patronage positions from the University of Havana and to obtain its institutional autonomy. Several young writers carried out the public Protesta de los Trece (Protest of the Thirteen) in the forum of the Academy of Sciences. Business leaders organized the Asociación de Buen Gobierno (Association of Good Government) to later be a political platform for their interests. Prominent intellectuals and professionals formed the Junta Cubana de Renovación Nacional (Cuban Committee for National Renewal), issuing a manifesto for national reform.[7] The membership represented a socially and politically influential constituency, including the anthropologist Fernando Ortiz, the architect Pedro Martínez Inclán, the philosopher Jorge Mañach, historian Emilio Roig de Leuchsenring, and Professor Ramón Grau San Martín, who would serve as president of Cuba. As a whole, such agitations consolidated a general impetus for fundamental reforms in the civic sphere and, in addition, gathered a cast of individuals who would continue to advance this project of reform over the next quarter century. The diverse activities of these protagonists as an informal coalition prompted the convergence of different disciplines, resulting in an overlap of the professional, intellectual, and aesthetic discourses of Cuban civil society. Jurisprudence, or public hygiene, or literature—a practitioner in any one of these fields could find in the others a parallel effort toward modernization framed in a similar language of civic reform.

The convergence of disciplinary and political concerns became readily visible in 1927, when the founders of the Grupo Minorista published a declaration in the magazine *Carteles* advocating the "new art" and the "latest artistic and scientific doctrines, theories, and practices" and denouncing "Yankee imperialism" and "outrages of pseudodemocracy."[8] Mañach and Roig de Leuchsenring signed the declaration, as did the writers Alejo Carpentier and Francisco Ichaso, the sculptor Juan José Sicre, the critic and dramatist Luis A. Baralt, the journalist Armando Maribona, and the publisher of *Carteles,* Alfredo T. Quilez. By this time the presidency was held by Gerardo Machado. An enormous program of public works underwritten by loans from American banks had gained him an initial stage of public approbation, but in 1928 his already corrupt regime became a dictatorial one as Machado illegally extended his term in office without reelection. Violent confrontations with his political opposition commenced, with bombings and assassinations daily events in Havana by the end of 1932, and the United States began to press for Machado's resignation under the threat of intervention. Machado resisted for several more months, but finally ceded power in August 1933 to a collective government formed by opposition groups. This short-lived government was overthrown in September in the Sergeants' Revolution, a military rebellion led by Sergeant Fulgencio Batista that had begun as a petition of grievances within the ranks but by circumstance developed into a political coup. Promoted to colonel and chief of the army, Batista held power behind a succession of presidents whom he installed during the next year.[9] The various revolutionary groups and constituencies that had opposed Machado consolidated and dissolved numerous alliances as these formal governments were removed through force or impeachment. In 1934, the U.S. government was finally willing to recognize the new administration (now nominally headed by Colonel Carlos Mendieta) and signed a treaty with Cuba to abrogate the Platt Amendment. With the abrogation, Cuba acquired actual sovereignty, a basic prerequisite for the national aspirations formulated by the advocates of reform.

The remaining prerequisite—a stable, and ultimately democratic, civil society—depended on the resolution of the constitutional question. One of the first reforms of the 1933 revolution had been the provisional restoration of the Constitution of 1901, which Machado had altered to extend his unelected term. But the Platt Amendment still rendered the original text a flawed charter. Moreover, the 1901 constitution, drafted in the very different context of independence from colonial rule, had not addressed the social and economic issues that were now primary concerns of political debate and that many partisans desired to resolve into fundamental law. Inadequacies in the prevailing constitution were mitigated partially by the abrogation of the Platt Amendment and by more than a dozen provisional constitutional laws and their accompanying modifications, but the haphazard compilation that served as the fundamental charter during the later 1930s seemed to reflect the uncertainties of the political situation itself. Fulgencio Batista, intent on retaining power, announced a number of social and economic reforms in 1937. Interviewed by the newspaper *Diario de la Marina*, Batista defended his view of such interventions: "Others want to see in me a simple guardian of order. But what do they understand by order? Because, I view this more as a concept of architecture rather than police work."[10]

By this time, with the presidency occupied by Federico Laredo Bru and an uneasy balance, though not an actual truce, struck between partisans of different political alignments and varying degrees of radicalism, a consensus had emerged that the next event in the political development of Cuba must be the drafting of a comprehensively new constitution. This process would not be solely a political event, for though the projected constitution was obviously a political instrument, it would assume an influential significance and value in relation to other cultural dimensions of civil society as professional practices and intellectual activities contributed directly and indirectly to the formulation and the propagation of a new constitutional basis. In the city of Havana—the political capital and also the cultural and financial center of the nation—a relatively small group of individuals engaged in extended exchanges and debates on issues of nation and history and modernity that set cultural events in close parallel with political ones, often enough through the work of a single person. Jorge Mañach, for example, was at once a leader of the radical ABC political party, organizer of the radio broadcast *Universidad del Aire*, a writer for *Diario de la Marina*, an editor of *Revista de Avance*, and a delegate to the constitutional convention. Political reform and artistic modernism were joint endeavors to Mañach, for whom the definition of *cubanidad,* or Cuban identity, would emerge equally through the articles of a constitution as in essayistic articles like his own "Indagación del choteo" (Investigation of mockery, a famous explication of the tenor of Cuban humor). Few could match Mañach's range of activities, but many of the individuals involved did circulate in more than one constituency.[11] Emilio Roig de Leuchsenring trained as a lawyer and early in his career participated in commissions charged with revising the civil code Cuba inherited from Spain. Named Historian of the City of Havana in 1935, Roig de Leuchsenring for the next three decades wrote prolifically in popular and scholarly contexts about the history of Havana and Cuba; his major works adopted an unhesitating political cast as purposeful contributions to a strengthening nationalism. Fernando Ortiz, an anthropologist and ethnographer by discipline and a politician and reform leader by deed, disseminated ideas into virtually every salient discourse in Cuba. The influence of his *Contrapunteo cubano del tabaco y el azúcar (Cuban Counterpoint: Tobacco and Sugar),* published in 1940, with its defining perspective on Cuban culture, and his studies of folklore and Afro-Cuban traditions carried into paintings and novels, into legislation and scholarship.[12] Ortiz was a central figure in the many *tertulias* (salons) that gathered individuals with similarly wide-ranging careers, whose discussions extended outward through essays and lectures, government committees and professional associations. From the early 1930s until the late 1950s, the smallness of professional and intellectual circles, and their predominantly middle- or upper-class *habanero* membership, fostered the overlapping endeavors and exchanges between these institutional localities, exchanges that were often further disseminated through radio programs, newspaper articles, and public exhibitions.

The precocious engagement with modernist practices that occurred in Cuba coincided with the widespread initiative toward reform. Indeed, that engagement occurred in part because of the advocacy for reform. The revolutionary change of political institutions, the modernization of the city, the transformation of social relations—the affinity between these central motives of the modernist discourse to which Cuban intellectuals were turning and the programs of reform those same intellectuals were initiating was distinct and unmistakable. The architect Pedro Martínez Inclán, a member of the Junta Cubana de Renovación Nacional, had argued for the modernization of Cuban cities in the 1920s and in 1949 published a *Código de Urbanismo* (Code of urbanism) that applied to Havana the doctrines of urbanism developed in modernist discourse in Europe. While his own designs held to a strain of neoclassicism, Martínez Inclán also, as a member of the Colegio de Arquitectos and of the faculty of the School of Architecture, supported the entry of modernist architectural discourse into the academy. The younger architects whose programs and practices Martínez Inclán supported sought out direct contact with leading international figures. Nicolás Arroyo and other recent graduates, for example, took advantage of the temporary residence of José Luis Sert in Cuba in 1939 to create a Cuban chapter of CIAM (Congrès Internationaux d'Architecture Moderne). Sert, who was then completing the manuscript for his polemical study *Can Our Cities Survive?,* argued that modern architecture was the crucial means to revive the physical and social health of cities, and the subsequent collaboration between a circle of Cuban architects, Sert, and Sert's partner Paul Lester Wiener was predicated on a determinate link between design and reform. Another Cuban architect and planner, Eduardo Montoulieu Jr., came into contact with modernist ideas at the Graduate School of Design at Harvard, where he studied and where Dean Joseph Hudnut and Walter Gropius and later Sert as well espoused an understanding of the progressive capacities of architecture and urban design to accommodate and induce change. Montoulieu's articles for Cuban newspapers, his pamphlets, and the seminars he taught disseminated this central tenet as the promise of modernism in Cuba.[13]

Examining the entanglement of architecture and law in Cuba thus enables also a close consideration of the relation between modernism and reform, a relation that is inescapable and yet also insufficiently defined. A second question, then, to follow the initial one posed by this book, would be: how did modern architecture participate in processes of reform and change? In Cuba, as in the world more generally, modern architecture was certainly offered as a privileged discipline for the possibilities of reform, combining as it did technological innovation in its deployment of materials, methods, and forms; the management of human habits and desires in its accommodation of individuals and groups; and the organization of collective life in its urban configurations. Yet, when viewed separately, as it often is, through the isolated practices of a discourse, this capacity for reform and, more particularly, the impulse toward an idealist or utopian social and political reform held by modern architecture seems starkly diminished, with its projects depicted as naive, or ineffective, or complicit with other less emancipatory programs of change—naive because it failed to account for the density and idiosyncracy of real human behavior; ineffective because it neither possessed nor controlled the mediating instruments and institutions through which change would be conducted; and complicit because so many of its projects appeared over time to be channeled into the consolidation of managerial or technocratic regimens. Such diagnoses have not been wholly inaccurate, yet the reasons for such outcomes, the concatenation of events that precipitated such consequences, cannot be sufficiently elucidated without an explication of architecture's participation within larger contexts of reform. Conversely, a history that describes a process of change through the structures of implementation such as technical bodies or autocratic leaders, by eliding the influence and actions of frameworks or concepts from seemingly subordinate disciplines, describes that process as a determinism of cause and effect that obscures the refractions through which events occur.

Within modernism, the discipline of law, with its purview over the present and future course of social and political relations and with its relative independence from the constraints of materiality, was seen to hold a capacity for acts of reform similar to that held by architecture, a capacity perhaps even more extensive in its reach, though arguably less immediate in its physical effects. It is in the tangled confluence of these two—architecture and law—that the modernist project of transformation can be rendered with a finer and more accurate grain. In the historical context of the Cuban Republic, to describe reform and the potentiality of reform necessitates discerning events both in the institutions and governance of the real city and in the protocols and plans of *la ciudad letrada*. This book examines both spheres through the conjunction of architecture and law—a conjunction that had the city as its inevitable object and planning and urbanism as its corollary practices—in order to locate the refractions and exchanges between these spheres as the operations of reform. Given the inseparability of modernist practices from the central motive of reform, these refractions and exchanges may be regarded also as the operations of modernism itself.

Architecture and the Construction of History

Between the revolutions of 1933 and 1959 that bracketed the period of the Cuban Republic, the project for the formulation of civil society was sustained at times by and at times against prevailing political and social conditions.[14] These years included periods of democratic governance and periods of dictatorial rule, years of economic prosperity and years of economic constraint. The argument that follows traces the discursive reciprocities of architecture and law through the concept of constitutionalism in order to arrive at an understanding of the role and the potential of architecture in these contingent, changeable circumstances. In the late 1930s, there was, even among political opponents, a clear and common adherence to the goal of a stable legal order; in the 1940s, elected presidents and other civic figures attempted to instantiate the principles of democratic governance; and even during the 1950s, with the conflict between Batista's dictatorship and an opposition that included Fidel Castro's guerrilla rebellion precluding any similar concordance, the civic project still remained an evident and coherent aspiration. During these three decades and up to 1959—when the Cuban Revolution swept away existing political and social structures and with them this project of civil society—the future envisioned by the advocates of reform never did arrive at any full resolution; nor was the Constitution of 1940 ever more than partially implemented and enforced; and many of the architectural and urban propositions of those years remained unrealized projects. This book, therefore, is as much a history of potentialities as it is a history of actualities. Read from the perspective of architectural history, it will reveal how the modernist concepts and arguments that developed as an international discourse before the second world war evolved into the particular actions and consequences of modern architecture and urbanism in Cuba. In recounting the participation of familiar as well as less known figures of modernism, and in retracing the movement of familiar disciplinary tendencies, it will suggest how the abstractions of modernist architectural discourse came to be bound mutually to realities of governance, customs, and locality. Read from the perspective of Cuban history, or legal or cultural history more generally, the book will explain how not only the material products such as buildings or monuments, but also the immaterial disciplinary frameworks and methods of architecture as a cultural practice, produced representations that had a conditioning effect on their historical context. In proposing the concrete significance of this capacity within the apparent abstractions of architecture, it will suggest too the concrete significance of possibilities present in the Cuban Republic, the possibilities of other intentions and other consequences than those that transpired.

The book consists of three parts, each of which examines events in the full chronological span of republican Cuba from the early 1930s through to 1959 while focusing on a discrete object of the disciplinary exchanges that occurred in the project of civil society. The first part, "Constitution," presents both the history and a theoretical understanding of the Cuban Constitution of 1940, describing the principles and the intentions of constitutionalism that were derived from the format of the constitution and revealing the tangency between these principles and concurrently developing debates about national planning. An advocacy campaign undertaken through journalism and exhibitions by the Patronato Pro-Urbanismo (Pro-Urbanism Association) commenced shortly after the promulgation of the new constitution. This campaign and its eventual consolidation as the rationale for the creation in 1955 of a Junta Nacional de Planificación (National Planning Board) are retraced alongside the crucial rediscovery in Cuba of the Laws of the Indies as a model for the juridical origination of urban form. Legislative and architectural understandings of planning are shown to have been more than parallel conceptualizations; intertwined through the structuring means of diagrams and charters, they were the projective impetus for the reform mandated by the constitution.

The second part, "City," examines urban plans proposed for the city of Havana through the lens of constitutionalism; it considers the form and the probable effects of these plans as corollaries to the normalizing intent of constitutionalism and as the future sites of civil society. Starting with partially realized city plans designed by the French urbanist J. C. N. Forestier, the reorganization of Havana and the regulation of its growth became the central concern for architects attempting to refashion civic life through the physical form of streets, buildings, and districts. The Pilot Plan for Havana produced for the Junta Nacional de Planificación by the firm Town Planning Associates (in collaboration with Mario Romañach and other Cuban colleagues) provides the legible trace of a pursuit through design of the normalizing aims of the constitution. In the plan's proposed reconfiguration of the colonial quarter, Habana Vieja, the propositions of urban design are revealed to contain also the evidence of a complex articulation of history that was provoked by historicist presumptions underlying the constitution.

The third part, "Monument," discusses two architectural proposals, one built and the other unrealized, that were to represent civil society; it analyzes the capacity and the consequences of architecture within the context of constitutionalism.

The Monumento a Martí, a national monument to honor the Cuban patriot José Martí, designed by Jean Labatut, is examined first. The prolonged debate over the form this monument should take, and the varied course of its eventual realization, are deciphered for evidence of polemical antagonisms between alternative conceptions of modern architecture, and for underlying conceptions of how citizens themselves might be construed for and by an architectural object. The second project, the unrealized presidential palace designed by José Luis Sert and Mario Romañach with the engineer Félix Candela, offers an additional and concluding understanding of constitutionalism's temporal capacities. The figurative regimen of the palace, which consisted of abstracted royal palm trees symbolic of Cuba, is here exposed in its broader relation to a mimetic structure on which the constitution itself depended.

The three trajectories, and the textual, graphical, and physical artifacts that provide their orientation, have an analogical function, revealing through their commensurabilities the processes of representation, normalization, prefiguration, and deferral that are the composites of constitutionalism itself. In each part, the categorical object—the constitution, the city, the monument—serves to arrange and thereby bring into view what was a dynamic circulation of propositions, definitions, and intentions among a group of institutional and individual actors (several of whom appear in more than one part, and in more than one significant role). While numerous artifacts such as urban plans and monumental buildings, or expository texts and model regulations, are placed under examination, the method and indeed the aim pursued in this book is to make legible the discursive exchanges, to render the translations and transpositions between disciplines into meaningful objects in themselves. The artifacts are effectively the material evidence of a constellation of less tangible occurrences that are the primary subject of the book—they are the material evidence, in short, of constitutionalism. The sequence of three parts can be seen to descend in scale, in deceptively familiar fashion, from the expansive scale of planning and of the nation, to the scale of urban design and of the citizenry, and then to the scale of architecture and of the individual citizen. At the same time, however, the sequence of the three parts with their reiteration of the same decades in different perspectives is assembling the larger object of constitutionalism, and thereby assembles a distinctive concept of history formulated by the agents of constitutionalism, which architecture not only reflected, but helped to construct.

I

Constitution

1 The Idealized Republic

The Constitution of 1940

On July 1, 1940, the seventy delegates of the Constitutional Convention traveled to the eastern province of Camagüey, to the small town of Guáimaro, to ratify the new Cuban constitution with their signatures. The convention had met without interruption in the Capitolio Nacional in Havana for the preceding five months, and now that the fundamental law had been drafted and approved, the signing of the constitution was to be a historical performance, a recapitulation and a confirmation of the founding of the Cuban Republic. The very first republican constitution, declaring a sovereign national existence independent of Spanish colonial rule, had been drafted and signed by Cuban revolutionaries in Guáimaro in 1869. To pay homage to that precedent, and, equally important, to cast the new constitution as the fulfillment of the aspirations and intentions of the earlier one, delegates signed two handwritten copies of the document in a schoolhouse at the same site, and with the same table used by their revolutionary predecessors. One of the participants later described the surrounding festivities: spectators from the nearby countryside and from other provinces flooded into the "hamlet of wooden houses and colonial roofs." Local residents and visitors displayed the national colors on their traditional *polainas* and guayaberas, and the *guajiros* rode on horseback in the streets. This jubilant crowd followed the proceedings "under the cobalt canopy in which a sun, full of creole summer, warms the crowd already glowing with patriotic enthusiasm."[1] Spectators' shouts of "Viva Cuba Libre" were heard throughout the nation by citizens listening to the radio broadcast. Patriotic enthusiasm was summoned again in Havana four days later when the constitution was formally promulgated from the portico of the Capitolio Nacional. Delegates, joined by representatives of the government and armed forces, faced an "immense crowd that filled the flight of steps and overflowed into the sidewalks, streets, balconies, and rooftops of the surrounding buildings."[2] Speaking to the crowd and to the radio audience, the president of the convention officially promulgated the constitution. "The nation applauds," wrote the observer. "The future opens to the interrogation of destiny."[3]

The subtle formulation of this phrase, foreseeing both an open future and a destined national trajectory through that future, revealed the particular temporal responsibility of the 1940 constitution; it supplied a hinge between past and future, an armature to join together instances of national destiny already transpired and those still possible. The paired ceremonies for its ratification confirmed and made visible this temporal function by constructing an associative environment of contextual details. One event, held in a rural province in the countryside that had fostered the independence movement in the nineteenth century, was tied to the past. Morning in a small town, houses with "colonial roofs," spectators in customary dress, the iconic *guajiros* on horseback, in the diffused landscape of a "creole summer"; delegates approaching one by one the table, the tangible artifact of the past that transformed each present gesture of signing into a historical reenactment. The second event, held in the urban center in a capitol building inaugurated just eleven years earlier, embraced the future. Afternoon in the capital city, the huge stair opening to the plaza framed by tall commercial buildings, a dense crowd filling "streets, balconies, and rooftops"; the proclamation spoken and broadcast into the air summoned the future nation into the present. Either event on its own would have been insufficient to satisfy the temporal obligation borne by the constitution. Only when enacted through these two purposefully paired ceremonies, illuminated by the contrasting scenographies of their architectural backdrops, could the present act of constitution fuse these two temporal orientations.

At the same time, delegates and audience acknowledged the constitution to be directly a product of its own historical moment, distinct from past and future. Speaking of the first revolutionary constitution, one delegate sought to fix the "parallel between the spirit of Guáimaro and that of the new constitution" by proclaiming that both were inspired by the "desire to establish the idealized Republic." Yet, he said, an urgency distinguished that first constitution from the present one: "what in Guáimaro was haste, impatience, summary, here has been excess of precaution, of checks, doubt, delay, study, detail, remedy."[4] Regardless of whether or how long it endured into the future, he asserted, the new constitution would "always remain the faithful reproduction of an epoch and of the expression of the dreams of Cuba in those moments."[5] The moments marked by the constitution were understood to be moments of national transcendence in which the debilitating factionalism of Cuban politics had been overcome by a strong, common determination to erect the structure of a stable civil society.

Constitutions and Governance

In 1936, the Cuban government had, with the consent of Colonel Fulgencio Batista, commenced the process of constitutional reform by creating special commissions in the House of Representatives and the Senate to draw up proposals for a new constitution to be debated, modified, and ratified by a subsequent constitutional convention of elected delegates.[6] The commission of the House of Representatives based its draft on the 1901 constitution, proposing significant changes in the guarantees of individual rights and the addition of new governmental institutions. As the basis for its draft, the Senate commission adopted a text proposed by Dr. Gustavo Gutiérrez y Sánchez, who was the commission's technical adviser. Gutiérrez had previously served in the House of Representatives, been the secretary of justice, had taught in the Faculty of Law and Social Sciences at the University of Havana, and had written extensively about law and economics. He participated in the reform movements prior to the 1933 revolution and was associated with the Grupo Minorista. The text Gutiérrez proposed was a comprehensive reformulation of the constitution, with detailed proposals for the organic structure of government and for securing individual social and economic rights. After further modifications by both commissions, the full congress approved this text at the end of 1936 as the *Proyecto de reforma integral de la constitución* (Draft of the comprehensive reform of the constitution).[7]

In establishing a means to compose civil society, the articles of the *Proyecto de reforma integral* placed a new and special emphasis on social and economic dimensions in the form of progressive policies regarded as the gains of the revolution. It supplemented the individual rights that had been defined in the 1901 constitution with social rights ("derechos sociales") categorized under four "cornerstones" of Cuban society: family, culture, work, and property.[8] Articles divided under these headings asserted rights such as the freedom of the arts, sciences, and teaching, the universal right to education, a fundamental right of employment, and the rights of property. This last had been a point of particular contention, with political groups, business coalitions, and individuals with large landholdings all anxious to have their respective interests installed at the core of the constitution. The text offered a difficult compromise, with the fundamental guarantee of property secured but tempered by the recognition of its social function: "The State recognizes private property; but its use and exploitation have to be realized according to the inclinations of the Cuban people."[9]

The 1936 *Proyecto de reforma integral* formally initiated the constitutional process, and over the next three years other alternative drafts, along with numerous commentaries and partisan manifestos, hypothesized the substance and structure of the new constitution.[10] One such text, published under the title *La forma técnico-funcional de gobierno* (The technico-functional form of government), advocated for the new constitutional government a technocratic organization designed to represent broad constituencies rather than the narrow interests emphasized by partisan politics. Its author, an economist named José Luis Abalo, subscribed to the corporatist view that government should be organized into groups directly representing the competing interests of a society. He recommended the recognition of three broad constituencies, to be formally manifested as political bodies: *trabajadores capitalistas* (owners), *trabajadores no capitalistas* (workers), and *trabajadores profesionales y artísticas* (professionals and artists). In a new bicameral legislature, a Cámara de Representantes (Chamber of Representatives) would have 45 percent of its members elected from each of the first two groups and 10 percent from the last, while a Cámara de Senadores (Chamber of Senators) would be composed of thirty "specialists" selected by test or competition: ten economists, six engineers, six jurists, two hygienists, two educators, and four "individuals nationally or internationally famous for possessing exceptional culture and mental capacities."[11] Abalo contended that the representatives would be "a source, the most complete, specific, and exact, of information about the nature and form of the determinant factors of national life";[12] they would reveal the precise contours of the conflicts between the different interests that created the economic and social life of Cuba. The senators, by contrast, were to be technical assessors who, "because of their dedication to a specialty, [could be] divorced from the surrounding reality";[13] taking into account only specific facts and fundamental principles, these neutral assessors would determine the viability of the representatives' solutions and their likely effect on collective welfare.

Abalo's proposal aimed to establish social stability by formalizing an equilibrated relationship between social constituencies calibrated by a regulatory body of impartial experts.[14] This recourse to expertise through a "technico-functional" form of government was undoubtedly a response to existing partisanship and the corruptions of patronage. Gutiérrez had reacted similarly, suggesting in his original draft of the *Proyecto de reforma integral* that the bicameral legislature be composed of one chamber of "representatives" and a second chamber of "economic character called the 'Economic Council of the State'" that would replace the "antiquated" Senate.[15] (The final version restored the Senate as the second chamber, but still included the Economic Council as a separate organ responsible for defining the socioeconomic policy of the Republic.) But the inclusion of these technical organs in the constitutional proposals also corresponded to a more general prewar trend toward scientific governance. Positivism had pervaded Latin America in the latter half of the nineteenth century; one of its leading proponents was Enrique José Varona, a leader of the Cuban independence movement and central figure of the first republican decades. Even as Latin American intellectuals began to turn away from positivism and its perceived materialist affinity, the neighboring example of Franklin D. Roosevelt's Brains Trust and the extensive programs of the New Deal would have reinforced in Cuba a faith in the ability of the visible hands of technicians to mitigate the imperfections of political systems. The consequence of these models of a managerial government in Cuba was to create a direct connection between the constitutional project and professional activities. By proposing to replace antiquated parliamentary bodies with modern technical bodies, Abalo and Gutiérrez drew professionalism into the center of constitutional discussion, and professionals themselves into the cultural project of the constitution.

The strongest juridical influence on theories of constitutionalism in Cuba during this period was one specific strand of positivism, the legal theory of the Austrian jurist Hans Kelsen.[16] Founder of the Vienna School of legal philosophy, Kelsen formulated and propounded his Pure Theory of Law against the then competing tendencies of the metaphysical claims of natural law and the empirical analyses of legal sociology. His Pure Theory of Law asserted law's independence from both the transcendental ethics expressed in the former and the actual behavior of individuals and societies scrutinized in the latter, for the proper structure of law, he argued, was normative, a hierarchical order in which any given norm is a presupposition, understood to be validated only by a superior norm. A legal order might consist of any set of presuppositions with a basic norm (conventionally expressed as a constitution) at the apex of their pyramidal structure, where it provided the primary or root presupposition: "A norm the validity of which cannot be derived from a superior norm we call a 'basic' norm. All norms whose validity may be traced back to one and the same basic norm form a system of norms, or an order. This basic norm constitutes, as a common source, the bond between all the different norms of which an order consists."[17] Although a system of norms existed as a legal order only in relation to a particular social context, it was not equivalent to that context. Norms, as presuppositions, could be neither consequences nor causes of actual events. They were only "the expression of the idea that something ought to occur," not assertions about actual behavior that is or is not occurring:

> Whereas an "is" statement is true because it agrees with the reality of sensuous experience, an "ought" statement is a valid norm only if it belongs to such a valid system of norms, if it can be derived from a basic norm presupposed as valid. The ground of truth of an "is" statement is its conformity to the reality of our experience; the reason for the validity of a norm is a presupposition, a norm presupposed to be ultimately valid, that is, a basic norm.[18]

Kelsen's Pure Theory of Law thus proposed that a legal order could be constructed from any set of presuppositions; not bound by transcendental principles or by social reality, it was a form that neither prescribed nor proscribed a particular content.

Cuban legal philosophy absorbed Kelsen's influence critically rather than imitatively and challenged the relativism of his Pure Theory of Law. In the preface to *Teoría general del derecho* (General theory of law), Antonio Sánchez de Bustamente y Montoro confronted the implication of Kelsen's theory: "'The Law can have any content . . .' Is this acceptable? Can we the men of this generation accept it?"[19] Against the backdrop of fascism in an international context, and the recent Machado dictatorship in a national one, Bustamente y Montoro found such relativism difficult to abide, arguing that the dry objectivism of Kelsen's theory prompted a "new thirst for justice."[20] Other legal scholars in Cuba were equally unwilling to accept Kelsen's theory as a conclusion. It would have been difficult to support a relativist posture in the context of nationalism and self-determinism that preceded and accompanied the project of the constitution; and in addition, legal philosophy in Cuba had already encountered the philosophical currents of phenomenology emerging from Europe, which provided an additional avenue to critique Kelsen's positivism.[21] In 1939, Miguel Jorrín published an essay titled "La fenomenología y el derecho" (Phenomenology and law) in the journal of the University of Havana.[22] He credited Kelsen with opening a theoretical path away from the limitations of earlier positivism and from those of natural law, but asserted that this was only an initial step. Pursuing Kelsen's thesis on the presupposition of norms, Jorrín identified the key difficulty as *apriorismo,* the necessary establishment of an a priori presupposition. Solving the problem of *apriorismo,* he argued, required taking up the phenomenological method. From the scrutiny of the objects of experience, the facts of real lives and events, one could distill the "essence" of those experiences, the ideal to be rendered as the a priori presupposition of law. The firm ground would be objective reality itself, but reality transformed, with the contingencies of historical life sloughed off to reveal only the essential contours. Through such a method, Jorrín contended, it was possible "to construct a juridical science upon a material a priori, still replete with content."[23]

Jorrín conceived this methodological stance as a synthesis of normativism and phenomenology, and most of the positions articulated in Cuban legal philosophy similarly alloyed different theoretical strains of argument. From these combinations emerged a persistent validation of the role of historical reality within a legal order. Bustamente y Montoro, for example, while adhering to Kelsen's assertion of the autonomy of law, still insisted on the importance of "customs" in its actual performance. Not only was social custom itself a normative system that regulated matters outside the law, but as such it influenced the behavior and judgment of subjects within a legal order. Among several juridical norms, he discerned a specific hierarchy: "1, the Constitution; 2, the law; 3, the custom of the place; 4, jurisprudence; 5, general principles of Law."[24] For participants in constitutional debates, including those who commented on them, defining the relationship between the real and the normative, between facts and principles, was a crucial issue. In itself, this argument was not at odds with Kelsen's theory, which conceded that the content of norms would necessarily be elucidated from social circumstances.[25] The process of that elucidation, however, and the claims of legitimacy derived from it, remained to be formulated. According to Bustamente y Montoro, it was necessary "to insist forcefully upon Cuba's historic urgency for a close sympathy between its vital exigencies and its juridical norms. In few social realities is this problem posed so seriously."[26]

Writing in 1938, in the introduction to his book *Historia del derecho constitucional cubano* (History of Cuban constitutional law), Gutiérrez emphasized that in the 1901 constitution, independence and the U.S. occupation had been the overriding issues. Now, he argued, the primary concern was the delineation of a socioeconomic system for Cuba, not only because of transformations in Cuba, but because "a new constitutional epoch" had emerged.[27] The older concepts that underlay the 1901 constitution, derived directly from the revolutionary transformations of the United States and France at the end of the eighteenth century, had been superseded by the doctrinal advances of the revolutions of the twentieth century. The Weimar constitution of 1919 and the new Spanish constitution of 1931 exemplified the new form of modern constitutions that now defined and guaranteed socioeconomic regimens. Yet while Gutiérrez approved this new constitutional epoch embraced by modern nations, he insisted that the Cuban nation must also recognize its own irreducible composition. The special commission of the Senate, possibly prompted by Gutiérrez, echoed this argument, acknowledging the exemplary value of the other modern constitutions, but characterizing them as the manifestations of particular "psychological, cultural, biological, social, economic, political, geographic, and educational factors"—in short, as the products of a "difference in the environment of reality."[28] They could not serve directly as models for the Cuban case. Invoking José Martí's declaration that the "Cuban people ought to govern themselves taking into account natural elements," the commission concluded that "if the Constitution principally organizes the government of a people, it is indisputable, then, that to draft it natural Cuban elements should be taken into account."[29]

By the 1930s, José Martí, the leader of the Cuban independence movement who had died in battle in 1895, often served in justifications of social, cultural, and political positions in Cuban discourse.[30] In 1933, Jorge Mañach published *Martí, el apóstol* (Martí, the apostle), a concise and widely read biography that sought to define the *modernista* poet's central significance as a political thinker to the intellectual structure of Cuban independence. For the title, Mañach used the common epithet that suggested the national reverence with which Martí was regarded. Citations of Martí's writings now appeared in a variety of contexts, in books, newspapers, and political speeches, in order to explain or expound a current attitude or intention, sometimes with tenuous fidelity to Martí's own beliefs. In citing Martí to make a claim about the importance of an essential Cuban identity, the commission accurately attached a central preoccupation of Martí's philosophy to a prevailing debate in prewar Cuba: To what extent should Cuba and other Latin American nations draw upon the cultures of Europe and North America? How should the models offered by international political or social or artistic movements be received into the nationalist context of Cuba? Martí had lived in exile in Spain, Venezuela, Mexico, and New York City; his strong mistrust of North American influence was tempered by a measure of admiration. Foreign cultural influences need not be rejected summarily, he felt, but their hegemonic supersession of local culture should be resisted. With this stance, Martí famously identified the hybrid character of "mestizo América" as its strength. Yet, in the political sphere (with Cuba's colonial situation in mind), Martí had insisted on the correlation between government and the situation of the governed, which he believed to be rooted in physical conditions of nature and climate that produced the nation's cultural forms and institutions:

> One must see things as they are, to govern well; the good governor in America is not one who knows how government is conducted in France or Germany, but who knows the elements of which his country is composed and how they can be marshaled so that by methods and institutions native to the country the desirable state may be attained wherein every man realizes himself . . . The government must be the child of the country. The spirit of the government must be the same as that of the country. The form of government must conform to the natural constitution of the country. Good government is nothing more than the true balance between the natural elements of the nation.[31]

With an echo of Montesquieu, Martí defined an organic relation between governmental forms and environmental, physical, and habitual conditions. The natural elements he invoked were not just the physical climate of organic and inorganic material, but the properties and behaviors that emerged in this milieu. Writing to incite a revolution, he avoided specific prescriptions for political structures in favor of a rhetorical appeal to republican virtue and civic conscience, but the link Martí fashioned had renewed relevance in Cuba following the revolution of 1933 when political and aesthetic pursuits in different disciplines converged with a reinvigorated and pervasive nationalism. In such a factional moment, political consensus to resolve a new national government required (alongside motivations such as economic gain) the general motive of a perceived national interest, which, variously cast as national pride, community obligation, or simply progress, was accompanied by arguments about Cuban history and culture that had in turn been explicated even prior to independence through the concept of *cubanidad*. *Cubanidad*, as an assertion of national identity and as a summation of the defining characteristics of Cuban life and experience, could be invoked to sanction revolt against Spain, foster antipathy to North American influence, lament political indifference, and deplore political partisanship. In the wake of the 1933 revolution, *cubanidad* became in effect a medium for the expression of critical perspectives, and so as *cubanidad* became a central preoccupation for art, literature, sociology, and other disciplines, its invocations remained inseparable from their surrounding political context.

Martí was concerned that the embodiments of environment and government should be commensurate, as exemplified in the figure of the "natural man" whose instinctive equilibrium Martí contrasted to an authority acquired from books. When applied to the project of drafting a new Cuban constitution, Martí's equation was supplemented by a third embodiment, the constitution itself. Where Martí posited only the relation between environmental balance and concordant governance, the argument made by the commission situated the drafting of a constitutional text, and the constitution itself, as a mediation between these two. The commission's conclusion—"if the Constitution principally organizes the government of a people, it is indisputable, then, that to draft it one should take into account natural Cuban elements"—construed the writing of the constitution as drawing from the conditions of physical and social environment to produce a document that would then organize the actual governance of the nation. This process was more than a sequential movement from existing conditions to future ones. Because the constitution would itself come into being and would continue to exist as a mediating term between environment and governance, its drafting was fundamentally a process of representation in all senses. To "take into account" the inherent constitution of Cuba in drafting a written constitution was to transform existing elements, features, and customs into the formal terms and orders of the charter, to reveal them in distilled form, to make them legible as a text that described the condition of Cuba itself. The commission minutes succinctly posited this representational role with a telling metaphor: "the Commission has placed before itself the Cuban fact *[el hecho cubano]*, focusing its view on the whole in the sense that it is reflected in the Constitution as in a mirror."[32]

Like a mirror, the constitution could reflect "el hecho cubano" without being identical to it—as a representation, the constitution would not be reducible to that which it represented. The deliberate distance between the constitution, the reality from which it would be derived, and the political forms that it would compel could have been asserted literally (as in Abalo's suggestion that members of the senatorial chamber would be "divorced from the surrounding reality")—or confirmed obliquely, as with the references in both Abalo's and Gutiérrez's proposals to external principles and concepts such as justice or will, which were deemed to either transcend or precede the evidence of their specific local effects. The distance would, in any case, be secured by the formal tropes of the constitution itself, a written text subject to codes and precedents, conforming as might a novel to the conventions of a style or genre. Through such distinctions, the constitution could manifest the organization of Cuban political and social structures without being synchronized to their activities or consequences, loosed from a historical situation on which it nevertheless depended. Conceived as a faithful instrument of representation—as a mirror—the constitution rendered as a cultural medium opened affinities to disciplines participating in the formulation of the civic sphere.

The Debates of the Constitutional Convention

Delegates were elected at the end of 1939 to represent nearly a dozen political parties at the Convención Constituyente (constitutional convention). In the years since the 1933 revolution, the diversity of political interests had not been reduced, though their degrees of influence varied.[33] For the convention, delegates grouped themselves in two coalitions, one in support of the government (which was still controlled by Batista) and the other opposed. Batista did not attempt to forestall the convention, even when the opposition parties won more delegate seats. Indeed, an atmosphere of compromise surrounded the constitutional debates. Three days before the convention opened, the leaders of the parties had pledged themselves to cooperation by signing a formal pact of conciliation. The inauguration of the convention on February 9, 1940, attended by a crowd at the Capitolio Nacional and broadcast by radio, included a series of speeches promising the elevation of nation over party. Mañach, a delegate for the ABC revolutionary party and leader of the opposition coalition, vowed that dogmatism and demagoguery would be foresworn in favor of sincere, substantive action. Partisan calculation was not entirely suppressed during the convention, of course, but it was diminished to a remarkable degree, so that the constitution that emerged at the end of two months of debate, drafting, and revision could be agreed upon and approved by a broad range of political constituencies. It was not entirely satisfactory to any one group, but precisely for that reason it could be raised as a symbol of a new stage in Cuban political life—indeed, as the first moment of a new Cuban republic.

As the product of sustained debate between disparate political agendas and perspectives, the constitution ratified and promulgated in the ceremonies in Guáimaro and Havana attained neither the succinctness of the 1901 constitution nor the polemical clarity of draft proposals such as Abalo's technico-functional order. Nearly three hundred articles and additional transitional dispositions produced a detailed formulation of the organic structure of government and lengthy specifications for its corresponding social responsibilities.[34] The Constitution of 1940 confirmed the existing tripartite division of powers between a legislature, an executive, and a judiciary, with the judiciary in particular regarded as the indispensable authority to maintain a state of law, key to providing greater stability to Cuban politics. In addition, and admitting the inheritance of the colonial system of government, the charter also granted autonomy to municipalities in Cuba. This armature of national and local government authority was to be erected upon two categories of fundamental rights, individual and social. Individual rights, most already guaranteed in the 1901 charter, consisted of equality, property, habeas corpus, and freedoms of association and religion. Social rights, most newly defined in the 1940 charter, were classified under the four cornerstones: family, culture, work, and property. These categorizations recognized the family as an organizational element of society, sanctioned culture and its free expression as a fundamental interest of the state, guaranteed social assistance and the regulation of labor. The fourth, acknowledging the social function of property, aimed to promote a republican ideal of civic community while also confirming the liberal presumption of the inviolability of property. These new dimensions signaled a fundamental change in the relationship between the state and the nation; the passive government construed by the 1901 constitution, designed to protect the individual from the state, was supplanted by the active government of the 1940 constitution, calculated to produce individual benefit from the operations of the state. To formalize the progressive goals of the 1933 revolution entailed an active state, as numerous articles made clear: article 79 assured that the state would develop low-cost housing for workers; article 83 gave it authority to regulate the placement of industrial areas; article 134 gave the legislature responsibility for dictating regimens for national development; article 215 required each municipality to establish a Comisión de Urbanismo (commission for urbanism); and article 271 declared that the state would direct the national economy to ensure that its benefit accrued to each individual.

The density of the constitutional text could be explained in two opposed ways. Gustavo Gutiérrez argued on the one hand that the political immaturity of the nation compelled a more detailed charter. A simple definition of constitutional principles was insufficient because it was not supplemented by the established laws and customs that would sustain those principles; therefore, the constitution itself had needed to provide supplementary guidance to coordinate political and social behavior. Other modern constitutions provided the precedent for this case, as did the broadening influence of managerial forms of government.[35] On the other hand, though, the complexity of the constitution could also be explained by the political maturity of the nation; that is, by the prior existence of developed social practices, cultural institutions, and bodies of legislation in Cuba. Many of these derived from the colonial past—the building code was one of the elements of the Spanish civil code still in effect in 1940, for example—yet directly shaped aspects of the modern urban society. The habits inspired by these laws and institutions were threads woven into the details of the new charter, as Gutiérrez seemed to acknowledge by arguing that the new constitution could supply an armature to transform the underlying principles of these unrelated and unregulated elements into a "methodical assembly *[conjunto metódico]*." Gutiérrez chose his words carefully, explaining that the constitution "includes and focuses, in reality, a plurality of facts and laws *[hechos y derechos]* that, appraised globally within its fixing and regulation, determine a whole";[36] its plural parts "have, or ought to have, a close coherence among themselves in the function of the organisms and activity of the State that they try to regulate, which determines the existence of a true method rather than a capricious and invertebrate collection determined by chance or by similarities of another order."[37] In this light, the 1940 constitution would not be seen as a novel beginning or as the elaboration of organs of government from first principles, but rather as the distillation of principles from the existing historical context and the assembly of existing institutions into a comprehensive schema.

Following Kelsen's fundamental distinction between the "is" and the "ought," the "is," or "el hecho cubano," was regarded as the environment from which the "ought," the normative system, could be distilled through the mediations of constitutionalism. Through this process of mediation the constitution would assume its full representational function, which was to describe *and* to project. Exceeding the autonomous role Kelsen conceived and surpassing also the passive reflection of descriptive representation, the representational imperative of the constitution was in fact transformative; it was to reveal the necessities and exigencies of the real (what the Cuban nation is) and then to convert those to the ideal (what the Cuban nation ought to be). In 1941, Gutiérrez succinctly conveyed the representational extent of the new constitution when he wrote that "our fundamental Charter [is] an index and a program."[38] An index registers and records already existing conditions; it marks the fact of a past event. A program proposes conditions to be produced in the future; it choreographs a future event. The movement from the first to the second, from index to the program, is a movement from the retrospective to the prospective. The revolutionary emphasis on reform, manifested in socioeconomic propositions and guarantees, had made the programmatic aspect of the constitution indispensable. Yet it was not simply in its overt proposals—free education or minimum wages—that the constitution was projective, or, to use Gutiérrez's significant choice of word, a "plan," but also in its conceptual structure. The constitution was to project the object that it described: the Cuban nation. Although the nation could be (and was) relentlessly invoked as a signifier, it had no instrumental capacity, no organs or agents through which to act. One commentator writing about the constitution proposed that the nation "constitutes the peristyle of our fundamental Charter," an architectural metaphor that suggests the manner in which the nation both preceded and bracketed the constitution, but without providing its essential structure.[39]

Within this peristyle the constitution would produce an instrumental space, the space of civil society, which it conjured through its projection of two figures, "el estado" and "el ciudadano," the state and the citizen. The state was constituted by the structure of elements and procedures established in the constitution—such as the three branches of government, the *consejos* (councils), the delegation of municipal powers, or the provisions for amendment. According to Kelsen, the state was simply the legal order produced by the prevailing normative system—not an entity subject to the legal order, but rather the actual expression or embodiment of that legal order circumscribed spatially and temporally by three elements: the territory in which the legal order was valid, the persons to whom that order pertained, and the powers with which the order manifested its validity and efficacy. In the legal order defined by the 1940 constitution the third of these translated into the form of the plan. Where the articles of the Constitution of 1901, with its legal order to be expressed in a passive state, included no such presumption, those of the 1940 constitution, with its contrasting formulation of an active state, literally compelled the formulations of plans. The word *plan* itself occurred only infrequently in the constitutional text, but various articles required the legislature to direct the economy, municipalities to manage their development and create commissions for urbanism, schools to be built and curricula devised, and land uses to be constrained and encouraged. Each of these instanced a concept of plan: an inventory of current facts assessed in order to project in the future a specific course of possibilities, events, and consequences. The constitution itself could have been understood as a plan, in the sense that it proposed to constrain some future possibilities and compel others, and certainly its very existence was understood by some as a recasting of the future. Writing in 1938, Gutiérrez regretted that the preceding years had been "a state of provisional conditions . . . No one dared to make plans for the future. Much less carry out projects that looked to the future."[40] But in 1940, the improvisational was overcome by the planned; contingency and causality would be managed by the state, if not with the precision Abalo claimed for his technico-functional form of government, then still with unprecedented deliberation and forethought.

The constitution also projected the second element—persons subject to the normative legal order—in the figure of the Cuban citizen, who was constituted in several articles that sanctioned the acquisition of citizenship by birth or by naturalization, and that detailed the accompanying rights and obligations to be regulated by law.[41] Through their exercise, a citizen acquired standing within the legal order. The first element, the territory of the legal order, was established in article 3: "The territory of the Republic integrates the Isle of Cuba, the Isle of Pines, and the other adjacent isles and keys that with them were under the sovereignty of Spain under the ratification of the Treaty of Paris."[42] Here even the physical dimension of the nation was documented in reference to a historical moment in the narrative of independence. Out of these constitutional figures—state, citizen, and spatial extent—and their respective attributes, the contours of civil society were defined such that the "civic" would be the reciprocity between individual citizens and the legal order that encompassed them. Civil society would consist in their relationship of mutual engagement, in which the state would regulate its citizens and citizens would regulate the activities of the state. One legal commentator put it as follows: "The relations between the citizen and the State imply a double juridical aspect: the individual as the end of the activity of the State presumes the study of the rights of citizens, and as a means to achieve the superior ends of the State involves the study of the obligations of citizens."[43] With this distillation of the interaction between state and citizen, the structure of reciprocity forced an emphasis on the events and institutions that would enable that interaction. Municipalities, colleges, councils, professional societies, these would be the sites of the mediatory operations required by reciprocity. Indeed, such institutions would be fully responsible for contriving the efficacy of the constitution in the years following the convention; for, as many commentators noted, the new charter presumed that a substantial set of enabling legislation and organic reform would follow from its promulgation.

Enacting the Constitution

As the first article of the 1940 constitution demonstrated, it is the particular characteristic of any constitution that it projects the object that it represents: "Art. 1. Cuba is a sovereign and independent State organized as a unitary and democratic Republic, for the enjoyment of political liberty, social justice, individual and collective welfare, and human solidarity."[44] This article described Cuba by specifying the characteristics that were the inherent and permanent compositional substance of the nation. The description was also performative, because the text itself endowed the nation of Cuba with these characteristics. This first article of the constitution summoned into being, and so literally constituted, the Cuban nation whose intangible constitution it represented in text.[45] The paired functions of the constitution pointed to an apparent contradiction: description refers to an object that already exists, while performance aims to produce an object's existence. The paradox of the Cuban constitution was its claim to constitute something that already existed. Cuba had been a republic for four decades, a coherent cultural entity for four centuries, and yet the Constitution of 1940 was to be as much the instigation as the affirmation of its existence.

The ceremony in Guáimaro to ratify the 1940 constitution made manifest the desire to bind the charter to a sequence of historical contingencies, not only to evidence the *cubanidad* of the charter but also to assert its legitimacy, to sustain its a priori claim of validity. No referendum would be held to ratify the new constitution; because the delegates had been selected through popular election to represent the political parties at the convention, their signatures provided in an immediate sense the authority of the constitution. As the representatives of political power—power to persuade and to coerce, power to enact and enforce the constitution—they sanctioned the charter on behalf of the Cuban people. However, with an incomplete franchise, with the deep political schisms that persisted, and with the decision made by some parties not to participate in the convention, only a tenuous legitimacy could be asserted on the basis of present events. The authorization of "el pueblo" (the people) might be better obtained by a different process of legitimation, one that fixed the constitution within a historical trajectory. Consequently, much of the rhetoric that surrounded the drafting of the constitution described the charter as the realization of an earlier project and the fulfillment of a historical process. Considered in a short temporal frame, the constitution fulfilled the project of the 1933 revolution. "The revolutionary conquests," said Gutiérrez, "manifested themselves in the constitutional text."[46] In this respect, the charter actually derived its legitimacy from a precise historical contingency. Bustamente y Montoro pointed out that the assumption of constitutional powers by the provisional governments had no justification in law, only in circumstance; the subsequent legal order therefore "originated from a revolutionary fact," which was one of the instances that Kelsen suggested could propound a basic norm.[47] But the signing in Guáimaro invoked a broader temporal frame, in which the 1940 constitution fulfilled the revolutionary effort initiated in the nineteenth century—the republican movement for which José Martí had been martyred, and which had been only partially consummated in the 1901 constitution. This extended historical trajectory conformed as well to Kelsen's theoretical construction, which held that a sequence of constitutions would be traced back to "some constitution that is the first historically." Subsequent constitutions then "postulated that one ought to behave as the individual, or the individuals, who laid down the first constitution have ordained."[48]

The mimicry of the signing of the 1869 revolutionary constitution at Guáimaro—the table, the site, the landscape—made the historical lineage and ordination implicit in the text of the constitution visible and concrete. The legitimacy of constitutionalism, in other words, had to be produced, constructed through historical narratives and through events designed with significant spatial and physical characteristics. Emilio Roig de Leuchsenring and other historians had begun to consolidate what would soon emerge as revised narrative of Cuban independence.[49] Other disciplines, from the arts to the social sciences, made parallel endeavors. The designation of the prior sequence of revolutionary moments as the origin of the 1940 constitution distanced the newly ratified charter from its present moment just as its promulgation asserted its contemporary role. The ceremonies in Guáimaro and Havana, hinged between past and future, signified the charter's pivotal importance in the nation's history. But while the convention had seemed to offer a respite and a solution to recurring instability, once signed the constitution was returned from the conciliatory sanctuary of the convention to the turbulent environment of Cuban politics. Many commentators cautioned that it could produce enduring effects only if it were immediately supported by the creation of complementary legislation to enact and enforce its principles.[50] Some elements of the constitution required the creation of new institutional bodies with their own accompanying regulations, and while the text incorporated many more elements of a legislative character than did other constitutional precedents, much of the structure of colonial statutory law remained in force. Attention was also paid to the provision in the constitution allowing for an emergency suspension of constitutional guarantees, a provision that allowed the temporary dissolution of the constitution itself. Although events in the immediate wake of the convention appeared to justify considerable optimism about the capacity for constitutionalism to maintain equilibrium in the Cuban political sphere, this provision confirmed its inherent fragility.

2 Better Cities, Better Citizens

The Political Function of Planning

In 1942 the polished propaganda of a new civic organization, the Patronato Pro-Urbanismo (Pro-Urbanism Association), initiated an appeal for a synthetic program of planning to be instituted under the authority of a national planning law, with the group's manifesto pointing out that nine of the articles of the new constitution either required or presupposed regulatory activities commensurate with the concept of planning.[1] The Patronato was founded by five individuals with overlapping concerns in civic and professional activities: architect Pedro Martínez Inclán, who served as the association's first president; Eduardo Montoulieu, an architect who had recently studied city planning at the Harvard University Graduate School of Design; Ana Arroyo de Hernández, already involved in campaigns for the preservation of monuments and soon to join the faculty of the University of Havana; Alfredo T. Quilez, the publisher of the journal *Carteles;* and Luis de Soto, a prominent critic and historian of art at the University of Havana. Its organization resembled the various reformist groups founded during the Machado regime, and indeed some of its founders had played a role in those earlier organizations—Martínez Inclán had signed the manifesto of the Junta Cubana de Renovación Nacional, and Quilez the declaration of the Grupo Minorista. Several former members of the Grupo Minorista soon joined the Patronato Pro-Urbanismo: Armando Maribona, Luis A. Baralt, Juan José Sicre, and Emilio Roig de Leuchsenring, each of whom participated simultaneously in other cultural institutions, as did other members such as Lilliam Mederos, the founder of the Lyceum y Lawn Tennis Club, Joaquín Weiss, the leading architectural historian at the University of Havana, and Agustín Sorhegui, the president of the Colegio de Arquitectos.[2]

Through this professionally diverse and influential membership, the Patronato began to conduct a systematic publicity campaign in support of national planning, a campaign that explicitly linked planning to civic reform. The Patronato's prospectus, which itself imitated the form of a constitution, stipulated seven objectives, pledging to promote the knowledge and application of "the science of Urbanism"; to support "the promulgation of Laws, Regulations, Ordinances and all measures that are favorable for the urban improvement of the nation"; and "To encourage patriotism and civic pride by means of the enlargement of our cities"[3] (Figure 2.1). These aims presumed the possible and necessary coordination of urbanism, law, and civic consciousness, a presumption merited, according to the group, by the objective benefits of modern planning but also legitimated more authoritatively by the 1940 Constitution. Extending the claim broached in the manifesto, Montoulieu argued in an article for the *Havana Post* that article 277 of the new constitution obliged the state "to foresee, guide and design scientifically the safe, beautiful, economical and utilitarian growth of its towns, cities and regions."[4] A few months later, Montoulieu published in the magazine *Carteles* an even more concise claim: "Articles 211, 213, 215, 273, and 277 of our new Constitution imply the creation of a National Commission of Urbanism, which is the fundamental objective of the law that this Patronato Pro-Urbanismo of Cuba proposes."[5]

The membership of the Patronato and the audience that it addressed represented numerically and demographically a relatively narrow constituency and so did not depict the social circumstance or political standing of all Cuban citizens, but it did closely correspond to, and indeed depended on, the aspirations projected in the 1940 constitution. Members' natural regard for constitutionalism as the currency of civic discourse prompted the Patronato's ambition to raise citizens' awareness of the advantageous promise of planning. Its campaign of articles in daily newspapers and popular magazines, and lectures and exhibitions for the general public, aimed to persuade bodies of citizens—the Club de Leones, for example, or groups of property owners—of the urgent need for a national planning law and thus to encourage those bodies to lobby independently for the legislation as a benefit to their own activities.[6] But as the further ambition of the Patronato "to encourage patriotism and civic pride" revealed, the group also sought to produce, as a correlate to planning, a civic consciousness. For its motto, the Patronato adopted a succinct slogan: "Mejores ciudades, ciudadanos mejores"—better

ESTATUTOS DEL PATRONATO PRO URBANISMO DE CUBA

CAPITULO I

NOMBRE

Esta asociación se denominará PATRONATO PRO-URBANISMO DE CUBA. Su sede oficial será en la ciudad de la Habana.

CAPITULO II

FINES

Los fines del Patronato son los siguientes:

Primero: Estimular, promover y divulgar el conocimiento de la ciencia del Urbanismo, fomentando el interés por su aplicación a las ciudades y los poblados del territorio nacional.

Segundo: Velar por el desarrollo y embellecimiento urbano y rural en el territorio de la República de acuerdo con planes científicamente estudiados.

Tercero: Promover la promulgación de Leyes, Reglamentos, Ordenanzas y cuantas medidas sean favorables al mejoramiento urbanístico de la nación, así como la modificación y modernización de aquellas ya existentes que resulten ineficaces o anticuadas.

Cuarto: Propender a evitar que se cometan infracciones de planes, Leyes, Reglamentos, Ordenanzas y disposiciones vigentes y de las que se dicten en el futuro en materia de Urbanismo.

Quinto: Atraer a su seno representaciones de todos los intereses nacionales y locales relacionados con los fines que persigue el Urbanismo moderno.

Sexto: Mantener relaciones de intercambio y contacto con corporaciones análogas del Extranjero.

Séptimo: Estimular el amor patrio y el orgullo cívico mediante el engrandecimiento de nuestras ciudades.

CAPITULO III

CLASES DE SOCIOS

El Patronato estará formado por cuatro clases de socios: de Honor, Protectores, Correspondientes y de Número.

Serán socios de Honor las personas que, a juicio del Patronato, tengan méritos para ello, de acuerdo con lo que determine el Reglamento. Los socios de Honor estarán exentos de toda contribución.

Serán Socios Protectores las personas que deseen contribuir a los fines del Patronato sin tomar parte activa en el desenvolvimiento del mismo y de acuerdo con lo que determine el Reglamento.

FIGURE 2.1 Statutes of the Patronato Pro-Urbanismo. Courtesy of the Frances Loeb Library, Harvard Graduate School of Design.

cities, better citizens—a phrase that bound together physical order and social order, cleverly employing grammatical symmetry to construe a reciprocal relationship between cities and citizens in which the latter were both the consequence and the prerequisite of the former. The slogan sounded a constitutional resonance not only in the state's obligation for planning, but in citizens' obligation to civic conscience. The 1940 constitution defined the Cuban citizen, sanctioning the acquisition of citizenship by birth or naturalization and granting standing in its legal order to citizens with articles that detailed accompanying rights that allowed residency without discrimination in Cuba, suffrage, and the receipt of public assistance. But in advance of these rights, the 1940 constitution stipulated the obligations of citizenship; along with military service and the payment of taxes, they required each citizen "To comply with the Constitution and the Laws of the Republic and to observe civic conduct, instilling it in one's children . . . promoting in them the most pure national conscience."[7]

Some earlier drafts of the new charter had, like the 1901 constitution, required military service and the payment of taxes, but the clause obligating the cultivation of civic conduct and conscience appeared for the first time in the 1940 constitution. During the Constitutional Convention, the clause prompted opposition from several delegates who argued that while compliance with the constitution and its enabling laws could be juridically mandated, moral or behavioral suasion lay beyond the purview of the charter. In a rhetorically formal but quite charged exchange typical of the convention, delegates debated this point. Juan Marinello, representing the Communist Party, argued that "We should reject, from now on, formulations of a moral type in the text of the Constitution. It is a matter of making a constitutional text with truly juridical, perfectly exacting characteristics."[8] Jorge Mañach, who had proposed the wording of the clause, retorted that there were prevailing "hungers and preoccupations" of such importance to national life that the character of the constitution must, regardless of their insufficient juridical aspect, address and cultivate them. Several years earlier, in an essay titled "Condiciones de civismo" (Conditions of civic responsibility), he had argued that the "sense of civic responsibility *[civismo]* is not a natural attribute in an individual or in a people, but a result of more civilized coexistence."[9] Now, to inculcate this attribute and redress the grave problem of "civic absenteeism *[el absentismo ciudadano]*," Mañach appealed to his fellow delegates: "We must not forget that the Constitution has a didactic efficacy, an indirect, normative effect on the national conscience."[10] The specific obligation toward civic conscience was further supported by additional articles, including several relating to education that mandated that courses be taught on civics and the constitution and that all teaching tend to inspire "in a spirit of *cubanidad* . . . the love of country [and] its democratic institutions."[11] Cumulatively, these articles fashioned a constitutional intention not only to define citizenship and thereby produce citizens, but also to project a citizenry with full awareness of its standing and its duties. To the extent that the constitution was to serve as a means to reconcile individual and collective interests, awareness of citizenship might be further characterized as an inducement toward community, one aimed at overcoming what was then seen as the nation's fatal characteristic: *particularismo,* or factionalism.

Montoulieu (who took the lead in the Patronato Pro-Urbanismo's publicity campaign during 1942 and 1943) presented the regulatory capabilities of planning as a remedy for the piecemeal approach to public works that had occurred in the Machado regime and that persisted in privately financed urban developments. In such developments, the uneven and unbalanced representation of interests invariably resulted in the absence of a coordinated accounting of varied "points of view *[puntos de vista].*" In the properly regulated development of a city, Montoulieu wrote, "one should not neglect the needs of the shopkeeper in favor of those of the tourist, nor those of the industrialist in favor of those of the poor worker, nor those of the public employee in favor of those of the rich owner, because these and many other interests should be defended for the good of the majority."[12] Without a comprehensive assessment, one or another individual interest would be advantaged, perhaps unjustifiably, at the expense of others. (Montoulieu did not need to state explicitly for his readers that his critique was a condemnation of the corrupting influence of political patronage that subordinated public interest to the financial benefit of individual partisans.) Another failing he identified in the improvisational, uncoordinated approach to development was its susceptibility to unintended consequences. Because such an approach failed to adequately assess its potential ramifications for other areas or its likely effects over time, it risked compounding problems rather than alleviating them. Even to fulfill clear, specific needs, Montoulieu wrote, "city planning cannot and must not be attempted at such a random rate, because no sooner would one measure be taken to fulfill or correct an individual need than a new one would arise perhaps in conflict with the preceding recent action."[13]

These flaws could, he asserted, be remedied with the objective projection of a larger order, a *conjunto* that encompassed the totality of individual points of view, and that regulated their relationship at any moment in time and their interaction over a temporal span from the present into the future. Such "true plans of the whole *[verdaderos planes de conjunto]*" along with the agencies and techniques that produced them—such as urbanism and architecture—represented "the best proof of the spirit of collective organization that prevails in all the civilized nations of the world where urbanism directs the growth of their population centers."[14] Montoulieu suggested that scientific planning and urbanism would mitigate distortions of influence in a manner similar to the creation of a professional civil service stipulated by the 1940 constitution, by providing a disinterested evaluation of all points of view in regard to a specific issue. By producing and maintaining the organizational frame of the *conjunto,* planning could guide the transaction from present to future, or, in Montoulieu's words, from "that which is *[lo que hay]*" to "that which ought to be done *[lo que deberá hacerse].*"[15]

La Exposición sobre Urbanismo

Constitutionalist ambitions were in evidence when, in September 1942, the Patronato Pro-Urbanismo presented La Exposición sobre Urbanismo (Exhibition on urbanism) at the Lyceum y Lawn Tennis Club. The attendant publicity boasted that the event was "the first exhibition of urban planning" to be organized in Cuba, an unprecedented demonstration of the arguments in favor of planning.[16] Conceived and designed by Montoulieu with the assistance of Miguel Gastón, with whom Montoulieu collaborated professionally, the exhibition presented a didactic series of panels combining text and graphics to illustrate the main concepts of planning. These were supplemented by drawings and a model of a proposed Plano Regulador (Master plan) for the town of Varadero, a beach resort east of Havana. Montoulieu and Gastón had developed this plan a few years earlier for the Cuban government; it was not implemented, but served as an illustration of the beneficial consequences that would follow from adopting the principles presented in the other materials. The exhibition opened with Montoulieu's lecture on "La necesidad y conveniencia de los Planos Reguladores" (The necessity and advisability of master plans) and closed with a roundtable discussion on urbanism; both events were reported in popular publications.[17]

Even visitors who did not attend the lectures would have found themselves addressed, quite directly, as citizens, for even in preliminary sketches of the exhibition Montoulieu employed a clear appeal to a constitutional subject. In his sketch for the first panel, a pointed finger confronted the viewer—the citizen—to ask, "You plan your clothes, your house, your hobbies, your work, studies, travels, food budgets, in short, your life . . . but . . . who plans the surroundings? The streets, parks, schools, hospitals, shops, industries, houses, theaters, museums, etc. . . . in the cities, in the country?"[18] (see Plate 1). Why, the question obviously implied, tolerate improvisation in the public sphere if you would refuse it in the private? Both are dimensions of a continuous human environment—your studies and the school you study in; your clothes and the street you wear them in; your pastimes and your parks. Both contexts are improved by—indeed, are made functional by—the conscious activity of planning. The pointed finger confronted the viewer again in another sketch to exhort, "You as an important part of the citizenry can and should participate in the planning process by means of an active civic conscience!"[19] The active citizen, knowledgeable about neighborhood and nation and motivated by same civic conscience required by the constitution, should identify needs and shortcomings to be addressed by technical authorities, while always subordinating individual interest to collective benefit.

The role of the citizen was conclusively assigned in a third sketch, a diagram of three constituent elements of the planning process: citizens educated about the intentions of planning and able to define their future needs and ambitions; technicians able to assess the demands of citizens and devise the means for their satisfaction; and branches of government interpreting and resolving the demands of citizens without recourse to political exigencies (see Plate 2). Montoulieu's sketch provided a diagram of civil society construed as the reciprocity between state and citizen, here with the additional specification that that reciprocity is to be contrived through the mediating mechanism of planning. The citizen, equipped with the reflexive awareness of an "active civic conscience," elaborates demands addressed to the state, while the state, armed with the instrumental capacities of the plan, regulates the environment of the citizen. The diagram made visible the functional reciprocity—which is to say, it manifested the civic sphere—in the form of the third constituency, the technicians responsible for the agencies and methods of planning. Planning, it seems, was to become the operative mechanism, and technicians the very embodiment, of civil society.

In additional sketches explaining the necessary characteristics of this conception of civil society—its adequate conjunction of citizenship, its preparation through a plan, and the application of expertise—Montoulieu asked that professionals and academics recognize their responsibility to fulfill a social function. In addition to acting as citizens, he argued, they must apply their respective expertise to the needs of community and nation (see Plate 3). The techniques pertaining to their disciplinary practices could be coordinated in the larger disciplinary and conceptual framework of a national plan. This coordination was to have an organizational manifestation of its own, a "central planning organism *[organismo central planificador]*" that would direct all planning activities. Montoulieu devised a diagram suggesting that, while other government bodies could retain their portfolios, a new Junta Nacional de Planificación (JNP, or National Planning Board) should be the central entity responsible for assessing and arbitrating their various programs and proposals (see Plate 4). This board "does not intend to eliminate other state organisms or to interfere with their departments, but rather to collaborate with them." Coining the name that would be adopted a decade later, Montoulieu proposed that "A JNP so conceived and endorsed by the Executive = The best instrument of government."[20] It would be, he imagined, an objective, nearly invisible instrument, mediating the respective prerogatives of agencies and branches of government without imposing the characteristic practices or techniques of one or other professional discipline.

Montoulieu's polemical sketches extended the argument of the Patronato beyond the ideas of city planning and toward a continuing program of national planning overseen by a national planning board. Abstract aims of civic improvement, collective benefit, and "patriotism *[amor patrio]*" were equated with, and even transformed into, a concept of planning. The Patronato thus advocated urbanism not as an end in itself, but as a means to achieve the higher and more consistent degree of social order promised by the 1940 constitution yet undermined by the inadequacies of the political sphere. The group initiated the project of planning in Cuba and diffused the principles of that project into a variety of disciplines through the equally varied affiliations of its membership, adopting its clever motto—"Mejores ciudades, ciudadanos mejores"—to convey as its fundamental principle the idea that order brought to bear upon the city would produce self-regulating order in the citizen. From this idea followed the two conceits of Montoulieu's sketches, the interpellation of the Cuban citizen and the reliance on a characterless expertise. The sketches correlated the normative terms of constitutionalism with those of planning—another caption stated that to plan is "to know what is, to define what should be, to define what is to be done," joining to the constitutional "is" and "ought" a third term, that which must be done. In a more summary statement, Montoulieu underscored this sequence of transformation: "To improve we need order, for order we need a plan. Isn't it true?"[21]

Sources of Cuban Planning Discourse

In national elections held in June 1940, Fulgencio Batista won the presidency through the first democratic process completed in Cuba since the Machado dictatorship; a cabinet of ministers was sworn in and a new Congress seated. Ramón Grau San Martín and his Auténtico Party supporters formally assumed the opposition role. The Cuban economy, dependent on the export of the sugar crop, improved considerably as a result of trade constraints and scarcity caused by the war. Sources of instability remained, however. With extensive North American ownership, the national economy was still bound to the economic policies of the United States. Organized political violence persisted, and Batista maintained a strongman's hold on instruments of political power and patronage. In 1944, Batista's handpicked candidate—who would have permitted Batista to retain control of the government—lost to Grau in the presidential elections. Batista defied expectations by neither rejecting the result nor imposing military rule, instead ceding power to his elected successor and removing himself from Cuba for an extended tour of Latin America and life in Florida. This peaceful transition seemed to evidence the mature progress of the political process, but it was followed by increasing corruption and decreasing government competence and by the recurrence of what was termed *gangsterismo*.

The public activity of the Patronato Pro-Urbanismo lessened after 1943, but individual members of the group continued to work toward the goal of national planning, independently and within professional organizations such as the Colegio Nacional de Arquitectos and the Sociedad Cubana de Ingenieros (Cuban Society of Engineers). Articles about planning appeared in newspapers and journals, and the several members who taught architecture or the history of architecture at the University of Havana were able to present their expansive theories of urbanism to the first postwar generation of architects.[22] Gradual consolidation of a discourse on planning was the consequence less of general tendencies than a quite deliberate attention. It was sustained in large part by a rather narrow set of professional relationships and by particular moments of political opportunity. The moments of political opportunity resulted from the continuing disruptions within the political sphere—and the public reaction to them. The relationships included personal friendships among several younger Cuban architects who became increasingly familiar with and engaged in the international architectural discourse that emphasized the importance of planning and its relation to architecture.

The manifesto of the Patronato Pro-Urbanismo described planning as "the greatest social advance of our century," one whose value had been proven in other modern nations whose exemplary practices Cuba should not ignore.[23] Just as modern constitutions had (according to Gutiérrez) provided precedents for the incorporation of social and economic policies into a constitutional text, modern urbanism according to Montoulieu and Martínez Inclán offered methods to suppress the improvisational urban development that prevailed in Cuba. The manifesto cited legislative examples, in France, Germany, England, and Mexico, where a scientific urbanism was promoted in collaboration with governmental initiatives. Physical examples were not identified, but the leaders of the Patronato would have had in mind several strands of thought circulating in North America and Europe. Martínez Inclán followed the legacy of the City Beautiful movement in the United States, and his 1925 book *La Habana actual* (Havana now) had accounted the merits of the combination of systematic urbanization and aesthetic embellishment that he referred to in the text as Civic Art. The more recent theories of Werner Hegemann would also have been an important influence, just as they were elsewhere in Latin America. Martínez Inclán had read Hegemann's treatise *City Planning, Housing,* which began with the proposition that national planning was a "basic conception of the American Constitution," which had been "conceived as an expression of these planning efforts"; the relevance of the connection asserted between a constitutional project and a planning program would not have escaped Martínez Inclán's attention.[24] In its propaganda, the Patronato did emphasize that by applying the new "scientific" urbanism to the development of cities not only the cities would be substantially improved, but also the regions they integrated, and hence the nation as a whole. Incremental projects that were manifestly problematic at local levels could, according to their arguments, be tempered by incorporation into larger frameworks of planning in which the multiple criteria and consequences of any single project could be assessed. Such accumulated frameworks would ultimately correspond to the scale and the structure of the nation itself, so that planning, as conceived by the Patronato, did have the national ambition identified by Hegemann.

Montoulieu had also been exposed to Hegemann's ideas when he began his graduate studies at Columbia University, where he first met Joseph Hudnut, dean of the School of Architecture and a protégé of Hegemann.[25] When Hudnut moved to Harvard University in 1935 to become the dean of the Graduate School of Design, Montoulieu followed and spent the next three years there. In 1938, he developed a collaborative thesis with his fellow architecture student Miguel Gastón on a plan for the development of Varadero, the origin of the project that would become the basis for their later submission to the Cuban government. That summer, he also attended as a Cuban delegate the City Planning and Housing Congress organized by Carlos Contreras in Mexico City. At Harvard under Hudnut and the new chair of the architecture department, Walter Gropius, Montoulieu focused his studies on regional planning, absorbing the lessons of the Tennessee Valley Authority and the National Resources Planning Board, as well as the ideas of urbanism recently propounded by CIAM (Congrès Internationaux d'Architecture Moderne) and disseminated by Gropius and others at Harvard.[26] Montoulieu, who continued to publish articles promoting aspects of planning even after the activities of the Patronato Pro-Urbanismo had diminished, customarily identified himself as a planner, but he did practice architecture in Cuba and was closely associated with a group of young architects then emerging as the primary protagonists of modern architecture in Cuba. Under the leadership of the slightly older architect Eugenio Batista, Montoulieu, Gastón, Nicolás Arroyo, Rita Gutiérrez, and Mario Romañach began to advance the modernist discourse arriving from Europe, Brazil, and the United States.[27]

Together they founded a Cuban chapter of CIAM named ATEC (Agrupación Tectónica de Expresión Contemporánea [Tectonic Group of Contemporary Expression]). ATEC issued its manifesto in 1943, although it was likely organized earlier and as a direct result of a prolonged stay in Havana by José Luis Sert, a leading member of CIAM who met and became close to Eugenio Batista and the others in 1939.[28] Eugenio Batista and Arroyo would travel to England in 1947 to attend the sixth CIAM congress as the Cuban delegation. There, they heard the "Reaffirmation of the Aims of CIAM," which reiterated the organization's prewar declaration that planning would organize community life and proposed that the postwar period was witness to the emergence of "a new conception of integrated planning."[29] The two Cuban architects would also have observed that many of the CIAM groups were involved with city and regional planning at a governmental level. England itself offered a prime example; the new Town and Country Planning Act had just been introduced, and members of the British chapter, MARS (Modern Architectural Research Group), were employed as advisers to the Ministry of Town and Country Planning. The experience impressed upon Eugenio Batista and especially Arroyo the expansive scope of contemporary planning and, more importantly for these Cuban delegates, its necessary proximity to political processes and institutions. Members of ATEC who did not attend the congress still had ample exposure to CIAM polemic and its declarations regarding new concepts of integrated planning. Books like José Luis Sert's *Can Our Cities Survive?,* published in the United States in 1942, and his essay "The Human Scale in City Planning," published in translation in the journal *Arquitectura* in 1946, conveyed the principles.[30]

Further exposure to modernist debates in the 1940s was provided by visits to Cuba made by prominent practitioners. Richard Neutra, who came in 1944, was then working in Puerto Rico as a consultant in the design of dozens of rural schools and health centers, a model highly relevant to the Cuban situation. These projects were part of development programs being undertaken by the new Junta Nacional de Planificación de Puerto Rico created by Governor Rexford Tugwell and led by Rafael Picó. While Neutra exemplified for the Cuban architects a new style of architecture—a regional modernism—his work in Puerto Rico explicitly tied that architecture to a larger domain of planning.[31] Visiting in 1949, Walter Gropius discussed in formal lectures and informal meetings his adherence to a scientific approach to design. Gropius argued on principle for the coordination of disciplines that would be essential to a national planning effort—the same coordination depicted in Montoulieu's appeal to technicians. Jean Labatut, professor of architecture at Princeton University, traveled frequently to Cuba in the 1940s and 1950s after winning the commission to design a monument to José Martí in Havana. Although Labatut had a quite different stylistic and rhetorical predisposition than the members of CIAM, he did share the belief that architecture and urbanism were conjoined endeavors. As the founder of Princeton's Bureau of Urban Research, organized to collate research related to urban planning, Labatut brought architectural study to bear on the larger concerns of planning. For example, under his direction the bureau organized and published a symposium on the topic "Highways in Our National Life." Eugenio Batista, who had studied and been a teaching assistant at the Princeton University School of Architecture, remained in close contact with Labatut, as did Mario Romañach after meeting him during reviews at the University of Havana. Montoulieu meanwhile continued an informal dialogue with Sert, returning to Harvard for a planning degree and a teaching assistantship in the early 1950s. Cuban discourse thus absorbed a genealogically broad range of planning concepts that included the City Beautiful movement, New Deal policies, and CIAM polemic. Once in circulation in Cuba, and bound up with concurrent discourses on modern architecture, they emerged as a newly refashioned modernism, indebted to sources in Europe and North America, but no longer in close resemblance to them. The signal distinction lay in the political complexities of the Cuban context and the civic aims of the groups that invoked them. Some Cuban architects, with their colleagues in the arts, had begun to adopt the forms and the polemics of modernism in the 1920s, though they remained a minority in the profession as a whole. Modernism spread more widely during the 1930s but now in company with these other influences and entangled with the civic ambitions of national formation. In this circumstance, modernism was not conceived in relation to existing political and social structures, but instead emerged in association with the creation of new structures. Political and aesthetic aims underwent modernizing transformations in parallel rather than sequentially.

The Politics of Planning in Cuba

The manifesto of the Patronato Pro-Urbanismo asserted that no Cuban city was embellished with civic centers and that no real consideration had been given to the artistic and functional aspects of waterfronts and railway stations. Such claims were arguable: by 1933 the Cuban government had realized several elements of a plan for Havana by the French urbanist and landscape architect J. C. N. Forestier commissioned a decade earlier; and work had also begun on the Central Highway, a new transportation artery running along the spine of the island.

After the war, President Grau initiated a further portfolio of public works documented in a government publication, *Memoria del plan de obras del gobierno del Dr. Ramón Grau San Martín.*[32] A new road network for Havana, hospitals, and new infrastructure were included, but even ambitious public works such as these were less evidence of planning than proof of established patronage practices. State sponsorship of these various programs, certainly symptomatic of modernization but of political expediency as well, was not a sign of their functional coordination. The Patronato Pro-Urbanismo manifesto, citing nearly a dozen articles of the new constitution, forecast the opening of a novel political moment in the nation's history, a moment in which the relation between planning and politics might be fundamentally altered.

The central instrument the group envisioned for such a transformation, a national planning board, would necessarily have as much a political tenor as a professional one. In 1944, *Arquitectura* published an essay by Joseph Hudnut titled "Urbanismo y Política," a translation of his recent article "The Political Art of Planning." In the essay, Hudnut advocated for a vigorous engagement between planning and politics, arguing that the prevailing tendency to regard such engagement as inappropriate threatened to diminish the efficacy of planning. The recent abolition of the National Resources Planning Board in the United States epitomized such a consequence but would not, Hudnut believed, curtail a continuing evolution from informal or unofficial planning associations toward official planning authorities. Such an agency would be able to realize the artistic and the scientific aims of planning by taking, as Baron Haussmann had done in Paris, "the machinery of government as [its] paper and crayon. Committees, senates, and constitutions, finance, law, and human necessities [would be] the prime components of [its] art."[33] Hudnut's arguments clearly corresponded with the aims of the Patronato Pro-Urbanismo, expressing them more overtly as the desires of a profession rather than the recommendations of technicians, at the seemingly propitious moment of new governance in Cuba.

The transfer of power in the 1944 elections had given cause for optimism about the coalescence of political and civil stability, just as the publicity for Grau's public works program seemed to promise the adoption of a planning regimen. Both were illusory, however. Corruption under the Auténtico Party continued to foster political antipathies and public works were implemented in a partial and uncoordinated manner. In 1948, Carlos Prío Socarrás succeeded Grau as president, extending the rule of the Auténtico Party and also its exploitation of the economic prosperity of the postwar years as political stability deteriorated into *gangsterismo.* Eduardo Chibás, the founder of the rival political party known as the Ortodoxos, lost to Prío in the 1948 election but began a vocal campaign for reform of the disintegrating political sphere, denouncing corrupt officials by name and with details in regular radio broadcasts. In the same election, Fulgencio Batista won a seat in the Senate and returned to Cuba and to some degree of political influence. In 1952, he announced his candidacy for a return to the presidency in the next election. The electorate faced a choice between the ruling Auténtico Party, the weakened opposition Ortodoxos (Chibás had committed suicide the year before), and former president Batista. Before they could choose, Batista seized power in a *golpe de estado* during the night of March 9, 1952. The next day, he suspended the 1940 constitution.

Through the 1940s, national planning remained only an aspiration for the design professions as they pursued political opportunities rather than actual plans. In the realm of economics, though, a limited scope of national planning had begun to be realized. As in other nations, the relationship between the state and the economy was profoundly affected by mobilizations and controls during the second world war, and, like other nations, Cuba had turned to planning as a solution. To manage Cuba's economy during the war, President Batista created the Junta de Economía de Guerra, and appointed Gustavo Gutiérrez as its director. After the war, this agency was transformed into the Junta Nacional de Economía (JNE), and Gutiérrez remained as its head for the following decade, through the succession of elected presidencies and the 1952 *golpe de estado.*[34] The JNE acted as an advisory council for the executive, compiling economic data, monitoring the sectors of the Cuban economy, and recommending government actions and even legislation related to the economy. The board was not isolated from political concerns—economic policies continued to be distorted by political expediency and by the political influence of the *latifundistas,* the enormous landed interests that controlled agricultural production—but it was responsible for the first systematic efforts to define coordinated programs of economic development in Cuba.

Gutiérrez became involved in this initiative toward planning after earlier work and writings on internationalism and law, after involvement in practical politics as a representative, and, importantly, after participating in the drafting of the 1940 constitution. Gutiérrez formulated several general proposals for Cuba's economic development, each argued within a historical perspective. He diagnosed many structural problems in the Cuban economy as the residue of its colonial past and repeatedly underscored Cuba's urgent need to extricate its economic policies from political caprice, and throughout his tenure in the JNE, Gutiérrez maintained the constitutional project as an aspiration toward which the nation might continue to develop. It was Gutiérrez who had once described the 1940 constitution as "a multiple, radial plan," and among the several imperatives that followed from the constitution the understanding of the plan as an inventory of current facts assessed in order to project in the future a specific course of possibilities, events, and consequences resonated most profoundly in Gutiérrez's efforts to define the responsibilities of the JNE.[35] Under the presidencies of the late 1940s, Gutiérrez persistently attempted to install a planning function within Cuba's political sphere, winning a series of partial successes but not acquiring any extensive directive capacity.[36] Gutiérrez directed many proposals toward a professional audience and to the political leadership, but some exhortations on his vision of a path toward "progress and welfare" were addressed to citizens. In March 1950, he presented a lecture titled "El presente y el futuro de la economía cubana" (The present and future of the Cuban economy) to the Sociedad de Amigos de la República at the Lyceum in Havana. In the *Diario de la Marina* the following day, Jorge Mañach appraised Gutiérrez's talk as a lucid and authoritative exposition. From Gutiérrez's "central point of view *[punto de vista central],*" Mañach wrote, "the Cuban economy could be viewed as a landscape in the round *[paisaje de la rodonda],* as a system of multiple interests that need to be coordinated with a sense of responsibility and a sense of nation in order for Cuba to be able to take advantage of the moment of economic maturity."[37]

Different disciplinary spheres, however, had not yet been integrated into the central point of view capable of seizing this advantage. In 1949, Pedro Martínez Inclán insisted once again that the articles of the 1940 constitution compelled the existence of a national planning authority, and that "without local and national *planos reguladores* [master plans], it is materially impossible to fulfill the postulates of the Fundamental Charter of our nation."[38] But throughout this period, advocates of planning contended against the ramifications, perceived and real, of further integration of planning and politics. Some opposed to planning saw integrated planning as indistinguishable from the administered society of socialism or communism. Friedrich Hayek's widely disseminated *Road to Serfdom* summarized the attitudes of those who feared that even partial concession of central governmental planning authority in social and economic realms would result in such a society.[39] Proponents of planning attempted to overcome this view with reasoned descriptions of the possible synthesis of planning and liberalism. Joaquín Martínez Sáenz outlined such an argument in an address broadcast in 1949 on the *Universidad del Aire,* the radio program hosted by Mañach on current cultural and political affairs. Sáenz (one of the signatories of the 1940 constitution and later the director of the Banco Nacional) proposed that it was a fallacy to counterpose planning with an unadulterated liberalism because the latter existed nowhere in the modern world; the state exercised extensive authority over economic activity, especially during the war years, but also subsequently in the forms of trade tariffs and other artificial controls, without compromising individual liberty. Deliberate shaping of new institutions of planning would, Sáenz argued, lead the nation toward a "synthesis of political liberty and economic security."[40]

Planning also posed a challenge to existing political realities. Although an authoritarian government would be able to implement planning by fiat, the creation of planning agencies and corresponding planning legislation would likely constrain the proliferation of public works projects used to reward partisan interests. In this regard, advocacy for planning would have seemed antagonistic toward prevailing political practices, which by the late 1940s had reached new levels of financial corruption, and which, immediately following Batista's imposition of autocratic rule, seemed to obviate independent planning endeavors. From a perspective lodged between such opponents—between those who saw planning as an entry to socialism and those who recognized its challenge to existing political habits—Mañach offered a defense of planning. In a series of articles published in *Diario de la Marina* and the *Revista Lyceum* in 1952 and a longer essay published the next year he argued the relevance of the pragmatist thought of John Dewey as an appropriate basis for the democratic order that Mañach desired to see established in Cuba.[41] Cuba had lost all but the formal devices of its democratic structure just before Mañach published his essay, and the preceding decade under an admittedly imperfect democratic system had not seen any significant mitigation of the deleterious effects of capitalism. Lacking from Cuba's democratic system of the 1940s, Mañach suggested, was an adequate degree of authority, an authority capable of producing and enforcing the requisite disciplinary effects. Turning to Dewey, Mañach wrote:

> The remedy to [the effects of capitalism], according to Dewey, cannot consist of brutal planning, which suppresses liberty . . . What we need is not so much a severely planned society as a society *capable of planning [capaz de planificar]* or of planning intelligently *[proyectarse inteligentemente]*, which is not the same. He returns here to applying the experimental criteria. "We need an authority that, abandoning the old forms in which it operated, favors the capacity to direct and make use of change, and at the same time we also need a type of individual liberty distinct from that which unrestrained economic liberty has produced and justified—a liberty of general participation, under the guarantee and control of a socially organized authority."[42]

Mañach thus retrieved a sense of planning not as the authoritarian desire for regimentation to be imposed upon a society, but as a more fundamental "capacity to plan" to be embedded within the society itself. Mañach had already given his approving report on Gutiérrez's 1950 lecture, in which the economist described the coordination of collective interest as the prerequisite for the final maturation of Cuban society, and here drew a passage from Dewey that unmistakably framed that coordination as the volition of a participating citizenry. (An echo could be heard also of Gutiérrez's lament that during the revolutionary period and its aftermath, without the sanctions and limits of a constitutional framework, the nation lacked the capacity to plan.)

Mañach's invocation of planning as the instrument by which such participatory governance could be achieved augmented the political and cultural relevance of planning discourse in Cuba. In disseminating this view of planning into public discourse, his essays added a different layer of political implication to what was more often proposed as a professional science. His argument particularized the general distrust of planning's authoritarian potential, proposing that in the Cuban context planning could in fact serve as a defense against authoritarianism by soliciting a voluntary delegation of an extensive administrative role. At the same time, and in accord with his own continued defense of the suspended constitution, Mañach was presenting a more critical judgment of Batista's new government, though he pointedly implied a preference for evolutionary rather than revolutionary transition. Dewey's pragmatism, he cautioned, outlined a process of progressive change and gradual adjustment by which a new society could arise without passage through another revolutionary period. Joseph Hudnut's article ten years earlier addressed the planning profession, whereas Mañach directed his essays to a lay audience, but both contained a similar appeal for the political viability of planning. In the earlier moment, planning held the potential to overcome divisive factionalism; now, Mañach perceived in the wake of the *golpe de estado*, planning might guard against a consolidated authority.

The Junta Nacional de Planificación

During the early 1950s, Cuba's economic prosperity propelled a building boom, and the rapid urban expansion of Havana only exacerbated the problems of unregulated, speculative development that the Patronato Pro-Urbanismo had condemned ten years earlier. New subdivisions extended the city fabric to the west and south, while traffic congested the streets of central Havana. The passage of a Ley de Propiedad Horizontal (condominium law) accelerated the speculative real-estate market, and added the new building type of high-rise condominiums to the Havana skyline.[43] Now, against the backdrop of an unelected but relatively stable administration, the combination of these dramatic physical transformations and the fragility of a speculative economy brought the concerns of economists like Gutiérrez and architects like Montoulieu into ever greater proximity. The haphazard construction activities that Montoulieu condemned in the 1940s had only increased in scale and pace; the risks of Cuba's single-crop economy that Gutiérrez identified were only exacerbated by the boom in speculation.

The two constituencies they represented finally joined in 1953, brought together by the shared issue of planning. In April of that year, a conference titled "Sobre la Conveniencia de una Ley de Planificación Nacional" (On the advisability of a national planning law) gathered representatives from three professional institutions, the Colegio Nacional de Arquitectos (which convened the meeting), the Sociedad Cubana de Ingenieros, and the Junta Nacional de Economía; the government was represented as well, by the architect Enrique Luis Varela, who was undersecretary of public works, and by two members of the Consejo Consultivo. (With the legislature suspended by General Batista, the Consejo Consultivo, or Consulting Council, acted as an executive advisory council to help formulate government policies and legislation.) Most in the audience were affiliated with one or more of the professional groups, and were already convinced of the necessity of national planning; the audience to be persuaded of the advantages of a Ley de Planificación were the members of the Consejo Consultivo (one of whom was the journalist Armando Maribona, who had been a member of the Patronato Pro-Urbanismo), and through that body, Batista himself.

Recent actions by the Consejo Consultivo had precipitated the meeting—legislation then under review by the council had a direct bearing on economic and fiscal policies. The moment appeared decisive for a transformation to a coordinated form of government planning, and speakers emphasized the urgency of immediate action. Gutiérrez, speaking as the head of the JNE, rehearsed the details for the audience.[44] A year earlier, the JNE had conceived a trilogy of laws related to economic management: a Ley de Alquileres (rent law), a Ley de Viviendas (housing law), and a Ley de Urbanismo y Planificación (planning and urban planning law). Gutiérrez, believing that the issues of finance and housing policy could not be considered separately from a more comprehensive policy of planning, had established committees within the JNE to study the physical and financial dimensions of planning. The financial planning committee included representatives from the Banco Nacional and BANFAIC and an economist in the JNE, Luis José Abalo. Maribona was a member of the physical planning committee, as was the architect Honorato Colete.[45] Colete was instrumental in formulating a final proposal for a Ley de Planeación Urbana y Rural del Desarrollo Económico y sus Financiamientos (law for the planning and financing of urban and rural economic development) that, as its lengthy title suggested, incorporated financial policy into a comprehensive planning regimen; when he addressed the 1953 conference, he confirmed Gutiérrez's criticism that this law might be fatally undermined by an alternative proposal submitted to the Consejo Consultivo in which financial aspects would be addressed in separate, rival legislation. Gutiérrez, Colete, and the other speakers insisted on an integrated planning, a comprehensive managerial scope adjacent to, but insulated from, political policies and activities. They proposed, in essence, that integrated planning become a functional governmental power. From the point of view represented by Gutiérrez and Colete—the economists' perspective—only an integrated planning could properly guarantee the effective and responsible realization of proposals; only integrated planning could adequately assess the dynamic effects of the interaction of fiscal and physical regulation. If financial policy were, through such a scientific planning regimen, made independent of political policy and also linked to programmatic development, the misdirection of governmental expenditure by political exigency would greatly diminish.

Agustín Sorhegui, president of the Colegio de Arquitectos, offered the audience a parallel history, rehearsing the consolidation of planning advocacy from the architects' perspective. Where Gutiérrez had listed his own efforts and accomplishments in the economic sphere beginning in 1943, Sorhegui recalled the work of the Patronato Pro-Urbanismo and the persistent effort by Cuban architects to impress upon successive governments the urgent necessity of a national planning law. He agreed that more than urban planning was required; an integral planning that took account of national resources and national aims was the only adequate solution. He also agreed that it would be necessary to ensure the autonomy of planning in relation to political activity, and to convince governments that planning would assist rather than impair programs of public works. His support for planning, though, derived fundamentally from his dissatisfaction with, even abhorrence for, the disorderly development of the city: "Had there existed a Planning Law, our cities would not have grown in anarchic form in which they have been made, without prior zoning, without study of the principal routes of communication, slovenly for having neither strips of land with sufficient width nor grand open spaces for parks, which constitute the lungs with which cities breathe."[46] These features were the same symptoms earlier denounced by the Patronato Pro-Urbanismo, and suggest that for the architect, planning promised the amelioration of a social rather than political pathology. This suggestion implied in turn the belief that through the techniques of planning, a transformed physical environment could produce a transformed social environment, a sequence of transformation presented to the conference in a different fashion by Alberto Prieto Suárez, dean of planning at the School of Architecture at the University of Havana. Suárez argued that an unbroken chain of planning procedures extended from "the simple elements of aesthetic ordering" all the way to coordination at a regional scale.[47] The claim that such a transaction could be effected provided the basis for an emerging architectural rendition of planning with three salient characteristics: first, it gave precedent to the physical environment as the object of planning work; second, it proposed a direct causational relation between physical and social environments; and third, it introduced into planning an aesthetic standard of valuation.

With this formulation came a preliminary consolidation of professional roles. A recurring theme during the meeting was that an idealistic or selfless commitment to the nation was not only an individual but a collective professional responsibility. Suárez phrased it in the grandest terms, declaring that "the Planning of a nation . . . is one of the most noble initiatives that a people, its Government, and its institutions ought to consider."[48] Speaking to and on behalf of the Colegio de Arquitectos, Sorhegui cast this sentiment in terms of professional obligation: "The Colegio de Arquitectos, in holding this function, is complying with one of the inescapable duties fixed upon it by the Decreto-Ley de Colegiación that originated it, that of always dedicating to the nation and to the society in which we live the cooperation of the technical knowledge of its professionals in order to carry out in full the social function that corresponds to it."[49] (Montoulieu's earlier assertion of the obligation of technicians to recognize and fulfill their social function and to commit their expertise to the collective interest had given a precedent for such claims.) At this moment, with the equal standing of professions assumed, the summoning of professional allegiance could still be a natural corollary to a more general appeal to civic conscience and could effectively circumvent the potential distraction of political affiliation in favor of presumptively objective skills. In fact, planning would become an arena of significant contention between these professions, as architects, engineers, economists, and lawyers refined their concepts of planning with distinctive rival emphases. As different professionals pledged their mutual cooperation in the shared endeavor of planning, each simultaneously delineated its scope of exclusive expertise within planning. The conflation of order in a social environment with perceptible physical order insinuated into planning an aesthetic dimension alongside its economic and political dimensions, and the invocation of professional allegiance reinforced architects' singular disciplinary claim to matters of aesthetic valuation.

In April 1953, a more present concern than the standing of the professions in relation to one another was their standing in relation to the government. As individuals, the conference participants possessed disparate political views and different degrees of proximity to Batista's administration, but the projects—legislative, economic, physical—they proposed as professional groups would inevitably compel a participatory role in its activities. The planning advocacy pursued over the preceding decade had consolidated a standard of professional objectivity that could now be summoned as a sense of political disinterest, and though to some extent a merely rhetorical claim, this assertion of disinterest did enable the distantiation of professional and political pursuits. While power remained firmly lodged in Batista's hands, the independent practices and discourses of the professions were still needed to translate that power into viable and operative forms. At a second event, the "Fórum sobre la Plaza Cívica y Monumento a Martí" (Forum on the Plaza Cívica and the Monumento a Martí), held in Havana in May and June of the same year, the government's failure to situate a proposed monument to José Martí into the context of a comprehensive urban plan was construed as further evidence of the necessity of planning legislation. This debate included a brief but influential foreign intervention in the form of a telegram sent by José Luis Sert. The architect Eugenio Batista, attempting to solidify the argument that flaws in the design of the Plaza Cívica evidenced the urgent need for planning, solicited the intervention in a telephone call and letter to Sert. Optimistic that the Fórum might succeed "in introducing into the mentality of the people and Cuban politicians" a conviction of the advantages of planning, he requested that Sert help by offering his official views as president of CIAM.[50] Sert obliged, responding with a telegram presented at the next session of the Fórum. Sert concurred that a master plan or a pilot plan should be devised in advance of the siting and design of a complex of buildings. "A civic center of this type," he concluded, "which ought to be the heart of the city, should be planned in accordance with the most advanced technical knowledge, thereby avoiding the repetition of errors that, knowing what technical solutions the circumstances require, are inexcusable today."[51] Eugenio Batista reported back to Sert that when he had read aloud Sert's telegram, the Fórum had "applauded enthusiastically," in spite of rules against such displays.[52]

The organizers of the Fórum unanimously agreed on a six-point official statement by the Colegio de Arquitectos based on the criticisms voiced. The statement concluded that the lack of any "true planning *[verdadera planificación]*" at any point during the long evolution of the project for the Plaza Cívica was to be blamed for its several eventual shortcomings: the lack of formal and functional coordination between the various buildings to be sited around the plaza; the absence of regulation over the zones of influence of the plaza to prevent the development of inappropriate or harmful speculative projects in its environs; and the failure to consider the economics of the project, from the initial acquisition of land to the later realization of buildings, in relation to the overall economic capacities and needs of the nation. In consequence, the Fórum statement reiterated the now familiar pronouncement of "the urgent need and advisability of providing for the Nation a *National Planning Law that really* creates conditions for its *Planning.*"[53] A delegation from the Colegio de Arquitectos met with General Batista to present the conclusions of the Fórum and, according to the journal *Arquitectura,* Batista agreed to advance planning legislation within the month.

That particular promise went unfulfilled as professional forums ceded their position in civic debate to reports on the July 26 assault on the Moncada Barracks at Santiago de Cuba, which, though unsuccessful, marked the beginning of the revolution against Batista's regime. The trial in September of the surviving rebels and their leader, Fidel Castro, was intended to demonstrate the defeat of the rebellion, but in a speech later known for his claim that "History will absolve me," Castro recapitulated the illegitimacy of Batista's regime by defending his actions with an eloquent denunciation of Batista and an avowal of his desire to restore the 1940 constitution. Although overshadowed by this political turn, planning remained the focus of professional concern throughout the year. Rafael Picó, the director of the Junta Nacional de Planificación in Puerto Rico, visited Cuba during the summer. Lectures he gave on the structure and accomplishments of national planning were received with special attention because of the physical and cultural similarities of the two islands. In July, Nicolás Quintana, a younger architect who would soon assume a role as a leading proponent and practitioner of urban planning, attended the 1953 CIAM congress in Aix-en-Provence, where he met and traveled with Sert. In August, Sert arrived in Havana where, in a lecture to the Colegio de Arquitectos and in a subsequent interview with Maribona for *Diario de la Marina,* he expanded on the summary argument of his telegram, discussing the requirements of a pilot plan, the importance for cities of a classified road network, and the need to identify and address the specific social and economic factors of the region in order to effectively plan its development.[54] No less important than this public advocacy were the appeals and suggestions he made personally and directly to Cuban architects. Sert spoke from a position of institutional authority, as the president of CIAM and as the new dean of the Graduate School of Design at Harvard, and professional authority, as a partner in Town Planning Associates, which had entered a second decade of practice focused almost entirely in Latin America. Sert had opened the firm with Paul Lester Wiener and Paul Schulz in New York City in 1942, and by 1953 Town Planning Associates had developed several (for the most part unrealized) pilot and master plans for new and existing cities in Latin America.[55] Sert and Wiener had also collaborated on smaller projects, including two private commissions in

Cuba. In 1952, a group of New York investors solicited a design for a typical sector of low-cost housing to be submitted to a Cuban National Housing Program sponsored by the Instituto Cubano de la Vivienda. Town Planning Associates produced drawings and models of two-, three-, and four-bedroom units, along with a site model for a hypothetical neighborhood, which were exhibited in Havana. Sert took his trip to Havana in 1953 for the second commission, the design of a beachfront resort hotel with two adjacent private cottages on the Isle of Pines, off Cuba's southern coast.[56]

Neither project was executed, but they allowed Sert to renew contact with his Cuban colleagues and as a direct consequence he and Wiener became closely involved in the creation of a national planning organization in Cuba. Their relationship with Nicolás Arroyo proved pivotal. Arroyo had been appointed as the director of the Comisión de Planificación Centro Turístico de Varadero, a new regional planning board responsible for formulating and regulating the development of Varadero, the small town and a beach resort on a narrow peninsula east of Havana used by Montoulieu as a prototypical planning case in the 1942 Patronato exhibition. Batista's government had chosen Varadero for development as a primary tourist area, as a model for the expansion and diversification of the Cuban economy through a larger and more profitable tourist industry. More important, Arroyo had attracted the attention and sufficient confidence of General Batista to be in a position to address him directly regarding the architects' campaign for national planning.[57] After a meeting with Arroyo in New York, Wiener and Sert drafted a memo for him outlining the feasibility and desirability of a "Pilot and Master Plan for Metropolitan Area of Habana."[58] The memo, which Arroyo intended to use as part of a presentation to Batista, described the central benefit of planning as the management of the growth of cities without the chaotic effects of financial waste, slums, traffic congestion, and other familiar problems of the modern city. It provided general definitions of master plans and their contents, and suggested that along with a plan for Havana, regional and national plans should be prepared as well. Wiener and Sert concluded the memo with a proposal for their retainer as consultants for the master and pilot plans, including an outline of fees and a scope of work.

In the spring of 1954, while awaiting the outcome of that proposal, Town Planning Associates commenced two professional collaborations with Arroyo, designing a new subdivision on the outskirts of Havana with his architectural firm, and acting as advisers to his government office for the master planning project about to commence in Varadero. The Varadero plan had been under discussion for some time, but Batista had finally given orders to Arroyo to proceed with what would be the first comprehensive master plan in Cuba since Forestier's work in Havana nearly thirty years earlier.[59] Town Planning Associates also pursued unsuccessfully a promising commission for the planning of Habana del Este, an area of undeveloped land on the eastern side of the Havana harbor, but that commission was offered to Skidmore, Owings, and Merrill (SOM) in late 1954. For Sert and Wiener, their disappointment was likely mitigated by the imminent culmination of the long campaign for national planning. Arroyo's proximity to government officials and his direct contact with General Batista had supplied the final necessary link, and he was asked by Batista to prepare an enabling act of legislation for a national planning office. In November, Arroyo and Wiener agreed that Town Planning Associates would assist, with the two firms sharing the cost of consulting fees.[60] A friend and colleague of Sert's, Professor Charles Haar of the Harvard Law School, was recruited to supply a draft of the legislation to be forwarded to Cuba. In December, Wiener asked Paul Schulz to draw up contract arrangements for Town Planning Associates to act as consultants for Pilot Plans for Varadero, Havana, Trinidad, and as advisers to the National Planning Office.[61]

Ley-Decreto No. 2018, signed by Batista on January 27, 1955, created the Junta Nacional de Planificación (JNP).[62] The preamble of the enabling act cited article 264 of the Constitution of 1940, which directed the state to increase national prosperity through the development of public works.[63] It also cited the studies of specialized organizations such as the United Nations and the experience of other nations as having demonstrated the necessity of planned development and technical coordination to achieve such prosperity. And it acknowledged the long campaign undertaken by professionals and specialists from diverse scientific, civic, and cultural institutions to enumerate the advantages of planning. In consequence, the decree established the new agency (described as "an autonomous technical organism, in the nature of a consultant and adviser for the Executive Power") to conduct a comprehensive portfolio of planning activity:

> La Junta Nacional de Planificación (JNP) will have as its principal object the preparation of a *Plan Regulador Nacional* and such *Planes Reguladores y Urbanos*

> as are necessary for it, and that will serve to guide the scientific and economic development of the nation, with the goal of sponsoring, in the most effective form, improvement in housing, sources of jobs and communications, obtaining greater efficiency and economy in the use of land and the exploitation of natural resources, with a view to attaining the greater welfare of all citizens.[64]

This national planning program would be conducted by implementing several procedures: the acquisition and compilation of data on existing conditions; the study and analysis of resources and objectives; the assessment, recommendation, and projection of plans of actions; and the coordination of related activities conducted by other public or private agencies. Compilation, analysis, projection, and coordination—these were the fundamental tasks, as defined by the enabling act, that together constituted the mechanism of planning. Within the JNP, responsibility for supervising these tasks was assigned to a Consejo Ejecutivo, an executive council composed of two architects, two engineers, and one economist (to be nominated by the president of the Junta Nacional de Economía). The minister of public works would be president of the JNP ex officio, thus securing a close proximity between the agency and the executive.

This prominent role was given to Nicolás Arroyo, who, having choreographed the creation of the JNP, was appointed by Batista as minister of public works and president of the JNP. Able to determine the internal structure of the junta and choose the staff for its executive council and various departments, Arroyo was now in a position to act on the lesson learned at the 1947 CIAM congress, the need to integrate professional and governmental planning activities. Joining Arroyo as members of the executive council were the engineers Vicente J. Salles and Armando Pérez Cobo and the architect Agustín Sorhegui. The president of the Junta Nacional de Economía, Gustavo Gutiérrez, nominated Luis José Abalo as the economist required for the remaining council seat.[65] Arroyo himself made appointments to the departments within which almost all of the work of the JNP would be carried out: he named Eduardo Montoulieu as Jefe del Plan Regulador Nacional, Mario Romañach as Jefe del Plan Regulador de la Habana, Nicolás Quintana as Jefe de los Planes Reguladores de Varadero y Trinidad, and Jorge Mantilla as Jefe del Plan Regulador de Isla de Pinos. (Each was paired with a young architect to act as an assistant; these "Segundo Jefes" were, respectively, Felipe Préstamo, Pelayo Fraga, Osvaldo Tapia Ruano, and Guillermo Núñez.) Eduardo

Cañas Abril and Armando Maribona assumed positions as public relations and press officials for the junta. The final role, the position of expert consultant to the JNP, was filled by Town Planning Associates. On behalf of the Cuban state, Arroyo signed a contract with the firm on July 1, 1955, agreeing that in return for consultations and collaborations with the JNP, Town Planning Associates would receive an annual retainer of $120,000 plus expenses.[66] Town Planning Associates would encounter persistent delays in receiving payments from the Cuban government over the next few years, but the agreed sum suggested a deep commitment to the transformation of processes of physical and economic development on the island, for these fees were ostensibly appropriated for planning, for assessment, and for projection, rather than for capriciously conceived building projects and political programs. They also represented an enormous sum for Town Planning Associates, a small firm with few employees, making the Cuba commission central to the office's work and its stature. The JNP was a source of professional authority for the Cuban architects on its staff as well, and promised the extension of the architectural modernism they developed in their private commissions into a larger field of activity.

Now that a national planning office existed and the project of planning could commence, a new specificity of definition was needed, both of professional roles and of planning itself. Immediately after the enabling law was issued, as part of what must have been a concerted campaign of publicity accompanying the creation of the JNP, several representatives made appearances to discuss the new agency and its role. A daily television program called *Comentarios Económicos* (Economic comments) conducted interviews with Arroyo, Sorhegui, Abalo, Cañas Abril, and Maribona, and also with representatives from professional associations of architects and engineers, to solicit their judgments. What would planning accomplish? What would be its tangible or visible effects? What roles would be played by the different professions and what benefit would accrue to them? The rationale and the promise of planning were presented in much the same general terms as they had been over the preceding years: planning proposed an alternative to the deleterious effects of improvisation, lack of foresight, and demagoguery that had persistently compromised Cuban civil society. This characterization was offered by Cañas Abril, who declared the planning law "the most transcendental and important measure that has been promulgated in Cuba in recent years, because it tends toward a national legislation directing all constructive activities to favor the collective good."[67] The others interviewed on the program expressed a similar belief that the planning law offered a vital instrument for Cuba's social and economic progress but also pointed out that many of its specific details remained uncertain. Abalo noted that the earlier draft law projected by the JNE had included a considered proposal for developing and managing fiscal dimensions of planning and policy (thus implying a shortcoming in the actual decree). The president of the planning commission of the Colegio de Ingenieros, José Luis Sust, sidestepped questions about whether architects should have more responsibilities than engineers with the ambiguous response: "There are conductors who are pianists and conductors who are violinists. Now, all one needs to know is how to be a conductor."[68]

For his part, Arroyo offered reassurances that civil engineers would be centrally involved in the work of the JNP, but the predominance of architects was evident, as was the sense that the JNP was the fulfillment of the efforts of the Colegio de Arquitectos, regardless of the support for planning from other fields. The architect, as the technician who Montoulieu proposed would play a mediatory role in civil society, had become a political figure. At its inception, the JNP contained potential weaknesses tied to its central mandate to act as a coordinating authority connecting virtually all fields of professional endeavor. These weaknesses would become apparent as its work commenced, exposing the seemingly irreconcilable differences between professional and political spheres. The fundamentally architectural cast of the JNP and the way in which its architectural perspective dominated the work of planning undermined the idea of integral planning and the possibilities for synchronized disciplinary approaches. At the same time, both inside and outside the JNP, concern persisted that integral planning implied an ambition of regimentation characteristic of totalitarian states, or that the inescapable affiliation of the JNP to General Batista rendered its activities political, even authoritarian, rather than exercises of objective expertise. This circumstance seemed evidence that integral planning had achieved political sanction at a disabling cost. Hudnut's assertion, made a dozen years earlier, that planning should aspire to executive authority and consequently to political accountability, had been realized but in association with a government that was itself removed from civil structures of accountability. In a sense, then, as Martínez Inclán and the other members of the Patronato Pro-Urbanismo desired, the postulates of the Fundamental Charter had been fulfilled, but they had been fulfilled in a manner that seemed to reinscribe their divorce from the civil sphere that the constitution had aspired to produce.

3 A Perfect Structuring

Representing the Nation as Plan and Purpose

HAVANA was among the first cities to be founded in the new territories of the Spanish empire, well prior to the 1573 compilation of the royal ordinances known as Las Leyes de Indias (Laws of the Indies), so it was not as a matter of causation that the Laws of the Indies would have caught the attention of twentieth-century Cuban architects or planners.[1] But in their other respects—as historically contingent constitutive statutes, as reminders of the continuous presence of the law as a discursive form in Cuba, as earlier examples of attempts of the ruling elite to manage in advance the unfolding of social events—the ordinances would have resonated as a precedent for the latest legal instrument of order, the 1940 constitution. In the 1930s and 1940s, several historians of Latin American urbanism debated the instrumentality of the Laws of the Indies. The Argentinean historian Miguel Solá began his *Historia del arte hispano-americano* (History of Spanish-American art), published in 1935, with quotations from several articles of the Laws of the Indies that suggested their influence over the disposition of colonial cities. In 1942 and again in 1948, the architectural historian George Kubler discussed the "famous urban statutes," arguing that existing settlements likely provided models of urban form incorporated into the ordinances.[2] Other historians had taken up the genealogy of the ordinances and considered alternative possibilities, launching a study of the influence of the Laws of the Indies on urban morphology that continued through the 1950s and on to the present moment.[3] The historical examination pursued during the 1940s and 1950s persistently sought to establish what had provided the model for the new cities of Spanish America, whether it was the physical forms of existing gridiron urban layouts in Spain or in pre-Columbian America, or the conceptual forms described in Renaissance treatises by Alberti and Filarete. Little consideration was given, however, to interpreting the ordinances themselves as a model. The Laws of the Indies were regarded either as a transcription of architectural theory or as a description of existing conditions, and the constitutive and mediatory properties of the ordinances—their projection of a programmatic plan, the motivations and potentials of their legal form—were not acknowledged. The progression of this historical research ignored the critical synthesis that the ordinances embodied: the discursive reciprocity of law and architecture.[4]

Writing in 1938 on the history of Cuban constitutionalism, Gustavo Gutiérrez adumbrated Ángel Rama's later conception of two civic actualities, the real city and *la cuidad letrada*. Gutiérrez argued that every nation has two constitutions: "one *theoretical* or *literary* that lives in the formalities of the Fundamental Charter, and another *real* or *practical* formed by life itself in the development of national institutions."[5] The first category, which Gutiérrez also called the "formal," existed in the textual material of the charter; the second, which he called the "biological," was the sum of interactions of events and institutions. The inherent potential of any historical moment, he claimed, was measured and revealed by the degree of correspondence between these two levels, between the two constitutions. Correspondence, not reduction or identity, was the goal: "While the constitutions separate themselves more, the more difficult is constitutional life and more disposed to disturbances and revolutions. While they draw closer and mix more, the life of a nation is made easier, and social welfare *[bienestar social]* more likely and more lasting."[6] In 1952, Gutiérrez would reiterate his postulate of the coexistence of two constitutions, the formal and the biological, and conclude with regret that the "Cuban formal Constitution is in many aspects superior to and more advanced than the biological constitution."[7]

At the same time Gutiérrez proposed his idea of constitutional correspondence, there was in fact a precocious awareness of the Laws of the Indies in Cuba among persons concerned with the overlapping spheres of law and architecture. This awareness may have originated in exchanges between Cuban and Mexican professionals, through events such as the sixteenth International Congress of Planning and Housing held in Mexico City in August 1938. Its organizing committee included a representative from Cuba, Francisco Carrera y Jústiz, professor in the School of Social Sciences at the University of Havana, who specialized in municipal law and had published essays considering urbanism as a municipal science. Martínez Inclán and Montoulieu were among the several Cuban architects and planners who attended the congress.[8] Studies published by the congress included a portfolio of historical plans of Mexico City, with analyses by Federico Gómez de Orozco and Justino Fernández (a historian and an urbanist, respectively) whose analytic approach deliberately aligned historical studies and contemporary planning as parallel endeavors. Although without specific reference to the Laws of the Indies, their methodological approach married a historical understanding of legislation with analysis and projection of urban morphology, so that it resembled the concept of the ordinances themselves.[9] Carrera y Jústiz, as his writings made clear, already recognized the instrumental potential of the proximity of law and urbanism (and in 1940, he would publish notes on the relation between municipal law and the new constitution).[10] The analyses presented at the congress could have sharpened the perception of that critical relation for those who, like Martínez Inclán and Montoulieu, had approached urbanism from the perspective of the architectural profession.

A passing reference to the Laws of the Indies in the Patronato Pro-Urbanismo manifesto—to emphasize the careless nature of developments in the contemporary city—was the first indication of their cognizance of the precedent. But the tangible evidence of a precocious comprehension of the Laws of the Indies in Cuba emerged in 1945, with the publication of a short essay titled *El urbanismo en las leyes de Indias* (Urbanism in the Laws of the Indies), by Francisco Domínguez Compañy.[11] In this essay—the first theorization of the ordinances since their prior obsolesence—Domínguez Compañy argued that the Laws of the Indies should be seen as an equivalent to "the Science of Urbanism"; their regulation of circulation, sanitation, and social and formal configuration—the "material contents *[continente material]*" of the city—consisted of the same scope of activity, albeit on a less complex scale than in the modern era. He recognized, moreover, that "the Ordinances . . . constitute an organized plan, a perfect structuring, in accord with the principles maintained by the modern Science of Urbanism, in containing a generating and regulating plan of the urban landscape, or, the image of the city."[12] The Laws of the Indies would have taken on particular significance in the shadow cast by the 1940 constitution and its associated debates. As statutes that projected a plan to produce the image of the city, they were quite obviously analogous to the new fundamental charter that projected a plan to constitute the civic sphere. A discursive synthesis between law and architecture already perceptible—in the work of Carrera y Jústiz, for example, and equally in the two ceremonies to ratify and promulgate the constitution—might be explicitly recognized as a mechanism through which the institutions and practices of architecture could be coupled to the project of the constitution.

The historical example of the Laws of the Indies made this potential explicit to the *letrados* of postwar Cuba—Martínez Inclán and Montoulieu, as well as Gutiérrez, Mañach, the historian Roig de Leuchsenring, and others—who were already engaged in the formulation of new bases for civil society. If conceptual norms and experiential realities were both actualities, equally objects of substance or influence, then to reform them similar means would need to be devised. Here, Mañach offered a caution. In lectures delivered and published in the late 1940s, Mañach identified a perennial disposition that he suggested had emerged in Latin America following the independence wars of the early nineteenth century as the new nations began to define their political and social structures.[13] Their inheritance from Spain met with the American environment, combining a contemplative idealism and a determined sense of action that Mañach called *quijotismo* to acknowledge the paradigmatic representation of a relentless determination to summon up the ideal as reality itself. *Quijotismo* was an "affirmation of the ideal against the grain of experience, and often behind its back; an essentially contemplative attitude, that the cervantesque paradigm wanted to bring to action."[14] Mañach admired this tendency toward the "ideal pragmatism of Don Quijote" for its decision to produce goodness rather than contemplate the good. However, this same resolve for action—for *quijotismo* over *quijotidad*—was equally a conflict, a "tenacious conflict between the more or less ideal norm (learned in the books of political chivalry) and the . . . primary reality of America, of which Sancho continuously reminded us."[15] Riding so roughly over the facts and evidence of experience, Don Quijote could never truly reconcile them with his idealism. "America," Mañach concluded, "is in need of an idealism more sober in its words and more moderate in its deeds."[16] The Laws of the Indies maintained parallel to the "primary reality" of the actual city an "ideal norm" in the form of an originary diagram endowed with similarly redemptive aspirations. And the slogan of the Patronato Pro-Urbanismo, "Mejores ciudades, ciudadanos mejores," could likewise sponsor a renewed *quijotismo,* with each half of its formula divided again into a real and an ideal existence. In order to consolidate a unified civic sphere, the distance between the two cities had to be bridged, Gutiérrez's two constitutions had to be drawn closer together, by some means necessarily imbued with *quijotismo* and tempered by the mordant realism of Sancho Panza.

From the Athens Charter to the Havana Charter

For Cuban architects committed to and working to extend the precepts of modernism, a modern parallel to the Laws of the Indies—and a transition from their monarchical privilege to a technical authority—could be found in the Athens Charter of CIAM. Derived from the carefully edited deliberations of the fourth CIAM congress held in 1933, the Athens Charter laid out the requisite conditions of the Functional City as deduced from dozens of analytic studies of existing cities presented at the congress. In a format that counterposed observations of existing conditions to requirements for future alternatives, the document condemned the rapid, haphazard development of cities caused by industrial and economic modernization, and proposed a new mitigatory regime of urbanism. Most famously, the Athens Charter defined the city as a composite of four "functions"—dwelling, leisure, work, and circulation—each assigned to its own sector and accommodated by a prescribed architectural solution. The Functional City consisted in the rational regulation of these four functions by architecture, with the provision of space and form adequate to each, so that they operated in harmony as an urban environment. (The four functions were soon understood as the summary proposition of the charter as a whole.) Implicit throughout the document, and at times explicitly stated, was the presumption of a political transformation from laissez-faire capitalism either to managed economies, or, preferably, to socialized ownership of land and production. These political dimensions of the Athens Charter would have been received in Cuba, as they were by the CIAM membership, with varying degrees of approbation. But in Cuba the form and example of the document provided a relevant and useful model distinct from its political content—for the Athens Charter was unmistakably a constitutional text, a constitution for the modern city. José Luis Sert published one version of the text in New York in 1942 as an appendix to his book *Can Our Cities Survive?*, and the successful propaganda of CIAM distributed the Athens Charter further in the postwar years, through the academic and professional work of CIAM figures.[17]

The Athens Charter largely refrained from supplying specific or detailed recommendations; its contents were a set of principles, to be comprehensively applied to specific cases. Its very name posited its constitutional nature, an outline of the general presuppositions of conditions that ought to obtain in the future. Those conditions, once met, would constitute the Functional City. The Athens Charter opened with a preamble that asserted the interrelation between the city and its political, economic, social, and physical surroundings; with the disruption of the equilibrium of these factors by mechanization, the preamble concluded, cities had been seized by chaos. Four sections followed, each divided into observations and requirements, in which a series of articles established the principles relevant to each of the four functions. The section on housing, for example, observed that the population densities compressed into unsuitable congested sectors in the present-day city required planned residential sectors oriented to the provisions of the natural environment. But the requirement was set in the normative terms of a principle, not the methodical terms of technique. A supplementary category on the Historical Parts of Cities (apparently added to the Athens Charter with some circumspection) mandated the protection of historical elements in cities as long as their preservation did not cause any detriment in terms of the four functions and as long as their preservation was not considered a sanction for the use of "styles of the past" in new structures.[18] Reluctance to consider these articles integrally part of the charter obviously stemmed from CIAM's doctrinal repudiation of eclecticism and academicism in favor of modernism, but their inapposite quality also testified to the constitutional nature of the document. As a constitution brings its object into existence, any existing realities must be integrated into the framework of the constitution, a process that can only be effected by their transformative accommodation to the narrative terms of the constitution. In 1940, the delegates recast the historical Cuba as the initiation of a process, and reworked "el hecho cubano" (the Cuban fact) as the raw material for the normative framework of the fundamental charter. Because its own drafters saw the historical city as the problem to be overcome rather than the project to be fulfilled, the Athens Charter could not fully incorporate that reality, but only quarantine its residue.

The Athens Charter did not endeavor to produce the image of the city so much as its organization. Certainly, the architects who drafted the document had images in mind, but those were not translated into the text; had they been, they would have fixed its principles too firmly and too precisely, rendering it not a constitution but a statutory code. Its articles aimed to establish what ought to be, and so, without selecting among formal or physical approaches, stipulated the organizational principles of the cities in the classification and the distribution of the four functions. The charter also situated the city in terms of its relational connections, to the surrounding region, to economic imperatives, and to political and social exigencies, describing its organizational hierarchies as the physical mediation of these contextual forces, again much like a foundational charter. In two articles of the concluding section, the constitutional (as opposed to statutory) premise was confirmed by these hortatory statements:

> 85: It is a matter of the most urgent necessity that every city draw up its program and enact the laws that will enable it to be carried out.
> 86: The program must be based on rigorous analyses carried out by specialists. It must provide for its stages in time and in space. It must bring together in fruitful harmony the natural resources of the site, the overall topography, the economic facts, the sociological demands, and the spiritual values.[19]

Constructing the image of the city was a task to be undertaken by technicians within the framework of the charter. So, as the Athens Charter was disseminated, the recipients of its mandate had either to fill in its framework of broad principles with the finer grain of instrumental proposals for the city or to extrapolate only the principles themselves, raising them to the level of fundamental presuppositions that defined their object, the city, even in the absence of the city itself. These two options were not exclusive, but were linked dimensions of a process of reconceptualizing the city in legal terms.

The direct influence of the Athens Charter manifested in Cuba in 1948, when Pedro Martínez Inclán published his *Código de Urbanismo* (Code of urbanism). Subtitled *Carta de Atenas, Carta de la Habana* (Athens charter, Havana charter), the book offered, as explained on its title page, "A contribution to the promulgation of the Carta de América, taking as a base that of Athens, by the French CIAM group, which already constitutes an organized body of urbanistic doctrine"[20] (Figure 3.1). As the legal pretension of words such as *code, charter,* and *promulgation* suggests, Martínez Inclán's *Código de Urbanismo* not only traced its own provenance to the Athens Charter, but would also have been associated with the awareness of the Laws of the Indies emerging in Cuba at exactly that same moment, in the wake of the Constitution of 1940. It participated in the circulation of themes and significances between three charters—the Laws of the Indies, the Athens Charter, and the 1940 constitution—taking on their presumption of a discursive binding between law and architecture, but absorbing as well the compound of modernism, history, and nationalism that they together represented. The *Código de Urbanismo* brought into the formal apparatus of the Athens Charter specific contextual concerns derived or adapted from the corollary debates on the Constitution of 1940 and the imperial ordinances, foremost among them the project to realize the Cuban nation first envisioned by the Guáimaro revolutionaries and now poised in the ranks of modern democratic nations.

For his urban code, Martínez Inclán took verbatim the text of the Athens Charter published by Le Corbusier, and then added, modified, and excised articles to mold the original charter to the Cuban situation. New and modified articles were distinguished with italics, so that the adaptation of the model constitution was visibly evident, and Martínez Inclán's additions were extensive enough that his charter contained twice as many articles as its predecessor (Figure 3.2). The additions began at once with a new article inserted after the original first one: *"2: The urbanistic problems of the region are closely linked to those of the province and those of the nation."*[21] The first article of the Athens Charter had stipulated that the city was not an isolated object, but part of the larger whole of the region; and at one level, Martínez Inclán's addition merely makes the unremarkable point that Cuba's size, insular condition, and the dominance of its capital city created a direct relation between the city and the nation. But a more remarkable, second representational level was conjured up as well by the parallel textual currencies of the constitution and the Laws of the Indies, in which the organization of the city both embodies and represents the normative organization of the society. The city thus was wed to the larger project of the nation not only as the product of a politico-economic system but also as the representation charged with projecting the future condition of the nation itself. Like the constitution, the *Código de Urbanismo* envisioned the civic sphere as a reciprocal process, in this instance as an exchange between the city and its inhabitants and the nation and its citizens. Martínez Inclán's text brought the ideal of the civic explicitly forward, inserting the adjective into articles of his text and its functional space into the organization of the city.

Martínez Inclán also understood the political charge of the Athens Charter, and preserved its demands that the social function of land be acknowledged and balanced with, not subordinated to, individual interest. Martínez Inclán signaled

To one of the most famous Architects of our Century from an ancient colleague of Cuba

P. M. Inclán

Habana-4-49-

Código de Urbanismo

CARTA DE ATENAS

CARTA DE LA HABANA

(Una contribución a la promulgación de la Carta de América, tomando como base la de Atenas, del grupo del CIAM francés, la cual, constituye ya un cuerpo organizado de doctrina urbanística).

1949

IMP. P. FERNANDEZ Y CIA., S. EN C.

LA HABANA, CUBA

FIGURE 3.1 Pedro Martínez Inclán, title page of *Código de Urbanismo*, with Martínez Inclán's inscription to Walter Gropius: "To one of the most famous architects of our century from an ancient colleague of Cuba." Courtesy of the Frances Loeb Library, Harvard Graduate School of Design.

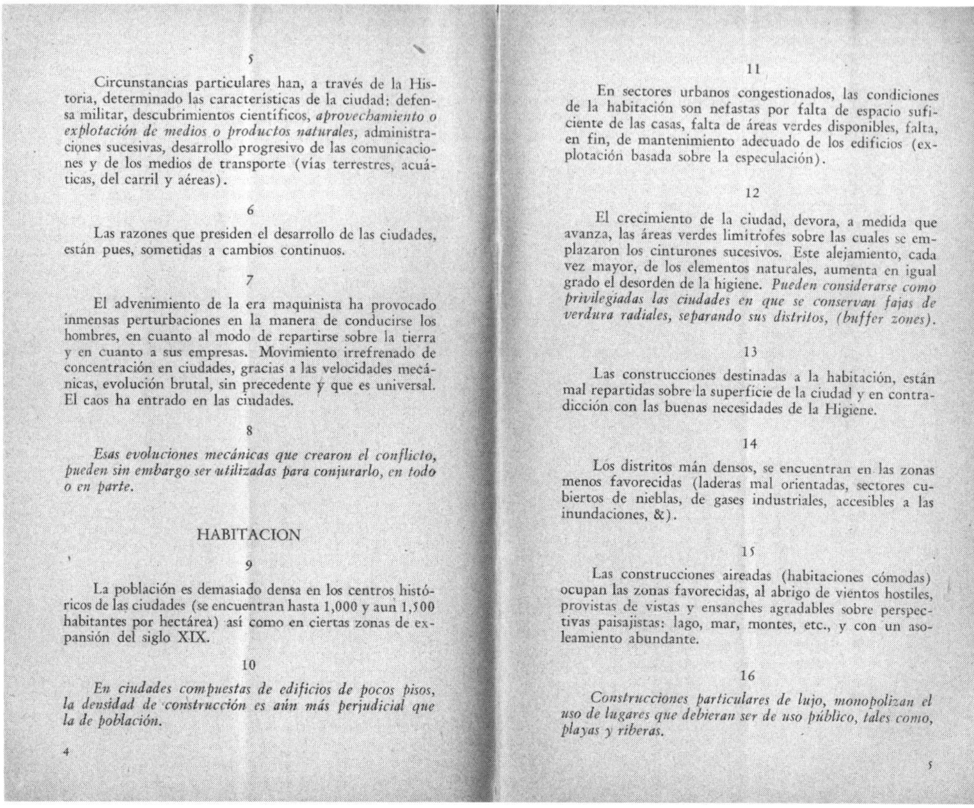

5

Circunstancias particulares han, a través de la Historia, determinado las características de la ciudad: defensa militar, descubrimientos científicos, *aprovechamiento o explotación de medios o productos naturales,* administraciones sucesivas, desarrollo progresivo de las comunicaciones y de los medios de transporte (vías terrestres, acuáticas, del carril y aéreas).

6

Las razones que presiden el desarrollo de las ciudades, están pues, sometidas a cambios continuos.

7

El advenimiento de la era maquinista ha provocado inmensas perturbaciones en la manera de conducirse los hombres, en cuanto al modo de repartirse sobre la tierra y en cuanto a sus empresas. Movimiento irrefrenado de concentración en ciudades, gracias a las velocidades mecánicas, evolución brutal, sin precedente y que es universal. El caos ha entrado en las ciudades.

8

Esas evoluciones mecánicas que crearon el conflicto, pueden sin embargo ser utilizadas para conjurarlo, en todo o en parte.

HABITACION

9

La población es demasiado densa en los centros históricos de las ciudades (se encuentran hasta 1,000 y aun 1,500 habitantes por hectárea) así como en ciertas zonas de expansión del siglo XIX.

10

En ciudades compuestas de edificios de pocos pisos, la densidad de construcción es aún más perjudicial que la de población.

4

11

En sectores urbanos congestionados, las condiciones de la habitación son nefastas por falta de espacio suficiente de las casas, falta de áreas verdes disponibles, falta, en fin, de mantenimiento adecuado de los edificios (explotación basada sobre la especulación).

12

El crecimiento de la ciudad, devora, a medida que avanza, las áreas verdes limítrofes sobre las cuales se emplazaron los cinturones sucesivos. Este alejamiento, cada vez mayor, de los elementos naturales, aumenta en igual grado el desorden de la higiene. *Pueden considerarse como privilegiadas las ciudades en que se conservan fajas de verdura radiales, separando sus distritos, (buffer zones).*

13

Las construcciones destinadas a la habitación, están mal repartidas sobre la superficie de la ciudad y en contradicción con las buenas necesidades de la Higiene.

14

Los distritos mán densos, se encuentran en las zonas menos favorecidas (laderas mal orientadas, sectores cubiertos de nieblas, de gases industriales, accesibles a las inundaciones, &).

15

Las construcciones aireadas (habitaciones cómodas) ocupan las zonas favorecidas, al abrigo de vientos hostiles, provistas de vistas y ensanches agradables sobre perspectivas paisajistas: lago, mar, montes, etc., y con un asoleamiento abundante.

16

Construcciones particulares de lujo, monopolizan el uso de lugares que debieran ser de uso público, tales como, playas y riberas.

5

FIGURE 3.2 Pedro Martínez Inclán, typical page spread of *Código de Urbanismo,* with Martínez Inclán's textual additions in italics. Courtesy of the Frances Loeb Library, Harvard Graduate School of Design.

the direct parallel between his proposed urban charter and the 1940 constitution, which had qualified its recognition of private property with a definition of property's social function.[22] Other overt parallels included specifications for low-cost housing programs, calls for government recovery of *plusvalía* (unearned increment), and opprobrium of political partisanship, all of which correlated with constitutional articles or convention debates. These elements confirmed the formal character of Martínez Inclán's charter by strengthening its already implicit connection to the 1940 constitution, but they also provided its realism, its instrumental adaptation to the Cuban situation. Although the *Código de Urbanismo* maintained the normative intention of the Athens Charter, it inevitably assumed a more prescriptive quality because of its specific intention to be a Carta de la Habana (Havana Charter). The obvious difference from the Athens Charter was

Martínez Inclán's focus on an existing city, a focus that enabled him to introduce thematic concerns derived from his own theories of urbanism. His concern for traffic circulation, for example, was far more emphatic and detailed than that expressed in the Athens Charter. Similarly, planning of the city was discussed not merely as a general benefit, but in the precise terms of the Cuban planning debate; the text called for a national planning law, the creation of a national planning board, and the supercession of municipalities by coordinated regional and provincial divisions. These elements were presented in a section titled "Legislation," one of two full sections that Martínez Inclán added to the seven divisions of the Athens Charter. Ten articles explained the components required for the systematic planning of a city, region, or nation, including expropriation laws, laws for recovering *plusvalía,* and other undefined regulations and ordinances. The final article of Martínez Inclán's charter recapitulated the established thesis on planning: *"184: Of fundamental importance is the creation of Ministries of Urbanism completely independent of those of Public Works and provided with full and well-defined legal faculties, including that of determining the use of all useful land to carry out the general planning of the nation."*[23]

The section on legislation followed another new section titled "Estética Urbana" (Urban aesthetics). Given Martínez Inclán's role in the planning debates, it is no surprise that he used the *Código de Urbanismo* to advance the campaign for national planning, but given the explicit modernist affiliation of its model, the Athens Charter, aesthetics may have been a more awkward insertion than legislation. Urban aesthetics—or what Martínez Inclán also tellingly referred to as "Estética Ciudadana" (civic aesthetics)—had provided the central theme of Martínez Inclán's first treatise, *La Habana actual,* as well as the focus of courses on "The Architecture of Parks, Cities, and Gardens" that he taught at the University of Havana. Martínez Inclán included without apparent hesitation the word *beauty (belleza)* as a necessary urban quality, an appeal to the nonscientific that the drafters of the Athens Charter would not likely have tolerated. He elevated the quality of beauty to something like a function of the city, affirming its value in a crucial appendage to one of the concluding articles of the Athens Charter:

> 156: The cycle of daily functions: dwelling, work, recreation, will be regulated by Urbanism with the strictest economy, with dwelling considered to be the very center of urbanistic concerns and the focal point of all measures.

> 157: *This does not mean, however, that of the three graces of Contemporary Urbanism, hygiene, circulation, and beauty, the last should be sacrificed in any considerable manner for economic reasons. Spiritual values ought to balance material ones in social life and therefore in the Planning of Cities.*[24]

These spiritual values and their consequent expression in qualities of beauty were an encompassing standard of aesthetic valuation, which appears with Martínez Inclán's rhetorical emphasis to precede the functional. Or, if it does not take precedence, then at least the functions are, without the graces, simply unredeemed reality, not yet synchronized with the superior representational order. The seeming anachronism of Martínez Inclán's emphasis on graces and beauty, at a time when he acted as one of the strong defenders of modernism in Cuba, can be attributed to several factors. His support for modernism was always tempered by an acceptance of a wider range of stylistic variation than among his younger followers, and he had in fact been closely associated with J. C. N. Forestier and his civic designs for Havana in the early years of the Machado regime. Viewing the city rather than the building as the object of design predisposed Martínez Inclán to accentuate the monuments and boulevards that had been part of Forestier's proposals. The most important factor, though, was his concern for the expressive value of those same elements—that is to say, their civic character—which prompted him to detailed recommendations in the *Código de Urbanismo.* In this concern for the expressive role of monuments and boulevards, Martínez Inclán combined a retrospective impulse for the city beautiful with a prospective impulse toward the projection of the civic sphere that corresponded to the influence of the constitutional project. Moreover, Martínez Inclán's emphasis adumbrated, and gave strength to, the disciplinary assertions of architecture that would be made in the pivotal events of 1953—for the aesthetic valuation that would at that moment be claimed by architecture was in Martínez Inclán's argument already embedded within the formulation of the civic sphere. The functional city, his arguments implied, might be a modern *urbs,* but without further architectural elaboration it would not be a modern *civitas.*[25]

Martínez Inclán began the section on urban aesthetics with the qualification that its stipulations would be "sufficiently general and flexible so as not to cancel initiatives that break with established routine."[26] Its terms would not, therefore, prohibit forms and solutions yet to be invented by modernism in favor of forms already habitually familiar. The remaining articles made clear that Martínez Inclán did not actually consider history and historical forms part of the category, for his text still included the separate section titled "Patrocinio Histórico de las Ciudades" (Historic heritage of cities) that had appeared in the Athens Charter, with new articles placing restraints on restorations and preservations of historic buildings. He moved only one article from that section of the Athens Charter to insert it under "Urban Aesthetics": "The use of styles of the past, under aesthetic pretexts, . . . will not be tolerated in any form."[27] The positive recommendations of the section on urban aesthetics, in addition to minor concerns for cornice alignments and the removal of kiosks and billboards, consisted of proposals for civic expression. The artistic dimension of the city was "indispensable" and must especially be addressed, Martínez Inclán argued, in the "vestibules" of entry into the city, in any civic center such as a plaza or a grouping of buildings, and in monuments. For residential neighborhoods, he recommended that in lieu of municipal regulations, "commissions of neighbors" advised by professionals should be responsible for evaluating "aesthetic matters."[28] In Martínez Inclán's view, it seems, civic consciousness was not a historical force already present *in* the city; civic consciousness was to be produced *by* the city as citizens encountered its buildings, environments, and processes. This production would first entail careful attention to the accommodation of the four functions (housing, leisure, dwelling, and circulation) that supplied the requisite materials of the civic consciousness, but these would then be supplemented by an explicitly representational function—the aesthetic—to make the civic sphere visible.

Martínez Inclán's rewriting of the Athens Charter mirrored the broader transformation of modernism in Cuba under the effects of constitutionalism. The political exigencies—the climax of the 1948 elections with the accompanying sense that the process of civic reform was once again receding—confirmed the view that a fundamental national consciousness which ought to underlie such processes, and which had been constituted in 1940, had not yet been sufficiently substantiated in the Cuban citizenry. Therefore, modernism in Cuba, though inseparable from the scientistic thinking embedded within the Athens Charter, could not be reduced to technocratic practices and solutions; it would not stage a confrontation between technocratic and traditionalist perspectives. Martínez Inclán's *Código de Urbanismo* outlined a synthetic modernism that could activate an aesthetic dimension not in the service of nostalgia or conservatism but rather as the motive force of a new civic sensibility. If conceived as a domain of technicians, modern architecture could only lay a claim to the tangible or quantifiable aspects of political and social reality; conceived in Martínez Inclán's terms, modern architecture claimed a right to participate in the design of the structures and images of the lettered city as well.

Diagrams of *la ciudad letrada*

By the time they began to participate in the planning debates in Cuba, Paul Lester Wiener and José Luis Sert had already attempted to realize the precepts of the Athens Charter in a number of Latin American cities. In Brazil, Peru, and most extensively in their Pilot Plan for Bogotá, Colombia, Town Planning Associates proposed the four functions as the organizational conceit for its city planning projects and experimented with the charter as an analytic framework and prescriptive instrument.[29] Their work in Latin America also introduced them to the historical precedent of the Laws of the Indies. Sert and Wiener recognized the significance of the orderly composition of the colonial cities when working on their proposed plans for Lima. In 1947, they made a careful study of the old colonial core of that city, including its central Plaza de Armas, laid out according to the strictures of the Laws of the Indies. In September of that year, just before leaving New York to attend the sixth CIAM congress, Wiener sent a request to the librarian of the Harvard Graduate School of Design for "a copy of the town-planning chart proclaimed by Charles V King of Spain."[30] By 1950, he and Sert wrote with confidence about the significance of the imperial ordinances in an article about their work in Latin America. They noted how the "colonial legislation formulated by Spain for the new cities to be founded in America specifies with great detail how these new cities should be built," providing a model pattern of *cuadras* (blocks) punctuated by plazas. Although they regarded this pattern as "outmoded," they remarked approvingly that "many articles of the Recopilación de Indias could be written into modern social legislation."[31] Wiener's characterization of the ordinances as a "townplanning chart" hinted at an analogy that he made explicit in an essay titled "History of Planning." The Laws of the Indies were to be substituted by a modern equivalent: "the principles and doctrines have been devised for our time by the great work of the CIAM. Its Chartes d'Athène can serve us as the Charte of Charles the V did in colonial days."[32]

Although perhaps equivalent as normative charters that provided principles and doctrines for the formulation of cities, the two charters could be distinguished by several consequences of their historical distance from one another, as Wiener elaborated in a lengthy passage:

> The TOWNPLANNING CHART BY CHARLES V OF SPAIN, devised about 1560, serves practically all latin-american cities. It gave accurate measurements for the founding of towns, allocated the various functions in terms of so and so many Cuadras, located small manufactures, and the civic functions, recreation and church around the Plaza de Almas. It is a formidable, thoughtful document, probably devised for the court with counsel of the leading architects of Spain and was sensible within the limits of the primitive colonial life of the people.
>
> Its very effectiveness for its time proves its inadequacy for to-day. The fact that it was a rigid grid iron pattern should also prove that it could not be flexible to accommodate the changes that have since occurred.
>
> The haphazard and tremendous growth of the latin-american cities coincides with the industrial age which came upon us in great rapidity. Our cultural thinking is in most parts even today incapable of grasping its impact. OUR CITIES ARE AS CHAOTIC AS THE REST OF THE WORLDS POLITICAL AND ECONOMIC CONFUSION. The cities are the true physical reflection of the tensions, strains, and stresses of our times. Our minds as well as our cities must adjust and relearn. I believe CITY PLANNING is the *barometer*, the *indicator*, as well as the *physical* and often *spiritual* of our epoch.[33]

The efficacy of either charter, according to Wiener's critique, depended on a direct correlation to the realities of its epoch. Both the royal ordinances and the Athens Charter attempted to instantiate order within or against a background of chaos, but a chaos specific to its historical moment. In the colonial instance, the chaotic environment was the wilderness of the new continent and the unredeemed state of its aboriginal inhabitants, and the ordinances combined imperial ambitions with missionary intent to tame both disorders. In the modern instance, chaos was the condition of industrial society itself, in both physical and emotional effects of uncertainty and a frenzied pace of change. Obliged to confront its respective reality, the program of royal legislation had provided the detailed directives listed by Wiener, inadequate for industrial society precisely because of their powerful efficacy for that former historical circumstance. But Wiener failed to note that the Athens Charter did not contain a similarly precise program, or indeed any detailed prescriptions, and so needed to be filled in with directive programs devised by technicians. By the early 1950s, the insufficiencies of the Athens Charter were clear to Wiener and Sert, and to other members of CIAM.[34] The question, as Martínez Inclán had apparently understood in 1949, was that of supplemental means. If, as Wiener desired, city planning was to act as "indicator and ordinator" of the epoch, the Athens Charter had to be elaborated with the relevant barometric and ordinal instruments.

In 1953, at the ninth CIAM congress, Wiener submitted a paper titled "Man's Habitat" in which he categorized the human environment at different scales of association.[35] In a later version of the paper published in *Nuestra Arquitectura* he included a diagram that resolved this environment into four components: the physical habitat, the productive habitat, the social and spiritual habitat, and physical communication (Figure 3.3). It further specified a scalar series linked by these zones, with four squares representing the home, the neighborhood, the city, and the region. These squares were contained in turn by two circles representing the world and the cosmos and resolving a diagrammatic statement of order that would have been comprehensible to a colonial *letrado*. By representing the levels of association from the home to the region as an increase in scale through the concentric squares, it emphasized the continuity between them, suggesting that the same criteria of analysis and prescription could be applied to each. At the scale of the world and cosmos, the graphic changed to a circle, indicating a perceptible distinction. The four zones of the diagram corresponded roughly to the four functions of the city specified in the Athens Charter—the physical to dwelling, the productive to work, the spiritual to leisure, and communication to circulation—but the values assigned by this diagram differed from those in the charter. Not only did the diagram describe the full compass of man's environment beyond the city—even representing the metaphysical cosmos as a physical territory—but it also emphasized the relationship between elements as much as, if not more than, the categories themselves. The physical and productive zones mirrored one another, forming a background that set the scales into relief; the communicative and the sociospiritual zones acted as ligatures binding the scales together, with the greater width of the latter band revealing its paramount importance. In this respect, in contrast to the Athens Charter,

Wiener's diagram concludes rather than presumes the organization among and between elements, representing as a precondition the "fruitful harmony" that the charter had posited as a goal.[36]

In notes assembled two years earlier for a "Report on the Future," Wiener had tested various names for the function categorized as leisure in the Athens Charter. In one alternative, he referred to it as "Cives," a misspelled Latin presumably

GRAFICO DEL AMBIENTE HUMANO. — **Rojo:** Habitat físico. Lo natural y lo hecho por el hombre. — **Verde:** Habitat productivo. El hombre actuando sobre su contorno físico para producir y mantener su subsistencia, y elevar su nivel de vida. — **Azul:** Habitat social y espiritual. Actividades culturales, intelectuales y metafísicas. — **Amarillo:** Comunicaciones físicas.

FIGURE 3.3 Paul Lester Wiener, diagram of the human environment. *Nuestra Arquitectura,* no. 320 (1956).

intended to mean the civic, in which category Wiener included the functions of improvement of body and mind, and programs such as libraries, schools, and museums.[37] The sociospiritual ligature, then, equated to the civic, making the civic sphere both a function of the city and an organizational pattern of the social environment. Wiener described his diagram as part of a projective plan of action, arguing that by representing the natural and social order in which any planning activity would take place, it would "help clarify present problems and signal the guidelines and procedures to be followed in future considerations."[38] Disputing any narrow limitation on the role of architecture, moreover, Wiener insisted that it would make broad, essential contributions to this new, more adequate human habitat, with an extension of the responsibilities of architecture both represented and enacted by the diagram. "My chart," he claimed, "is a step forward into the human environment to expand the area of [architects'] aspirations and humanistic utility"; its "practical value" lay in its graphic representation of the expanded territory of architecture and its succinct definition of "the basic interrelation of everything that influenced the human environment. In all the levels or cells these are the things that we ought to project in two- or three-dimensional terms, that is to say, the house, the neighborhood, the city, or the region."[39]

The cellular scales of Wiener's diagram had several direct antecedents. Sert had employed similar categories in his 1944 essay "The Human Scale in City Planning," beginning with the neighborhood unit and ascending through the township, the city, the metropolitan area, to the economic region.[40] In that essay, which was also published in Cuba, Sert provided what was essentially a diagram of the Athens Charter. Ostensibly a real proposal for the organization of satellite cities, the diagram was more important as an illustration of "new patterns based on a principle of classification of functions, and subdivision into different parts or units" that integrated as an organic whole. He aimed to produce an urban pattern adequate to the epoch by "transforming the actual inorganic shape of our cities into an organic and living body." By this reasoning, the Athens Charter's four functions required units of aggregation, as well as relational systems commensurate to an organicist arrangement of parts. Sert continued to regard the elements defined in the essay as the basic "units" of planning, conceptual elements with a direct relationship to the actual structure of the (organic) city. "Every city," he later explained, "is composed of cells" and the role of planning was to orient these "cells or units" in "some kind of system or relationship."[41]

For the eighth CIAM congress in 1951 the MARS Group had proposed that the theme of the meeting, the civic core or the "Heart of the City," be studied at five "scale-levels" of community: the urban housing group, the urban residential neighborhood, the urban sector, the city, and the metropolis. According to Jacqueline Tyrwhitt's description in the associated CIAM publication, *The Heart of the City*, each of these scale-levels was a unit of social aggregation that, when combined as an urban environment, created the "area within which a full life can be lived with freedom of opportunity for the development of the potentialities of each individual."[42] A related diagrammatic instrument, the MARS Grid, provided a standardized presentation format to be used by delegates to display their work at the congress, as in, for example, Town Planning Associates' presentation of its plan of Chimbote, Peru.[43] In the orderly configuration of a grid, six columns organized information pertaining to the core, the social center that existed in some form at each scale-level and thus served as a unifying conceptual element. The first three columns called for the same scalar series as Wiener's diagram, descending from the region, to "the place"—which might be city, village, or neighborhood—to the core itself. The fourth column provided spaces for illustrations of the core, and the last two columns coordinated diurnal and historical temporal depictions. The MARS Grid did not actually function fully as a grid, because the rows were not indexical categories and therefore did not link the content of adjacent columns. But the format did illustrate the intention to classify and order disparate and variable elements into a coherent and stable representation by enforcing a continuity between scalar relationships and temporal sequences.

In this regard, the MARS Grid was actually "a simplification" of the CIAM Grid designed by Le Corbusier for the seventh CIAM congress.[44] Like the MARS Grid, it arrayed standard cells to permit visual comparisons between disparate types of information, but unlike the later version, the CIAM Grid operated as a grid, indexed both vertically and horizontally. Five vertical columns corresponded to the four functions, with an additional miscellaneous category. Horizontal rows encompassed various dimensions of planning, from climate and land use, to economics and legislation, to public opinion. These rows were separated into two groups, one representing the proposition itself and the other representing rational and sentimental public reaction. For presentation, the CIAM Grid was to be displayed horizontally, with its axes inverted, and with the relevant cells filled with maps, drawings, text, or photographs. Although capable of incorporating information pertaining to any scale, the CIAM Grid did not employ the scalar structure of the preceding examples, pursuing instead a broader classificatory ambition that attempted to fix myriad types of data into a coherent schema. The resulting representation portrayed the discrete parts as fungible, homologous elements, so that a relationship between, for example, legislation, climatic conditions, and public enthusiasm would be readily apparent. The organization of the grid suggested that all of the information was commensurable, or was made so by the universal ordering format of the grid itself, a presumption evident in Le Corbusier's descriptions of its efficacy: the two coordinates of the grid, he claimed, would accommodate "all forms of analysis and commentary (public opinion, public authority, specialists, sociologists, economists, technicians, etc. . . .)," in effect translating between their different modalities. Moreover, its scope spanned "the environment of a kitchen and the environment of a continent," and the modest dimensions of the grid, he boasted, were "all the space necessary to contain the graphic presentation of our civilization."[45]

As Wiener would do for his own diagram, Le Corbusier insisted that his grid was not only an analytic method—a "science of measurement," a "tool for analysis"—but also a projective device—an "instrument for thinking," a "tool for synthesis." "The Grid," he readily conceded, "does not pretend to make fine town planning schemes of itself," but it imposed a structure on the dense and disorderly material of a planning problem and enabled its user "to construct a mental architecture amid the chaos."[46] Although offered as analytic methods, discursive artifacts such as Wiener's diagram and the CIAM Grid contained a predisposition commensurate with the lettered city and so positioned architecture within a larger matrix of urban activity. More significant than their presumption of universality—evidence of a pervasive insistence on scientific, rational thought as a shared fact of contemporary life and also relevant as the modern rendition of the epistemological claim of the Laws of the Indies—was the capacity of these diagrams, charts, and orders to connect architecture to the larger domain of planning and thereby open planning to systems of aesthetic valuation. Sert had made this aspiration evident when, in the opening chapter of *Can Our Cities Survive?*, he specified the narrative structure of his analysis: "Let us take note of what we see in our city, as a pedestrian would in its streets and parks, or visiting its dwellings, offices, factories, and shops. By assembling our observations, we should arrive at a view of the whole which will help us understand the urban organism in all its functions."[47] Like the constitutional *conjunto,* the process Sert described was not simply inductive analysis but an assertion of the interrelationship of scales and modalities that endowed such representational artifacts with projective potential. Sert's narrative structure privileged architecture ("what we see in our city") in this experience of the sequence from part to whole, just as the artifacts privileged architecture as a discourse capable of representing the whole through its parts, and therefore capable of configuring the order of the whole through the manipulation of its parts. Significantly, each of these artifacts proposed a continuous field of operations, with no points of disjuncture or incommensurability, by deploying two structures of order—one of scale, the other of typological classification—both of which encompassed the full dimensions of planning without interruption. The order of scale traveled from architecture, to urban design, to the regional plan, while the typological order bound together the heterogeneous content—be it technical, linguistic, visual, or emotional—of any single scalar instance.

Yet each of these representational artifacts already contained moments that eluded its apparently stable order. In Wiener's diagram, there was the subtle distinction between his recoded four functions and those of the Athens Charter; Wiener's differentiation disrupted the causal relationship between physical environment and form to which a technocratic vision would seem to subscribe (and was in this respect similar to Martínez Inclán's rewriting of the Athens Charter). In the MARS Grid, precisely the failure to actually function as a grid left space between unconnected categories, such as the break between physical and temporal parameters. In the CIAM Grid, the forced equivalence of "rational" and "sentimental" categories only highlighted their incongruence, while the inclusion of both a column and a row categorized as "miscellaneous" strove to contain unanticipated ambiguities. Even Sert's five units of planning, when compared to the MARS Group's scale-levels and to Weiner's cells, show that while scalar logic prevailed, the prime component of aggregation was inconstant—the neighborhood unit in one instance, the core in the next, and the home in the last. These equivocal moments marked potentially productive points of conjunction between conceptual ("lettered") and real ("visible") orders. The representational codes were not pure signifiers of the lettered city; they were attempted translations between the tangible city and its figurative image. The Laws of the Indies inscribed an ideal civic space to be superimposed willfully on a real physical and cultural geography. In their historical time, the city constituted almost entirely in itself a political armature identical to the empire or the crown. In the later reincarnation of the instrumental idealism of the Laws of the Indies—Martínez Inclán's *Código de Urbanismo,* Wiener's diagram, and other representational artifacts of Cuba's postwar *ciudad letrada*—the projected political armature was the nation. These modern substitutes construed a whole composed from coordinated parts—not the fixed, hierarchical, and consistent structure of the royal ordinances, but a flexible, inconsistent configuration. Nevertheless, the nation, too, would be constituted through urban form, and the value of devices such as Martínez Inclán's code and Wiener's organicist diagram lay in their visualization of an idealized form in terms easily converted into professional instruments and practices.

The overarching political venture of the constitution of civil society was readily assimilated to the composite of modern norms and expert discourse layered upon the newly recovered and validated conceptual form of the colonial ordinances. The Constitution of 1940, the prerogatives of professional organizations, and the untenable instabilities of the Cuban political sphere all required the projection of a process of social maturation in order to reorganize the present; and the formulation of a juridico-architectural armature was if not compelled by, at least a direct answering to the contours of Cuban circumstance. Made apparent in these configurations of legal and architectural forms that constructed the image of the lettered city was also the intent to privilege architecture in an organicist representation of the city and its civic dimension. Given a privileged position coordinating the reciprocal engagement of norm and reality, architecture was to prompt an ever tighter proximity between the figurative city and the real city. The charters and diagrams would, like the surface of a photographic plate, be imprinted with the data of the real city ("el hecho cubano") while their organizational orders of articles, grids, or concentric fields, situated this real city within standards of evaluation—legal *and* aesthetic. Here architecture assumed a mediating role, through which facts could be shaded or glossed according to the signifying terms of the law, and the significance of the law could be tested and modified by facts. The distinctive disciplinary claim made by architecture was its capacity to operate in both the realm of signs and the realm of properties with equal fluency. Seen through the disciplinary lens of architecture, the nation appeared both as a work of art, to be construed by aesthetic practices with regard to its past history, and as a complex function, to be scientifically managed according to its underlying order and its potential organization. The application of these aesthetic and technical practices, conceived as general disciplinary capacities, still required, however, an effective engagement with political machinery.

Planos, Planes y Planificación

When the Junta Nacional de Planificación was established in 1955, the Spanish word *planificación* still counted as a neologism, and competed with the rival terms *planeamiento* and *planeación* as translations of the English term "planning." In a television appearance as a press official for the JNP, architect Eduardo Cañas Abril explained why *planificación* should be adopted as the appropriate term:

> The word *planificación* still doesn't exist in the dictionary of the Academia Española. It is a neologism, but to our mind it is the most correct term; it is a word that is formed from two Latin roots: *Planis:* one will plan, and *Fiscare:* to build. So already the word itself through its own roots is a simultaneous concept of planning and realizing. The term *planeamiento* is too vague a term and so we adopt this term of *planificación,* because it is the simultaneous concept of something that is planned but is inside the terms of construction, of realization. So it is a concept that is not theoretical, but practical.[48]

Cañas Abril's attributing to the practice of planning these paired dimensions of plan and realization followed the constitutionalist conjuncture of representation and projection. Evaluative assessment of reality could not be neutral in either representation or plan; it would assume the contours and predilections of its medium, mode, or technique, and the formulation of any transformation of that present reality into a future one would likewise be shaped, limited, and illuminated by the disposition that gave rise to its initial description. The constitutive act implies the simultaneity of description and performance, however, while plan and realization are separate moments in a process of planning (although the plan does contain already the image of its realization). But what was significant in the parallel between the constitution and planning was the indication that the production of the civil society in either medium would be both functional *and* aesthetic, occurring in the movement from one to the other, with the aesthetic made functional and the functional recovering its aesthetic foundation. The definitional complexities of *planificación* did not end there. What is planning? What will planning do? These questions were directed at every proponent of the Ley de Planificación (planning law), each of whom drew in turn upon the array of definitions and illustrations that had accumulated over the previous half-century. Cañas Abril, after dissecting its etymology, supplied a surpassingly general account of *planificación* according to which no factor or dimension of human life could be excluded from the scope of planning consideration; once this total environment was seen as a whole, its abundant range of potentials would become apparent and susceptible to management. Cañas Abril's understanding of planning was illuminating, if not as a definition, then as an illustration of planning's immodest aspirations, and as a revelation of its particular concern for relationships, influences, and interactions. His etymological dissection was used in an explanatory brochure that the JNP published in the fall of 1955 as part of its continued program to raise public awareness and support for its activities; the brochure also distilled a more concise definition of planning as the anticipation of the future and the ordering of the present.[49]

More precise definitions elaborated the significance of this temporal emphasis (and the significance of planning more generally). Montoulieu regarded planning "as 'a thought process'" that oscillated between the three temporal moments of future, present, and past, seeking to predict and then calibrate a set of events in each to a set of events in the others.[50] This goal, he pointed out, compelled one to recognize the central importance of process—"To plan is much more than to draw plans *[planos]*, it is to make plans of action *[planes]* and every plan implies a program, that is to say, how the plan will be put into action."[51] Here, Montoulieu contributed his own etymological distinction by segregating the two Spanish words for plan: *plano,* which refers to a plan in the sense of graphic representation, and *plan,* which means a plan in the sense of a program. Planning conjoined both, conjoined description and performance, and included as well the connective tissue of a third term, the plan of action resulting from their conjuncture. The *plano* was an instrument of mediation similar to the constitution in its efforts to delineate the relationship between what is, what ought to be, and what will be. Like the constitution, it must be admitted to have its own form, its own structure, whether graphic, textual, or a combination of both. The drawn maps, statistical charts, and written policies of planning were types or genres possessing dispositions and orientations, as well as incapacities and limitations, that placed an emphasis on the transitive character of planning, the translation from plan to realization. This understanding of planning could pertain to distinct realms—the economic, the social, the physical—though Montoulieu seemed to instinctively use architecture and urban planning as illustrations for the most general concept of planning.

As director of the Office of the National Plan within the JNP, Montoulieu's work embraced the broadest connotations of planning—its social and economic intentions at a national scale—and his work with the Patronato Pro-Urbanismo had already convinced him of the need to educate and apprise the public of the ambitions and benefits of planning. Montoulieu was therefore concerned with producing both functional and illustrative narratives of planning. The JNP did assemble a campaign of publicity, devised by Maribona and Cañas Abril, with educational aspects. The brochure on the Ley de Planificación was one such effort, as were the television interviews and newspaper articles, and in 1957, the JNP presented an exhibition of its work at the new Palacio de Bellas Artes (Museum of Fine Arts) in Havana. The text of the brochure that accompanied this exhibition glossed the 1955 law to insist that the purpose of "the modern science-art of integral planning" was to promote the general welfare of all citizens by organizing effectively the social and economic development of the nation.[52] A year earlier, Montoulieu published lecture materials (from a seminar course on planning that he taught for the architecture students at the Universidad de Santo Tomás de Villanueva) as a lengthy pamphlet titled *Planificación,* the most comprehensive statement on planning produced in Cuba in relation to the work of the JNP.[53] Montoulieu distinguished between "true" and "pseudo" planning; the latter adopted the approach of assessment, projection, and realization, but without the actual capacity to coordinate the many factors such an approach set in motion. True planning existed only when all fields of endeavor coordinated their efforts as a larger, encompassing sphere of planning. Only then was planning truly "integrated" planning because only then were all the necessary functional elements at the disposal of the plan. Pseudo-planning, in his view, occurred when practitioners of a single profession (architects in his example) failed to incorporate their planning practices into this wider sphere, and thus actually curtailed the possible effects and influences of those practices. From this distinction, of course, proceeded Montoulieu's distinction between *planes* and *planos,* between integrated plans and isolated drawings, as well as the resonance with constitutionalism's *conjunto,* the whole methodically assembled out of constituent parts.

Montoulieu favored integral, or true, planning for more than its greater efficacy; it was also a better comprehension of the purposive knowledge to which planning aspired. The multiplicity of planning, he argued, reflected directly the complexity of modern society and its specializations. Although an architect himself, he did not join with colleagues who conventionally argued that architects were predisposed to adopt the larger role of planner, which he viewed as a distinctive role with an analytic and projective scope aggregated from other disciplines. Montoulieu selected a quote from the British planner William Holford to make the point: "The essential town planner is therefore one who knows how to make a case. What the barrister achieves by advocacy, the scientist by research, and the architect by the drawing of designs, the planner has to achieve by using all three methods at once . . . Town and country planning is architectural planning extended into the field of government, it is estate management on a regional scale, and it is sociology expressed in three visible dimensions."[54] This compound of perspectives becomes in effect a second-order perspective, the *punto de vista* of the *planificador* (planner). Although Montoulieu made ready reference to the figure of *planificador,* it is not at all certain that this figure was, or even could be, embodied in a person. It might have been easy enough to imagine the function of coordinator to be so embodied, but the additional assignment of such varied productive technical (and epistemological) capacities seems to make clear that the *planificador* was understood as a type of fiction, a characterization for a less defined configuration residing in the background, composed of relations, interactions, and incommensurable modes.

The JNP itself was conceived in such terms (although in practice it was closely tied to the discipline of the architects who staffed it) as an "autonomous organism" capable of functioning in and through the diverse environments of law, architecture, engineering, and economics. As an agency, it might exceed or circumvent the limitations of its particular constitutive elements by translating analyses and projections from one mode to the next, constructing a case in the terms of the lawyer, the scientist, and the architect. Montoulieu derived such a model of the planning agency from the source of many aspects of his planning philosophy, Rexford Tugwell, who as governor of Puerto Rico had created a national planning board that was regarded at the time as one of the most successful such agencies. In a series of lectures titled "The Place of Planning in Society" delivered and published in 1954, Tugwell declared:

> The planning agency is a coagulator, a putter-together, a conjoiner which brings hopes into focus and promises into possibility, a protector of reason among competing imaginative conceptions, a reducer of vague expectations to measured charts, tables, and maps, a filler-out of strategies with the stuff of tactical reality. It is sometimes a kill-joy; but sometimes also a fulfiller of dreams.[55]

Tugwell made clear that he thought planning activity should be assigned to an independent institutional body in order to take advantage of the rarified expertise of modern specialist disciplines, but also, and more importantly, to mitigate the provincialism and self-interest inherent in other branches of government, particularly the legislature. To be faithful to the requirements of its scientific disciplines, the planning agency would have "to accept, from those who define the general aspirations, their definition of what ought to be," and then determine how practically to proceed toward that outcome.[56]

Initial definition of aspirations would remain the prerogative of citizens and their government representatives. For the 1942 exhibition presented by the Patronato Pro-Urbanismo, Montoulieu had rendered planning as a tripartite organization of state, technician, and citizen. He repeated this formula in his 1956 pamphlet, arguing that citizens must be educated on the nature of planning in order to fulfill their responsibility within the planning structure. Citizens, he expected, would define for the state their own lacks and surpluses, their actions and intentions; the state would evaluate collective necessities and capabilities; the technicians, directed by both the definition and the evaluation, would project plans oriented toward these national aspirations. Planning, as a process, facilitated an "effective embodiment *[plasmación]* of the objectives of the 'collective mind.'"[57] In the form of an agency, it also functioned as that collective mind. In the terms set by the debates on planning in Cuba and by the subsequent planning activities of the JNP, the efficacy of planning still depended on political variables. Planning might assume the capacity to shape the *conjunto,* to conceive and articulate the form of the whole and to regulate the highest order of its structure; or planning might assume the ability to shape the part, such that changes within that part ramified predictably through the whole, transforming it in desired fashion even though the whole itself might never be visualized concretely.

In its legislative form, the JNP appeared to possess the former, sweeping capability to control the whole, despite its deliberately constrained executive power, and its initial staffing seemed likely to provide the JNP with vital political ties to real executive authority. Nicolás Arroyo had been able to instigate the creation of the JNP precisely because of his proximity to General Batista, and the requirement that the minister of public works be the head of the JNP created a seamless connection from the architectural profession (or the part of that profession Arroyo represented) to the JNP and from the JNP to the ministry and to Batista himself. Paul Wiener for one was fully aware that Arroyo's position was inescapably political. In memos to his partners he explained that Arroyo was juggling the short-term demands of the ministry—new roads, existing patronage works, and similarly political projects—with the long-term professional concern for scientific planning. These competing interests might be a liability initially, but Wiener seemed to have faith in Arroyo's commitment to planning and his ability to insinuate it into the political domain.[58] Regardless of the greater or lesser support among its individual members for Batista's administration, the relation between Batista and Arroyo bound the JNP to the political regime. Some internal political conflicts did emerge, between Arroyo and Montoulieu over Montoulieu's independent prioritization of the National Plan; and between Montoulieu and Abalo over the theoretical scope of planning, with Montoulieu defending the idea of integral planning against Abalo's accusations of communism.[59] The partners of Town Planning Associates avoided participation in internal disputes, but fostered when they could the close proximity between the JNP and Batista's administration. Wiener and Arroyo accompanied General Batista for a two-day trip to the Isle of Pines at the end of 1955, a trip that must have been the only prolonged contact during which the case for planning could be argued directly to the president.[60] Wiener and Sert were certainly aware from their prior decade of experience in Latin America that their work could be realized more readily under an authoritarian executive, but their own firmly held progressive convictions were utterly at odds with Batista's second regime, which had retarded a promising progress toward consistent democratic governance in Cuba.

The elections Batista had promised for 1954 were perfunctory; with other political parties refusing to participate, Batista ran unopposed. Some groups were willing to endorse elections provided that Batista restore the 1940 constitution; others demanded that he step down before elections. Batista would eventually restore the constitution (formally at least, though as in the preceding decade, the constitution was never in full effect), but he refused to hold new elections. The *diálogo cívico* (civic dialogue), an attempt by a group called the Sociedad de Amigos de la República (Society of Friends of the Republic) to broker a compromise between Batista and his moderate opponents, ended unsuccessfully in 1956. By then, a new underground revolutionary organization, the Directorio Revolucionario Estudiantil (Student Revolutionary Directorate), had formed in Havana; and before the end of year, Fidel Castro, who had been exiled following his imprisonment after the Moncada Barracks attack, returned to Cuba with a small guerrilla force and established an encampment in the Sierra Maestra mountains of eastern Cuba. His insurgency would expand slowly over the next year, establishing control over an increasing area of territory, while in Havana and other cities bombings and assassinations once again became regular events, along with peremptory violence carried out by the government. On March 13, 1957, members of the Directorio Revolucionario Estudiantil and another rebel group, the Organización Auténtica, attacked the presidential palace in central Havana. This attempt to assassinate Batista failed but at the same time underscored the rising intensity of resistance to Batista's dictatorship. Some civic leaders adopted clear stances against the government, without endorsing revolutionary groups. Jorge Mañach, who had left Cuba for the first three years of Batista's rule, returned under amnesty in 1955. He helped organize the Sociedad de Amigos de la República and formed a new civic opposition group, the Movimiento de la Nación (Movement of the Nation) before leaving Cuba again in 1957.

Although no explicit pronouncements were offered at the time by its personnel, as an institution the JNP opposed revolutionary change and maintained an uncomfortable position that combined an advocacy for reform with an extensive participation in Batista's regime. To the extent that the senior members of the JNP—Arroyo, Montoulieu, Romañach, Abalo, and Quintana, as well as Wiener and Sert—shared a common interest or impulse, it would have favored gradual reform guided by a technical or professional class. But degrees of difference could be discerned within the group's political interests: Arroyo, as minister of public works, was a member of the government (and in 1958, the last year of Batista's rule, he was serving as Cuban ambassador to the United States); Abalo's memoranda for the JNP conveyed an implacable hostility to communism, though in Cuba the Communist Party turned against Batista only during these late years; Nicolás Quintana made clear that he did not support Batista (and was apparently willing to assist revolutionary efforts against him), while Mario Romañach tried to remain at a distance from political affairs; as foreign consultants, a different gauge might have applied to Sert, himself an exile from dictatorship who disapproved of Batista's regime and was optimistic that it would be short-lived, and to Wiener, who would, shortly after Batista's fall, tell a colleague, "You can imagine our awkward situation with respect to the Cuban Revolution. Here we are good liberals and democrats and are probably identified in the minds of some people as Batista men."[61]

Yet that identification was not an entirely implausible one. With the exception of Arroyo, the members of the JNP would not be labeled *batistianos* (close supporters or collaborators of Batista), but their connection to the government was undeniably immediate. The classification of technical or professional work therefore posed a salient distinction. The JNP gathered practitioners who had for several years, and under several different governments, claimed the goal of national planning as their defining disciplinary interest. Sert and Wiener, linked to this group by personal ties and by disciplinary affiliation, were likely also motivated by professional expediency and by progressive optimism. Even as it forced their proximity to the government, the JNP also created a formal institutional setting somewhat distanced from personal and political interest. The ministry of public works occupied the old Convento Santa Clara in the colonial quarter, while the JNP was housed separately in an office building in the newer district of Vedado. The institutional organization of this setting, and the work to be undertaken within it, were to be further insulated by the practices that had defined them. Town Planning Associates delineated these practices in a series of charts designed to explain the organization of the agency and to propose divisions for its working tasks.[62] These charts also revealed the enormous scope of activity presumed to fall within the purview of the JNP. One diagrammed the articles of Ley–Decreto No. 2019 in order to illustrate the hierarchies of the included activities (Figure 3.4). It made evident the direct vertical line of authority between the JNP and the executive and between the JNP and the myriad elements that would fall under the "control" of a national plan—nothing less than "el hecho cubano," or social and physical reality. Horizontally, the scope of the JNP extended out into regional

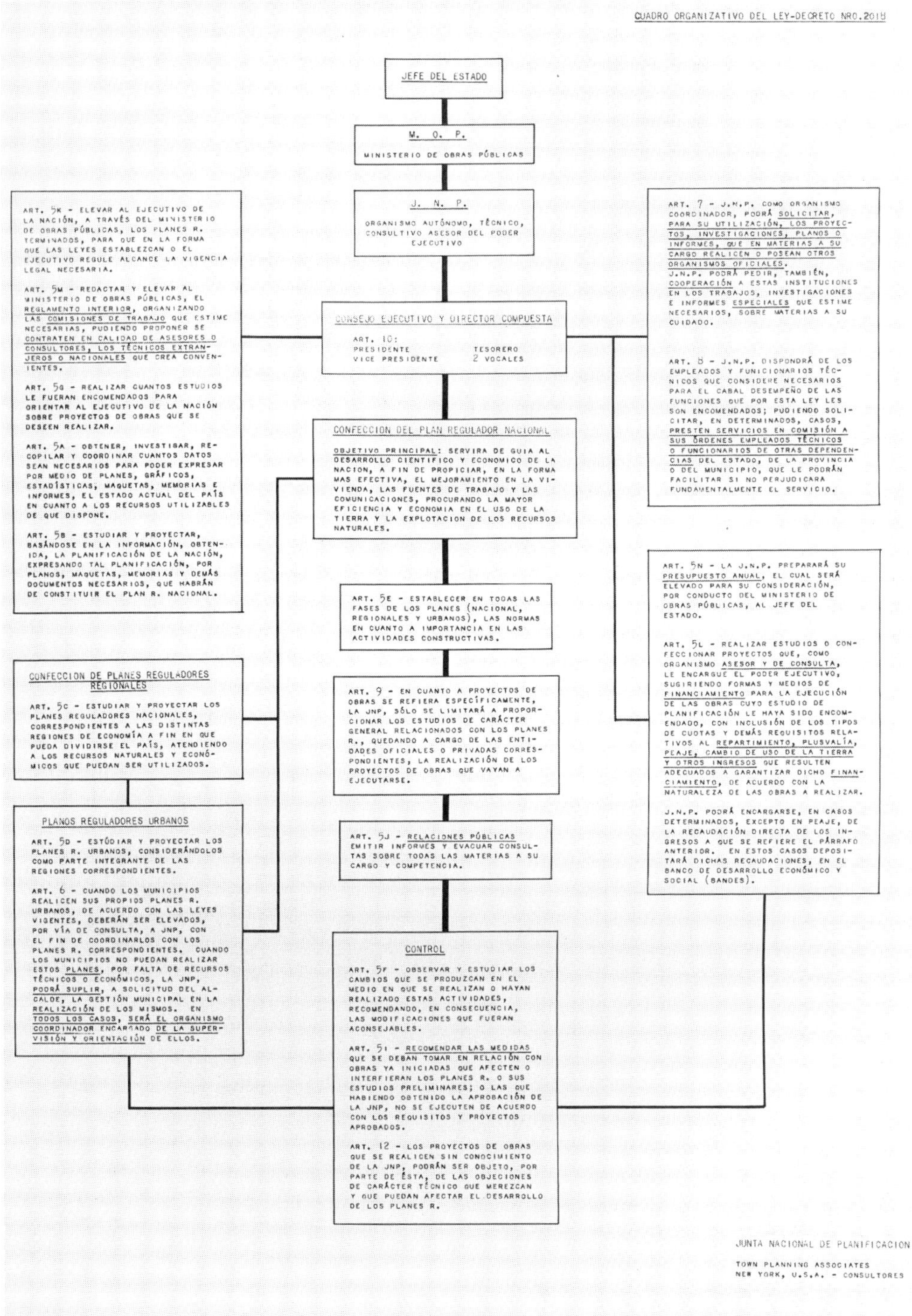

FIGURE 3.4 Ley–Decreto No. 2019 depicted as an organizational chart for the Junta Nacional de Planificación. The individual articles of the law are placed in a hierarchy of responsibilities descending from the head of state to the internal departments of the JNP. Courtesy of Paul Lester Wiener Papers, Box 155, Special Collections and University Archives, University of Oregon Libraries.

and urban plans, into fiscal policies, and into the research work of other government agencies. Other charts detailed the internal composition of the junta, broken down into specific tasks and personnel. The Office of the National Plan, for example, would have divisions for economics, statistics, and social studies, while the Office for Regional Plans would consist of divisions responsible for transportation, public services, natural resources, and education, health, and housing. Proposed personnel numbered near a hundred, far more than the dozen people who actually worked, often only part-time, at the JNP between 1955 and 1958. Such an enormous staff might have been able to accomplish the analysis, projection, and regulation of the Cuban environment, but as actually staffed there was little chance the JNP could acquire a full comprehension, much less control, of its extents.

But if the JNP fell short in the implementation of functional integral planning to regulate the socioeconomic *conjunto* of Cuba, it did make progress toward its representation, toward producing an image of the whole. Despite Montoulieu's persistence, the office did not project a national plan, or any substantial proposals for development that were national in scope, apart from the continuation of road-building projects already under way. But Montoulieu and his assistant, Felipe Préstamo, completed a quantity of analytic work, compiling statistical data on population, income, industry, and agriculture and laying it out in graphic form on new base maps of Cuba. They compiled topographical surveys, surveys of water and mineral resources, and surveys of agricultural production, all to be used to assist in the formulation of the future national plan. A new Cuban Institute of Cartography and Cadastral Survey created by executive decree in 1955 began work on a new topographical map of the island and a detailed map of Havana, both based on new aerial photographs and surveys. For its exhibition in the open courtyard of the Palacio de Bellas Artes in March 1957, the JNP displayed panels with photographs and analytic maps related to a prospective national plan; information on the master plans under way for Havana, Trinidad, and the Isle of Pines; and general statistics on energy, housing, and other public services, as well as the Plan Piloto for Varadero. Taken together, these graphic data offered the provisional representation of Cuba, present and future, that Montoulieu made clear he regarded as the basic functional element of planning.

In February 1958, a different exhibition held in the same venue addressed the theme of Cuban natural resources with an accompanying symposium of expert discussion. This symposium was organized by the Junta Nacional de Economía, under the direction of Gustavo Gutiérrez. Its organizers belatedly invited representatives from the JNP to collaborate in developing the exhibition, which presented information on Cuba's resources under eleven headings that included tourism, industry, and socioeconomic and natural resources. At the symposium, each division was the basis for a panel discussion between Cuban authorities and invited foreign experts. With a wide array of categories and depth of expert information, the symposium and exhibition approached a representation of the whole ecology of Cuba, not only its natural dimensions but its socioeconomic ones as well. The exhibition panels, all designed by Montoulieu and his assistant, attempted to describe with graphics and text the interaction of natural environment, social customs, and economic prerogatives, with such a descriptive representation understood as prerequisite to regulating that ecology. These panels did not adopt the rigid systematic classifications of the CIAM Grid, but their scope was similar—the same comprehensive and synthetic view claimed by Wiener's diagram of the human environment. Such a view was, though ambitious, certainly plausible given the size and insular condition of Cuba, and its importance would have been to identify points of connection between disparate realms of data and discipline.

Montoulieu was deeply dissatisfied with shortcomings that the event revealed, the sum of which, he regretted in an unpublished critique, was the complete absence of a "coordination and definition of aims" in regard to Cuban resources.[63] Montoulieu's disappointment was motivated in part by his desire to defend the prerogatives of the JNP, which should, he believed, have been the sponsor of the event and not merely a collaborator in the public propaganda of the exhibit. He hoped that through participating in that exhibit, and in presenting a paper at the symposium, he would be able to convince other Cuban officials of the proper role of the JNP as the coordinator of all activities related to management and development of Cuba's tangible and intangible resources. Coordination—or rather, the lack of coordination—emerged as the central point of criticism in Montoulieu's response. Each panel discussion, he argued, was in itself a highly accomplished study of the division topic, yet completely disregarded its relation to any other division topic. Representatives in each division were unwilling to concede a superior position in the hierarchy of planning to any other division, and the result, Montoulieu feared, was a situation in which each government agency advanced exclusively its own interest without any compensatory regulation by a coordinating body.

If planning opposed improvisation, then, as a corollary, coordination worked to prevent the debilitating effects of *particularismo,* a word Gustavo Gutiérrez had employed to describe the Cuban situation in the 1953 conference on planning. The Spanish philosopher José Ortega y Gasset had coined the term *particularismo* to depict the disintegration of a social whole into its separate parts so that no dynamic relation to the whole remained. "The essence of *particularismo* is that each group loses the sense of itself as a part, and, in consequence, stops sharing feelings with the others."[64] Ortega applied this concept to the study of Spain, in which, he argued, a process of regional disintegration over the preceding four centuries had progressed to the point where the nation no longer had a recognizable cohesion. Ortega did not advocate the suppression of the part in favor of the whole, but believed that a suitably "vertebrate" structure existed only when a dynamic system obtained between them, only when a unifying impulse and a dispersing impulse acted mutually upon one another. The condition of "invertebrate" Spain was, contrarily, a constellation of disconnected parts.

In the Cuban case, *particularismo* was evident not in regional dispersion, but in the dispersion of institutional and professional interests. In 1953, Gutiérrez worried that Cuba had inherited from Spain this same tendency, and prescribed the willful coordination imposed by planning as an effective curative. In a properly vertebrate structure, different professional constituencies could maintain their independent disciplinary prerogatives without being uselessly disconnected. Specifically contrived connections and hierarchical orders would permit coordinated function and the development of the whole as an effect, not a cause. But evidence of the factionalism of professional interests appeared at many points in the four-year life span of the JNP. It was the critical weakness of the 1958 symposium, according to Montoulieu, and it certainly helped provoke the disputes between Montoulieu and the economist Abalo. In 1956, in a formal consultants' report submitted to the JNP, Wiener and Sert pointed out that the conflicting perspectives of economic planners and physical planners could hinder properly integrated planning. Diplomatically, but with unmistakable preference, they described the two perspectives:

> The economic planners often presume that all planning must first of all be economically sound by traditional and known standards, and that it must first provide the productivity and means by which public works can be carried out.

> The physical planners, on the other hand, first of all project the needs of the future in coordinated fashion and give them physical expression in terms of comprehensive plans for regions, cities, etc.[65]

While their statement did not disparage the approach of economic planners, it did suggest that only the perspective of physical planners—the perspective of architects and urbanists—was endowed with capacities for coordination fundamental to successful planning.

Planning for Civil Society

The events of 1958 gave rise to the apparent certainty that General Batista would soon be forced to relinquish control of Cuba. Castro's insurgent force had gained control of large areas of the eastern provinces, including swaths of sugar-producing lands, and announced its intention to undermine economic production. Batista committed thousands of troops to regain the provinces, but a successful counteroffensive by Castro's guerrillas indicated a turn in momentum. The United States had begun to distance itself from Batista, imposing an arms embargo on his government, while rebel organizations joined together in an official anti-Batista alliance under Castro's leadership. Toward the end of the year, another staged election was widely boycotted, and the United States refused to endorse the legitimacy of the Cuban government. As Batista's hold on power eroded, the JNP and its consultants continued their work with little overt recognition of the possible effects that would accompany the end of his dictatorship. The development of the National Plan and the Pilot Plan for Havana continued, as did the preparation of the topographical map of Cuba. The staff of the JNP attended international conferences, maintained their thriving private practices, and even commenced work on new, large-scale commissions. Their expectation that such work would continue under whatever political authority succeeded Batista was an understandable one; since 1933, similar transitions of power had altered the contingencies that surrounded planning, but without disrupting the overall trend toward planning (as evidenced by the creation of planning institutions and the adoption of planning methods).

Then, early on New Year's Day 1959, General Batista fled Cuba, consummating but also commencing the Cuban Revolution. As Fidel Castro assumed control of government, it soon became evident that a different transformation of the political sphere was taking place. Hundreds of decrees issued over the following months affected all aspects of Cuban society. Property and infrastructure became instruments of the state as the revolutionary government first placed limits on ownership and rates and then moved to a policy of nationalization the following year. In May 1961, Castro announced that the Cuban Revolution was a socialist revolution and that the 1940 constitution was therefore obsolete; it would be replaced with a new charter. With the new government focused on agrarian reform and housing, and markedly biased against urban centers, the nature of planning was radically redefined as a revolutionary instrument (Figure 3.5). The JNP, which had initially remained intact, soon lost most of its members as they moved into exile. First recast as the Revolutionary JNP, in 1960 it was replaced by a new organization, the Department of Physical Planning, headed by Montoulieu's former deputy Felipe Préstamo.[66] A year later, he and almost all

FIGURE 3.5 Brochure published by the Revolutionary JNP in 1959, with captions promising the success of the revolution through planning. Courtesy of Eduardo Montoulieu. Photograph by the author.

the protagonists of the planning movement begun in the wake of the 1933 revolution had left Cuba.

From its creation to its dissolution after the Cuban Revolution, the JNP persistently focused an architectural perspective on planning, even when challenged by Abalo's criticisms or by Montoulieu's persistent reminders that "to plan is much more than to draw plans." To the extent that it fostered the *particularismo* that retarded the construction of a planning regimen, this disciplinary hegemony constrained the instrumental potential of the JNP. That potential, though, was constrained in advance by political circumstance. Batista's dictatorship incorporated as a republican gloss some of the organs of government that preceded it, including autonomous agencies such as the JNP, but the very proliferation of such agencies betrayed their capricious genesis. Soon after he was deposed, Batista attempted to exculpate himself with a narrative account in which he claimed credit for the extensive economic and social development of Cuba under his administrations. He titled his book *Piedras y leyes* to denote the integration of the laws *(leyes)* that had established order in the nation and the stones *(piedras)* that had been assembled into its structures. The chapters described hundreds of decrees, expenditures, and programs and an appendix listed the JNP as one of seventy-four autonomous organizations created by his government.[67] Despite the seemingly extensive vision this list implied, the actual consequences of these agencies were constrained by the piecemeal and often corrupt processes of implementation—Arroyo made regular appearances as minister of public works at groundbreakings and openings, yet did not successfully collate these various projects into a coordinated scheme as president of the JNP.

The proliferation of agencies into a collage of acronyms was also a symptom that Ángel Rama would identify of the disparity between the symbolic systems that evolved out of colonial legal frameworks and the cities that grew from foundations laid by the conquistadores:

> The evolution of the symbolic system did not lose momentum with the passage of time, and it seems to have reached its apotheosis in our own era, replete with schemes of signals, indices, acronyms, diagrams, logotypes, and conventional images so many of which imitate, or even aspire to replace, language. The component symbols in each of these systems respond only vaguely to particular, concrete facts of daily life. They respond, instead, to the needs of the symbolic

> system wherein they were originally conceived, the choice of signifiers being something of an afterthought, indispensable to expression but not essential to their genesis. Their function—founded on reason and instituted through legal mechanisms—is to prescribe an order for the physical world, to construct norms for community life, to limit the development of spontaneous social innovations, and to prevent them from spreading in the body politic. Their profusion in contemporary Latin America lends enduring testimony to the work of the lettered city.[68]

This symbolic realm, of agencies substantiated first as acronyms, with prerogatives tending more to representation than to realization, was always susceptible to the force of political caprice and certainly to authoritarian influence. And there would be no shortage of such component symbols after the Cuban Revolution—from acronymic institutions to legal decrees to posters—though they served a fundamentally different symbolic system. To categorize as ineffective the representations formulated in relation to planning—Martínez Inclán's *Código de Urbanismo,* Wiener's diagram, Montoulieu's charts—or to dismiss the 1940 constitution as unrealized, would define their efficacy, or lack of efficacy, too narrowly. An idealized image—the codes and diagrams and the constitution itself—went unfulfilled insofar as its correspondence with reality was not made close and the distance between Gutiérrez's two constitutions was not narrowed, but still it possessed an important register of effect. In one instance that took place after Batista seized power and suspended the constitution in 1952, university students in Havana held a funeral for the constitution, burying a copy of the document beneath a bust of José Martí. This collapsing of its representational and material dimensions served to illuminate the contrast between the civil society it embodied and the one within which it existed. When the popular magazine *Bohemia* solicited from several participants in the 1940 constitutional convention their opinion of Batista's arrogation of the presidency, most described the 1940 constitution as its counterpoint, as evidence of an authentic delegation of power from the people to the government that now embodied a deferred hope of the Cuban people. When Francisco Ichaso, a prominent writer who had been a delegate in 1940, eulogized the constitution after the 1952 "golpe de estado," he argued that the great accomplishment of the charter was to have created a new consciousness in its subjects:

> But the most important aspect of the Convention of '40 was the refinement of the collective feeling that it produced and that has translated into a more alert civic awareness, into a more correct political sense, into a fuller love for civil and democratic institutions . . . After the Constitution of 1940 came into effect politics was not for politicians, but rather the function and preoccupation of all the people.[69]

Ichaso intended, of course, this valorization of the constitution to demonstrate the illegitimacy of its suspension, but he also expressed strongly his optimistic belief that the "new civic spirit" and the "new Cuban conscience" could preserve the advances of the constitution even in the context of a politics saturated with "fatal remnants of the old plutocratic, opportunistic, *caudillo* [strongman] politics."[70] The Constitution of 1940 acquired a referential status to represent, to embody, the civil society as yet unrealized in Cuba and thus motivated the pursuit of practices that would assist its fulfillment—in short, it continued to motivate constitutionalism.

Constitutionalism, in the historical setting of the Cuban Republic between 1933 and 1959, should be understood first as a discursive milieu that oriented actions and inflected consequences by attributing to them a constant valence of meaning: the formulation of civil society. Immersed in this milieu, political structures, social realities, and disciplinary practices were all subject to its mediatory effect, marked most vividly by constitutionalism's emphasis on the "is" and the "ought." The measurement of the relative difference of these two and the evaluation of the translation from the former to the latter, also signaled during this period the presence of constitutionalism as a discursive mode—an assemblage of specific tropes employed to correlate norms to facts. Among these tropes the pairing of "is" and "ought," the valuation of the a priori, and the conflation of representation and projection predominated as traits of constitutionalism. As both milieu and mode, constitutionalism pervaded the disciplinary frameworks of professional, intellectual, and political actors of the period. It loosened the practices housed within those frameworks from their disciplinary confines, redefining them as elements within the larger civic environment. At the same time, as those disciplines participated in the construction of civil society, constitutionalism often confirmed the assertion of their specific prerogatives as irreducible contributions to the character of that civic environment. Constitutionalism deeply influenced professional and intellectual disciplines as an insinuated motive, but equally depended on those disciplines as means of actualization.

During the later years of the Cuban Republic, the proximity that had seemed apparent between the civil society projected by the 1940 constitution and the realities of the political sphere decreased, though without lessening the strength of the 1940 constitution as an embodiment of a future, and perhaps imminent, civil society. Meanwhile, though, new agents of constitutionalism such as planning had been adopted as means to formulate the underlying criteria for political and cultural debate; and as planning, in the form pursued by the JNP, struggled to produce from these criteria a coordinated civic environment, it did produce representations—diagrams and codes—with a sufficiency of purpose and concreteness that they might be applied and acted upon. The effort to construe a political system, occurring alongside the emergence of the aesthetic movement of modernism, produced the unique entanglement of law and architecture. Developing tenets of modernism had an affinity with those of constitutionalism (the problematic concern of *apriorismo* and normativism chief among them), and so an exchange or imbrication of tropes readily occurred. The consequence of constitutionalism, then, was not only the formulation of civic possibilities across a range of disciplines, but also in conjunction with those possibilities the distinctive evolution of modernism.

II

City

4 Public Works

Constructing the Urban Spaces of Civil Society

In 1928 in Havana, in a small park ringed with palm trees and facing the south hemicycle of the Capitolio Nacional, a ceiba tree was planted and dedicated as the Árbol de la Fraternidad Americana (Tree of American Brotherhood) to represent not only a union of nations, but the narrative of Cuba's emergence into that community (Figure 4.1). It had been grown from a seed planted at ceremonies held in 1902 to inaugurate the new republic, a ritual that itself recalled the traditional founding of the city of Havana in 1519, the "tradition that, in the shade of the big ceiba that had been there before, the first mass and the first *cabildo* of the new city had been held."[1] The newest ceiba carefully placed within an urban landscape thus forged a lineage from the foundation of Havana, to the founding of the republic, to the entry of Cuba into the international community of American nations; it evoked also a parallel lineage of civil society, one whose significance varied as much as its visibility. The original ceiba tree had been located in Habana Vieja—a neoclassical pavilion called El Templete was built in 1828 to commemorate the spot—and in 1948, Bernaldo de Quirós revealed that that first tree had also served as an *arbor infelix*, a *picota* for the punishment of condemned slaves. In the eighteenth century, he wrote, the governor of Havana "erected, over the location of the old ceiba, . . . a commemorative column relating the historical complex with the memory of the dead ceiba (first mass, first *cabildo*, although these are hypothetical; real and effective *picota*, supposed *rollo jurisdiccional*)."[2] A *picota* was a post or stone column placed in the main plaza of colonial towns, used as a pillory and for capital punishments and serving as a symbol of the enforceable authority of the law. Subsequently described as the *rollo jurisdiccional,* the stone column represented the law's jurisdictional extent. Inheriting these significances, the successive markers described by Bernaldo de Quirós acted as condensations of the encompassing environment of civil society. The Árbol de la Fraternidad Americana, a living tree, was another such punctuation, a perpetuation and a constitutive act to be witnessed within a civic landscape, a landscape whose presence was only indicated by the tall circular railing of elaborately wrought iron that surrounded the ceiba, and a landscape which was itself the object of extensive processes of modernization that would also be drawn toward constitutionalism.

By 1928, when the Árbol was dedicated, Havana had already undergone significant transformation from its colonial form, with a pattern of growth established that would persist into the 1940s (Figure 4.2). The original walled district, known as Habana Vieja, occupied the projection of land facing the sheltered bay and its narrow entrance; the city's nineteenth-century core, Centro Habana, had grown alongside, filling in the land outside the walls and establishing an urban edge on the northern coast. In the twentieth century, economic development had stimulated industrial growth, population increase, and real-estate speculation,

FIGURE 4.1 Árbol de la Fraternidad Americana. Postcard, circa 1931. Author's collection.

which together had prompted further expansion in two cohesive fabrics of development that extended outward, one westward along the coast, and the other south, along the edge of the bay and reaching inland as the topography allowed. Between these two extensions, lying either side of the railway branch leading into the city, a large area of undeveloped land remained, some of which had been platted by American military engineers as part of infrastructural improvements carried out during the U.S. occupation. Continued expansion of the streets and blocks of the city both into this vacant area and still further along the western and southern arms was presumed by a few visionary plans of the future city: a thesis

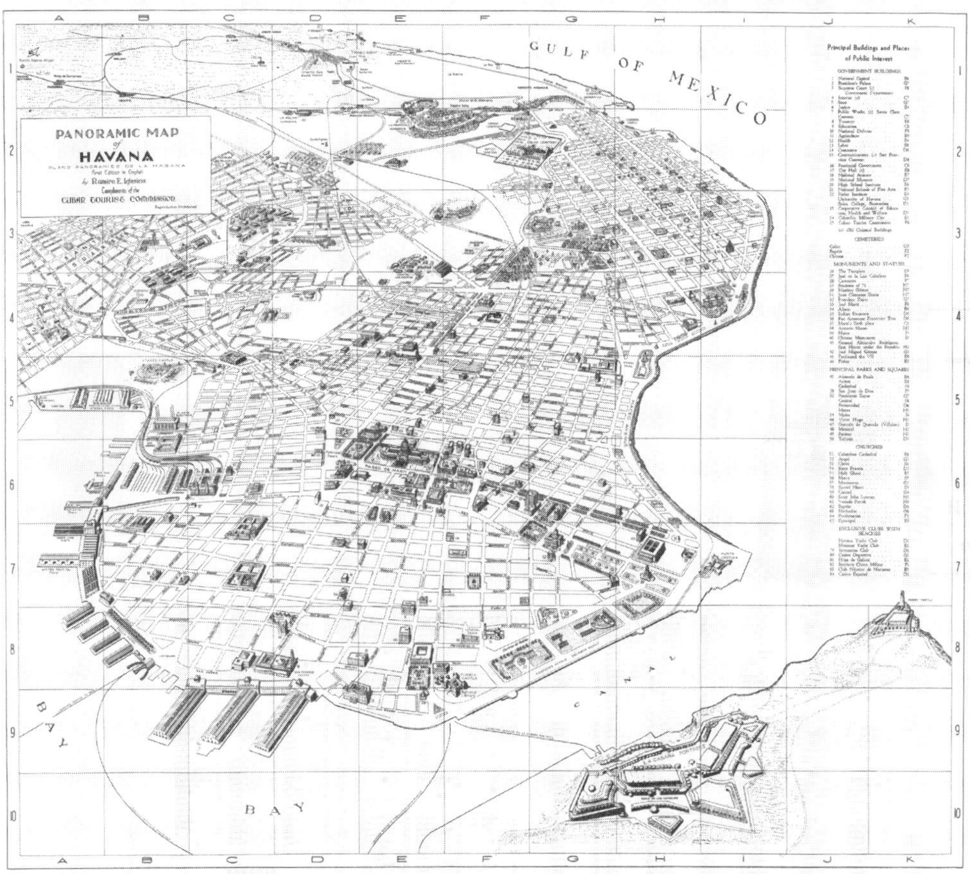

FIGURE 4.2 Map of Havana, 1940. Habana Vieja, the colonial quarter of the city, is in the foreground. Centro Habana is at the center of the map with the district of Vedado beyond at the upper right of the view. The undeveloped area within the city can be seen extending upward from the middle of the map. Courtesy of the Harvard Map Collection, Harvard University.

presented by Raúl Otero in 1905, a proposal formulated between 1915 and 1920 by Enrique Montoulieu, the city engineer, and, the most comprehensive, a plan published by Pedro Martínez Inclán as an appendix to his book *La Habana actual.*

Although the book was not published until 1925, according to Martínez Inclán the text and the plan were completed in 1919. In the prologue of his text, Martínez Inclán committed to produce "an exact description of our capital" requisite for comprehending its advantages and deficits. He therefore promised his reader

> A description without the passion of the poet: without the hatred or at least the contempt of the ignorant traveler so smug about the fame of his own land; without the opinionated nature of the artist disappointed in some undertaking; without the empty verbiage of the man of letters on the occasion that he writes much to conceal that he describes little, for lack of true technical preparation; without the preferences of the archaeologists or rather of the antiquarian, loving only old things; without the nonsense of the globe-trotter or explorer, determined to see characteristic particularities and rare phenomena in the most common and well-known things; in a word, with the strict scientific impartiality of the professional, somewhat tempered by the appraisals of the artist.[3]

In renouncing the variously distorted perspectives of poets, travelers, antiquarians, and others, Martínez Inclán implicitly claimed as distinctive the perspective that the architect or town planner directed toward the objects of the city. In 1924, Martínez Inclán had been named the first Professor of the Architecture of Cities, Parks, and Gardens at the University of Havana, and his claim had large significance in the Cuban context. Although artistic or aesthetic affiliations were usual, it was not uncommon for architects to assert the epistemic privilege of scientific objectivity. But in this instance that assertion was also a declaration of authority over Havana not only as a physical artifact but also as a social and a cultural space. In that regard, the renunciations in Martínez Inclán's claim were as significant as its presumptions, because the rejection of the descriptive modes of literature, travelogue, and archaeology carried away interpretive capacities and representational possibilities that were not (at least not explicitly) replaced within the architectural mode.

Martínez Inclán's proposed plan showed a network of radial streets superimposed upon the topography of the city (Figure 4.3). Its central hub, which he compared to the Étoile in Paris, was positioned in the area of undeveloped land southeast of Vedado and roughly equidistant between the old city center and the neighborhoods developing along the coast. From this hub, boulevards extend west to the Colón cemetery, north to the newly located university, east toward the bay, and northeast toward Habana Vieja; additional avenues reach out into as yet unoccupied land, connecting to lesser radial hubs, and forging a web of vehicular connections across the existing and future city. In his text, Martínez Inclán described the importance of individual buildings, parks, landscaping, and regulatory and economic initiatives. But as his plan makes clear, the system of circulation preceded these as the dominant element of organization. Most of the new boulevards he proposed cut through undeveloped land; he supported interventions in existing fabric, as in his proposed widening of two avenues in Habana Vieja, only when the advantage of improved traffic circulation and aesthetic embellishment outweighed the economic cost of such transformations. Preservation of existing elements was not one of Martínez Inclán's planning criteria, but a reasonable pragmatism of execution was. If such a plan "were to be realized," he wrote, "even if it went little by little, but with perseverance, in one hundred years, a brief enough term, Havana would be a sufficiently well-planned modern city."[4]

In December 1925, at the invitation of Gerardo Machado's newly elected government, the French urbanist J. C. N. Forestier arrived in Cuba commissioned to design a comprehensive plan for Havana that would improve the infrastructure of the city, embellish its physical aspect, and supply a framework for its apparently inevitable expansion. Forestier's reputation was that of an urbanist who could address both the technical and the aesthetic concerns raised by such an undertaking, or, as Martínez Inclán had posited, "the strict scientific impartiality of the professional, somewhat tempered by the appraisals of the artist."[5] To carry out the project, Forestier assembled a team composed of French and Cuban professionals who were directly responsible for many dimensions of the work. (Among them were two individuals who would later play leading roles in postwar urban projects in Havana: Jean Labatut and Raúl Otero.) The overall contours of his Plano del Proyecto de la Habana were conceived by the time Forestier left in February 1926; they were revised and further developed before and during his second prolonged stay two years later. During that visit, work progressed on a smaller urban scale as well, with the design and construction of specific elements of urban architecture, such as the Parque de la Fraternidad Americana in Centro

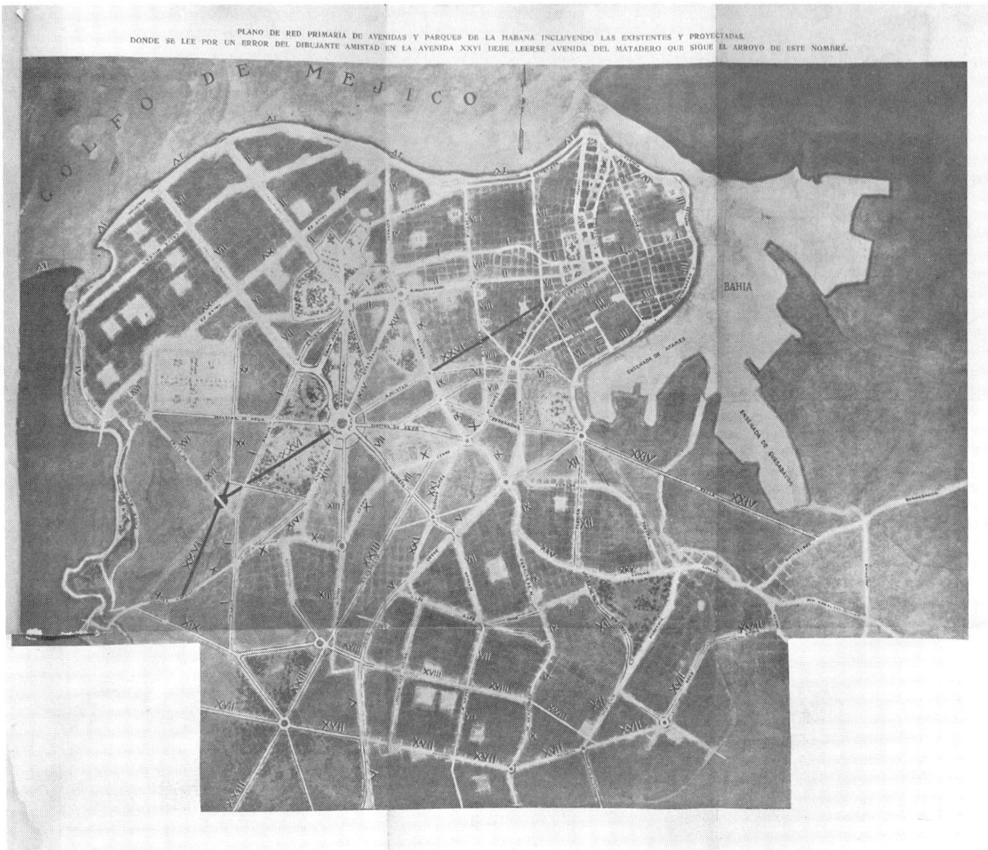

FIGURE 4.3 Pedro Martínez Inclán, Plan for Havana, circa 1919. Habana Vieja is the elliptical district toward the upper right area of the map. From Pedro Martínez Inclán, *La Habana actual* (Havana: P. Fernández y Cía, 1925).

Habana, as well as other parks and promenades on the Malecón and in Vedado. Several of these designs were set into execution by the time of Forestier's last visit, in the first three months of 1930. His death that October ended his participation in the planning of Havana, though not his influence on it.

Forestier's influence persisted not only through the Plano del Proyecto de la Habana, but also in the conception of the city that it defined. In Europe, alongside the emergence of a self-conscious avant-garde modernism in architecture and urbanism, as exemplified by Le Corbusier's City for Three Million of 1922 or the Weissenhofsiedlung in 1927, Forestier and his colleagues at the Société française des urbanistes (French Society of Urbanists) approached the city as a functional problem to be resolved by analytic examination and technical invention. They campaigned for modern urban legislation, administrative standards, traffic systems, and sanitary infrastructure, essential elements of the science of urbanism from which the artistry of the urbanist would construe a coherent whole, the plan of the city.[6] That this artistry typically followed the academic precepts and stylistic proclivities already being disdained by the avant-garde in Europe (although they remained the universal expression of cosmopolitanism in Latin America in the first few decades of the twentieth century) should not obscure the fact that the professional practices corresponded to modernizing tendencies. Cuba's capital city required streets, sewers, parks, and buildings commensurate with its progress from anachronistic colony to independent nation, and Forestier's Cuban patrons had selected him to construct the physical accommodation of the political and economic modernization of the republic.

The similarities between Martínez Inclán's proposal and Forestier's Plano del Proyecto de la Habana suggest that the French urbanist was as receptive to the ideas circulating in Cuba as the Cuban professionals were to the ideas of the foreign expert. (Martínez Inclán had traveled to France after the first world war and became acquainted with members of Forestier's professional circle and their work.) Like Martínez Inclan's, Forestier's plan described an armature that would primarily serve to shape the future expansion of the city rather than reorganize its existing elements[7] (Figure 4.4). His plan adopted some of Martínez Inclán's presumptions; the location of a new circulatory hub offset from the old city and from Vedado, for example, and the creation of secondary hubs in the southern outskirts. But while both plans emphasized circulation as the critical dimension of the urban plan, differences could be seen as well, and not only in the greater detail and precision that Forestier provided through his more extended period of study and design. In his preliminary sketches, Forestier distilled his transformative intervention to a simple figure, an axial cross formed by two enormous boulevards, one extending from a new civic center adjacent to the Colón cemetery eastward to a new rail terminus near the bay, and the other running southwest from the coast through the civic center to a new Bosque Nacional (National Forest) at the outskirts of the city. This gesture recalls (as Martínez Inclán's net of streets does not) the foundational impulse of the Laws of the Indies, the imposition of order, in this case with the *norma,* the right angle of a set square. The real conditions of the city, however, altered Forestier's cross at its conception. The location of the cemetery prevented the addition of a western arm, and the

FIGURE 4.4 J. C. N. Forestier, Plano del Proyecto de la Habana, 1925–30. From Comisión Central Pro-Monumento a Martí, *En memoria de José Martí* (Havana: P. Fernández y Cía, 1938).

implications, economic and social, of existing fabric would force the amputation of much of the northern arm as well; the figure could be connected to the coast only obliquely, through the already constructed secondary avenues that angled through Vedado.

In addition to the simplicity of its figure and the regulatory ambition that figure conveyed, Forestier's plan differed from Martínez Inclán's in the greater complexity of its punctuating elements, its plazas and monuments. Martínez Inclán, perhaps motivated by the judgment that a manifest pragmatism would afford his plans greater chance of realization, had noted that his central hub aimed to fulfill a traffic function and was not a "Centro Cívico" such as Enrique Montoulieu had proposed for that location in his own plan.[8] Forestier restored the idea of a civic center and added a grand monumental scale with upper and lower terraces linking a dozen avenues with two main plazas and several smaller squares (Figure 4.5). This articulated composition permitted maintaining axial emphasis while accommodating the variety of eccentricities produced when the avenues were positioned to connect with existing elements. Traffic assumed a secondary importance below that of civic representation. With the rendering of its plan outline over contour lines (or in another instance superimposed upon an aerial photograph of the terrain), the representational intention of Forestier's plan became apparent as the shaping of a civic environment out of the natural and artificial topography of Havana. His plan aimed to accommodate the functional requirements of the future city (as did Montoulieu's and Martínez Inclán's), but additionally it aimed to ensure the legible representation of that city. Consequently, the connection of the civic center to another grand plaza for the proposed railway terminus in the east and to a new campus for the university on the elevated

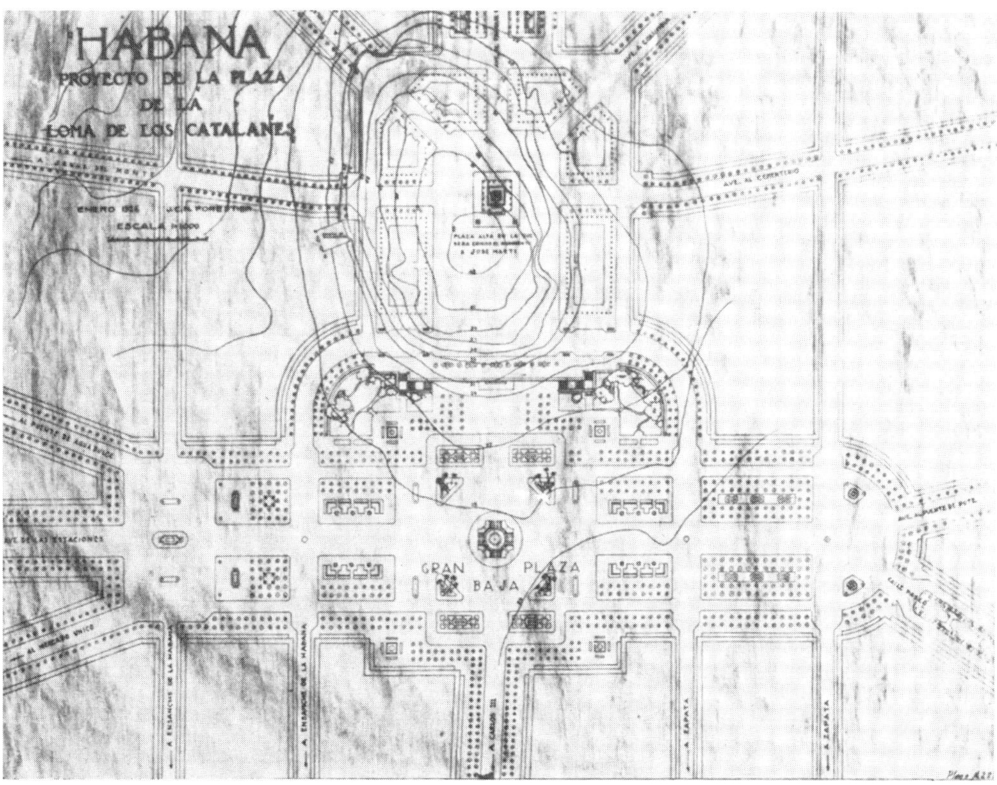

FIGURE 4.5 J. C. N. Forestier, proposed civic center for Havana superimposed over the existing topographic lines, 1926. From Comisión Central Pro-Monumento a Martí, *En memoria de José Martí.*

terrain to the north followed the principle that the major components of the city should be linked for vehicular movement and for visual continuity so that they could be seen and experienced as elements of the civic structure of the modern city. Because Forestier had to work within the constraints—historical, economic, and physical—of an existing city, this structure would necessarily be revealed either incompletely, abandoning some of its constitutive elements, or fragmentarily, with pieces complete within themselves but disconnected from other parts of the structure.

The latter proved to be the consequence of the plan, in part through intention and in part owing to the aforementioned constraints, to the political tensions in Machado's dictatorship, and to Forestier's death. Realized therefore as fragments, a number of elements were set into the overall context of the city. The civic center was realized much later and in different form, but Forestier's team succeeded in executing designs for the area around the university, for the renovation and embellishment of the Malecón, and for the blocks around the new Capitolio Nacional, the Parque Central, and the Paseo del Prado. These last three elements created an irregular axis joining the legislative house to the promenades and plazas that served as the theaters of public urban life; designs for the grounds in front of the presidential palace were also partially realized, linking that building to the newly refashioned Malecón. Carefully elaborated landscapes of royal palms and ceibas, elegantly appointed with street furniture such as benches made of coral, became durable sites for, and explicit representations of, civic life.[9] Architectural incidents realized within the larger perceived framework of the city, they assumed the aesthetic predisposition foreshadowed by the architectural emphasis of Martínez Inclán's *La Habana actual,* commensurate with the "the appraisals of the artist" embedded in the "art" of urbanism.

Architecture and Civic Culture

Forestier's designs conjured an urban landscape, a constructed environment of climate and organic and inorganic material, with prominence accorded to tropical vegetation, interconnected parks forming vegetal ribbons through the city, and the Bosque Nacional assuming clear importance in the overall plan. Nature supplied the referential properties of these elements as well. Some literally invoked natural elements of Cuba; others were deliberately bound to the natural forms of topographical contours. For example, one of the realized elements of the Plano del Proyecto de la Habana, the dramatic Escalinata (stone steps) of the university designed by Otero, emphasized rather than concealing an abrupt rise in grade to create the formal and imposing entrance to the campus. Other instances include the several plazas and boulevards designed to fix views of the sea either as terminuses or panoramas. And while the civic center location allowed the expedient extension of existing streets to the north and east to a crossing point, Forestier's civic center design also seized on the advantage of the small existing hill, the Loma de los Catalanes, in order to produce a sweep of stepped terraces. Such techniques were not only appropriations of the natural contour turned to aesthetic advantage but representational practices through which nature was revealed as the referential and legitimating ground of the city. Just as the coral benches and the Cuban laurels on the Paseo del Prado supplied the *cubanidad* of the otherwise universalizing classicist design, topographical singularities rooted the larger elements of urban architecture into a historical narrative that did not describe the growth of the city but rather the evolution of its site. The natural ground, in other words, would become the history of the superimposed architectural figures. The resulting formal synthesis of *ciudad* and *campo,* distilled with the nationalism of the initial decades of independence, produced a potent evocation of the nation, with revealed civic structures such as the movement and congregation of citizens, the university, and the Capitolio Nacional, all in effect naturalized by the architectural and urban forms themselves. But the capacity of such forms to serve as instruments of civil society was, even at the moment of their realization, undermined by the authority of the vicious dictatorship that commissioned them. With the legislature largely impotent during this period, the university perceived as a political threat, and political violence commonplace, the elements of the Plano del Proyecto de la Habana marked out a distance between the cohesive structure of nationhood and the more tenuous assembly of civil society.

After Machado's fall, the discernment of the civic potential of urban and architectural forms gained a new importance as such forms were recognized as constitutive elements, components in the construction of civil society. While Forestier's influence in Cuba remained, especially as conveyed through his collaborators, another lineage of influence emerged in the 1930s with a different emphasis on the civic role of urban form (and with a different stylistic disposition). Forestier's continuing influence derived in large measure from the construction of sites that became inextricably part of the social and cultural texture of the city: the Paseo del Prado, the Malecón, the Parque Central, the monumental stair of the university. But Cuban architects had also absorbed separately the influence of other writings on urbanism, particularly from North America, where many traveled and studied. Lessons from the work of Frederick Law Olmsted, Daniel Burnham's Plan of Chicago, and the City Beautiful projects of John Nolen were each imported into Cuba as contemporary theoretical positions. Martínez Inclán's book *La Habana actual* included numerous citations from Charles Mulford Robinson, whose own book *Modern Civic Art, or, The City Made Beautiful* had established many of the principles of the City Beautiful movement.[10] From that reading, Martínez Inclán derived the thesis articulated in his first book, that the city must be seen as an aesthetic expression of its social or community life and that political authorities and citizens, individuals and professions must acknowledge their obligation to contribute to its improvement through the practices of civic art. By 1936, during the period of provisional government following Machado's ouster, Martínez Inclán had encountered another theoretical position in the writings of Werner Hegemann, which diverged subtly but meaningfully from the precepts of the City Beautiful even while sharing the term "civic art."[11] Although an emphasis on aesthetics linked Hegemann to the ambitions of the City Beautiful movement, his writings demonstrated that he placed greater emphasis on the term "civic" than on the term "art." His interest focused from the start on the city as a historical object, rather than a canvas for expression. As early as 1915, Hegemann had determined that the expression of the civic should not be confined to surface, or style, or monument; all dimensions of the city, he argued, including necessities such as housing and transportation, had to be addressed together: "Today everybody knows that a really beautiful city can be created only by considering right from the beginning the proper co-ordination of all the needs and ideals of civic life and its physical expression."[12]

Daniel Burnham and other advocates of the City Beautiful had associated the city plan with the civic, but the incorporation of housing and transportation along with civic centers as the component parts of the city reflected the broader balance Hegemann sought in what he referred to as city planning, the balance between art and science. He championed art and aesthetics in the face of the critique of the city emerging in the social sciences and against the strengthening polemic of functionalism in architectural modernism, yet he also advocated science against the circumscribed artistic predilections of the academic traditions of architecture when those were offered as treatments for the crisis of the modern city. By 1936, Hegemann's writings had a markedly modern sensibility, foregrounding the question of planning, the necessity of housing, the instrumentalism of regulation, all as aspects of the conjoined practice of architecture and city planning. Stylistically, as his illustrations made evident, Hegemann remained circumspect, viewing academic and modernist examples with equal and comparable scrutiny.[13] It is Hegemann's early academic training that suggests the pertinent genealogy of his influence in Cuba. In 1904, Hegemann spent a year as a student at the University of Pennsylvania in order to study under the economist Simon Patten, whose ideas on progressivism, refutation of laissez-faire presumptions, and historicist economic theories all strongly shaped Hegemann's own later thinking on the city. Patten produced a similar effect on several of his other students who took up central roles in the planning discipline, including John Nolen, with whom Hegemann maintained a close association, and Rexford Tugwell, who, as discussed earlier, came to influence Cuban planning quite directly. The common thread was a belief in the advantages of planning exercised by an authority acting on behalf of the public, an authority concerned with the production of the civic sphere for comprehensive social benefits and as part of its own maintenance and reproduction. Hegemann, although never trained as an architect, added to this belief the claim that architecture would play a substantive role in any such production. Hegemann's arguments were easily assimilated into other disciplinary debates in architecture (seemingly to their detriment because such assimilations affiliated with more reactionary than progressive positions); indirectly, however, they also extended into architectural discourse through the writings of his protégé Joseph Hudnut.[14]

Hudnut's influence on professional discourse was limited, but his ideas did have some presence in Cuba on account of his association with Eduardo Montoulieu, who had been Hudnut's student. Hudnut contributed not only some dissemination of Hegemann's ideas, but also a more complex consideration of the question of the aesthetic dimension of city planning. At Columbia and more dramatically at Harvard, Hudnut championed the modern architecture of Gropius, Mies, and other European architects as attempts to accommodate not only the practical but also the spiritual necessities of the age. He argued early on against the reductive tenets of functionalism, considering the accommodation of function a prerequisite of aesthetic success but not its cause. In the pointedly titled articles "The Political Art of Architecture" and "The Political Art of Planning" (the latter published in Cuba in 1944), Hudnut also argued for architecture to engage vigorously with the problem of the contemporary city not from the vantage of an expert discipline but as a constituent of the social formation of the city:

> We are conscious of a participation in great tides of human behavior: and with what distinctness and force the great war brings that home to us! A habit of collective thought and action is daily confirmed as we face together the collective destiny which . . . we shall share together. Since our lives are to be lived, our happiness to be attained, as parts of a collective whole, we will inevitably become increasingly alert to whatever is of significance in the life of our community. Certainly city planning will be among those factors: and not as a biological science of shelter and physical health merely but as an art, interpreter of the human spirit.
>
> It appears then that we need not despair of an *architecture-of-cities*.[15]

The compressed hyphenation revealed an ambitious role for architects, who should not acquiesce to be subordinate to—or even merely equal to—technicians or social scientists in this project of the building of cities. To give form and significance to social organization through an architecture-of-cities, the architect faced a threefold task: first, to gain "a wider knowledge and understanding of the pattern of life in cities"; second, to assume responsibility for the social health, and "civic malformations," of the city; and third, to devise "programs of actions" and to "sketch the patterns of thought and conduct which might point the way to new social and economic equilibriums."[16]

Hudnut construed the connection between social configurations and architectural design in two brief essays, both prefaces to treatises on city planning, the practice within which that connection might be forged. One prefaced the first volume of Hegemann's *City Planning, Housing*. In these two pages, Hudnut employed the word *pattern* once to describe city planning as the "creation of patterns" and then to refer to citizens' inner "pattern of life."[17] The clear implication was that city planning was the coordination of one to the other, or perhaps more precisely the coordination effected by the extrapolation of patterns of form out of patterns of life. Hudnut wrote the second preface as a foreword to Sert's *Can Our*

Cities Survive? In spite of differences between Hegemann's principles of city planning and the CIAM principles set forth in Sert's book, Hudnut's two prefaces were similar, both emphasizing that a city should be defined not by an "aggregation of people" but by the "heart and content of society."[18] Cautioning that "It will be considered strange that I should find in a program for civic betterment . . . the basis for a new architecture," Hudnut nevertheless concluded, "I do not despair of an architecture of cities—by which term I mean cities which are patterned not only by those intellectual forces which seek to bend natural law to human betterment but also by those spiritual forces which throughout human history have left repeated imprints upon human environment."[19] For its part, the architecture-of-cities would take on a new character commensurate to the civic itself, in order to "exhibit not a principle of logic or of aesthetics merely but the true character and direction of our civic culture."[20] The word *direction,* which Hudnut also used with some frequency, conveyed an important significance, emphasizing the progressive condition of civic development. Civic culture was not a static element of the human environment; it evolved in conjunction with the forces of human history and with the pattern of cities. Moreover, civic culture was subject, to some extent at least, to orientations induced or fostered by those patterns, and consequently the plan of a city expressed in "streets and squares" could equally be the plan for civil society.

By the early 1930s, the administration had suspended the implementation of Forestier's overall plan for Havana. According to José María Bens Arrarte, an architect and critic, the plan had been enacted "dictatorially" without the involvement of representatives of property owners, businessmen, and professionals—in other words, without the central participants of civil society—and was thus unsuccessful in offering a persuasive direction or orientation for the future Havana.[21] The next similarly comprehensive direction was offered a decade later, following the presidential inauguration of Ramón Grau San Martín in 1944. In October of that year, his administration initiated the Plan de Obras del Gobierno del Presidente Dr. Grau San Martín, a broad and coordinated initiative of public works throughout the nation. Its seven principal categories incorporated the construction of roads, sanitation, schools, hospitals, ports, public buildings including housing and markets, as well as the general implementation of urbanism. These projects were distributed throughout Cuba in order to achieve a comprehensive modernization, but attention was focused primarily on cities and on Havana in particular, and the Plan de Obras del Gobierno included several proposed Planos Reguladores. All similar in their scope and their delineation of elements to be addressed, these master plans seemed to accord with a general urbanistic template: first, a new civic center was located adjacent to the core of the city and connected with primary avenues of circulation that were to be enlarged and improved; second, new parks including playing fields and playgrounds would be distributed throughout the city; third, secondary streets were to be straightened where possible and widened and paved to improve traffic circulation. Accordingly, the new Plano Regulador de la Habana was focused on improving the functioning of the city, although with a more concentrated sense of necessity. The capital city of the nation possessed the "physiognomy of a provincial city" with inadequate structures of circulation for its population and its commercial and governmental activities, and an accounting of the Plan de Obras del Gobierno published for the government in 1947 looked critically on prior efforts, Forestier's included, to improve this unfavorable condition:

> Until 1944, all of the plans for the embellishment of the capital were realized by means of arbitrary programs. They pursued the aesthetic, forgetting the functional. Havana was filled with plazas and buildings, streets and avenues, leaving aside communications with the furthest neighborhoods, the great conflicts that cause traffic congestion and the modern requirements of urbanism.[22]

While the embellishment of the seat of government was to be acknowledged as necessary, the functional problems of roads, population growth, and urban activities were the proper and vital focus of urbanistic attention. In suggesting this emphasis, the Plan de Obras del Gobierno adopts the position adumbrated by Hegemann and by Hudnut regarding the aesthetic improvement of the city as a corollary of its functional resolution.

Grau's presidency initially extended the apparent consolidation of a stable political environment, marking an electorally sanctioned transition of executive power. Grau's prior participation in the 1933 revolution gave his administration the cast of the progressive optimism of that moment. To the extent that Forestier's proposals would have carried associations to the prerevolutionary moment, they would have had to be reconceived in the terms of postwar progressivism. With the economic lift of the postwar sugar boom, Grau's administration was able to conceive such a possibility, and so the Plan de Obras's extensive array of public works thus reflected not only the necessity of modernization but also the desire for social progress as manifested through public health, education, and housing. The accomplishment of a physical planning effort commensurate to a new political circumstance was, however, deeply compromised by the political realities of the Grau administration and by the limitations of professional authority over planning. Patronage and graft, already habitual, assumed new dimensions, with an enormous increase in civil service positions and consequent expenditures almost inevitably rendering the program of public works an instrument for political manipulation. Articulation of a professional concern for planning was equally insufficient, with the emphasis on technical or functional considerations overshadowing their latent political implications. A plan for Havana proposed in 1951 by Eduardo Cañas Abril as president of the Comisión de Planificación del Colegio Nacional de Arquitectos conveyed an explicit concern only for issues of circulation, and lacked any new comprehensive vision for the city. So, while projects for infrastructure, roads, and buildings were carried out during these first postwar years, the connection between them and their collective association to a political register was not established.

From Civic Art to Urban Design

For a period of years, roughly between 1953 and 1957, the two modifiers "civic" and "urban" existed as uneasy synonyms in architectural discourse; they were not truly commensurate yet they did not convey distinctively different meanings. Some peculiar phrases resulted—such as José Luis Sert's redundant description of a "Civic City."[23] Difficulties emerged when the words became containers of critical significance in a debate about the architecture of cities. In his manuscript of "The Architect and the City," a lecture he presented in 1954, Sert redacted the very first sentence to read: "Architecture is 90% an urban ~~or civic~~ activity."[24] Was a perceived redundancy or an opportunistic banishment the cause of the excision? The sharpened spoken delivery of the sentence perhaps informed the decision, but Sert's editorial stroke in itself signaled important distinctions being made at that moment. The invitation to the First Urban Design Conference at the Graduate School of Design (GSD) in 1956 pointedly discarded the term "civic design" because it had acquired, according to the organizers, "too specialized or too grandiose a connotation."[25] The proposed substitute, "urban design," presumed to avoid these two hazards, one a self-constraining focus on monuments and the other a self-dissipating claim to social practice. Sert introduced the term "urban design" soon after he took over as dean, using it as the title of a lecture given to a regional conference of the American Institute of Architects (AIA).[26] The importance of the civic was not disregarded—he used that word a dozen times in his six-page text—but instead distinguished as a desired result (the environment of civil society) distinct from a practice (urban design). In other lectures during these years, Sert often repeated his narrative of the city in decline sliding inexorably toward the crisis hyperbolically posited by the title of his book *Can Our Cities Survive?* The increasing rate of suburbanization, the physical and economic deterioration of old city centers, and the decoupling of social life from its traditional setting in the city suggested to Sert that the fundamental idea of the city was being diminished, if not abandoned. The loss of the city, he warned, would be a loss of the physical dimension of civic life:

> Fly over vast continents, as we do today, and imagine cities disappearing: what would remain as an expression of our culture? This culture of ours is a culture of cities, *a civic culture*. It is in the central areas of cities where the landscape is really a man-made landscape that the past shows many examples of civic beauty, civic landscapes sometimes built in the course of centuries, where city planning and architecture are at their best. No isolated building can compete with them. They are a miracle repeated through the ages—the Acropolis, the Piazza San Marco, the Place de la Concorde, etc.[27]

The defining characteristic of civic culture, for Sert, lay in its articulation of a communal existence, a social existence of discourse and exchange. Sert wanted to replace the terms "civic design" and "civic art" in order to remove the association and influence of the aesthetic practices he considered anachronistic; his ambition was not to diminish the civic, but to disengage it from those standards. Civic culture, civic beauty, the civic landscape—these goals remained in force in Sert's arguments linked to a different set of standards and practices.

One association that Sert could neither remove nor diminish was the association of the civic with the political. Out of the large catalog of centers of culture and of public congregation to which Sert tended to refer, the three exemplary civic landscapes he selected in the preceding quotation underscored the political register: the Acropolis as the achievement of the first democracy, the Piazza San Marco as the seat of an oligarchic republic, and the Place de la Concorde as the stage first of royalty and then of regicide during the French Revolution. All explicitly connoted political environments, and the citizens who congregated in these spaces, as conceived in Sert's narrative, were political actors, participants in the production and reproduction of civic processes in various manifestations. But the political context of the 1950s, in the United States or internationally, was prominently absent from Sert's descriptions. In the political spectrum asserted in earlier CIAM polemic, ranging from communist to socialist to liberal affiliations, Sert had occupied a middle position; this stance had been tempered by Cold War realities into a left or progressive position that presumed democratic governance and citizen participation as a matter of course. When Sert spoke of the civic sphere to his audiences in 1953 and 1954, it would have been understood that the system of participation already existed, and that its expression, encouragement, and refinement were the civic intention of architecture.

Adopting "urban" as a new encompassing modifier entailed consequences other than disciplinary fratricides. First and perhaps most important, the urban did not inherently contain the political, whereas the civic inescapably did. The urban referred more descriptively to a physical condition rather than the sociocultural concept invoked by the civic. The urban therefore corresponded more smoothly with the assertion of technique, or of objective science, claimed as a basis of an urban design that would reconfigure what was now referred to as an environment:

> We cannot any longer talk or think in terms of buildings alone. We are aware that buildings large or small are an integral part of their environment and are shaped by that environment. Our environment is being radically transformed, or reshaped. The young men now coming to the schools of architecture, engineering, landscape architecture, those that are working hard to produce better painting and sculpture, the sociologist, educators, doctors, real estate men, business men, politicians, economists will have to make an important contribution towards the shaping of that environment.[28]

Similarly to planning, the concept of the urban formulated in urban design allowed the construction of an object—the city—that could be operated upon and regulated by a set of technicians, the various professions working in synchronized fashion. Sert described this object, and its center in particular, as a no-man's-land, because no profession claimed it as the site of practice and because modern architecture had so far failed to produce, or even attempted to produce, its solution. He urged architects to enter into this territory, to consider it a bridge between architecture and planning where the emerging tenets of urban design could be discerned and clarified.

Paul Wiener concurred, proposing to the audiences of his South American lecture tours that architecture and planning were integrated by the shared problem of the city. The significance of the isolated object of architecture had diminished and now the "problems of architecture . . . are originally and essentially connected with the new patterns that govern the Planning of Cities."[29] To the theoretical framework of urban design applied to Cuba, Wiener also contributed his singularly passionate faith in future technological transformation. From the years just after the war and on into the 1950s, Wiener frequently proselytized about the potential for this technological transformation to provoke similarly extensive changes in social formation. Writing on the topic "Future World's Fairs," Wiener suggested that these showcases of science and society should provide "a visualization of the kind of world we want to make . . . a dramatization of a Utopia, but a Utopia by way of experiment with the means already at our disposal."[30] His approbation of existing means was not a sign of conservatism, but rather evidence of his belief that those means, if only properly seen and deployed, already surpassed the capacity of citizens to absorb and adjust to the transformations they signified. An essay that Wiener contributed to the CIAM volume *The Heart of the City* a few years later made clear the extremity of his optimism: "The age of alchemy in which we live today means essentially that it is now possible to make anything—materials, machines, and energy—out of nothing, anywhere in the world, in any amount, almost without measurable cost in terms of time and labor."[31] This view had a social corollary, in that such capabilities might render current political tendencies obsolete, as Wiener suggested in personal correspondence in 1947:

> Life everywhere is full of political talk, it's a major pre-occupation. I for my part believe that both the left and the right are outmoded. I know that new atomic energies will be available in the next five years that will completely revolutionize

> life of everyone; that we are embarking on an epoch of abundance. We will have to revise all of our concepts including the political ones; a new philosophy and a new social system quite different from anything the world has ever known will soon begin.[32]

Wiener's polemical stance undoubtedly held implications for the work of Town Planning Associates in Cuba, both in the strength of its fidelity to modernization and in its potential articulation of a relationship between the architecture of cities and the political environment in which that architecture was produced.

With the creation of the JNP in January 1955, Town Planning Associates finally obtained the governmental sanction and authority for design work that Wiener and Sert thought was essential to the uncompromised realization of "architecture-of-cities" or urban design. Both men were aware of the contingencies involved in work undertaken at the level of national government (a lesson they had learned in Colombia), but in Cuba their friendship with Arroyo, and Arroyo's position in the JNP and the presidential cabinet, were grounds for confidence. Within a month, the firm's correspondence referred to the commission for a new "Plan for Havana," and work did indeed begin rapidly on several fronts within the JNP. Arroyo quickly staffed the agency, and Montoulieu, Quintana, and Romañach commenced work, respectively, on the National Plan, the Plan for Varadero, and the Plan for Havana. Montoulieu pursued work on the National Plan with some measure of independence, while Quintana took over the work in Varadero that had been initiated by Arroyo in collaboration with Town Planning Associates. It was a comprehensive plan for Havana, often envisioned after the war but never initiated, that was arguably the central component of the work of the JNP and Town Planning Associates. Havana dominated the cultural and political life of Cuba and contained a significant percentage of the island's population. For the Cuban architects and planners, it posed the problem of national and cultural definition; for Sert and Wiener it offered a challenge to produce precepts and practices of urban design through the conjunction of architecture and planning.

Work on the comprehensive plan for Havana took place in roughly three stages, with preliminary work carried out in the summer of 1955 and into 1956, followed by more detailed refinement later in 1957. The final stage consisted in the preparation of drawings, diagrams, illustrations, and text for the folio publication of the *Plan piloto de la Habana*. (The folio was completed and printed at the end of 1958, but not issued until after the revolution in January 1959.) Three stages of work were understood to correspond to stages of specificity and superseded regulatory control. First, a preliminary scheme would outline the premises of the proposed plan; then, a *plan piloto,* a pilot plan, would be developed to demonstrate the schematic organization of that plan and the interrelationship of its parts; finally, a *plan regulador,* a master plan, would present the structure of physical and regulatory implementation that would guide the future development of Havana. Within the JNP, the Oficina del Plan Regulador de la Habana (OPRH), headed by Mario Romañach and regarded proprietarily by Sert and Wiener, was directly responsible for its development. The significance of the plan as an example for other Cuban cities, Havana's cultural and political centrality, as well as the other architects' (all of whom were *habaneros*) profound interest in the city, made this work in some ways the common project of the JNP. Sert had previously prescribed the master plan as the first step of the practice of urban design ("The new redevelopment of sectors in our cities should be first determined by a master plan. It is this master plan which should fix their character, size and limits"),[33] while Wiener in his own lectures often quoted, without citation and with his own modifications, a general description of planning as the definition of a master plan:

> It is a well considered correlation of the immediate and long term needs, purposes and desires of the people which are suitable, feasible and capable of expression in physical terms. The Master Plan is presented as a guide to assist private individuals and public officials in the adjustment of beneficial objectives through coordinated action. To achieve its aims, the master plan must be realistic in origin; in scope it must be broadly inclusive; in outline it must be bold and imaginative; in detail it must be flexible. Such planning provides the basic framework for directing the development of the urban area in its growth, and prescribes interpretations to facilitate its realizations.[34]

Expansive definitions such as these not only reflected the potential vagueness of the term, but also indicated the ambitious scope of elements the master plan was presumed to regulate.

At the moment when the Plan Regulador de la Habana was initiated by JNP, Professor Charles Haar of the Harvard Law School was addressing precisely this conceptual expansiveness of master plans. Haar, who specialized in planning law and zoning law, joined the Harvard faculty the year before Sert was appointed dean at the GSD. The two became close friends and colleagues; Sert and Wiener brought Haar into discussions of the Cuban Planning Law in 1954, and he provided comments and the outline proposal for the law that Sert conveyed to Arroyo. Over the next few years, he consulted on additional aspects of the planning work in Cuba, traveling there at the end of 1956 to meet Cuban legal professionals to discuss strategies for highway, zoning, and subdivision laws that were to be developed by the JNP. Haar believed strongly in the transformative potential of planning and during the 1950s produced an extensive body of research on planning law in the United States, addressing its theory and its implementation in several articles and books, including an authoritative case-book on land-use planning that he began to draft in 1955.[35]

Two essays in particular examined the issue of the master plan as a concept situated between a more general sphere of normalization and a more specific realm of implementation. In the first essay, "In Accordance with a Comprehensive Plan," Haar took up the question of enabling legislation for zoning in the United States, observing that these laws adopted a common language requiring that zoning be carried out "in accordance with a comprehensive plan."[36] The exact object and meaning of that phrase, Haar pointed out, was undefined. Did the adjectival modifier imply that zoning must be geographically expansive? Or that the city was required to produce a temporally extensive plan? Or did it refer to analytic work, calling for complete study of all existing conditions prior to any enactments? The phrase could, he concluded, support any or all of those interpretations. This range of meaning would permit wide variation in the degree of instrumentality attained by a master plan, with a geographically extensive plan presumably resembling statutory zoning while a temporally extensive one would be an anticipatory statement of principles. The one inescapable function of the master plan was to prevent juridically the imposition of an arbitrary or arbitrarily conceived enactment by requiring some statement of the premises on which any specific planning proposal was asserted; the "comprehensive plan" provided the standard of juridical judgment, articulated to the degree necessary to render it useful as a criterion for the evaluation of facts. Like Sert and Wiener, Haar saw that the concept of the master plan assumed an interdependency of elements and motives complex enough to require prior regulation in order to achieve beneficial consequences, or at least to avoid deleterious or ineffective ones. But significantly,

Haar did not situate the master plan within an instrumental dimension, but in a normative one. The master plan, by "requiring an articulated statement of generalized relations, with supporting data and findings, lends assurance that . . . thinking in comprehensive terms has in fact gone on. The forced referral to previously formulated standards introduces a new and more sharply defined principle of legitimation for later legislative enactments."[37] In serving to legitimate subsequent decisions and actions, the master plan would assume an explicitly political role, at a remove from direct material consequences but still very much an effective force insofar as it bridged between the fundamental norms articulated at a constitutional level and statutory instruments such as zoning.

In the second essay, significantly titled "The Master Plan: An Impermanent Constitution," Haar noted that the purpose of a master plan, as outlined in the Standard City Planning Enabling Act used as a template by many jurisdictions in the United States, was that "of guiding and accomplishing a coordinated, adjusted, and harmonious development . . . which will, in accordance with present and future needs, best promote health, safety, morals, order, convenience, prosperity, and general welfare, as well as efficiency and economy in the process of development."[38] Was this best accomplished, Haar asked, by employing the master plan simply as technique, or by fixing it as actual legislation? The answer depended on how the purpose and the ambition of the master plan were defined, and Haar thus proposed that the master plan be understood as two conceptual categories, one concerned with the making of plans and the other concerned with their effectuation.[39] The first category he divided into six typical uses of the master plan: "(1) a source of information; (2) a program for correction; (3) an estimate of the future; (4) an indicator of goals; (5) a technique for coordination; and (6) a device for stimulating public interest and responsibility." Each of these types concerned theories of planning, that is, arguments about the nature of planning itself. The second category, effectuation, identified five types of master plan: "(1) a prophesy of public reaction; (2) a tool for the planning commission in making reports; (3) a guide to effectuating procedures and measures; (4) an ordinance regulating the use of the land; and (5) a guard against the arbitrary."[40] This category concerned the effects of planning on the physical environment, the realities resulting from planning law.

To the extent that it encompassed both of the two categories, the theoretical and the instrumental, a master plan signified the process of translation from planning to implementation. The paired modes of representation and projection are explicit in Haar's argument; an estimate or an indicator in the first instance becomes a prophecy or an ordinance in the second. (The parallels between Haar's dissection of the master plan and the CIAM Grid are also evident, in the distinction between analysis and realization, the distaste for the arbitrary, and the pointed emphasis on public reaction. Moreover, Haar's language accorded with that used to describe the CIAM Grid and Wiener's diagram of the environment—tool, guide, technique, device.) Haar pointed out that the "job" of the master plan was to define "goals and relationships," and that it functioned as "primarily . . . a philosophic guide to a way of life."[41] But as such a guide, the master plan pulled in two opposite directions, toward the normative and toward the real. It aspired to contain within one object a set of objective principles and a set of tangible effects, yet the dichotomous corresponding qualities of stability and flexibility would challenge its very basis. In response to this contradiction Haar offered the conceptual compromise of an "impermanent constitution."[42] The master plan would be enacted as a law, and to the extent that it controlled the enactment of implementing laws such as zoning, it would have "the cardinal characteristic of a constitution. But unlike that legal form it is subject to amendatory procedures not significantly different from the course followed in enacting ordinary legislation."[43] It would be "impermanent," susceptible to change in order to preserve the advantages of flexibility, yet a "constitution" to obtain the expansive privileges of normalization—a constitution as a snapshot, then, a momentary image of the organizational imperatives of the whole.

Haar recognized the necessary fragility of this compromise (the "touchstone values of master plan" must for the moment hang upon "so slender a reed")[44] but saw it as a means to endow the master plan with more, not less, significance as a set of authoritative guiding principles. Wiener was familiar with Haar's essays, and he, Sert, and Haar undoubtedly discussed the ideas they contained in relation to their work for the JNP commencing at that same moment.[45] Haar's conception of the master plan as an "impermanent constitution" explicitly framed the master plan within a constitutionalist context and elaborated its efficacy for the construction of potentialities in relation to uncertain conditions or events. In 1955, with Batista firmly in control of the government, Cuba's constitutionalist aspirations seemed at an ebb, and the fabric of Havana was much changed from 1940 (Figure 4.6). Haar's postulation of the impermanence of the master plan, however, did not suggest its supersession, but rather the means for its persistence. By forsaking rigidity, a master plan could maintain key values and aims over time in changeable political circumstances. Where the plans for Havana formulated under the dictatorship of Gerardo Machado illustrated the desire to fix concretely the orders and hierarchies of the city, the master plan as defined by Haar might open a different strategy for engaging with the political dimension of the city, a different strategy, in other words, for projecting civil society within the form and structure of Havana. Instead of a constellation of fixed images and inflexible relationships, the master plan might appear as the designation of an anticipatory process. The affinity of planning and law in this regard was clear to Haar: "The search for certainty has warped the function of the master plan; similarly, and

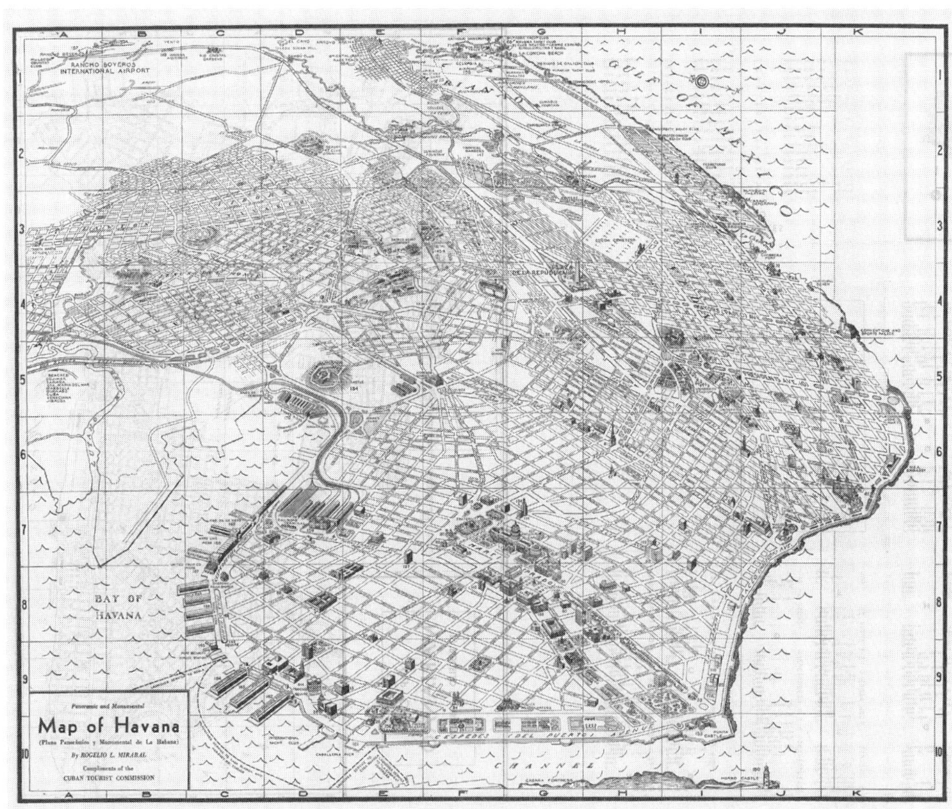

FIGURE 4.6 Map of Havana, 1953. The view is nearly the same as in the map from 1940 (FIGURE 4.2). The area of land at the center of the map is now almost completely developed, and the districts of Vedado and Miramar in the upper right extend farther west. Courtesy of the Harvard Map Collection, Harvard University.

paradoxically, the polar principle of flexibility has obviated its usefulness as a standard. An analogy to the field of law is not inappropriate. To the layman, there are clear rules of law that speedily resolve disputes and give ready answers; to the layman, too, the master plan can, with precision, solve all future land-use problems. To the professional, in both instances, life is far more complicated and in too much a state of flux to be handled in so slide-rule a fashion."[46]

5 Master Plans

The Retrospective Order of the Plan Piloto de la Habana

Paul Lester Wiener traveled to Havana in June 1955 and remained there for the rest of the summer working in the office of the JNP; he returned again in the fall, and stayed in Cuba from November through January the following year. During these residencies, Wiener helped devise the initial work program for the divisions of the JNP, specifying what data were to be acquired, what maps should be drawn, and what charts and diagrams should be developed. He also closely directed the design work of two master plan projects: the pilot plan for Varadero was roughly complete and was being refined as a master plan, and the research required for the Plan Piloto de la Habana was under way. Wiener remained in frequent contact with his associates Sert and Schulz at the firm's office in New York, where design work and drawings proceeded concurrently with the work in Cuba. Sert traveled to Cuba for shorter trips in the fall of 1955, and the partners relayed information, requests, and comments in letters, telegrams, and telephone calls to one another and at times directly to Arroyo. Because responsibility for each different plan was delegated among Mario Romañach, Nicolás Quintana, Jorge Mantilla, and Eduardo Montoulieu, all of whom were established practitioners and therefore more independent than subordinates, Wiener, Sert, and Arroyo in his official capacity provided the links necessary to unify the work as a coherent planning project.[1] Their exchanges of notes, memos, and sketches during this period reveal more an environment of design than a directed project. Decisions were made rapidly or else deferred entirely; work often proceeded based on availability of data or political interest rather than in determined sequences; authorship might be provisional or partial as disparate elements or different scales of work overlapped—in all, a set of diffuse circumstances that made evident and more legible the common intentions and techniques that structured the work.

During the summer of 1955, work on the Plan Piloto de la Habana focused on the two elements of the master plan defined by Sert: dividing the city into sectors and devising a classified road system. The determination of sectors and roads had two prerequisites: fixing the limits of the metropolitan area and an analysis of the land use within those limits. A preliminary sketch drawn soon after Wiener's arrival proposed a "perimeter" for an area of metropolitan Havana that encompassed the already developed areas to the west and south as well as less developed land situated southwest of the city and across the bay to the east. An annotation explained the necessity of perimeter limits: "Purpose=limit extension/check Real Estate & fringe development over 35–50 years."[2] Having diagnosed the rapid, uncoordinated sprawl of new *repartos* (subdivisions) outward from the city center as socially and economically debilitating for Havana, the architects aimed first to constrain and regulate such elements. In a later exchange of memos, Sert and Wiener discussed how the definition of metropolitan limits could be used as the basis for new legislative requirements. Such legislation would stipulate, for example, that the city authorities would provide utilities only for *repartos* within city limits; the city authorities had been in effect subsidizing new *repartos* by supplying utilities even though they had not been consulted during planning stages. More important, the legislation would specify a process by which the consent and approval of municipal government would be required for any new *reparto*. This process, they argued, would allow the imposition of specific design criteria, including the provision of utilities, open spaces, community uses, densities, and building types. They were aware that their proposal required considerable renovation of existing legal structures because the area they defined as metropolitan Havana was in fact composed of different independent municipalities. These, they suggested, could establish a joint authority that would enact measures to limit the location and design of *repartos* according to the principles proposed by the JNP and Town Planning Associates.[3]

Concurrently with the definition of the city limits, the Oficina del Plan Regulador de la Habana (OPRH) compiled an existing land-use map of the metropolitan area (Figure 5.1). This information would be applied to the work of the Plan Piloto, under Romañach, but its early stages were supervised by Montoulieu, an indication that the city was perceived as a regional economic and social entity. The color codes of the land-use map marked residential, commercial, industrial, and recreational uses throughout the city, producing a tapestry that highlighted how those functions clustered in large blocks, or formed corridors, or were isolated within other functions. With this information, legislation and design could be oriented purposefully toward segregating some functions, such as the industrial; juxtaposing others, such as the residential and the recreational; and nominating areas for future development or redevelopment. The four functions of the Athens Charter had merged in this case with techniques of land-use planning developed after the war in planning and legal discourse in the United States.

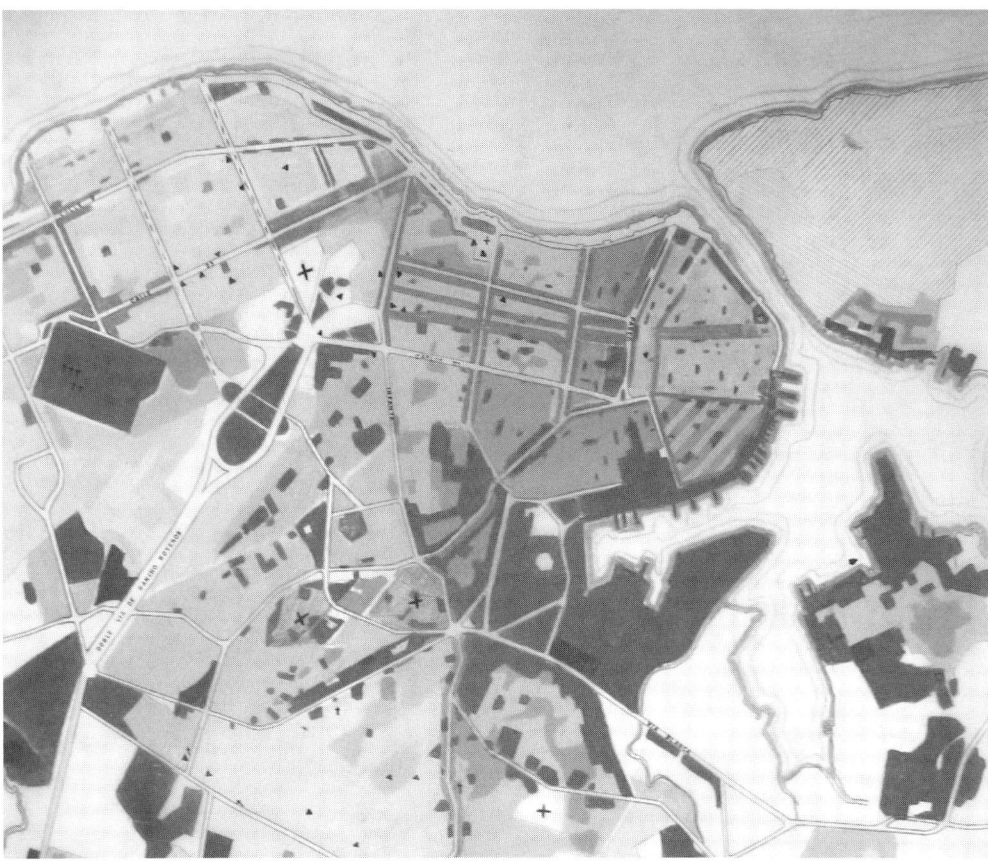

FIGURE 5.1 Junta Nacional de Planificación, Preliminary Land-Use Survey, circa 1956. Habana Vieja is to the right of the center of the map. The civic center then under construction is the teardrop shape to the left of center. Courtesy of Paul Lester Wiener Papers, Box 155, Special Collections and University Archives, University of Oregon Libraries.

The application of land-use planning and the attempt to define the regulatory apparatus of a metropolitan area distinguished this postwar plan for Havana from earlier, more technical approaches and from Forestier's proposal as well. These efforts, though, all confronted the same issue, the inevitable expansion of the city in size and population. In response, Forestier's Plano del Proyecto had extended the existing city outward, finding new circulatory nodes and networks to be projected from existing streets to establish an order in the outlying areas. The projects undertaken during the Grau administration also began from existing elements, adopting them as the basis for remedial or improving works. The design conceived by the JNP began from approximately the inverse presumption, first by defining the outer limit and then moving inward, back toward the existing city to address the area encompassed, and then by bringing into view the social and economic topography of the city as its existing reality. Where Forestier and Cañas Abril had emphasized networks of streets, the architects of the JNP emphasized an urban fabric as a continuous ground for the city. Without denying Forestier's grasp of the complete scope of the city, it is fair to suggest that Wiener, Sert, and their Cuban colleagues saw the city as a complete and complex object, all of whose interrelated parts needed to be revealed simultaneously. Moreover, they observed that housing, one element that earlier might have been regarded as derivative or as a consequence of the city, had now in fact become determinate, with the economic and physical influence of the development of *repartos* increasing each moment.

The Development of the Plan Piloto

Sert had previously listed the road network as the second constituent element of any master plan, and a new road system was incorporated into an early sketch, drawn in August 1955, labeled "Estudio preliminario de la estructura de Habana actual y futuro."[4] With this sketch, drawn over a map of the city, and also with a large-scale topographical model of Havana in its New York office, Town Planning Associates attempted the integration of a new road organization into the existing pattern of streets. As work progressed, the road network became the fundamental ordering gesture of the Plan Piloto, supplying together with the system of sectors the translation between the existing and the future Havana. A number of important road-building projects were already under way in the city and on its outskirts to alleviate traffic congestion and to accommodate the increasing suburban population. Although roads had obviously been central to earlier physical modifications of Havana, and had subsequently gained a near absolute value in plans for the city, they now attained a structural importance in the abstract conception of the city. In their first formal imposition of the new road network over an existing map of the city, Sert and Wiener were in general concerned less with the specific routes of their road network than with its system of classification, which followed "The Rule of the 7V," Le Corbusier's hierarchical system of circulation. "The Rule of the 7V" became widely known through Le Corbusier's design of Chandigarh, in which he employed the system, but he had proposed it first in 1950 for the Plan Directeur of Bogotá, which he developed in close collaboration with Sert and Wiener.[5] The rule classified roadways according to speed, attempting a decisive separation of pedestrian and vehicular environments. V1 was the classification for limited-access expressways, allowing the frictionless flow of traffic required by a modern city, while V7 identified a pedestrian route, guaranteeing the maintenance of a "human scale" in the urban environment. The five remaining categories spanned between these two to create a harmonious order of circulation. This abstraction of the circulatory function correlated with the smooth scalar transposition evident in analytic devices like the CIAM Grid. In the context of the master plan, such orders were instruments of normalization, or the introduction of an order of norms that regulated, and assigned meaning to, discrete aspects of the real city. But the rule also contained within its logic an encounter with existing urban patterns. The V4, lined with shops and streets according to Le Corbusier's detailed description, followed "existing bridal paths, easy, and usually winding roads, not made by human genius, but by the passage of much traffic." By incorporating these established routes into the overall classification, Le Corbusier argued, the 7V created a rational system adequate to new urban conditions, but also permitted "life [to] continue to flow along its old traditional route."[6]

Sert and Wiener made this same distinction in their Pilot Plan, introducing new expressways and improving existing roads, but also identifying existing "main streets" to serve as V4 roads. Their text specifies that "[t]hese main streets . . . follow the winding lines of the old roads opened between the property lines of the sugar plantations and large farms; they were never meant for the transportation means of today or those of tomorrow."[7] In the final plans published in the folio volume, V4 roads drawn in ribbed black lines wound unevenly through the red strokes of the new circulatory grid, apparently disrupting the sequential order of scale with the inconsistencies of use and habit (see Plate 5). The new roads had been laid atop existing ones in part for economic reasons; it was assumed that the expropriations required to enlarge the existing roads would be prohibitively expensive, more costly certainly than if new routes could be devised that minimized expropriation costs. According to Sert, this juxtaposition of old and new was not a compromise, but rather the refinement of the 7V system. The initial sketch of the roads had made him aware of the contrast:

> It also appeared from this preliminary or basic sketch . . . that a very interesting and new pattern for the city would come out of the co-existence of the old winding system of roads already developed—*"chemins des ânes"*—as Le Corbusier called them, contrasting with the straight line of the new highways which establish a clear system of sectors . . . This double system seems to us less rigid and more interesting than the one used in Bogotá. The existing main winding roads would, at a later date, become slow commercial streets and, in some sectors still unbuilt, lineal parks could be run at the sides.[8]

In Sert's regard for the resulting "new pattern for the city" there is an indication that the measure of the system was its capacity to absorb a variety of disparate criteria, a measure that is the fundamental pretense of a normative system; that is, the norm can incorporate existing elements and thereby modify their significance by coupling them to other elements and to the principle of the norm. It thus projects a future system of order and signification that can employ, without fully depending on, prior elements. New developed areas of the city, in other words, would contain these elements not as contingencies, but according to plan.

In the case of the 7V, the absorption of a scalar range was paralleled by a similar absorption of typological difference, evident in the contrast of the principle of the 7V with the statistical methods of traffic engineering. On behalf of the JNP, Sert and Wiener were authorized to retain as additional consultants experts in relevant fields and were responsible for integrating that expertise into the work of the JNP. For the Plan Piloto de la Habana, engineering recommendations were provided by the New York firm Seeyle, Stevenson, Value and Knecht, which, in 1956, helped design the details of the road network that was to be superimposed upon the existing city; their preliminary layouts indicated road types, but did not follow the rule of the 7V. Based on calculations of existing and anticipated traffic densities, their detailed proposal included four road types with typical roadway sections modified from the standards that the same engineers had developed for the Bogotá plan. This proposal was included with the formal consultant's report submitted by Town Planning Associates at the end of 1956, explaining how the proposed road widths and configurations related mathematically to speed and quantity of traffic. By 1958, when the drawings for the publication of the Plan Piloto were being prepared, the overall road layout remained roughly the same as in early sketches, but the engineers' classifications had been replaced with the 7V classifications. The road sections were keyed according to both systems, so that, for example, road type D-D was also captioned as type V4. The two classifications, however, did not actually correspond, and diagrams showed the V4 as a single street where the engineers proposed a divided roadway. A memo from Paul Schulz (who was responsible for some of the drawings of the road network) to Sert on the subject of road widths in Habana Vieja confirmed a certain malleability: "we used the Bogotá V3 standard. The Havana V3 standard . . . I thought too wide."[9] At one level, such changes demonstrated a disregard for precisely the application of expertise that was the fundamental claim of Sert's concept of urban design. To that extent, they expose an adherence to an architectural, or perhaps more properly an aesthetic assessment that undermined the more comprehensive ambitions of planning. At another level, these details expose a willingness to reconcile the conceptual system to existing conditions that reflects the desire to overcome the insuperable incommensurability of two typological orders, one mathematical and the other aesthetic. In this, perhaps, the potential of the normative system could be balanced against its cost. The normal order could achieve the smoothing out of rival differences and provide a comprehensive order of signification for at least one register of the city—circulation, in this instance—but could not do so neutrally. The norm, itself constructed out of a discursive or disciplinary context, would either directly or indirectly bring to bear the predispositions of that context.

The systematic road network also produced, or took into account, the division of the city into sectors. As Sert and Wiener used the term, a sector was an essentially autonomous neighborhood. A residential sector would have one or more schools, local commerce, recreation facilities, and some type of community facility, such as a library or a cinema; a commercial sector would include office space, parking facilities, and perhaps a transportation hub such as a railway station. A sector might also consist of a unique existing area of the city (in the Plan Piloto, the old colonial district would be such an instance). The classified road system bracketed the sectors, holding high-speed traffic to their perimeter so that the sectors themselves could maintain pedestrian routes and quieter roads. In the case of Havana, the sector system, which Town Planning Associates had developed for the Bogotá plan with Le Corbusier, offered a solution for containing existing and future *repartos*. Sert proposed that the "same basic principle that should govern the new 'Reparto' is the following: any such development is part of one or more sectors or units or can even be a totality of some sectors. In any case the property limits should not govern the street design as has been done in the past."[10] Conceived as roads and sectors (that is, not only roads but the territory between them) the organization of the city resembled an organic structure in the explicit interdependence of its parts. Because the sectors were to have specific dimensions, densities, and facilities and also specific proximities to one another, they affected the layout of roads. But the road network also had criteria of classification and orientation to be satisfied. Moreover, there were three existing factors to be accommodated by the organic structure: the topography, built and unbuilt, the various roads already in place and those under construction, and the prevailing system of development, subdivision through real-estate speculation. None of these was to be removed or abolished; instead, they would be bound into a regulatory system, a dynamic system of constraints.

From this set of decisions—the fixing of the perimeter, the land-use distributions, the road network, and the sectors—emerged a "preliminary" structure of the city depicting a concrete reality of future spaces and locations in the city. The road network and sector division would produce an even distribution of built fabric throughout the metropolitan area; its only differential would be density, which would decrease evenly with distance from the center of the city. Industrial development was segregated to areas on the outskirts of the city, and to the port area around the southern curve of the bay. Commercial streets would bisect many of the sectors, while new roads and an enlarged Malecón, the coastal boulevard along the northern edge of the city, would bring fast traffic from the west and south into the core of the city (see Plate 6). In the final version of the Plan Piloto, a lattice of lineal parks—V7 routes according to the classification system—

also bisected individual sectors and joined together to create continuous lengths of green space throughout the city, extending to the coast and to the city center; existing elements such as the embankment of the Río Almendares separating the neighborhoods of Vedado and Miramar, and the Malecón and the Paseo del Prado, were incorporated into this lattice as part of an even and apparently seamless distribution of the variables of urban life. Two distinctly idiosyncratic elements were proposed as well, although both were fixed within the overall structure of the Plan Piloto. One was an artificial island adjacent to the Malecón in Centro Habana, which would provide a self-contained platform for office buildings and hotels; the other was the extensive redevelopment of the old colonial quarter, Habana Vieja, with new blocks and areas of high-rise towers. The island linked to the park system of the overall plan, and the redeveloped old district was connected to the classified road network, yet both stood out markedly in the plan as indications of the possible extent of development in the center of the city.

New sectors were also included in the Plan Piloto to designate the development of Habana del Este (East Havana), although the exclusion of Town Planning Associates and the JNP from the planning of that area prompted merely schematic treatment in their drawings. Detailed proposals were, however, being formulated for the development of this large area of land whose proximity to the city center could be exploited once the tunnel under the bay was completed. One owner of large landholdings in East Havana retained Miguel Gastón to devise plans for subdivisions. Gastón in turn commissioned proposals from Skidmore, Owings, and Merrill (the firm originally hired by the tunnel company in 1954) and Franco Albini, a prominent Italian architect. The schemes they produced in the late 1950s included large areas of housing and a central avenue through a commercial district of high-rise towers. Drawings of Albini's proposal showed wide pedestrian areas bordered by low-rise concrete frame buildings, while Skidmore, Owings, and Merrill rendered the central boulevard as an urbane, polychromatic setting for habaneros and their cars. From this new sector of the city they could travel directly to the edge of the bay where, according to an unsolicited proposal by Jean Labatut for the embellishment of the tunnel entrances, the city of Havana would appear to motorists as a framed skyline (Figure 5.2). In addition to private economic forces, other institutions of government were also seeking to establish claims on the future form of Havana. At the end of 1956, the Director General del Departamento de Arquitectura y Urbanismo del Municipio de La Habana presented plans for accommodating the city's growth that recommended, among other measures, revised zoning codes, new satellite cities, and the reservation of open spaces within the city and along its coast. A year later, Batista's administration issued a decree sanctioning the development of the Malecón by using landfill to physically enlarge the coastal area, which, if carried out, would have created new and highly valuable real estate for the government to dispose of. (Hypothetical projects advanced in academic settings also participated in this activity of urban speculation; in 1953, for example, one of Pedro Martínez Inclán's thesis students had proposed reconfiguring several acres of the central city west of the train station as a set of superblocks.)

These policies and projects shared a strategy of significantly increasing the scale of the urban environment in contrast to its existing dimensions, by enlarging either land area, or buildings, or roadways, or all three together. Although the

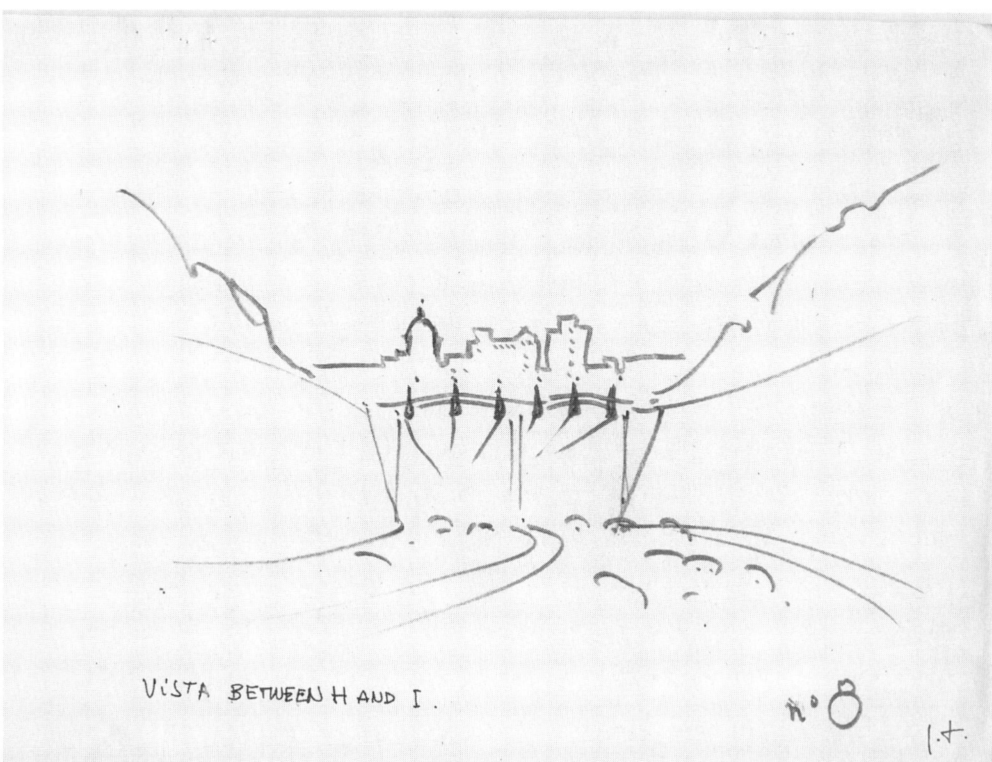

FIGURE 5.2 Jean Labatut, sketch, proposal for tunnel entrance, Havana, with skyline including the dome of the Capitolio Nacional. Jean Labatut Papers, Department of Rare Books and Special Collections, Princeton University Library.

JNP and its consultants acted as agents of Batista's administration, the plan for East Havana or the policy for the Malecón evidences the continuance of a strong economic pressure for development and speculation with which the work of the JNP would have to contend. The economic atmosphere of the Batista dictatorship was as permissive as its social atmosphere, with the real-estate speculation undertaken at a heady pace by investors adding new hotels, casinos, condominiums, and department stores in rapid succession to the city's streets and skyline. In this context, the provision of land area for construction—whether on new or reappropriated sites—would have been a pressing financial motive for Batista's administration, which depended on the increasing flow of legitimate and illegitimate capital into the country. The architects of the JNP were certainly cognizant of and influenced by this overwhelming sway of economic calculation—in fact, Wiener apparently spent some spare hours in Havana evaluating prospective building sites for the New York developer Paul Tishman—but they did not advance it as a central intention or conclusion of the Plan Piloto. Even as it engaged economic conditions, the work of the JNP framed its conceptions within a political focus, directing its claims toward the technicians who were to mediate between state and city rather than the investors, businessmen, or public who were ostensibly their beneficiaries. The Plan Piloto was, therefore, both an instrument of complicity, insofar as it would have accommodated and even assisted the unmitigated financial speculation of the period, and an instrument of regulation, in that it would have defined and delineated much of the physical outcome of that speculation in advance.

The political dimensions of the design of the city underlay the legible formal differences between the plans of the 1950s and those produced before the 1933 revolution, which is also to say that these political dimensions reveal the transition from civic art to urban design. Where the beaux-arts planning advocated by Forestier conceived the boulevard and its terminal points to be the functional and aesthetic key by which civic design could extend outward from and also intervene into the existing city, Sert and Wiener considered urban design as a process that began with systemic orders superimposed on the topographical whole of the city. This formal difference distinguishes as well the conception of the civic contained in the two approaches. The earlier emphasis on the path and the point corresponded to an intention to represent a civil society that was stable enough to be represented, while the distributed network proposed under the JNP corresponded to the aim of accommodating a civil society perceived to have changing orientations and motivations. Both proposals attempted to constitute a civic landscape, but where that civic landscape initially sought its sanction in the referent of nature, the postwar landscape claimed its sanction with participation in a normative order. Intervening between these two was the 1940 constitution, with its mandate for citizens to identify their aspirations as reciprocal with those of the nation and its promulgation of both temporal and atemporal structures of civic life. The 1940 constitution construed civil society as a condition to be constructed and therefore as an object to be designed. No longer a matter of art, then, the city too was to be designed through the mechanism of the master plan.

While Haar had already effectively renovated the concept of the master plan, the new civic landscape also suggested a more fundamental renovation of the concept of design, leaving behind a model that fixed upon the discrete connections between part and whole and turning toward a comprehensive model of interrelationships of urban scales. The relevant term here is *pattern,* a word that Sert and Wiener themselves used frequently in describing the city and civic life. Wiener had occasion to relate the political sphere directly to the concept of pattern in urban design in his report to the U.S. State Department after his 1956 lecture tour of South America:

> I took it as *my task* to clearly establish in the minds of my audiences, and the government officials with whom I had extended conversations, that the planning process must be democratic if it is to accomplish its aims and that it is *not* synonymous with socialism; that planning must *not* impose upon individuals authoritarian physical city patterns no matter how ideal they may seem and that the task is one of coordination and guidance.[11]

He believed that some correspondence existed between "physical city patterns" and administrative orders and social practices, and while rejecting authoritarian patterns as extensions of authoritarian government, he left open the possibility of other patterns to accord with more palatable forms of government. Sert also used the word *pattern* quite often when discussing cities and urban design, and, like Wiener, he used the term in order to marry physical and social configurations. For example, when pressing the importance of the city center in his address to the eighth CIAM congress, he suggested that "Many cities of the past had definite shapes or patterns, and were built around a Core that very often was the determining factor of those shapes"; and the city center, or core, was the expression and the enactment of the social and political life of the city, as Sert's favorite example, the Piazza San Marco in Venice, so clearly illustrated. The introduction of the rigid pattern of the gridiron through the ordinances of the Laws of the Indies offered an even more pertinent example. But in Havana, Sert and Wiener believed that they were introducing a new pattern to the city; and if it was a new pattern, it presumably contained if not the guarantee then at least the potential of new social or political configurations.

Jorge Mañach, too, had referred to patterns—using the English word—when suggesting the possible translation from prior traditions to new modes of experience, or specifically from past political incapacities to future political potentials. His desire for the integral transformation of "patterns of old experience" into "servants and instruments of the new desires and intentions" reflected a progressive historical thought apparent also in the understanding of the master plan advanced by Sert and Wiener.[12] In a meeting with the JNP in late 1957, they summarized their argument: "It seems to the consultants that we must in the designing of the Plan and Master Plan for the Metropolitan Area of Havana establish and pursue a complete new concept of city planning that will not only be applicable to Cuba but for all of South America . . . The doctrine is in contrast to the afore mentioned concept of extended walled city. A new doctrine starts with the principle of the explosive city" (meaning that the city did not extend outward incrementally from a stable center, but extended rapidly and with a corresponding deterioration of the center). "This is to say that attitudes toward 'suburban decentralization' on one hand, and 'urban renewal' on the other, will need to be welded to create new urban and rural norms."[13] The new patterns would calibrate extent and center within a set of norms that applied to both and that forced upon them a conceptual, and even a perceptual, continuity. For the pattern possessed an aesthetic value—as indicated in Sert's appreciation of the "very interesting and new pattern for the city" that would emerge in Havana from the contrast of new straight highways and the old winding roads—that would be legible as an expression of the normative structure itself. Its representational capacity would not be independent from either its functional or its performative capabilities, but rather, as the combination of all three, pattern would instance a representation founded on a normative claim that sponsored simultaneously its projective potential.

Housing and Typicality

"A village, a town or a city is the physical expression of the life of a community, it is built or shaped to contain that community, to protect it, to shelter it and to hold it together as a social structure."[14] This statement was the opening sentence of "The Neighborhood Unit: A Human Measure in City Planning," a report that Sert began to draft for the United Nations in 1951. Around that time, Sert had begun to make habitual reference in essays and lectures to the need for architecture to accommodate the social behavior of citizens, at the scale of the city and at the scale of the neighborhood. He had adopted from planning discourse the argument that the neighborhood unit constituted the basic element of an organic city structure. Its extent and population might vary according to cultural and physical conditions, but the essential concept remained the same: a collection of individual homes grouped together such that the physical fabric sustained the daily social lives of the families that lived in them.[15] The neighborhood unit might include basic community elements such as an elementary school, small shops or a market, and a gathering place such as a plaza or a community hall, and several units together would constitute an urban sector, with larger facilities such as a library or hospital. Because, in the modern city, the integral composition of the neighborhood had deteriorated with the dispersal of its elements and the inadequacy of its physical form to its social structure, neighborhood units had to be reorganized, Sert argued, and new forms designed, in order to resuscitate the organic structure of the city. New principles and codes formulated by urban design should "lay special emphasis on the Neighborhood Unit system which will be one of the basic elements of any Master Plan."[16]

The Plan Piloto de la Habana was to serve as a set of general directives or principles for the more detailed specifications of a subsequent master plan. But in some instances of these underlying principles, the considerable degree of architectural resolution made it possible to discern an armature of standards that consisted in typicality itself. One such instance was the design for a typical neighborhood sector included in the Plan Piloto. The typical neighborhood sector shown in the plan was in fact the proposal for Quinta Palatino, an *urbanización* (subdivision) that Sert and Wiener had devised in collaboration with Arroyo and Menéndez (with the work carried out for the most part with the architects Rita Gutiérrez and Jorge Mantilla). The pertinent pages in the folio volume of the Plan

Piloto included several contrasting plans—actually different versions of the Quinta Palatino project as well as the plan that Town Planning Associates had designed for the 1952 Cuban National Housing Program. These projects together formed a continuous arc of refinement of a housing scheme for Cuba initiated by the 1952 project. In that year, an investment firm in New York City had retained Town Planning Associates to develop a design to be submitted to the National Housing Program sponsored by the Cuban government.[17] Sert and Wiener accepted the commission and proposed a full neighborhood unit, with roughly three hundred housing units of various types grouped together with a school, community center, market, and landscaped public spaces on a hypothetical site (Figure 5.3). The housing units included two-, three-, and four-bedroom configurations, all single-story and paired together in rows. They shared a set of architectonic elements: a flat membrane roof, interior courts, and perforated wall surfaces to increase flow

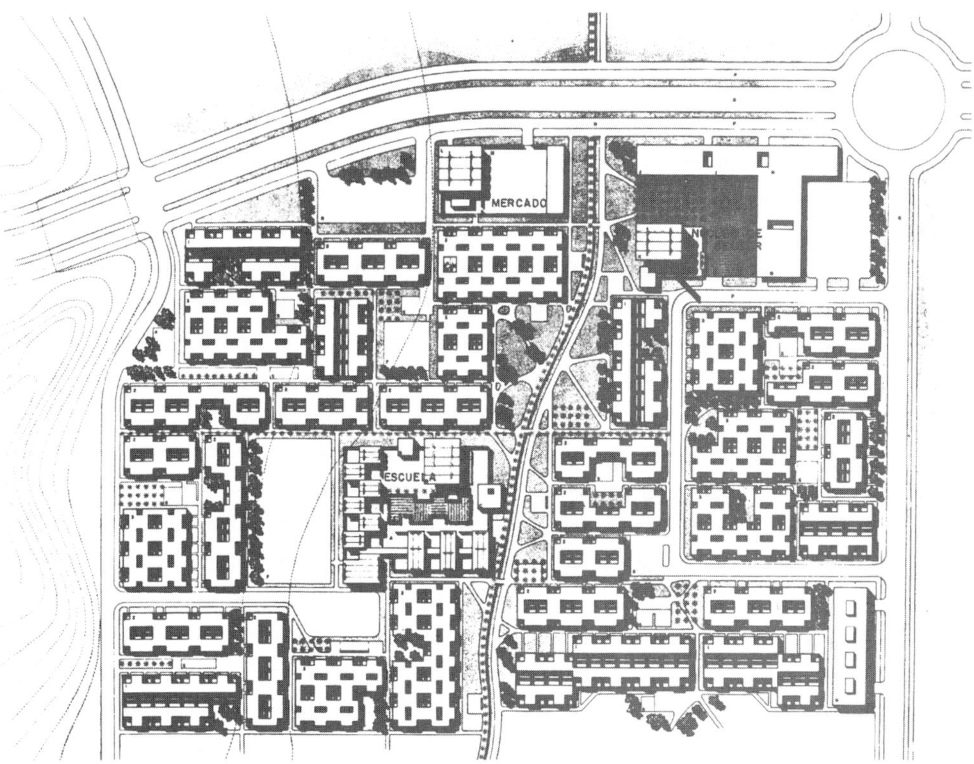

FIGURE 5.3 Town Planning Associates, site plan, Cuban National Housing Program proposal, 1952. Published in *Plan Piloto de la Habana.* Courtesy of the Frances Loeb Library, Harvard Graduate School of Design.

of air. In an accompanying text, Sert and Wiener described their proposal as the outcome of their previous experience in Latin America, and the scheme did in fact closely resemble the housing first developed for Chimbote, Peru, in 1948 and further refined in their projects in Colombia and, concurrently with the Cuba proposal, for Venezuela. In those projects, the partners had developed an inventory of typical housing solutions in which attached units were grouped together and arranged across a site to form a carpet of housing woven through with open public spaces ranging from a pedestrian walk to a shared courtyard to a larger plaza.

With such carefully arranged clusters of housing, Sert and Wiener attempted to address several aspects of the problem of economical housing for tropical climates. Layouts with detached houses, they wrote, required more infrastructure—sidewalks, roads, sewers, and utilities—because they had more street frontage. By attaching and grouping the houses, architects could reduce the costs of site planning and also improve living conditions by shortening walking distances within the neighborhood unit. Rows of houses could be oriented according to climatic needs, to take advantage of prevailing winds for ventilation through the louvered block walls. The clustering of the carpet house model also produced open areas that could be given over to formal and informal community uses. There was an aesthetic concern as well: "It should be noted that very small houses, such as we are dealing with, do not look well as detached units. Their small scale then becomes too noticeable. Houses of this type cannot be considered as isolated units—they must be studied as part of an all over pattern for better community planning."[18] In press reports of the exhibition of the National Housing Program submissions, the scheme by Town Planning Associates was singled out for having included a design for an overall neighborhood in addition to the design of housing units (which was all the competition had requested). General Batista and his Consejo Consultivo reviewed the submissions, and reiterated an intention to address the shortage of economic housing in Cuba through government programs (Figure 5.4). Lack of adequate housing had been identified as an issue more than a decade earlier, but only intermittent attempts to address the problem had been made. The only postwar housing project undertaken by the government was the Luyanó housing complex, built under the administration of President Grau and completed in stages in 1947 and 1948 (Figure 5.5). Sert and

Wiener obtained photographs of the Luyanó housing from their client, and must have had it in mind as they offered their critique of detached housing.

The Luyanó project, designed under the direction of Pedro Martínez Inclán by Mario Romañach, Antonio Quintana, and Jorge Mantilla, included four four-story housing blocks in addition to detached houses. The blocks faced a main highway, and the houses faced new looped internal streets; parks as well as provisions for a market and a school completed the scheme. A comparison between Luyanó (officially called Parque Residencial Obrero de Luyanó, or the Luyanó Workers' Residential Park) and the Town Planning Associates proposal reveals that the latter scheme does achieve a greater density of occupied land and reduces the area of streets. The housing units do possess a greater architectural presence than the bare boxes of the Luyanó project, although they would likely

FIGURE 5.4 Unidentified newspaper photograph showing General Fulgencio Batista (speaking, at center) viewing the exhibition of the Town Planning Associates proposal for the Cuban National Housing Program, 1952. Courtesy of Paul Lester Wiener Papers, Box 155, Special Collections and University Archives, University of Oregon Libraries.

FIGURE 5.5 Workers' housing at the Luyanó housing development in Havana, constructed 1947–48 and photographed circa 1952 by an unidentified photographer. Courtesy of Paul Lester Wiener Papers, Box 155, Special Collections and University Archives, University of Oregon Libraries.

have required the expenditure of the money saved by the careful site planning. But economic terms do not provide the most pointed comparison; the most significant characteristic in the Town Planning Associates project was its consolidation of a pattern. The Luyanó project had a system of arrangement—a standard setback from the street, a set spacing between houses, a compositional curve of streets—but not a pattern in the sense of an order reflecting a deliberate social organization. In the Town Planning Associates design, the units are grouped and arrayed so that the built elements also configure the open spaces, from the interior courtyards of the houses to the larger plazas framed by housing clusters. Pedestrian paths run between the clusters to provide a continuous connection between larger spaces, without forcing a loss in definition of those spaces. Parks or plazas at Luyanó, by contrast, were adjacent but not integral to the housing areas; the elements were held together only by the road layout.

The pattern that Sert and Wiener invoked in their description was the weaving together of the landscaped areas, community spaces, and private homes into an uninterrupted formal texture to cohere physical forms and social structure. The key to this cohesion was the element of the *patio,* or courtyard. In reporting on the gradual disappearance of the neighborhood unit from the city, Sert wrote, "We do find examples in the past, where the city-block was the container of a social structure. An example of this were the 'cuadras' or square blocks of many Latin-American cities. These 'cuadras' had a big patio in their center. This patio was used by the community of neighbors and it served as a gathering place for young and old, functioning as a recreation area, play lot, and public park or community club."[19] Sert had made a similar claim about the social function of enclosed urban space in his contribution to the eighth CIAM congress, where he spoke about the importance of the traditional plaza (which in his conceptual terms was also a *patio*) as a space for civic assembly. At the same time, Wiener and Sert also identified the importance of the *patio* to their carpet-housing typologies. In regard to their Cuban housing proposal, they wrote, "Another important element in these houses are the patios. The types here submitted have front and rear patios. The rooms opening onto these patios will appear much more spacious because of them. Further-more the people, by tradition, are accustomed to make use of these open spaces, spending many hours of the day and evening out-of-doors."[20] The courtyard house had been a subject of interest in modernist discourse since before the war, and Sert had encountered the *patio* as an element in his prewar studies of the vernacular architecture of Ibiza, while in Cuba the architect Eugenio Batista (with whom Sert was corresponding in 1952) had included the *patio* as one of the characteristics of the traditional Cuban house.[21]

The more significant claim advanced by Sert and Wiener in their Cuban housing proposal was the connection between these two scales, the civic and the domestic, through the formal element of the *patio.* Plans of the Cuban housing proposal appeared as the subject of the article "Can Patios Make Cities?" published in *Architectural Forum* in August 1953. The interrogative of the article's title succinctly conveyed the accompanying proposition that an architectural element was to be transposed into an instrument of urbanism, as the basis, in other words, for an architecture-of-cities. In their Latin American town-planning projects, the article reported, Sert and Wiener had developed the concept of using the *patio* as a "module":

> Because every element of these cities is related to the basic patio idea, each city plan has an underlying coherence, a kind of trademark visible in the smallest unit (the patio house), the intermediate units (patio greens, patio parks, neighborhood centers), individual public buildings (patio schools, patio churches, patio shopping centers)—all the way to the biggest unit, the monumental city center which is, invariably, a series of gigantic piazzas (or big patios) that form places of outdoor assembly for all the citizens.[22]

In thus spanning from the single dwelling to the civic center, or from the citizen to the citizenry, the *patio* extended its range to match closely Wiener's diagram of the human habitat, linking together the home and the city, and organizing intermediate scales as well. The underlying architectural or site-planning technique was the correspondence between built fabric and open space, or, in other words, seeing the ground and figure as a continuous whole. In an illustration for the article, the rendered plan of the Cuban housing proposal made clear the formal manifestation of the concept, with the different scales of *patios* highlighted so that the continuity of access between them was evident (Figure 5.6). The *patio* also proliferated as an architectural element at the scale of individual buildings, providing the basic unit for the organization of the school building at the center of the site and the market at its edge. By 1957, Sert and Wiener would describe this scalar concept as the "rebirth of the patio" and consider it to be a central conceit of their urban plans:

> *The patio becomes the predominant architectural feature* in these designs. They range from the patio for the one-family dwelling to those between apartments or row houses, to the public neighborhood patios of the small local square, or the larger patio of the local core, and finally the series of patios or squares of the main urban or metropolitan cores. *The rebirth of the patio* could give these cities a distinctive character. These patios would make use of a new architecture based on modern building methods.[23]

As the structural component that contained and then granted an "underlying coherence" to the disparate reality of the city, the *patio* was, according to Sert, capable of near-infinite variation in its manifestations, able to adapt through the treatment of materials, plantings, or water to assume the scale and appearance of formality or informality, intimacy or monumentality.[24]

An element of such mutable appearance and effect could possess the structural role that Sert and Wiener claimed only through its performance as part of a normalizing system, a conceptual framework that represented and projected the image of a social order. Within the formal pattern of the new city, the sequential hierarchy of the *patio* would create the binding, or the weave, that joined the physical environment with the social one to produce the civic landscape. As formulated by Sert and Wiener, a *patio* module therefore evinced the necessarily smooth flow of a scalar progression evident in diagrammatic constructions. But their description elided a crucial moment of transition from the private realm of

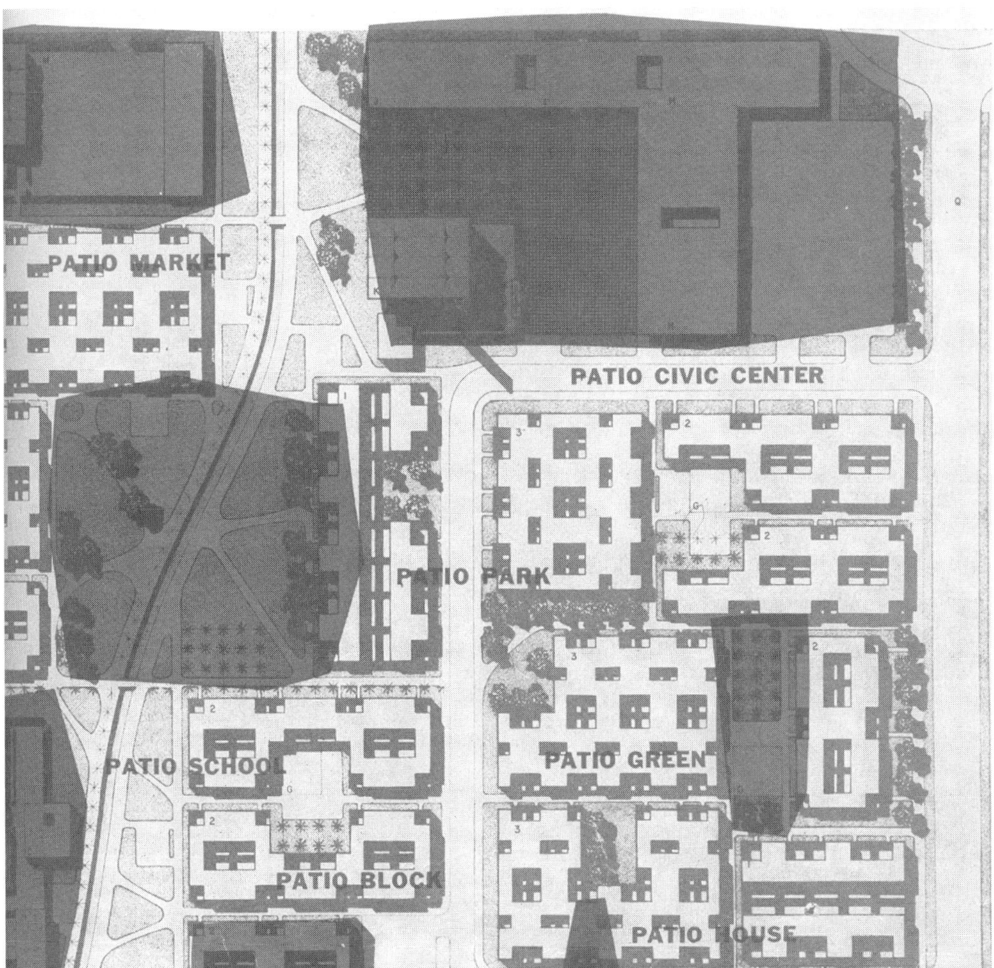

FIGURE 5.6 Illustration of *patio* module from "Can Patios Make Cities?" *Architectural Forum*, August 1953.

the individual to the social realm of the collective (just as did Wiener's diagram of the human environment). Sert, interested on the one hand in the formal figure of the *patio,* and on the other in the social potential of the civic center, did not observe any conflict between the scaling of the formal type and the equivalent scaling of the social context. But his writings and several of his designs made clear that a *patio* served two distinct purposes—at the scale of the house, exclusion; at the scale of the core, inclusion—a distinction that occurred along a seam in the graduated logic. The *patio* houses that Sert and Wiener developed in their Cuba proposals consisted of three defined spatial zones: *áreas cerradas, áreas cubiertas, áreas cercadas*—closed spaces, covered spaces, and enclosed spaces. The enclosed space, the *patio,* provided an outdoor room in which the family would enact daily life shielded from the public space of the street. They regarded this emphatic separation as essential, explaining that if "these outside spaces are not enclosed in patio form there will be no privacy and they will be useless."[25] In all of the housing types, a *patio* was located at the front of the house, with the street walls punctured only by doors or block screens. The private, protected interior was "contained within the walls . . . Behind them, once you enter the house, you can be in a different world—the world that each family can build for itself."[26]

At the civic scale, on the other hand, a *patio* was inclusive, drawing together and integrating the disparate elements of community. It remained an enclosed space, encircled by buildings such as the library, market, and church, but it would forge the symbolic and actual unity of these elements. As an urban architectural element, Sert asserted, the *patio* could render an awareness of interdependence, acting "both as a setting for the expression of this sense of community and as an actual expression of it."[27] Its civic role prompted a different state of enclosure in the civic *patio,* with a more permeable boundary and more differentiated space than at the scale of the house. Programmatic requirements influenced this change, of course, but Sert's elaboration of the *patio* enclosure conveyed greater significance than just functional complexity. While exclusion could be accomplished with a wall, Sert pursued the possibility of inclusion by staging a sequential relationship between central space and articulated programs. In the case of buildings such as the market or the school in the original Cuban housing proposal, later presented as "typical" civic elements in the Plan Piloto, a repetition of *patios* constructed the required mediation. At the school, for example, Sert used a boundary wall to demarcate the overall *patio* of the school complex and individual *patios* placed adjacent to every classroom to further subdivide the interior domain. The attempt to produce architecturally a connection between the individual realm embodied by the domestic interior and the collective realm embodied by the public plaza, while an aspiration quite broadly shared among postwar architects, had a precise valence in the Cuban context. It was the very basis for the assertion of the Patronato Pro-Urbanismo slogan "Mejores ciudades, ciudadanos mejores," and had already been invoked by Montoulieu in the exhortations he drafted for the Patronato's exhibition on urbanism: "You plan your clothes, your house, your hobbies, your work, studies, travels, food budgets, in short, your life . . . but . . . who plans the surroundings? The streets, parks, schools, hospitals, shops, industries, houses, theatres, museums, etc. . . . in the cities, in the country?"[28]

Cuadra and Norm

Early in 1954, after Wiener and Sert had begun working on their second Cuban commission, the design of the hotel complex on the Isle of Pines, Arroyo solicited their collaboration on a project for a new subdivision in Havana located just south of the site of the Plaza Cívica. The subdivision project was commissioned by one of the heirs to the property, Pedro Abreu, and was named Quinta Palatino after the *finca,* the ornate manor house that stood in one corner of the site. The Abreus were one of Cuba's old landed families, the owners also of the historic Palacio de Aldama near the Capitolio, and Emilio del Junco (one of the young architects active in ATEC and in professional practice) was married to Pedro Abreu's sister and had instigated the commission. The project proceeded on a somewhat erratic basis, as Abreu had to secure the permission of other heirs; at some point, the size of the subdivision was reduced, so that it occupied only a portion of the original property. In the end, the subdivision as conceived by Town Planning Associates in conjunction with Arroyo, and with Gutiérrez and Mantilla, was not realized. By 1958, part of the site was developed as the Reparto Santa Catalina under the direction of Emilio del Junco and Mario Romañach, with Town Planning Associates credited as the *urbanistas.*[29] Some of the conceptual potentials would emerge and survive in this succession of designs, while others remained latent.

Sert and Wiener acknowledged the receipt of site surveys in March 1954, and replied to Arroyo and Gutiérrez that they would "apply our housing standards and determine the number of dwellings—one-family houses and apartments—that could possibly fit on that site. Also, the percentage of road areas, green spaces, social services and shops."[30] They viewed the project from the outset as a neighborhood unit, and not only as a residential subdivision; housing was to be integrally related to the basic services of community life. They recognized as well the applicability of their early housing proposal for Cuba, and began by adapting its designs to the new site and programmatic requirements. The first site plans they sketched included a school and left ample open space; a "sector center" was indicated at the middle of the site. The architects were concerned with density of housing, calculating and recalculating the number of units as they experimented with different rosters of unit types. Single-story houses were, in these preliminary drawings, set back-to-back in bars, with three such bars positioned in parallel within a block surrounded by access streets. Sert and Wiener attended to economic aspects of the project as well, tabulating construction, material, and mortgage costs for the various housing types. Abreu responded to the initial plan with a request that the school be removed from the scheme and the quantity of open space be reduced. The subdivision was to provide primarily middle-income housing, with some more economical units distributed in the scheme as well. Sert and Wiener revised their plan accordingly, and in so doing developed a markedly different strategy of formal organization, one based upon a *cuadra* or block layout. The earlier version showed blocks separated by streets (in contrast to the carpet distribution of the Cuban housing proposal) but with the houses situated in parallel rows, so that no integral relation obtained between house and block. In the revised plan, the rows of houses set back-to-back run around the perimeter, reinforcing the *cuadra* forms and, crucially, leaving the residual open space, or *patio,* at the center of the block (Figure 5.7). These *cuadras* were then arrayed in a grid with the lots at the edges of the site simply extended to meet the limit of the property line. Two strips of narrower blocks divided the site into quadrants. One of these strips, running east–west, formed a linear park, in which larger apartment blocks of two or three stories could be placed with the necessary setback to prevent them from shadowing the lower buildings. At the crossing point of the two axes, additional apartment blocks were located adjacent to the sector center, rendered as a larger plaza enclosed by community buildings. The elements of the Cuban housing proposal (housing, community use, pedestrian access, and open areas) and the instrumental conceit of the *patio* organization (from house to *cuadra* to park to plaza) were both maintained, but with a different formal arrangement.

The formal arrangement was, of course, not new, either historically or in the work of Town Planning Associates. Wiener and Sert had recognized the *cuadra* as the essential unit of the gridiron plan of the Laws of the Indies, and regarded it as a concrete historical form in the Latin American city. Sert, moreover, had given considerable attention to the *cuadra* while working in Barcelona (although there his ambition was to overcome what he saw as the limitations inherited from the chamfered blocks of Ildefons Cerdá's 1859 plan). The *cuadra* had appeared in the Bogotá plan as Sert and Wiener developed their designs for the typical neighborhood sector for that city. In most instances, though, it appeared in that plan as a grouping of houses set within a larger superblock, rather than as the definition of a street edge as in the colonial Latin American city. Employing the

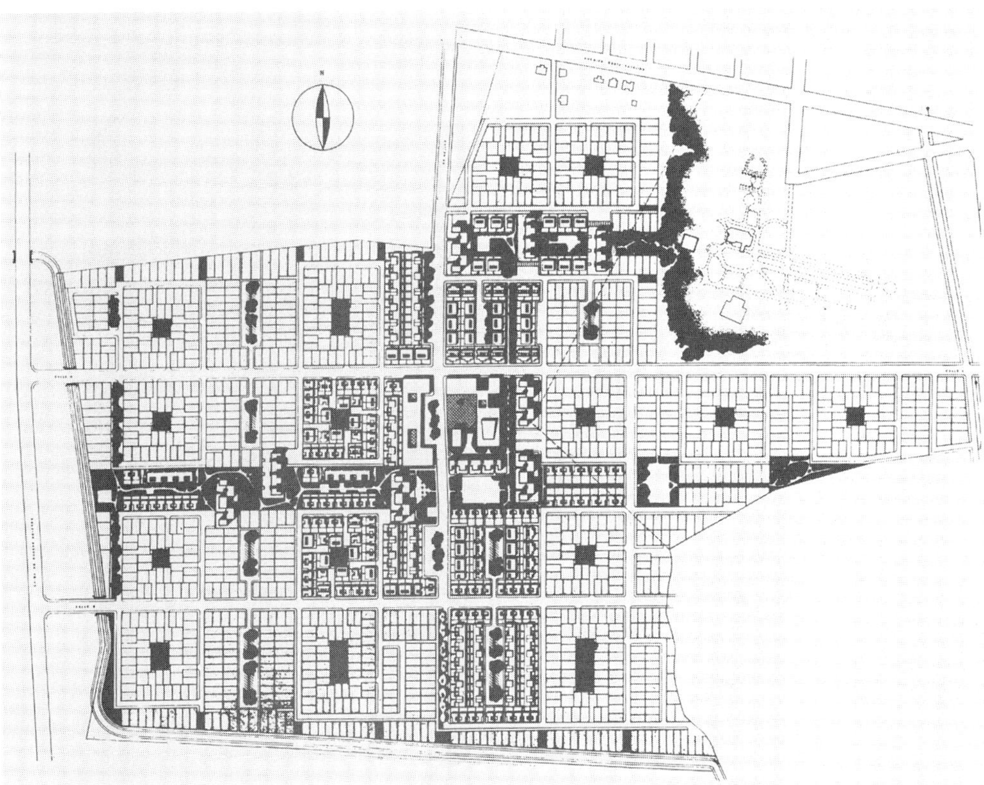

FIGURE 5.7 Town Planning Associates and Arroyo & Menéndez, site plan for Quinta Palatino showing *cuadra* layout, circa 1954. Published in *Plan Piloto de la Habana.* Courtesy of the Frances Loeb Library, Harvard Graduate School of Design.

cuadra as a formal arrangement for Quinta Palatino was therefore not unprecedented in terms of design, but in the Cuban context it did have theoretical implications that had not been raised in the prior work, firmly reinforcing with another formal register the overall framework of normalization as the constitutive basis of civil society. Through the *cuadra,* normalization obtained temporally, as the historic associations of the *cuadra* became absorbed into its present deployment, and its present deployment set constraints upon the future distribution of the physical fabric of the city. Through the *cuadra,* normalization also obtained spatially, by tying together the otherwise incommensurable urban architectures of the carpet-housing subdivision of Quinta Palatino and the colonial core of Habana Vieja. Between those two, other forms of urban architecture could be accommodated equally readily, such as the trapezoidal block of the Palacio de Bellas Artes in Centro Habana and the detached villas on the grids of Vedado and Miramar. The form offered, in effect, a rule of urbanism, a constraint upon the distribution of elements within the urban fabric. But this rule should not be conflated with the grid, with an abstract rational geometry; the grid accompanied the *cuadra* as its effect, not its cause.

Cuadras tolerated a high degree of variation, as evidenced by the various realizations proposed within the context of Quinta Palatino. Sert spent considerable effort testing different arrangements of housing within the perimeter limit, beginning with compositions developed for Bogotá and adding new ones in response to several different parameters (Figure 5.8). One fundamental issue examined in his comparison of O or H formations, or his comparison of a pinwheel distribution and a cross, was simply the number of units they allowed and the resulting physical relation of one unit to another. But Sert also considered issues such as local habits or predilections, debating with Gutiérrez, for example, whether there ought to be parking at the center of the *cuadras* to allow car access to the interior units: "Although I am in agreement with you I believe that it deals with a Cuban psychology *[un caso psicológico del cubano]* that can be taken into account, although I understand that would be sacrificing the small green space of the center or diminishing its convenience."[31] The open center of the *cuadra* was to accommodate other aspects of social life, however, and so could not be easily abandoned. Another arrangement, the pinwheel, offered the advantage of a clearly defined central *patio* with equally prominent openings to the exterior of the block. Architectural elements were evaluated here as well, as

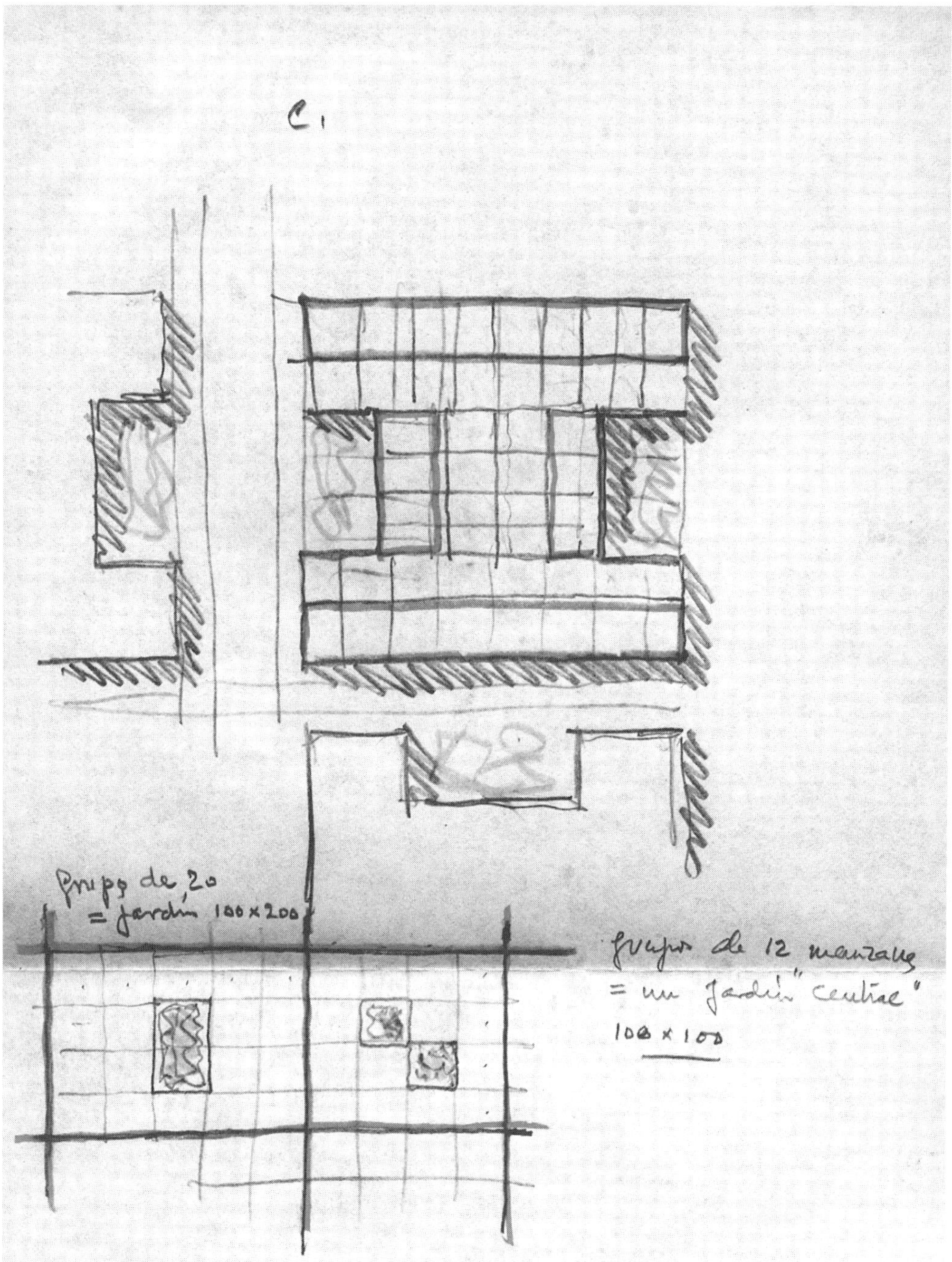

FIGURE 5.8 José Luis Sert, sketch of *cuadra* configuration, circa 1954. Courtesy of the Frances Loeb Library, Harvard Graduate School of Design.

Sert and Wiener wanted "to preserve in these houses the traditional elements of the Cuban house, like those for the porch and the patio."[32]

The normative frame of the *cuadra* could encompass or circumscribe these diverse contents, rendering them subordinate and comparable though not yet entirely commensurable. Commensuration was a possibility offered by one further conceptual register used to construct and sustain the normative system: the proportioning of the architectural elements. A sketch by Sert of a preliminary version of the apartment blocks showed a prospective section through stacked duplex apartments; an upper mezzanine in each apartment contained the bedrooms, and the living area was accorded additional height without requiring an additional flight of exterior steps (Figure 5.9). Sert drew figures in the different rooms and outside the block to suggest the relationship between the spaces and the activities they housed, a common drafting habit that in this instance resembles quite closely Le Corbusier's diagram of his Modulor proportional system as a chart of corporeal positions. The dimensions noted on the sketch confirm the resemblance, because they correspond to those of the Modulor system—the mezzanine levels would have had the dimension of the famous figure with outstretched arm.[33] According to Sert's own account, he had been using the Modulor scale since its preliminary introduction in 1948. Le Corbusier published the second volume *Modulor 2* in 1955, and altogether Sert supplied three separate testimonials for the two books. The first, written in 1948, exclaimed, "Working on a job for Lima (a town plan), I have tried out the 'Modulor'. What a wonderful find! In urbanism and all large-scale projects, it is a most valuable aid. With it, you can determine standard heights, dimensions and limit volumes, and by doing so lay the foundations for a legal code of urbanism."[34] The telltale dimensions of the Modulor appeared in their work in Cuba. For example, in the plans of housing that Sert sketched, the dimensions of several rooms were given as 2.96 meters by 1.40 meters, both of which are Modulor dimensions (Figure 5.10). The Modulor was also applied in the composition of facade elements in the architecture of Quinta Palatino and elsewhere—Wiener recorded in his diary that he had worked with Nicolás Quintana on revisions to a building design in Varadero and had "corrected their design—suggested facade treatment, roof treatment, etc. pivoting elements, subdivision of facade by Modulor geometry."[35]

Wiener's comment reveals that the Modulor was ready to hand for such design problems, and it did in fact serve as a drafting shorthand. But the range of its application—variously to plans, elevations, and block massing—demonstrates that the Modulor had additionally a comprehensive conceptual significance, offering yet another instance of scalar logic, similar to that of the *patio,* explicitly formal yet also analytic in function. The familiar details of the Modulor need not be rehearsed, but three points can be emphasized: first, the Modulor was a scalar system without any breaks or points of singularity—it did not begin from zero, but from a geometric relationship that enabled it to increase or decrease infinitely; second, Le Corbusier's assertion that the Modulor reconciled very disparate systems of measurement and proportion, overcoming the frictions between metric units, English units, and the human body, and uniting them into a coherent scale that provided a harmony of parts at any perceptual dimension—a synthesizing ambition that paralleled the typological binding of his Grid; and third, the

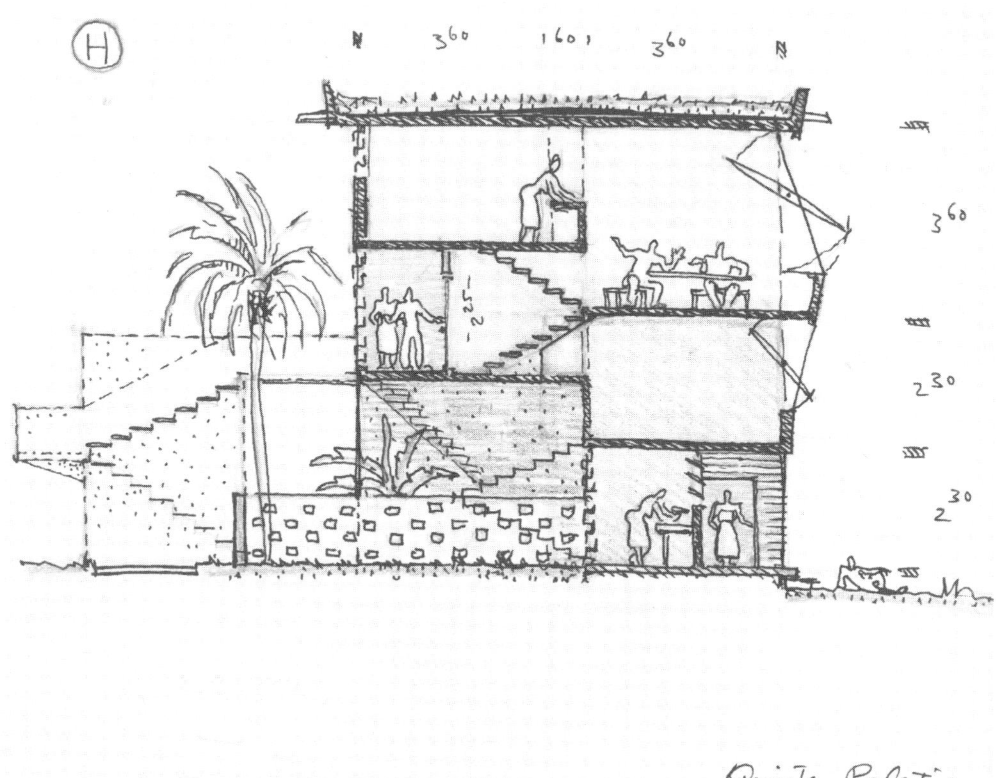

FIGURE 5.9 José Luis Sert, sketch of section of proposed Quinta Palatino apartment block, circa 1954. Courtesy of the Frances Loeb Library, Harvard Graduate School of Design.

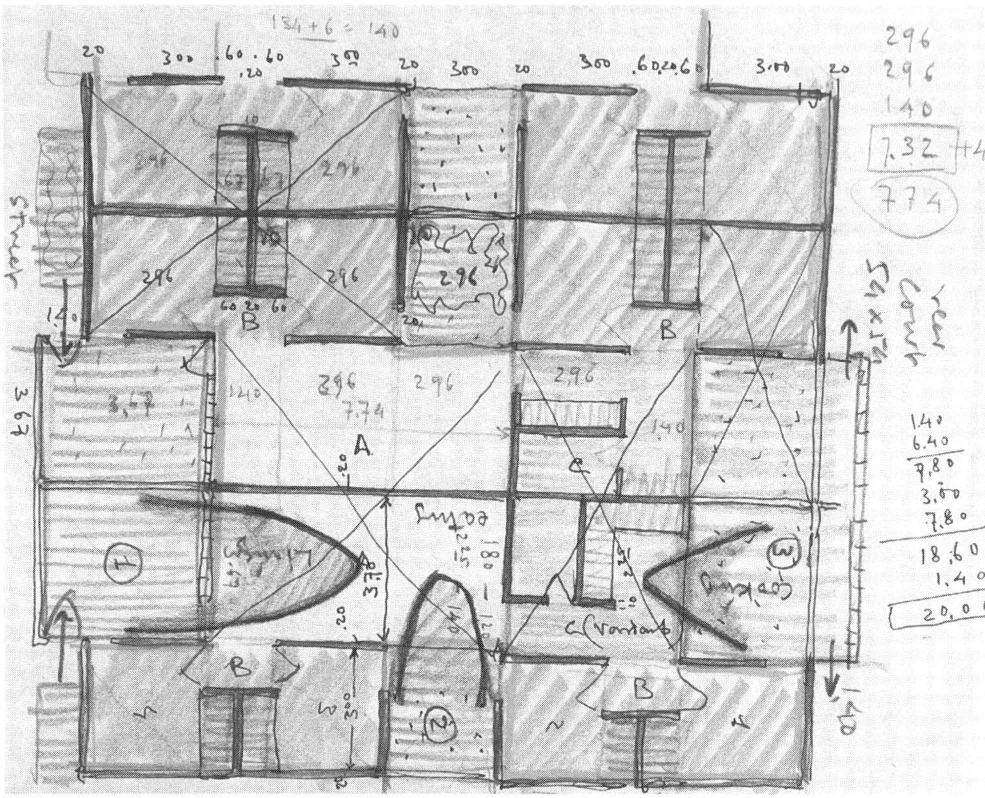

FIGURE 5.10 José Luis Sert, sketch plan of four-bedroom housing type, circa 1954. Courtesy of Paul Lester Wiener Papers, Box 155, Special Collections and University Archives, University of Oregon Libraries.

Modulor was based on a small but real mathematical mistake, the incorrect presumption of a geometric relationship between its two proportional series.[36]

The presence of this mistake, and the further compromise of the famously arbitrary adjustment of the "typical" height of the male figure, are moments of instability that betray the ambition of the Modulor—the attempt to imagine and construct a continuous field that united distinct elements. The Modulor, claimed its author, "is a flawless fabric formed of stitches of every dimension, from the smallest to the largest, a texture of perfect homogeneity."[37] But he offered the Modulor as more than an abstract concept; it was an instrument of design that could translate between classificatory analysis and objects of built form. When Sert declared that the Modulor could "lay the foundations for a legal code of urbanism" by governing *condicionales* (zoning or building regulations), he was expressing his desire for an operative correspondence between a conceptual and a social order, a correspondence through which the one would instantiate the other. Sert had for the previous decade argued the vital necessity of a human scale as the basis for configuring the spaces of modern architecture, by which he meant that a correspondence should be attained between absolute and experiential dimensions in a room, a building, a street, and a city. For Sert, though, this human scale implied more than a corporeal dimension and more than a ruled distance; it was also a social dimension, "a new measure related to man and to the social structure of the community."[38] This perception of an instrument that was at once a registration of the individual *and* the society was the concept of the human scale, and Sert embraced the Modulor as a technique to discern, represent, and produce the harmony between these elements.

In 1952, Sert gave the opening address for a symposium at the Museum of Modern Art on the topic of proportion in the arts. Using extensive research on proportion undertaken by Wiener, he asserted first that proportional systems, which "seem rooted in the human mind and constitute a tie between us and the world around us," had been adopted almost universally by cultures—"Geometry is rooted in the Americas as far as we can trace the history of this continent."[39] During the Enlightenment, he argued, such proportional systems had largely been replaced by "rigid modular systems" and these in turn had been appropriated by standardization and mass production. In parallel, some artists and architects had abandoned entirely all such limitations in favor of free form or expressionism. Now, Sert concluded, a return to proportion was urgently needed, as art and architecture faced an untenable choice between the monotony of standardization and the clashing contrivances of expressionism. "There cannot be," he concluded, "any beauty in a civic landscape without a certain harmony."[40] His language echoed the description of the Cuban housing proposal, with its emphasis on harmony and cohesion, and with the assertion of a balance between idiosyncrasy and monotony. As a scale that responded to the reality of standardization without reifying it, the diagram of the Modulor, Sert proposed, served "as a symbol and a promise."[41]

Standardization, as a trope of North American efficiency and pragmatism, had been stigmatized in Latin American intellectual movements at least since the publication in 1900 of José Enrique Rodó's essay *Ariel,* which juxtaposed utilitarian reason to interpretive spirit. In Cuba, the young architects of ATEC followed developments in international architectural discourse such as the renewed assertion of universalities during the postwar period even while they also pursued a deeper engagement with the historical legacy of Cuban architecture and the prevailing specific determinates of climate and culture. In regard to this pursuit, one especially salient aspect of Sert's deployment of the Modulor was his attempt to incorporate historical artifacts within its normative compass. Le Corbusier boasted of finding the Modulor dimensions in existing architecture, proving, he argued, the existence of an invisible proportional order. Sert may have succumbed to a similar perception when he annotated a sketch of a colonial facade in Trinidad with Modulor dimensions. Or perhaps he did indeed discover those dimensions, and because he saw the correspondence as a means of calibrating historical elements and the modern city, he proposed that they be employed in the new *condicionales* of the Plan Piloto de la Habana. But if the mandate for *condicionales* expressed his desire for a kind of embodied order, his advocacy for the incorporation of existing practices into new standards acknowledged the possibility that such ordering systems would establish norms, not universal absolutes. Such transformations, while they forestalled claims to universality, did not entirely restrain the ambitions and intentions expressed in the diagrams and charts that preceded urban design, but they dislocated those claims from the spheres of science and art and into the sphere of law. Entering into this sphere, they would necessarily enter into the realm of civic discourse and into the spaces of civil society, to install there a physical environment predicated not, or not only, on material utility nor on aesthetic effect but on typicality and normalization.

By the end of 1954, Sert and Wiener had, with their Cuban associates, developed detailed plans for several single-story housing types and three different types of apartment blocks. In these drawings, a set of similar details and compositional elements created a cohesion in the subdivision that remained consistent from the simplest, most economic of the housing units to the more complex arrangements of the apartment blocks. Interior rooms adhered to a set of typical dimensions, entries and rooms were accompanied by a *patio* or balcony, and the exterior walls were perforated with various assemblies of open brickwork to allow ventilation and to create partial views between the street and the interior *patios* (Figures 5.11, 5.12, 5.13). Modulor proportions were in evidence throughout—many of the layouts depended on a double square divided or supplemented

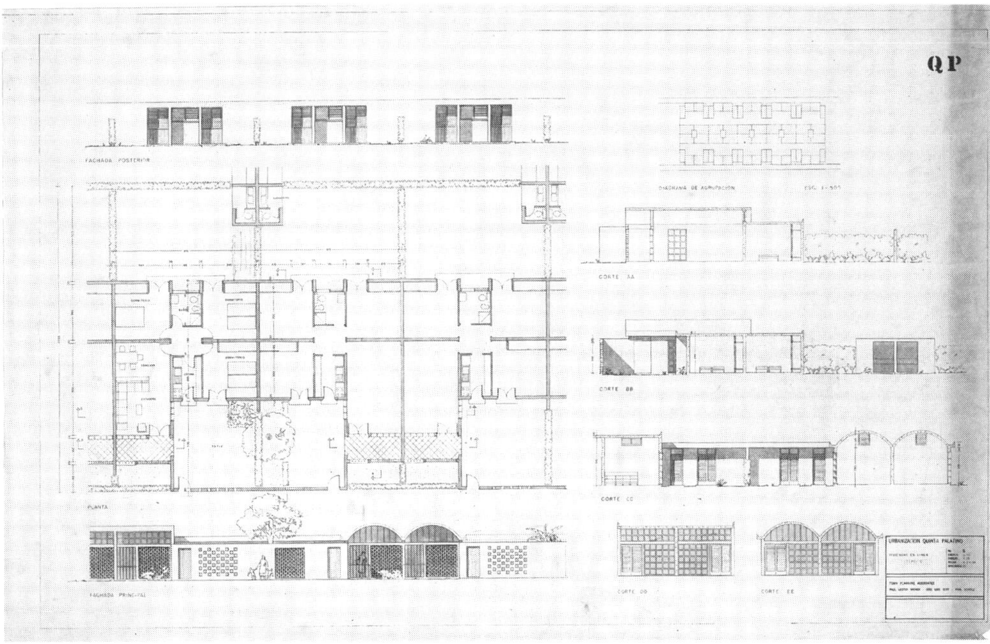

FIGURE 5.11 Town Planning Associates and Arroyo & Menéndez, three-bedroom housing type, Quinta Palatino, 1954. Courtesy of Paul Lester Wiener Papers, Box 155, Special Collections and University Archives, University of Oregon Libraries.

FIGURE 5.12 Town Planning Associates and Arroyo & Menéndez, model of three-bedroom housing type, Quinta Palatino, 1954. Courtesy of Paul Lester Wiener Papers, Box 155, Special Collections and University Archives, University of Oregon Libraries.

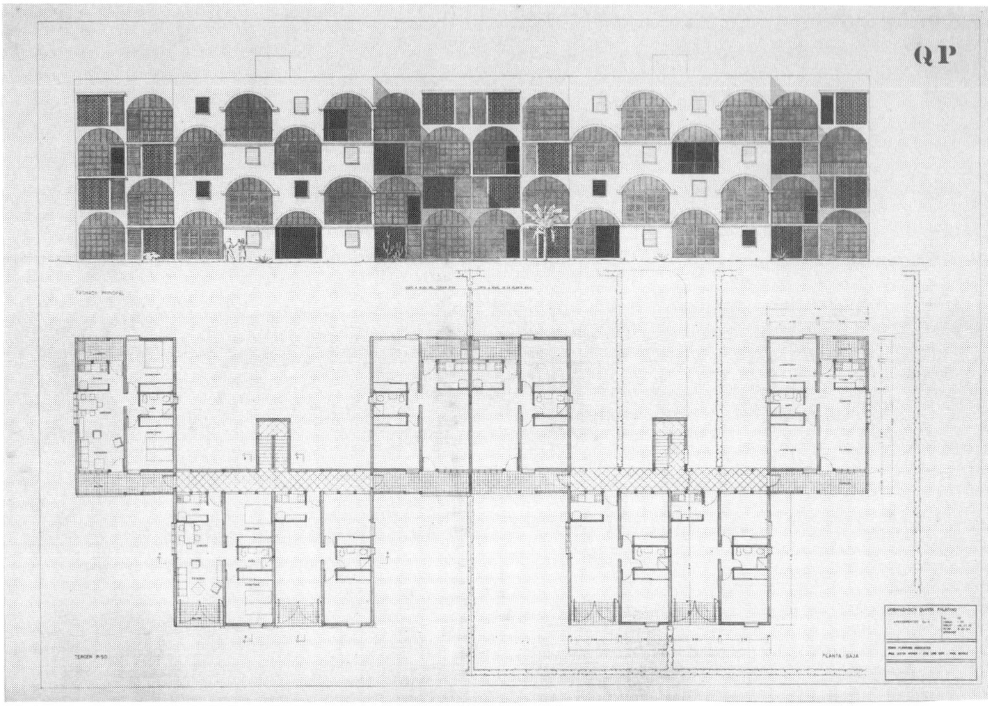

FIGURE 5.13 Town Planning Associates and Arroyo & Menéndez, apartment housing, Quinta Palatino, 1954. Courtesy of Paul Lester Wiener Papers, Box 155, Special Collections and University Archives, University of Oregon Libraries.

according to the Modulor—and in particular in the composition of the facades. The panels of open brickwork, for example, the extensions of the parapets, and the base and apex of the vault assumed either the platonic dimension of a square or the extension of one of the Modulor dimensions. The exterior wall of the houses stood at 2.25 meters, or the height of the Modulor figure's raised arm. Sert approached the design of the exterior walls with great deliberation, as these were the physical mediation between the distinct yet conjoined realms of the domestic and the civic. The privacy of the family interior required a solid wall, yet the cohesion of community life required some degree of either openness or transparency. In Cuba's tropical climate, the perforated wall provided the solution, with partial visibility permitting a sense of continuity between interior and exterior (or domestic and civic) without eliminating the distinction. *Persianas,* grills set above doors and windows, had been identified by Eugenio Batista and other architects as a definitive characteristic of Cuban architecture. Perforations along with other openings such as windows assumed a particularly figural aspect through Sert's developing architectural idiom. He had experimented with a catalog of formal elements in earlier projects, and in Quinta Palatino arrived at a formal technique that resulted in variety—the different shapes of the panels, the use of colors, and the avoidance of local symmetries even within the mirrored fronts of two adjoining units—but a variety contained within an overall order. The Modulor height of the exterior wall was to register experientially, so that the wall, the vital public element of the house, would correspond to the human scale, and at the same time to register conceptually, so that each component, from window, to wall, to facade, to *cuadra,* would be bound together, set "in harmony" within the larger encompassing rule of the civic landscape. In what should be considered in all senses the "patterned" surface of the apartment block facades, the ordering system was at once instrumental (proportioning the architectural object) and representational (linking the object, in the last instance, to the normative order of the Plan Piloto and hence to the city itself). It was both "symbol and promise."

The plan of Quinta Palatino completed in 1954—an arrangement of *cuadras,* linear park, and a large-sector center—did not survive as the basic plan of the project. As work progressed, surveys were carried out for roads, sewers, and utilities, and the architects tested the feasibility of building in phases, or building on limited portions of the property. A number of issues forestalled the project, including financial and ownership disputes outside the architects' purview. After the JNP began to formulate the Plan Piloto de la Habana, Quinta Palatino assumed a different potential role—that of typical neighborhood sector. As a *reparto* development, it was a manifestation of precisely the symptom that Sert and Wiener characterized as a threat to the future orderly development of the city. But it also prescribed a solution, as a properly designed *reparto* that could mesh seamlessly with other similar entities and with the classified road system and the sector divisions of the Plan Piloto. The Quinta Palatino proposal took on a highly important status in the overall plan as the reconciliation of architecture and planning through the medium of urban design. Eventually, however, the Quinta Palatino project succumbed to the prevailing conventions of subdivision projects, and over the next two years another plan evolved in which the *cuadras* were replaced by rows of housing set back-to-back. These rows created an almost solid built fabric, cut through only by the circular access roads that Town Planning Associates had earlier criticized as an excess of infrastructure. The linear park and the apartment blocks remained, as did a much smaller community center and the classified road system at the perimeter.

Even this diminished plan, substantially complete in 1957, was not realized in its entirety. At the end of 1958, *Arquitectura* published plans and a promotional text for El Reparto Santa Catalina, attributing the project to Emilio del Junco.[42] The plans showed the development of the northeast portion of the Quinta Palatino site, with a large central park and the indication of a future commercial center (Figures 5.14, 5.15). Despite the road system and the described characteristics of the *reparto,* which did not accord with the precepts advanced by Town Planning Associates, a vestige of the earlier schemes did remain in the clustered arrangement of the houses themselves. The houses, which were designed by del

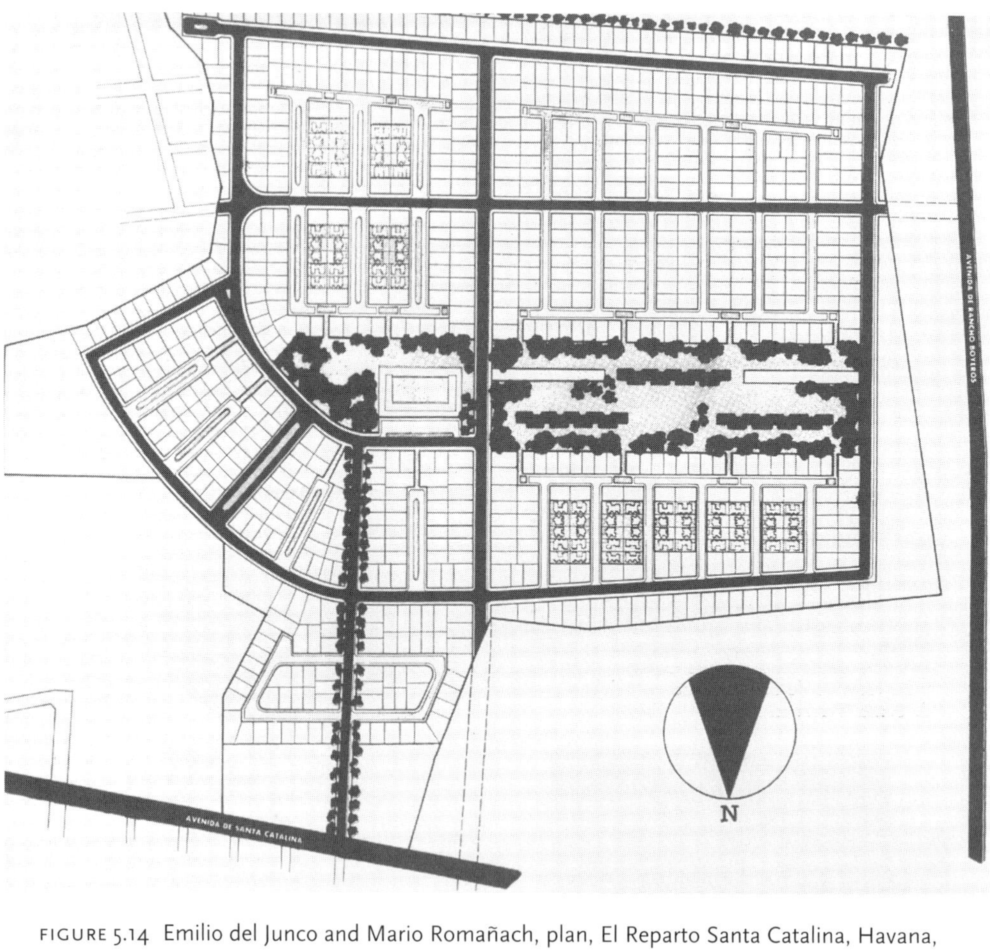

FIGURE 5.14 Emilio del Junco and Mario Romañach, plan, El Reparto Santa Catalina, Havana, 1958. *Arquitectura,* December 1958.

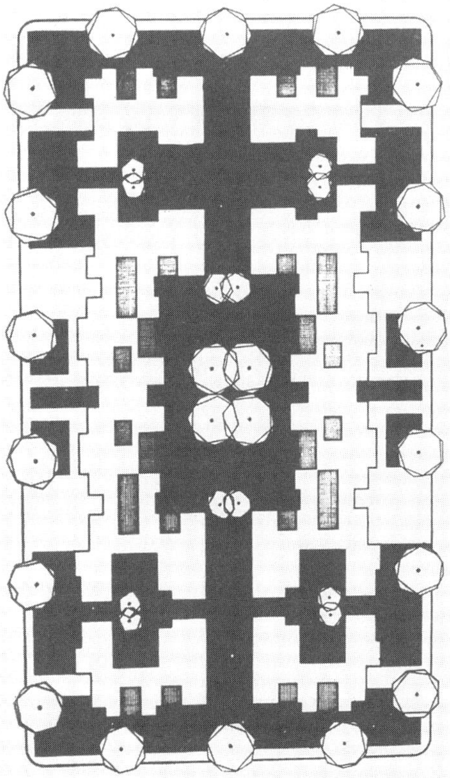

Distribución del terreno y situación de las casas con los jardines colectivos al interior de las manzanas. Emilio del Junco, Arquitecto.

DECALOGO DE PLANIFICACION INTEGRAL:

1
EDIFICIOS CONCEBIDOS PARA NUESTRO CLIMA

2
RESPETO AL ARBOL

3
ACCESO FACIL DE LOS PEATONES A LOS AMPLIOS JARDINES

4
DISEÑOS ORIGINALES QUE NO DESTRUYEN LA UNIDAD DEL CONJUNTO

5
AMPLIO ESPACIO ENTRE CASA Y CASA

6
APROVECHAMIENTO MAXIMO DEL TERRENO

7
PRIVACIDAD DE CADA VIVIENDA

8
VENTILACION CRUZADA

9
ELIMINACION DE PASILLOS LATERALES

10
PATIOS DE SERVICIOS AISLADOS

El grabado de la parte de abajo muestra la distribución de los terrenos y casas en otros repartos. El grabado de la parte superior señala cómo se distribuyen las casas en las manzadas del Reparto Santa Catalina, de acuerdo con la Planificación Integral de Casas y Manzanas.

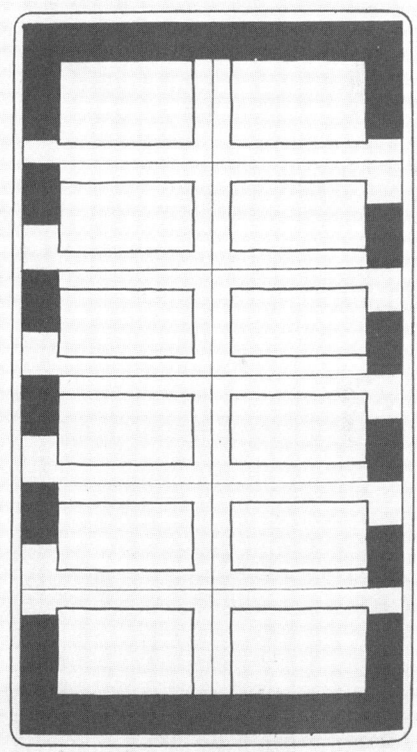

Planta de las corrientes parcelaciones que se hacen en La Habana y otras poblaciones del interior.

558 ARQUITECTURA

FIGURE 5.15 Emilio del Junco and Mario Romañach, diagram of block layout, El Reparto Santa Catalina, Havana, 1958. *Arquitectura,* December 1958.

Junco with Mario Romañach, and which were to be supplemented with houses by other architects to provide variety, did not abut at the rear. An open space for community use was left at the center of each narrow block, with access to the street and to the backyards of the houses. This space was not fully enclosed but was still recognizably a *patio* in Sert's definition, and an accompanying article compared the advantages of this layout to the dense infill typical of other developments in the city. The facades of the new houses, which were slightly separated to be offered as detached units with internal *patios,* revealed the characteristic traces of Romañach's idiom, influenced by yet distinct from Sert's earlier designs. Shallow gables replaced the curved vaults, and the structural frame subordinated the continuous wall. The projecting window frames and recessed doors might be taken for the residue of the modulations of the walls of Quinta Palatino, a residue that evidences the isolated, and therefore unrealized, attempt to constitute a vital connection not only between the scales of civil society, but also the habits and aspirations of civic life, through the projection of an architectural system of typicalities.

6 Historic Districts

The Regulation of the Past in Habana Vieja

THE comprehensive scope of the Plan Piloto de la Habana, its extension over the entire metropolitan area, depended on a regulatory framework that did not yet exist. It presumed the unification of the city at some level above the existing municipalities, and also presumed the consolidation of the authority of the JNP over rival agencies or interests. In perhaps no other area of the city were the claims as layered as in the old colonial quarter, Habana Vieja. Habana Vieja was the appellation that referred to the area of the city that had been contained within fortified walls. These had been demolished in the middle of the nineteenth century and the land built upon to weave together the *intramuros* and the *extramuros*. Major public works such as the Capitolio Nacional and the Paseo del Prado were constructed adjacent to this land in the twentieth century, modernizing the old center without disrupting its colonial core (Figure 6.1). The Plan Piloto de la Habana published by Town Planning Associates on behalf of the JNP proposed a nearly complete rebuilding of this district of the city; it was to be categorized as a sector and connected to the classified road system, with primarily office functions housed in linear blocks of high-rise towers and commercial programs on the ground floor of lower residential blocks. Elsewhere in the city new roads would, if realized, have required selective demolitions, and new areas of housing might have established new characteristics of design. But the proposal for Habana Vieja was of a different degree entirely—the seemingly total transformation of the original core of the city to accord with the norms of the Plan Piloto.

The proposal clearly shared premises with the program of urban renewal that developed in the United States following the passage of the Federal Housing

FIGURE 6.1 Ministerio de Obras Públicas, aerial photograph of Habana Vieja (upper right quadrant of image), with the former location of the fortified walls visible as a different urban fabric, circa 1956. The Capitolio Nacional is the large freestanding building near the center. Courtesy of the Frances Loeb Library, Harvard Graduate School of Design.

Act of 1949; through the lens of urban renewal the wholesale reconstruction of central areas, financed or subsidized by national government, was seen as an ameliorative to urban decline manifest in physical and social conditions. But a concurrent practice increasingly adopted during the 1950s—the establishment of historic districts in city centers—provided another set of premises, a different lens through which the preservation of historic buildings and neighborhoods was regarded as a brake against urban deterioration. In the context of nationalism, particularly as it emerged after Machado was deposed in 1933 and again following the promulgation of the 1940 constitution, the colonial district of Havana had begun to assume distinct representational value as a container of residual civic history.[1] Prompted directly or indirectly by the larger nationalist project, a number of disciplines with historical concerns began to direct attention toward the colonial period. Some of the artists associated with the Vanguardia movement, for example, incorporated details of baroque architecture in creating their new iconography of *cubanidad*, while ethnographers began to draw associations between the social habits of the colonial period and aspects of public and domestic architecture. Historians of architecture contributed as well. Even some who, like Martínez Inclán, supported the development of modernism in Cuba nevertheless regarded an understanding of colonial architecture as the only route to determine specificities of *cubanidad* that could be manifested in modernism. Two historians of architecture, Joaquín Weiss and Martha de Castro, published studies of colonial Cuban architecture in 1936 and 1940, respectively, while practicing architects also looked to colonial buildings.[2] Among the modernist group, Eugenio Batista by his example encouraged younger architects like Frank Martínez and Emilio del Junco to explore the lessons especially of traditional Cuban domestic architecture.

Two other architects, Luis Bay Sevilla and José María Bens Arrarte, who without opposing modernism remained somewhat more reserved in embracing it, made particular contributions to this historical awareness in essays published in *Arquitectura* and in the daily newspapers. They wrote about colonial architecture in detailed essays that combined a study of formal elements with accounts of historical events and personages to place architecture within its social context. In the early 1940s (in the wake of the constitutional convention and under Fulgencio Batista's elected presidency), Luis Bay Sevilla served as editor of *Arquitectura*. The journal's cover usually framed a sketch of an old building or street and the editor himself contributed a regular feature called "Viejas Costumbres Cubanas" (old Cuban customs) that discussed individual buildings and their settings within Cuban history. This column might describe a number of buildings that had existed previously on a particular site; sometimes it focused more on people than on architecture. Bay Sevilla also published contributions from historians, placing their arguments side by side with documentation of contemporary buildings and the administrative notes of the Colegio de Arquitectos. Some described the colonial architecture of other Latin American nations—Emilio Harth-Terré writing about viceregal Peru, for example—claiming the commonality of their historical context. Others were by Cuban historians such as Weiss, who examined techniques and tropes of colonial architecture not just with the familiar focus on churches and *palacios* but with studies of residential streets and architectural settings. An essay titled "Ventanas y balcones coloniales" (Colonial windows and balconies) considered the urban context of these discrete architectural elements, and the social life to which they corresponded. Weiss acknowledged the disappearance of this social life, but with a pivotal qualification:

> The times are what they are, and it is necessary to live according to their standard, making the most of all their possibilities; but History and Tradition will always constitute the foundations upon which are structured the future life of peoples, of that which will be in each moment their most valued patrimony. So, why should we stop, even for a moment, telling ourselves of our colonial windows and balconies?[3]

There was, in Weiss's self-consciously innocent query, a reflection of the wider poles of the question of historic patrimony, which at their respective limits advocated uncompromised modernization or retrospective nostalgia.

Designating National Monuments in the City

A polemical debate between self-avowed modernists and declared traditionalists had been carried out in the late 1920s in the pages of Cuban architecture journals, with Enrique Luis Varela emerging as a young advocate for the traditionalist position. It was perhaps possible to imagine the urban settings extrapolated from either of those two extremes, but the active participants in discussions about the architecture of Habana Vieja from the 1930s to the 1950s adopted more nuanced positions in pursuing this debate. Indeed, the calibration *between* these positions, and the cultural implications of these possible calibrations, became their central concern. The leading figure in the discussion of historic monuments in Havana was, by inclination and then by dint of his office, Emilio Roig de Leuchsenring, who in 1938 was appointed the founding Historiador de la Ciudad de la Habana (Historian of the City of Havana), a newly formed position granted general responsibility to foster the culture of the city of Havana. Roig de Leuchsenring became a member of the Patronato Pro-Urbanismo and supported its agenda, although he probably shared with two fellow members, Weiss and another leading advocate of preservation, Anita Arroyo de Hernández, a greater concern for the protection of historic buildings from the threats of speculation and development than for, say, the scientific study of traffic circulation. He wrote prolifically about diverse topics unified by the conceptual thread of Havana itself, or, more precisely, the continuous formulation of an image of Havana as a composite of past, present, and future, in myriad social and cultural forms. The physical fabric of Havana and its civic buildings in particular provided a critical component of this work; Roig de Leuchsenring sought to ensure the preservation of significant buildings in Habana Vieja, with the Catedral and the Casa de Gobierno foremost among them. He emphasized, though, that the preservation of the individual buildings was insufficient; their immediate surroundings—the other buildings that faced onto the Plaza de la Catedral and the Plaza de Armas along with the plazas themselves—were a vital part of the historical composition and also needed to be protected from development or demolition. The cathedral became the focus of an extended debate on the issue of national monuments, and Roig de Leuchsenring recited the history of this debate in a folio volume documenting the cathedral. This volume, published in 1959 under the auspices of the Junta Nacional de Arqueología y Etnología (National Board of Archaeology and Ethnology), accompanied a similar document published in 1957 on the Plaza de Armas. Together titled *Los monumentos nacionales de la República de Cuba* (National monuments of the Republic of Cuba), the two volumes represented the consolidation of a professional historical approach toward the nation's monuments.[4]

That consolidation had begun prior to the 1933 revolution, with the public debate over the cathedral and its plaza starting when, in 1929, Luis Bay Sevilla published a plan for the restoration of the existing plaza in a daily newspaper. In the accompanying essay, he argued: "This Plaza should be declared a national monument, and once the existing buildings there are expropriated, a colonial museum of furniture, books and periodicals, stamps, lithographs, etc., should be established in them."[5] Such a complex would be a valuable repository of historical artifacts within their original architectural setting; it would also, he believed, become a central attraction for tourists visiting the city. The same year, Forestier and his assistants submitted their own proposal for the restoration and embellishment of the plaza. In addition to creating a new geometric pattern of stone paving, they recommended that a nineteenth-century fountain located at the Alameda de Paula be moved to the Plaza de la Catedral to replace the existing fountain at its center. A drawing illustrating the proposed plaza bore a caption asserting that Forestier was "faithfully interpreting its traditional past." Bay Sevilla and Roig de Leuchsenring did not agree, however, and after Ley-Decreto No. 613 denominated the cathedral, the plaza, and the surrounding buildings national monuments in 1934, Forestier's proposal to move the fountain was rejected. The two critics offered the same justification: the statuary fountain, they pointed out, had been executed in the nineteenth century as a memorial to the Spanish navy; its military connotations had no place in the religious setting of the eighteenth-century structure of the plaza. Moreover, Roig de Leuchsenring contended, its height would obscure the view of the cathedral. Although the fountain was not moved, the plaza was restored under the supervision of Bay Sevilla, during 1934 and 1935. The cathedral itself was renovated, rather than restored, the following decade, between 1948 and 1949, extending the debate about the fidelity of efforts to preserve examples of colonial architecture.[6] While these developing efforts appealed to both the historical and architectural disciplines for their justification, explication, and implementation, the more important foundation on which they relied was the law.

In the two volumes of *Los monumentos nacionales de la República de Cuba*, Roig de Leuchsenring explained in detail the sequence of legal ordinances relevant to the study and preservation of colonial architecture. The prologue of the first volume provided a summary. No provisions had been established for national monuments in the 1901 constitution, nor in its subsequent revisions, nor in the constitutional laws of the post-Machado governments. The first legislative provision had been made in 1928, when Machado authorized the designation of national monuments "for the best and most effective protection of said monuments, of good historic, artistic, or patriotic character."[7] The first such designation was the one made in 1934 to protect the cathedral and its plaza, which explained the obligation of the state: "It is an obligation of every government to help maintain in its people the respect and love of their noble and extolled traditions, among which are accounted the architectonic works that are the ornament and honor of cities." The cathedral and its plaza were examples of this type of historical element, the decree continued, and should be preserved along with their surroundings for their "beauty" and "historic and artistic interest."[8] Three years later, in 1937, another decree created a Comisíon Nacional de Arqueología (National Commission of Archaeology) responsible for the "conservation and study of pre-Columbian and colonial monuments."[9]

Then, according to Roig de Leuchsenring's genealogy of legal dispositions, the Constitution of 1940 introduced a significant transition. Three articles of the new constitution pertained to the state's right and obligation to define and regulate the national patrimony:

> In fact, Article 47 declares that "culture, in all of its expressions, constitutes a fundamental interest of the State"; and Article 58 confers upon the State, by means of the Law, "the preservation of the cultural treasure of the Nation, its artistic and historic riches," also granting to it, in particular, the protection "of the national monuments and places notable for their natural beauty or for their acknowledged artistic and historic value." In Article 87, the Constitution, while acknowledging the existence and legitimacy of private property, taking into account the full concept of social function attributed to it, imposed limitations that the Law sets for reasons of necessity or public utility or social interest.[10]

This lineage thus tied the preservation of national monuments to the state's "fundamental interest" in culture, and by so doing claimed legitimacy derived from the presupposition of a basic norm: the desire to maintain the national patrimony rests on an interest in what "ought to be." In the appeal to article 87, the advocacy of preservation coincided with the advocacy of planning, for just as the members of the Patronato Pro-Urbanismo had asserted that the constitution's stipulation of the social function of property was the presumption that enabled planning, here preservation was authorized by that same stipulation. The physical fabric of the city, the existing buildings of the past and those that might be built in the future, would not be regarded as only the consequence of individual or commercial intentions; both the past and the future fabric would be considered as extensions of the social relations regulated by civil society. The advocates for protection of existing patrimony actually succeeded in achieving greater degrees of government sanction well before physical planning of future development would come to be embodied in the governmental structure. First, in November 1940, the municipal government of Havana created, at Roig de Leuchsenring's recommendation, a Comisión de Monumentos, Edificios y Lugares Históricos y Artísticos Habaneros (Commission of Historic and Artistic Monuments, Buildings, and Places in Havana) under the control of the Office of the City Historian. The following year, the Comisión Nacional de Arqueología was reorganized first as the Junta Nacional de Arqueología (National Board of Archaeology) and then, in 1942, once again as the Junta Nacional de Arqueología y Etnología (National Board of Archaeology and Ethnography). In addition to expanding the disciplinary range of the organization to include ethnographic research, the new board was created as an autonomous agency within the ministry of education, with the authority to nominate historic sites as national monuments. The membership roster likewise expanded, now including Martínez Inclán and Bens Arrarte but also leading anthropologists such as Fernando Ortiz and Lydia Cabrera. A range of disciplines as well as a breadth of cultural attentions now overlapped within an institutional context and with a focus on the physical artifacts of Cuban history. Coincident with the period immediately following the constitutional convention, such an institutional context also became a setting for formulating disciplinary extensions of the nationalist project of the constitution itself.

Following this new legal organization, President Batista signed Ley-Decreto No. 1932 in June 1944, authorizing the Junta Nacional de Arqueología y Etnología to compile an official register of national monuments and reasserting the status of the cathedral and its plaza as the first entries on that list. In addition, Ley-Decreto No. 1932 listed in detail which of the surrounding buildings came under the category of protected monuments. The legislation issued in 1934 had only stated that the buildings surrounding the plaza were part of the monument; this new law listed them by address and name, and also included buildings on the streets leading into the plaza as part of the vital context of the complex. So from the mid-1940s and extending into the 1950s, at least one professional organization viewed elements in Habana Vieja as historically situated, cohesive,

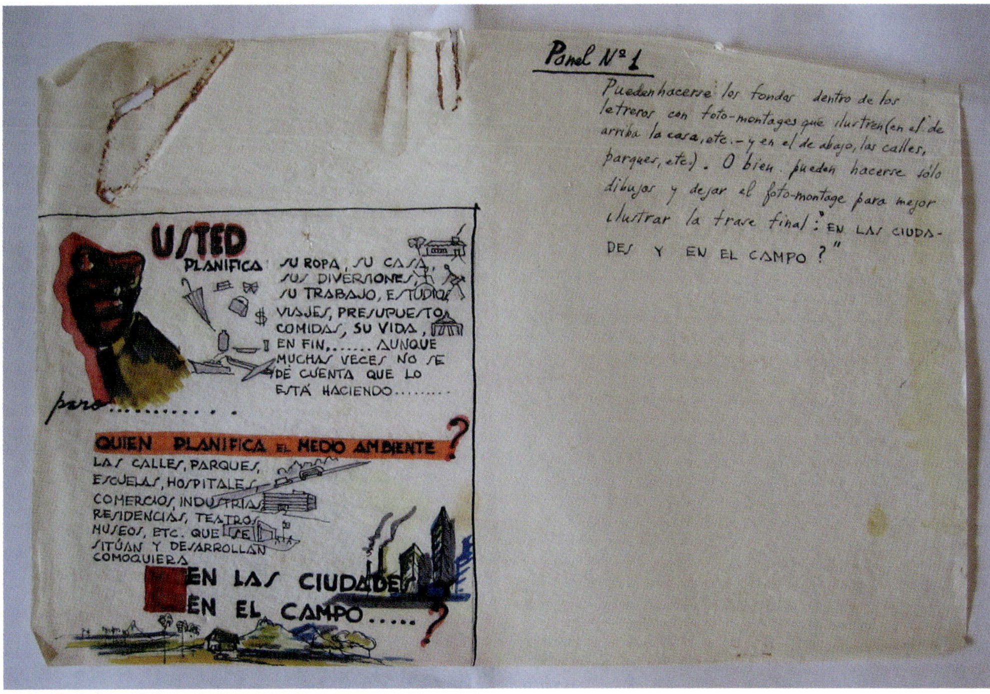

PLATE 1 Eduardo Montoulieu, sketch for exhibition panel no. 1, La Exposición sobre Urbanismo. Courtesy of Eduardo Montoulieu. Photograph by the author.

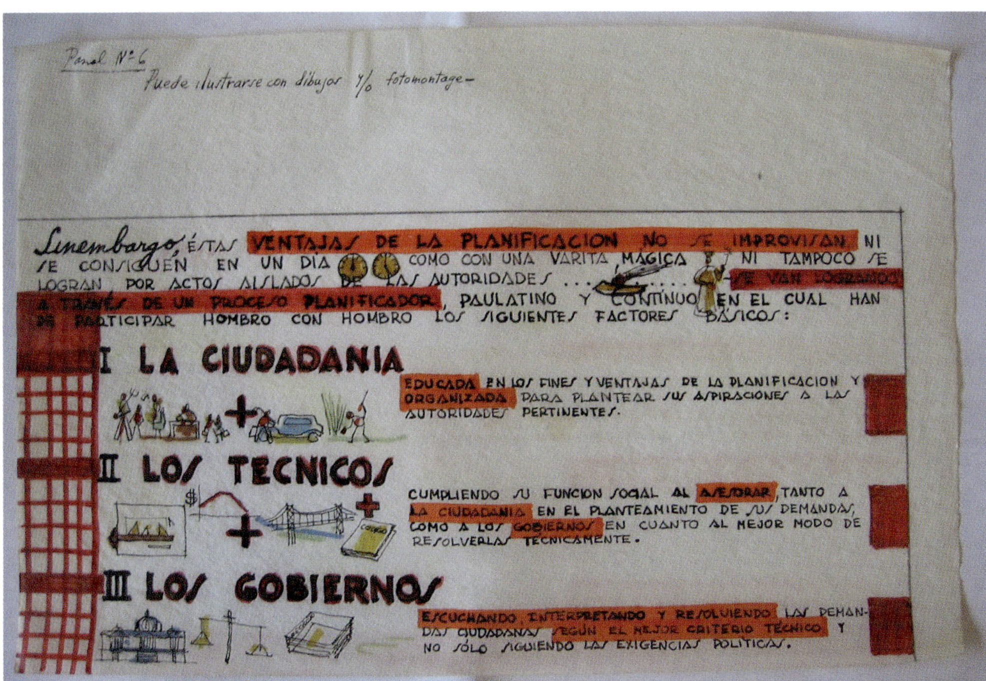

PLATE 2 Eduardo Montoulieu, sketch for exhibition panel no. 6, La Exposición sobre Urbanismo. Courtesy of Eduardo Montoulieu. Photograph by the author.

PLATE 3 Eduardo Montoulieu, sketch for exhibition panel no. 8, La Exposición sobre Urbanismo. Courtesy of Eduardo Montoulieu. Photograph by the author.

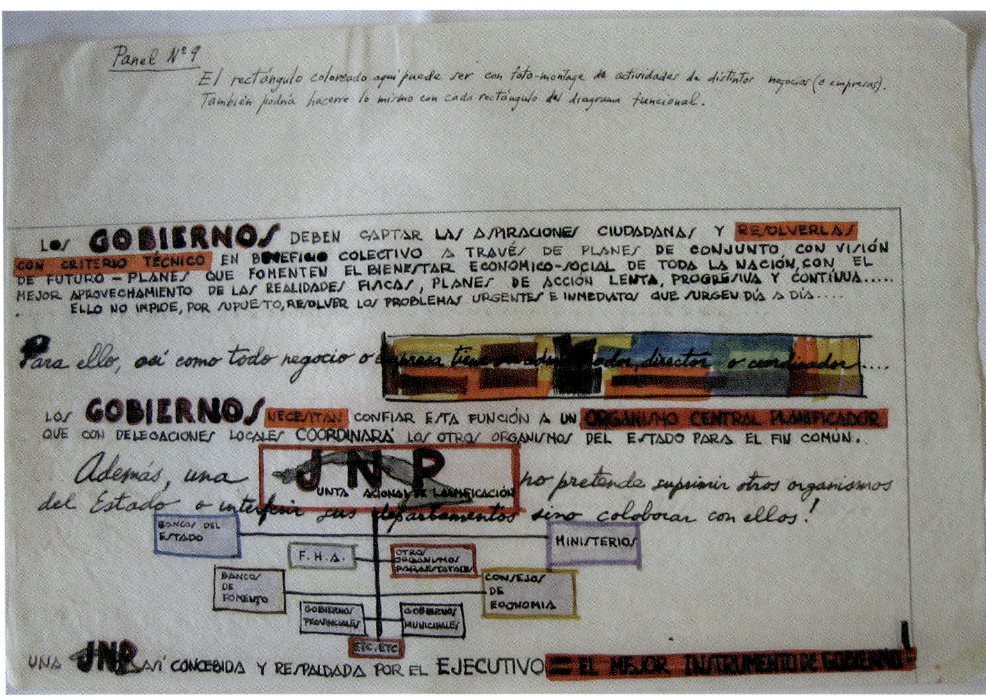

PLATE 4 Eduardo Montoulieu, sketch for exhibition panel no. 9, La Exposición sobre Urbanismo. Courtesy of Eduardo Montoulieu. Photograph by the author.

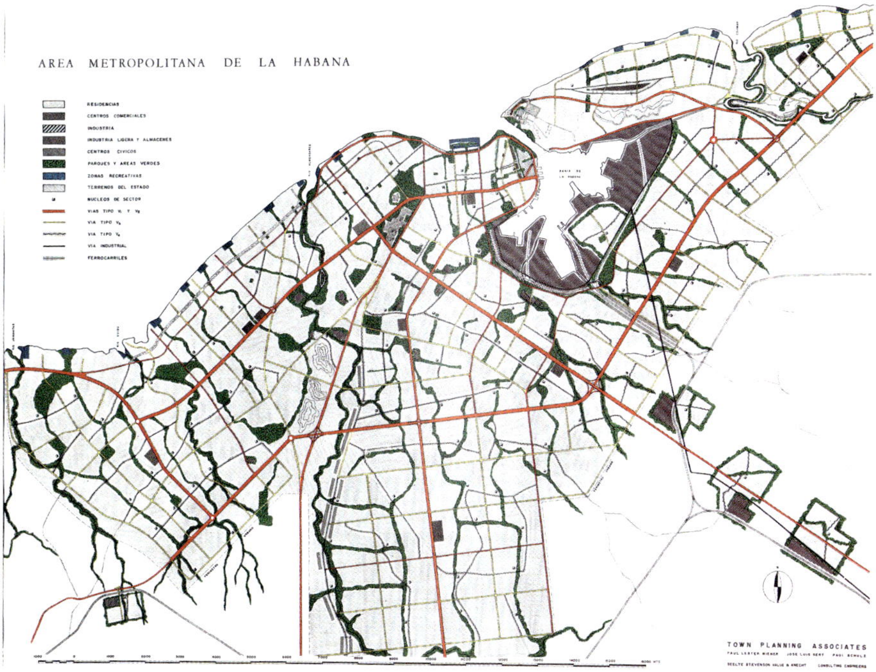

PLATE 5 Town Planning Associates and Junta Nacional de Planificación, Área Metropolitana, *Plan Piloto de la Habana,* 1955–58. Courtesy of the Frances Loeb Library, Harvard Graduate School of Design.

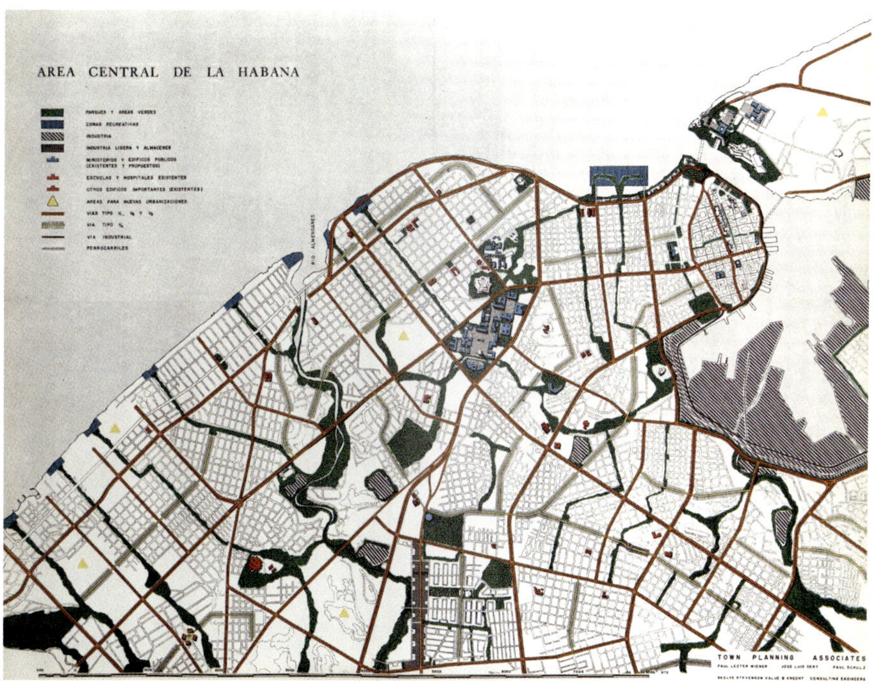

PLATE 6 Town Planning Associates and Junta Nacional de Planificación, Área Central, *Plan Piloto de la Habana,* 1955–58. The cluster of buildings shaded in blue at the center of the map is a proposed configuration for the civic center. Courtesy of the Frances Loeb Library, Harvard Graduate School of Design.

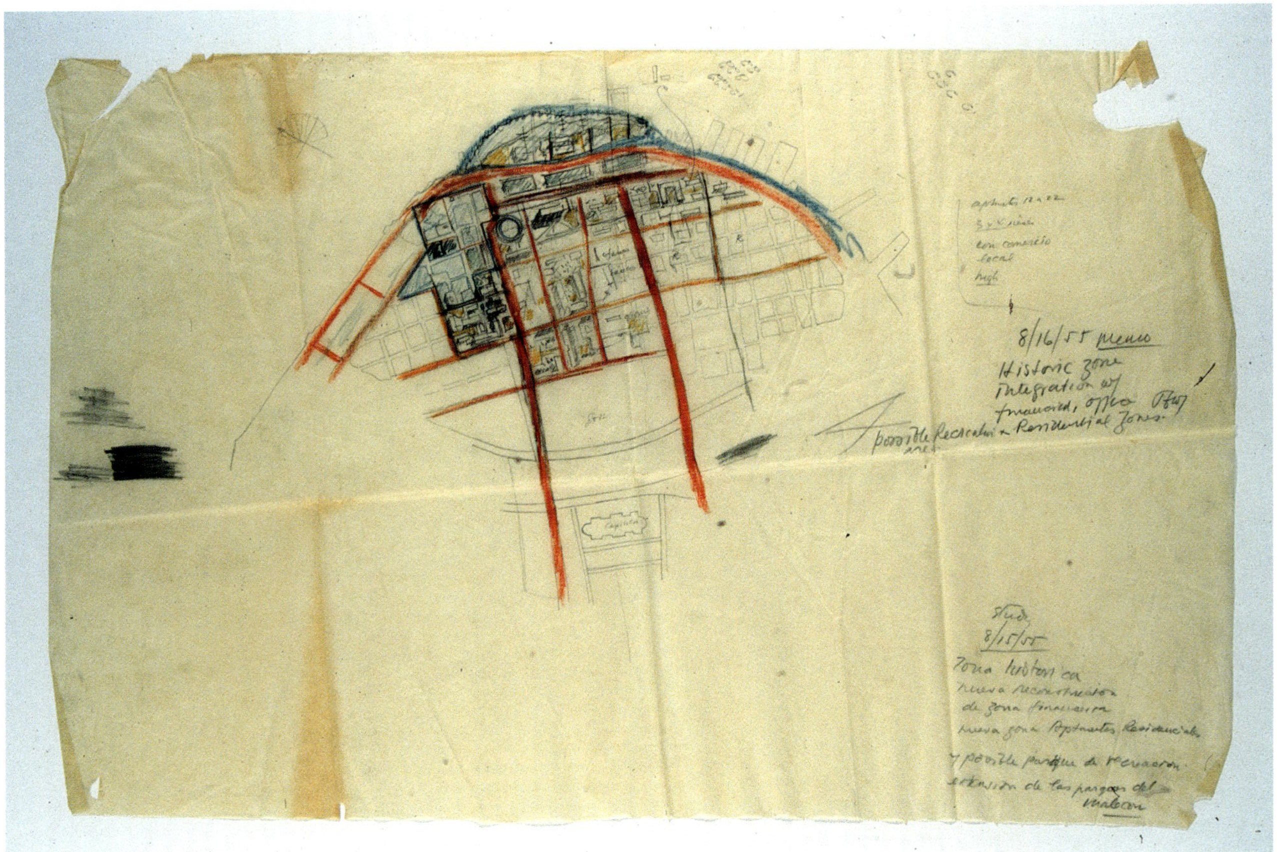

PLATE 7 Paul Lester Wiener, annotated sketch of proposal for Habana Vieja with "Historic Zone" shaded in blue at upper left, dated August 16, 1955. Courtesy of Paul Lester Wiener Papers, Box 155, Special Collections and University Archives, University of Oregon Libraries.

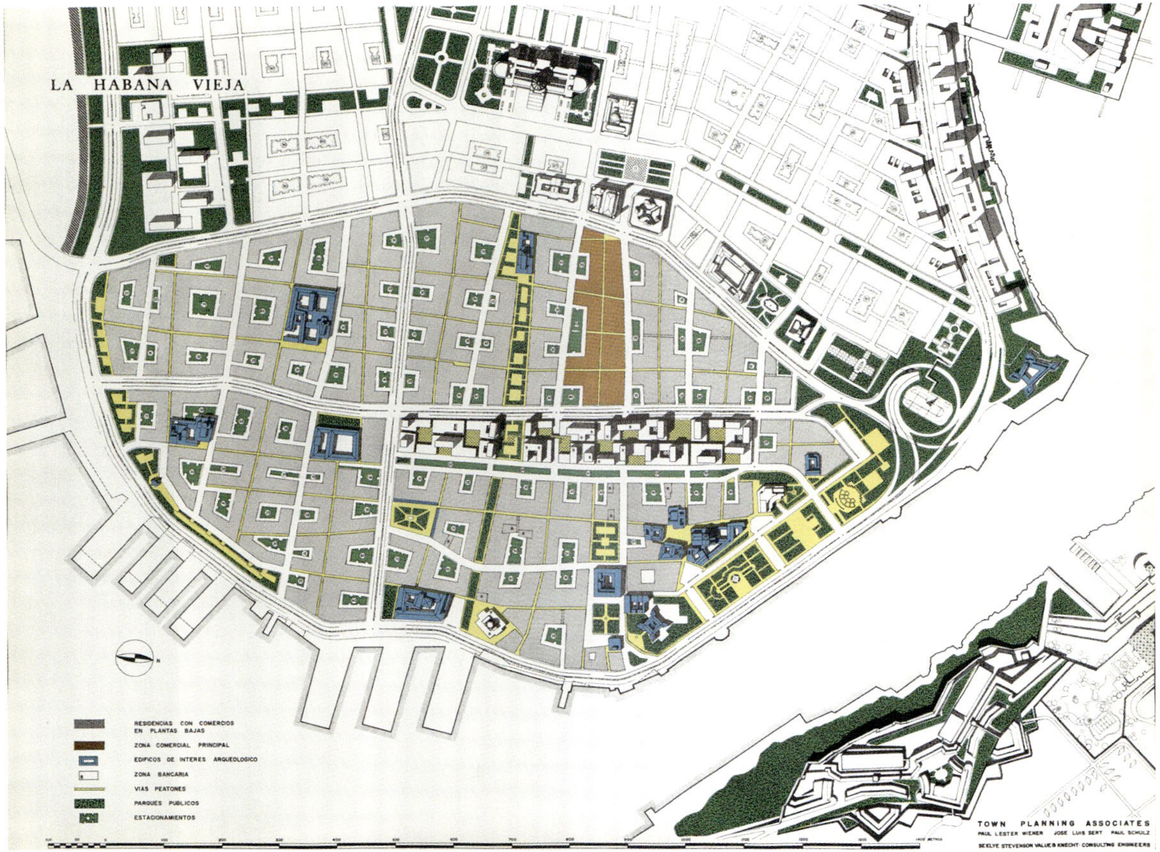

PLATE 8 Town Planning Associates and Junta Nacional de Planificación, final proposal for Habana Vieja, *Plan Piloto de la Habana*, 1955–58. Buildings of historical interest are shaded in blue and residential blocks are shaded in gray. Courtesy of the Frances Loeb Library, Harvard Graduate School of Design.

PLATE 9 Jean Labatut, photographs of illumination of Monumento a Martí at dusk. Jean Labatut Papers, Department of Rare Books and Special Collections, Princeton University Library.

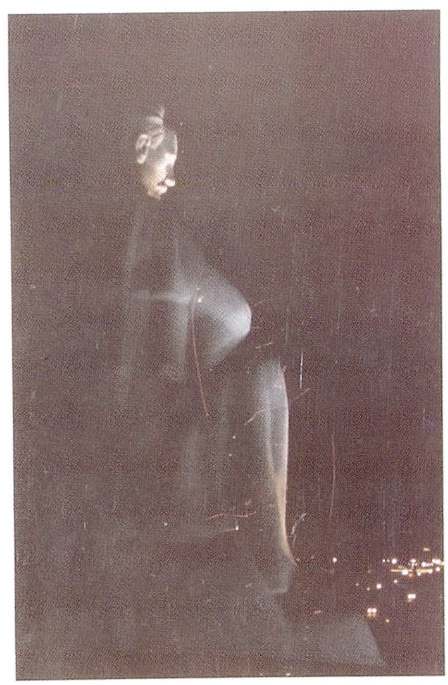

PLATE 10
José Luis Sert, Mario Romañach, Gabriela Menéndez, Félix Candela, and Hideo Sasaki, model, presidential palace, Havana, 1955–58. Courtesy of the Frances Loeb Library, Harvard Graduate School of Design.

PLATE 11 Carlos Enríquez, *Paisaje con caballos salvajes* (Landscape with wild horses), 1941. Oil on composition board, $17\frac{1}{2} \times 23\frac{5}{8}$ inches (44.5×60 cm). Museum of Modern Art, New York. Gift of Dr. C. M. Ramírez Corría. Copyright The Museum of Modern Art, New York. Licensed by SCALA/Art Resource, New York.

and expressive of national identity. The specificity of the 1944 legislation is its most notable characteristic, suggesting as it does a degree of research and scrutiny of the existing urban fabric and implying also a decision to *exclude* various other adjacent structures. Although Habana Vieja was regarded as the site of significant monuments, it does not appear that it was yet viewed in its entirety as a monument in a formal sense. However, some interpretive perspectives might have conceived the district as a complete fabric; for example, René Portocarrero's 1948 painting *Ciudad* must have drawn upon such a conception, seeing the city—here the historical city—as a figure in itself. For some writers and artists, Habana Vieja was the site of daily professional life. The journal *Orígenes,* founded in 1944 as a venue for the writing and artwork of the avant-garde, had its office in the quarter at the intersection of Compostela and O'Reilly, and contributors and colleagues like the architect Nicolás Quintana met in nearby cafés. The office used by ATEC was a few streets away on Empedrado, and several of the architects in the group had their offices in the district, which remained a business center even as the city expanded. It remained a center of government activity as well. Although the JNP would be situated in Vedado, the ministry of public works was housed in the former Convento de Santa Clara in the middle of Habana Vieja, and other ministries were similarly accommodated in converted buildings in the same area. Finance was the dominant commerce in the district. The Lonja de Comercio, the stock exchange, had been built near the quay in 1909, while the streets around Obispo and O'Reilly had long been the banking district of the city where several bank headquarters had been constructed in the first decades of the republic. These commercial buildings introduced the most significant changes to the colonial fabric in the prewar period. Within the tight constraints of small colonial lots, some were built up several stories high and described as the first skyscrapers in the city. After the war, an increase in automobiles quickly produced an intolerable congestion in the narrow streets of the district, which remained quite vital as commercial venues. Openings in the fabric such as the Plaza de la Catedral, the Plaza de Armas, and the Plaza Vieja provided necessary physical and experiential respites as much as historical instruction. They, like the rest of Habana Vieja, were viewed from very distinct perspectives in the 1950s, as resources for the daily functioning of the city or as settings for contemporary civic life.

Habana Vieja in the 1950s

In 1956, Bens Arrarte addressed the first Congreso Nacional de Planificación (National Planning Congress) on the subject of "Los problemas del tránsito y del estacionamiento" (The problems of transit and parking), which, despite its apparently technical concern, directly posed the question of how planning should intervene in Habana Vieja. Alleviating the problems of traffic congestion and parking shortages was, after all, one of the promises of planning, and those problems were at their worst in the central districts of the city. But after presenting various current proposals for street enlargements and underground parking, Bens Arrarte cautioned that any changes "need to take into account that the characteristics of Habana Vieja and its archaeological riches ought to be preserved."[11] Two proposals, one to remove the raised pedestrian walk from the Paseo del Prado to allow more traffic and the other to build underground parking beneath the Parque Central, would destroy that historical character, eliminating the array of royal palms in the latter and the public "salon" of the former. Bens Arrarte recommended that the problem be approached instead through a coordinated program of new aboveground parking structures, privately financed and judiciously sited. A new single-story parking structure, set a half-story underground, had already been constructed in the Plaza Vieja. This solution was not entirely dissimilar from his proposals, yet it was not an example he would endorse, for Bens Arrarte aimed primarily to defend the experiential dimensions of the physical fabric of the historic district. Perhaps, he suggested, streets in Habana Vieja should be dedicated to pedestrians, with buses and large automobiles excluded. One large central artery, an enlargement of the street Teniente Rey with new adjacent plazas, could provide the surgical alleviation of traffic congestion. As for the rest of Habana Vieja, "this part of the capital, for its historic value and for the old *palacios* that still survive, ought to be conserved as a Museum City, prohibiting the tall buildings that increase congestion." Certainly, he stated categorically, "Habana Vieja is not the zone suitable for complete demolition and for the erection over its areas a new neighborhood of tall buildings with wide green zones and spacious streets."[12] The projected enlargement of Teniente Rey to create a broad new Avenida del Capitolio extending from the steps of the Capitolio Nacional through Habana Vieja to the waterfront had been an element of Forestier's plan and more recently had been revived by the Departamento de Arquitectura y Urbanismo (Department of Urbanism and Architecture) of the city of Havana (Figure 6.2).

As designed by Carlos Maruri Guilló, head of the department, the avenue would bisect the colonial quarter, with adjacent blocks reapportioned and with an increase in property values for the district anticipated as a result.

The delegates to the National Planning Congress visited the offices of the JNP to see examples of the work being done, but it is not certain that Bens Arrarte was familiar with the agency's proposed Plan Piloto de la Habana. The preliminary version had been completed by the end of 1956, but was not published or circulated until the JNP hosted its exposition in March 1957. Given the close circle of the architectural profession in Havana, however, its details must have been known outside the planning office. Moreover, a likely future for the old city district had already been framed when, in January 1955, concurrent with the creation of the JNP and therefore prior to any of its proposals, Ley-Decreto No. 1996 sanctioned the "Rehabilitación de la Habana Antigua" (rehabilitation of ancient Havana). This law decreed that the president (General Batista) could, following "the necessary studies," declare "the public usefulness of the rehabilitation of the Ancient Zone of the City of Havana, rehabilitation that will consist in enlarging and improving its routes of communication and making provision in them for loading and unloading and for parking vehicles, enlarging the system of parks, playing fields, public gardens, and similar works."[13] A perimeter that encompassed the entire *intramuros* area as well as the first several blocks of the *extramuros,* including the Castillo de Atarés, the railway station, and the blocks

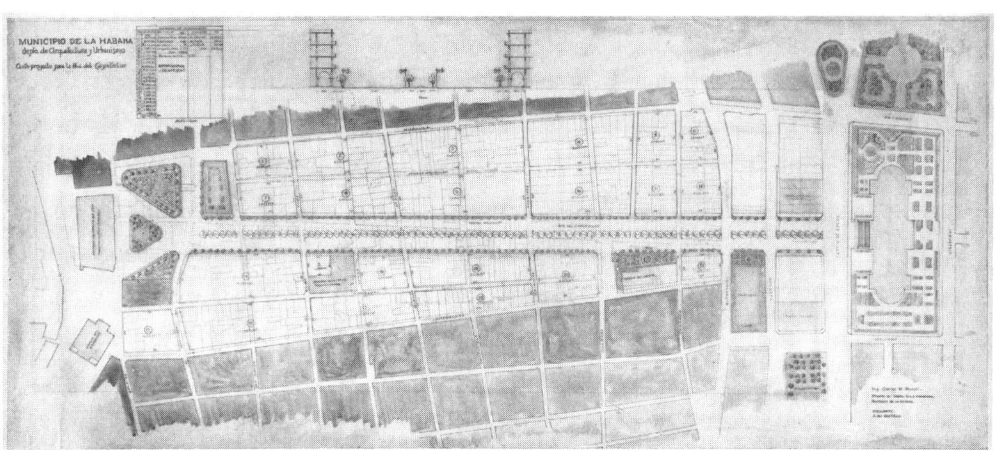

FIGURE 6.2 Proposal for a boulevard from Capitolio Nacional (at right) to the waterfront along the route of *calle* Teniente Rey, by Carlos M. Maruri Guilló as director of the Department of Urbanism and Architecture for the City of Havana. *Arquitectura,* January 1957.

in front of the Capitolio, defined the zone designated for rehabilitation. The law also specified the right to access any areas or buildings within that zone as necessary to produce studies and plans. Finally, it outlined a regimen for expropriation of properties and the granting of concessions for rehabilitation, both processes to be overseen by La Financiera Nacional de Cuba (Cuban National Finance Company).[14] From this beginning, the rehabilitation of Habana Vieja would have been susceptible to various forms of political and financial corruption. Property in the central area of the city was valuable and the speculative market continued to accelerate throughout the 1950s. Many buildings in the district were owned by the government, others by politically powerful banking interests. Ley-Decreto No. 1996 provided superficial government sanction for what could become essentially unregulated activity. Batista obtained the authority to define areas to be renovated; through the Financiera Nacional he would have the ability to make expropriations and award concessions. The likelihood of illicit dealings and patronage schemes must have been clear to the architects and planners of the JNP, although no explicit concerns were raised even as quite radical proposals for dealing with Habana Vieja developed during the summer of 1955.[15]

Two conceptual frameworks were available to the JNP and its consultants that would have placed the rehabilitation of Habana Vieja in a seemingly more objective professional perspective: urban renewal and historic districting. The implementation of urban renewal as a strategy for reviving deteriorating city centers had already commenced in the United States, and was an influential aspect of the planning discourse embraced by Montoulieu and by Sert and Wiener. For Sert in particular, the strategy focused on his particular concern, the city center; the urban-renewal process—the expropriation and financed redevelopment of extremely large areas of land—provided an opportunity for realizing the large civic centers that Sert regarded as indispensable to the recuperation of the city. Prewar concerns about slums, urban blight, and public health were consolidated in the policies of postwar municipal governments and the research of professional bodies in early renewal projects in Pittsburgh and Boston. Historic districting had also developed from its origins in a handful of prewar instances to gain more widespread attention in the first decade after the war. Although the explicit tendency toward preservation and the implicit tendency toward historicism would have set the idea of the historic district against some basic precepts of modernist planning discourse, its applicability to Habana Vieja could not have been disregarded. A nearby precedent for the rehabilitation of Habana Vieja was located not in the United States, but in Puerto Rico, in San Juan Antiguo, the colonial *intramuros* district of that capital city. Planning work undertaken in Puerto Rico had a direct influence in Cuba, through publications, symposia, and a lecture tour by the head of the planning agency, and while no explicit comparison between the two cities was recorded, some awareness of the San Juan example seems highly likely given the broader comparisons that were made and given the professional exchanges between the two countries. Proposals for the rehabilitation of San Juan Antiguo, in fact, included both urban renewal *and* historic districting. In legislation initiated in 1949 and consolidated in 1954, the Planning Board of Puerto Rico was given authority for the "regulation of ancient and historic zones." This legislation enabled the Planning Board to review proposals for the rehabilitation of historic areas to protect monuments, buildings, and streets, and to evaluate the appropriateness of new constructions. Under this set of legislation, the area referred to as the Historic Triangle of San Juan Antiguo was to be designated a historic district and to be rehabilitated. Consultants to the San Juan Housing Authority submitted "A Report on the Renewal Possibilities of the Historic Triangle of the City of San Juan" in May 1955 in which they recommended that specific portions of the district be conserved or restored, and that others be cleared and rebuilt with new building types such as apartment buildings, hotels, and parking garages.[16] The classifications to be made in the case of San Juan Antiguo, like those to be made in Habana Vieja, ranged along a spectrum from historic monument to dilapidated slum, and urban renewal was predicated on a diagnosis of the degraded city center as the latter.

While the monuments of Habana Vieja were valorized and legally recognized from the 1930s onward, the overall district was often described as typically consisting of buildings too deteriorated and living conditions too poor for a modern city. The preliminary JNP drawing of land use in the metropolitan area designated the southern third of Habana Vieja as *solares* (slums), using a diagonal hatching to distinguish these blocks, and colors that indicated that the rest of the district contained offices, with a concentration of commercial uses along Obispo and O'Reilly, and scattered artisanal industry and government buildings (see Figure 5.1). To accompany this kind of abstract diagnosis Sert and Wiener obtained a panel of photographs showing the conditions of life in the district (Figure 6.3). Sert had used the technique of photographic documentation of slum life in *Can Our Cities Survive?* to similar purpose, as evidence to support calls for architectural intervention.[17] Even if their initial diagnosis was based on superficial information, it was soon reinforced by detailed research the JNP conducted during the next two years. Extensive building surveys, proceeding block by block and including drawings and photographs to document the configurations and the entranceways of buildings, were compiled in large folio volumes. By the end of 1956, the JNP had produced a series of analytic drawings that assessed the housing types and typical morphology of the residential areas of Habana Vieja. Detailed land surveys of plots and ownership accompanied these, suggesting the convergence of both a social and an economic knowledge to support the drastic remedy of urban renewal.[18]

FIGURE 6.3 Photographs of conditions in Habana Vieja compiled by Town Planning Associates and Junta Nacional de Planificación, circa 1955. Courtesy of the Frances Loeb Library, Harvard Graduate School of Design.

But even before these comprehensive researches confirmed assumptions or presumptions, the JNP began to develop a series of master plan proposals, the first of which were devised during the summer of 1955 in meetings between Wiener and Romañach, with the participation of other members of the JNP. Wiener and Sert had by this time developed a shared methodology through their earlier projects in Latin America, but Wiener, who remained in Cuba for the summer, took the leading role in formulating these plans. While the overall composition of the metropolitan area and the new classified road system were being developed, specific areas of the city were also identified as special cases. The Almendares River between Vedado and Miramar was one such case, singled out for its potential to serve as an extended recreation area and because the traffic approaches to its crossings needed to be refined. Another was the area of the Malecón immediately west of the Paseo del Prado, where waterfront buildings were identified as potential sites of redevelopment (and where the possibility of claiming additional land from the sea had already been promoted by executive decree). Habana Vieja was a third such case. Wiener and Romañach considered the latter two in conjunction. In a sketch that he dated July 27, 1955, Wiener outlined programmatic areas on top of a plan of the existing Sector Central of the city (Figure 6.4). Several existing blocks of the Malecón are filled in with a new neighborhood unit of elongated slab buildings set within open blocks and widely spaced from one another. In Habana Vieja, a six-block area surrounding the intersection of Obispo and Habana streets is marked as the financial sector. The Plaza de la Catedral is marked, as are the Casa de Gobierno and Plaza de Armas, and the Plaza Vieja. Three encircled zones frame the *intramuros* area: the Paseo del Prado, the Capitolio Nacional, and the railway station, which is replaced with a sketched-in "helicopter port." Wiener recorded in his diary a meeting with Arroyo the previous evening, a discussion that must have accompanied the sketch. Arroyo advised Wiener of the possibility that the Paseo del Prado could be widened (which seems to be indicated on the drawing), and that a new building for the Banco Nacional by José Benitoa would be located nearby. In addition, the banking interests in Habana Vieja were interested in redeveloping the banking district. Arroyo asked Town Planning Associates to "supervise [the] scheme of Benitoa and of Banking interest to tie to Plan Regulador of Habana."[19]

A week later, Wiener recorded that he had "w/ Mario [Romañach] started study of financial area & corrected Malecón [and] started sketch 'Heart of the

City' in combination w/ Capitolio."[20] His mention of a sketch probably refers to one that shows the area immediately in front of the Capitolio as well as several additional blocks reconfigured as high-rise buildings set back from the streets in landscaped superblocks (Figure 6.5). These new blocks extended down to the hub of banking buildings located in the previous sketch, and thus proposed a considerably expanded area devoted to the new financial sector. Arroyo reviewed the new studies of the central area and recommended keeping the buildings opposite the Capitolio. Arroyo, Wiener noted, "found [the] scheme exciting—

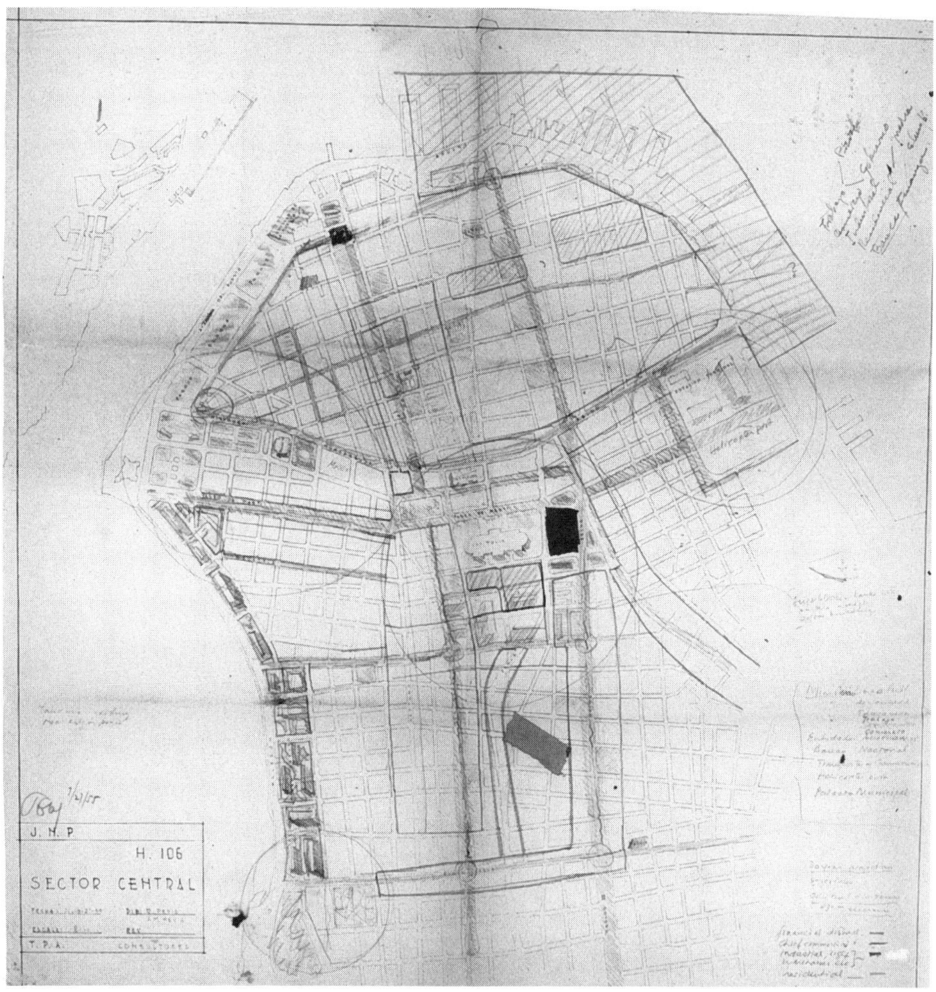

FIGURE 6.4 Paul Lester Wiener, sketch of proposed land use over map of existing districts of Habana Vieja and Centro Habana, 1955. Courtesy of Paul Lester Wiener Papers, Box 155, Special Collections and University Archives, University of Oregon Libraries.

[he] wants to have a financing study made to enable execution for whole of downtown area."[21] The Bankers Association had evidently commissioned its own design study at some point. Its proposal may have provided some of the programmatic and economic requirements, such as floor area and cost, but did not provide design direction for the JNP or Town Planning Associates. Wiener and Romañach, with Arroyo's encouragement, now considered possibilities for

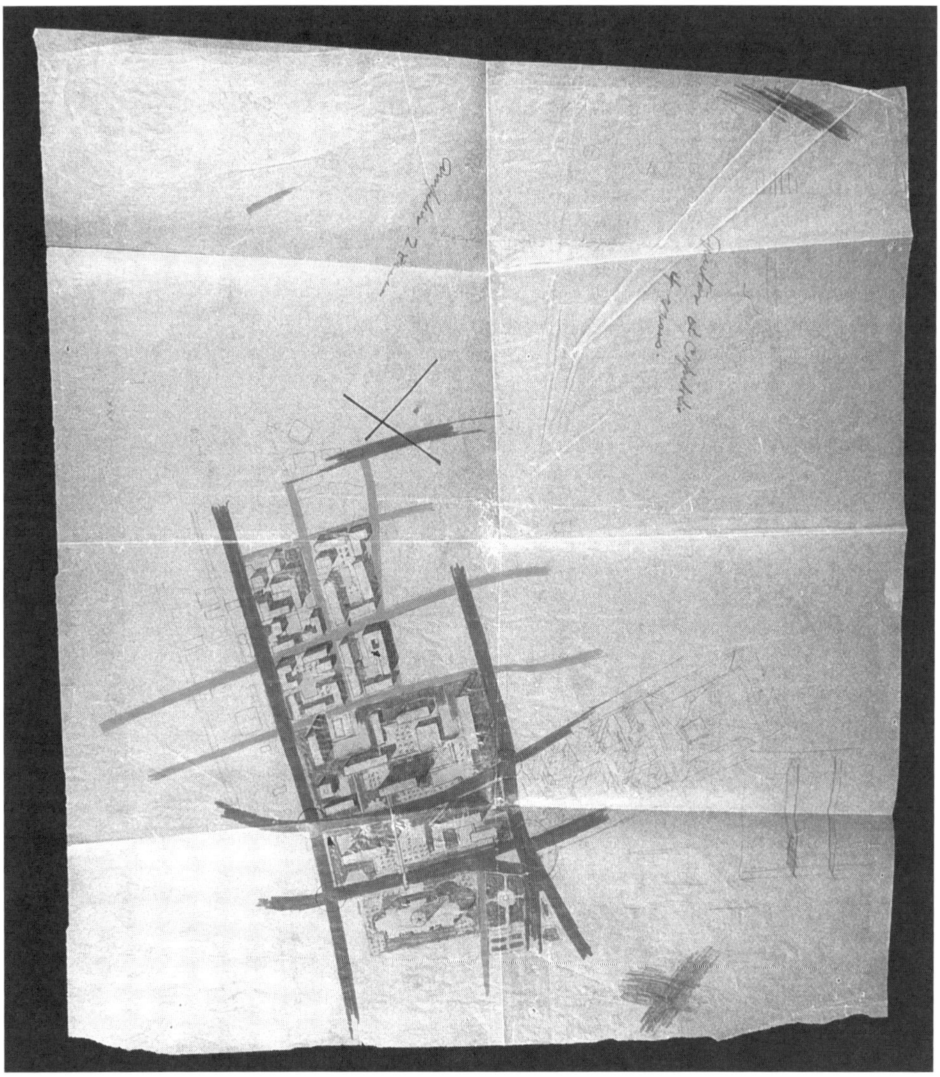

FIGURE 6.5 Paul Lester Wiener, sketch of Capitolio Nacional and proposed superblocks in Habana Vieja, 1955. Courtesy of Paul Lester Wiener Papers, Box 155, Special Collections and University Archives, University of Oregon Libraries.

the entire *intramuros* area. A pair of sketches showed their scheme sufficiently expanded that it now extended to the historical monuments in the northeastern corner of Habana Vieja. Here the significance of the colonial fabric was addressed for the first time—one indicated the monuments, markedly identified in blue, and in the other, Wiener's annotation proposed a "Zona Histórica" (see Plate 7). This zone would extend from the waterfront at the Castillo de la Fuerza to enclose the Plaza de Armas and Casa de Gobierno as well as the cathedral and its plaza. In the sketch annotated by Wiener, the zone extends a few blocks west of the Plaza de la Catedral, which would have provided a buffer between the historic monuments and the redeveloped area so that this proposal would have accorded with Roig de Leuschenring's exhortations that the adjacent buildings be considered part of the national monument, and would have accorded as well with the provisions of the 1944 decree to that effect.

Additional annotations mention the possibility of introducing areas of recreation as well as residential zones. Both sketches show the center of Habana Vieja given over entirely to new superblocks for the financial sector. Two new, larger roads extending from either side of the Capitolio frame this central zone. Like the central Avenida del Capitolio proposed by the city's Departamento de Arquitectura y Urbanismo as an enlargement of Teniente Rey, these two roads would bisect the district from west to east, but they would not have framed the central axis of the Capitolio Nacional itself. The two roads were to connect directly the larger framework of the classified road network and the reconfigured Habana Vieja. Some of the smaller streets in the sketches follow the route of existing streets for part or even all of their length; other existing streets are eliminated by the superimposition of the larger blocks. The various studies produced in these sketches were compiled in a larger drawing that included the arm of the Malecón that had been developed initially (Figure 6.6). The patchwork nature of this larger plan suggests a working document in which the various elements were tested and revised.[22] It possesses, however, a consistency of approach in that the dense, narrowly spaced existing fabric of Habana Vieja is largely to be demolished and replaced with superblocks that serve as plinths for towers and high-rise slabs. The spaces between buildings are to be landscaped plazas, connected one to the next as pedestrian routes through the district. Cars will be accommodated on fewer but larger roadways than in the existing arrangement of streets. The financial sector is three superblocks in a grid of two east–west and four

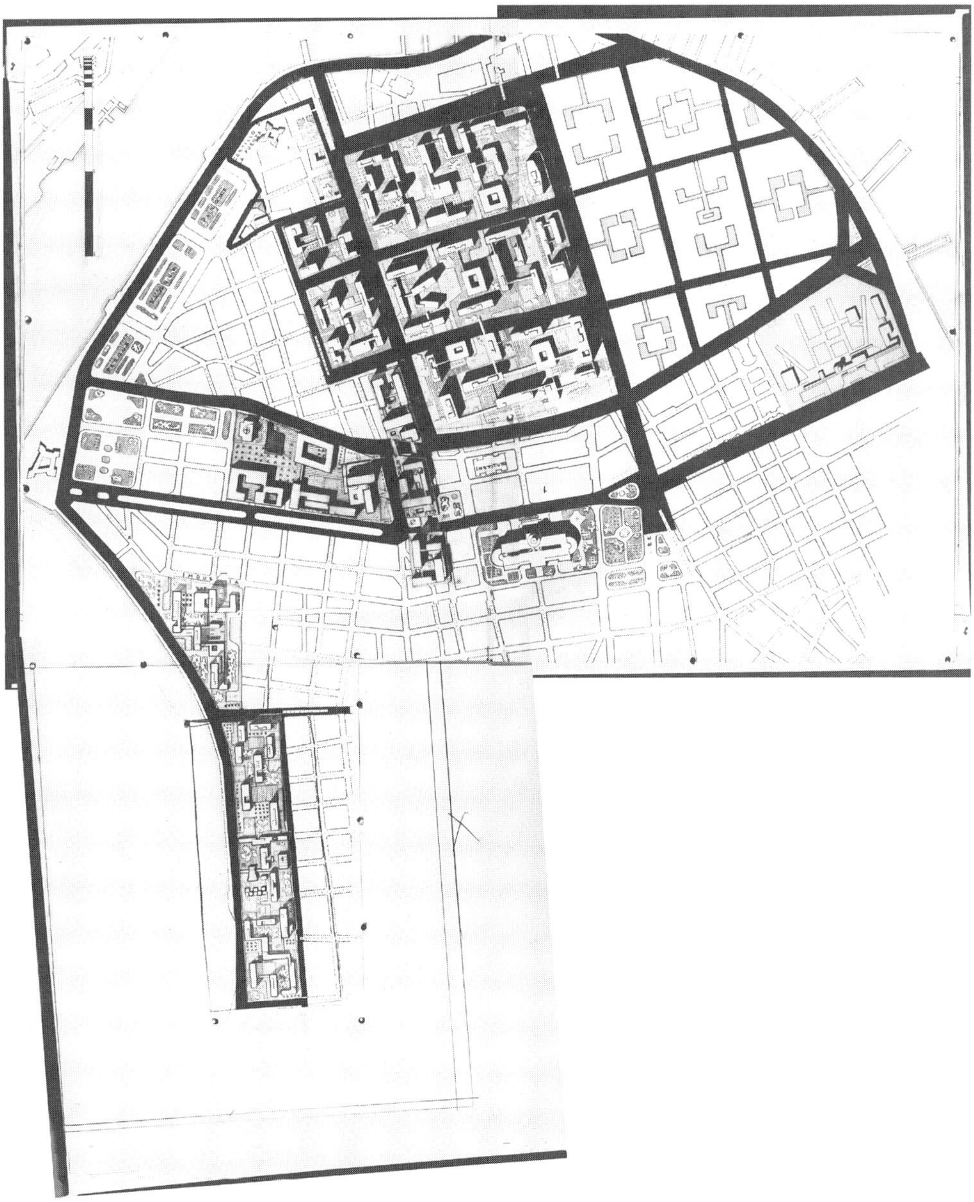

FIGURE 6.6 Junta Nacional de Planificación, composite plan of Habana Vieja studies, circa 1955. Courtesy of Paul Lester Wiener Papers, Box 155, Special Collections and University Archives, University of Oregon Libraries.

north–south roads. A spur of smaller, but still oversized blocks extends west to the Parque Central connecting to another superblock aligned with the Paseo del Prado. The resulting configuration would also have provided, underneath the towers and slabs, a carpet of landscape that cut away the dense, low fabric of much of Habana Vieja, connecting several of Forestier's monumental interventions, civic buildings such as the Capitolio and the presidential palace, and new commercial and cultural buildings. (The plan shows the recently completed Palacio de Bellas Artes on the superblock behind the presidential palace.) This new modern carpet would replace, of course, the consistency of the existing colonial fabric with a very different consistency derived from the typologies and polemics of CIAM discourse combined with the ethical and economic presumptions of North American urban renewal.

Two elements in the composite drawing suggest a degree of irresolution: the area identified as the historic zone between the Plaza de Armas and the Plaza de la Catedral, and the southern, residential zone. In crude outline, the composite drawing indicated that the small existing blocks of this latter area should be consolidated into seven larger blocks, with two partial blocks filling in the corners. A number of existing streets would be eliminated, and colonial structures such as the Convento de Santa Clara would be demolished. Access streets would penetrate to the center of these blocks, which were presumably otherwise solid midrise structures for residential units. Wiener traced a series of studies over this set of blocks, testing different arrangements of street and block, apparently seeking an appropriate balance between each block, an open, usable court at the center, and vehicular traffic and parking. In a few of these drawings, which he dated August 23, Wiener added a number of smaller alleys and courts to each block, reducing the apparent scale of division and creating a more specific diagram of relation between residence, court, and street. The second unresolved element, the representation of the historic zone in the composite drawing, outlined in black, shows the direct juxtaposition of the Plaza de la Catedral at its edge with the new superblocks, in contravention of the 1944 decree. The Plaza de Armas, also, would be open to the new urban fabric at its corner. It is possible that the juxtaposition revealed either a desire to minimize the unproductive land area to be occupied by the historic zone, or an indifference to the effect of the relationship between the new and the colonial structures. But at least one other sketch in the set of studies suggests that the design was approached quite carefully.

Drawn in a plan as an isolated fragment, the historic zone was rendered in detail, with all interior courtyards shown, and shaded to represent the buildings' height. Set in context against the new redevelopment, the open space of the plaza is clearly seen as related to the new urban landscape of the superblock. The desire evident here (distinct perhaps from the consequence) appears not to have been to stifle the historic buildings, but actually to integrate them fully into a new, encompassing civic landscape.

Habana Vieja and the Constitution of Norms

The irresolution of these two elements, the residential block and the historic zone, was perhaps a condition that influenced Sert's and Romañach's subsequent extensive revision of the scheme for Habana Vieja. The additional insights and specific knowledge of the surveys and analyses undertaken during 1956 and then compiled into reference volumes also had an effect on revisions to the plan. By 1957, Sert began to produce drawings of the new arrangement that was ultimately published in the folio *Plan Piloto de la Habana*. Sert had established his primary office in Cambridge as his responsibilities at Harvard made it increasingly difficult to work in the New York office of Town Planning Associates. He and Wiener remained in frequent contact, but the work of the firm was now divided between them. Sert developed the final version of the proposal for Habana Vieja in Cuba with Romañach (who also visited Cambridge and New York) and in his Cambridge studio with his assistant Joseph Zalewski and a small staff.[23] Also important to the context of the later version were the events that transpired in wider architectural discourse during these years. In 1956, the final CIAM congress was held in Dubrovnik, and the critique launched three years earlier by several younger members (the Team X group responsible for the program of the tenth congress) had begun to gain acceptance, not least as a rejection of the precepts of the functional city. The First Urban Design Conference at Harvard was also held in 1956, allowing Sert to move from the primarily European discourse of CIAM to a new primarily North American discourse of urban renewal and urban design.[24] The critique of the comprehensive urban reforms characteristic of early modernism appeared in that same venue as well, in comments by Jane Jacobs that foreshadowed her 1961 publication of *The Death and Life of Great American Cities*. Sert himself received important commissions at this time, beginning with the Baghdad embassy project, which enabled him to develop and refine his architectural idiom, but also to reconsider the role of architecture as an urban artifact.

In its final version, the proposal for Habana Vieja still recommended the comprehensive redevelopment of the old city (see Plate 8). It was still underwritten by the presumptions of urban renewal and by a willingness to adopt the heroic scale of intervention evident in prewar urban proposals such as the Plan Macià, an unrealized master plan devised by Le Corbusier and Sert for the expansion of Barcelona. Yet its configuration differed greatly from the first version; the carpet of landscape supporting segregated towers disappeared, as did some of the high-speed roadways proposed in that scheme. Two such roads remained, one following the east–west route of Calle Muralla to connect the Avenida del Puerto to the main boulevard Reina at the Parque de la Fraternidad, and the other running north–south roughly superimposed on the existing route of Calle Habana. These bisecting roadways, classified as V3, divided Habana Vieja into four quadrants. The northwest quadrant would still be anchored by a commercial area centered on Calle Obispo; the northeast quadrant would contain the banking interests, some in their existing locations, but most in a new financial sector running alongside the new Calle Habana. Towers set on low-rise buildings were arranged in a one-block-wide strip that extended into the center of the district. The original proposal for superblocks had been reduced down to this element, which, although still enormous in scale, especially in relation to the existing fabric, devoted far less land area to high-rise development. The remaining two quadrants were to be residential areas; the fabric of these areas, and of the two northern quadrants except for the financial sector, was to consist of low-rise blocks of four or five stories.

Compared to the earlier version, this final proposal suggested a greater degree of differentiation between parts of Habana Vieja, with the insertion of smaller and contrasting elements within larger orders. In fact, the district was still subordinated to an overall logic of organization, but one less overt than the superblocks of the earlier scheme. The key to this new logic was the road system. Unlike the earlier version, the new plan maintained almost all of the existing streets as routes through the district; the configuration of the existing city would be preserved in the relation of figure and ground. Existing streets, unchanged since the colonial period, contributed to the uniqueness but also to the disadvantages of the district. Sert, Romañach, and Wiener were attentive to both aspects, seeking to alleviate traffic congestion yet "still preserve the scale and charm of the old streets."[25] As a solution, they proposed a selective modification, in which the existing street pattern would be maintained, but alternate streets would be widened for improved traffic access, and parking and vehicular access to the block interiors would be provided off of these streets. The remaining streets would "serve exclusively as a pedestrian access opening to the traditional small scale street of Havana. These old streets are well protected from the tropical sun and can be covered with awnings and lined with arcades. The whole street will be one generous sidewalk where cafes can put chairs and tables and stores can display their goods. They can become even livelier than they once were before the automobile took over."[26] The reference to awnings invokes an image of the historical city, but in terms of social use, perhaps, rather than architectural style. Period photographs show the streets of Habana Vieja veiled with such awnings, and Sert's collection of personal photographs included similar settings that had captured his attention on Ibiza and Mallorca. But this image of the historical city is not a historicist one; it consists rather of an *imagined* social past, one with streets "even livelier that they once were."

Sert favored such informal trappings as a dimension added to architecture by social use and by the types of activities he felt architecture, particularly the architecture of a civic center, should facilitate or frame. He often used photographs of such scenes to elaborate his writings[27] (Figure 6.7). Yet the renderings of the alternating streets that were included in the Plan Piloto were ascetic and suggested only the outline of the idea described in the text. This restraint was in part a matter of format—the folio was a consultant's report rather than a polemical text—and the task of the Plan Piloto was to provide an outline or an armature to be filled in by a subsequent Plan Regulador. The restraint of many of the drawings reflected this condition, as well as what was likely a measure of self-conscious expediency in assembling the work. The asceticism of the diagrams also reflected a distinction between the objective of design, or the socially lived texture of the city, and the orientation of that objective to the construction of a normalizing order. A distinction that could largely be concealed by the conflation of social habits with civic ideals became evident when, through constitutionalism, the civic order was given priority.

Also included in the Plan Piloto were typical sectional diagrams to show the system of streets in Habana Vieja, diagrams that were to serve in part as the *condicionales,* or zoning specifications, for the district (Figure 6.8). These sections

FIGURE 6.7 José Luis Sert, photograph of village street in Ibiza, date unknown. Courtesy of the Frances Loeb Library, Harvard Graduate School of Design.

stipulated the width of the two street types, one to match the existing dimensions and the other several meters wider; the width of the street would also regulate the height of the adjacent blocks, in a set ratio limiting the height of the block according to the width of the street. The diagrams of the *condicionales* also introduced the second overall organizational logic of the scheme: the block or *cuadra*. Describing the street system as a "new approach to the 'cuadra' or grid pattern," the architects implicitly acknowledged a continuity with the original organizational schema of the Laws of the Indies, which had marked out a legal configuration of

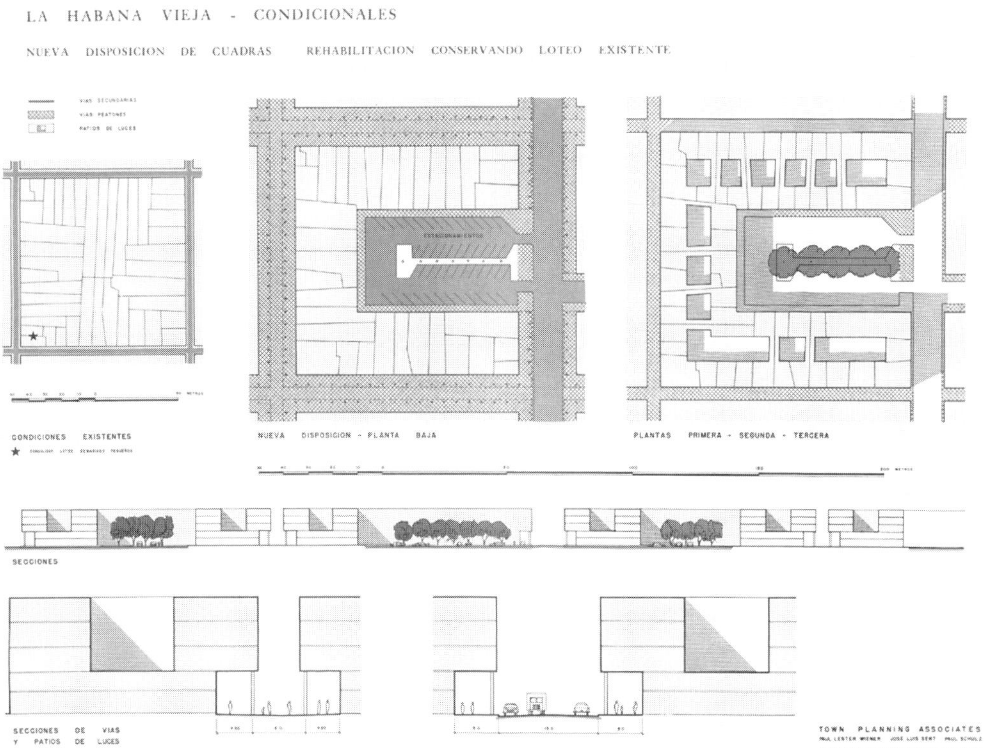

FIGURE 6.8 Town Planning Associates and Junta Nacional de Planificación, typical *condicionales* and block configurations proposed for Habana Vieja, *Plan Piloto de la Habana,* 1955–58. Courtesy of the Frances Loeb Library, Harvard Graduate School of Design.

social hierarchy and property ownership with the physical pattern of a grid. The rigidity of that grid was eased in the proposal for Habana Vieja and the irregularities of the existing arrangement of streets were incorporated. But this accommodation did not necessarily imply an abandonment of the underlying normative order. To the contrary, it permitted such a normative order to be imposed through the conceptual device of the *cuadra*. Each block of Habana Vieja would be conceived in the same fashion: defined by the encircling framework of alternating pedestrian and vehicular streets, a solid block of four- or five-story buildings with an open court at its center available for parking and other uses. The architects reinforced their claim of historical continuity in several ways: first, the open court at the center of the *cuadra:* "The centers of blocks should become public squares with gardens forming a park system that in a way would re-establish the old central patio or cloister pattern that would provide for play spaces and recreation areas besides adding charm to these forgotten parts of the city";[28] second, by introducing arcades along the first story of the blocks facing the streets, employing what they considered to be a characteristic compositional element in Havana directly responsive to the climate (the arcade was not inherently a historicist form, and so could be adapted to modernist idiom and remain suited to prevailing conditions); and third, in the potential maintenance of existing property lots even after the rehabilitation of the *cuadras*.

This last possibility was illustrated in plan diagrams that showed the irregular outlines of plots laid out in the colonial period coexisting with the more regular geometry of the center court and the smaller upper-story courts proposed for the rehabilitated *cuadras*. The maintenance of the existing lots was not necessarily preferred by the architects, who in other aspects of the urban planning work in Cuba argued for more radical revisions to existing property ownership and subdivision, but it offered a concession to a realistic assessment of property transformation. It also exhibited the characteristic advantage of a normative system, in the capacity to absorb the contingencies of the existing reality, "el hecho cubano," and transform their significance with a superimposed order. Sert and Wiener included in the Plan Piloto a model of a typical *cuadra* proposed for their Bogotá plan (Figure 6.9). In Bogotá, where their scheme had similarly divided the city into sectors with classified roads, the *cuadra* served as a unit of urban fabric, although without the historic engagement prompted in the proposal for Habana Vieja. The photograph of the model shows a structure similar to that recommended for Havana, with its lower story an arcade and its center an open court with vehicular access and elements of landscape; smaller upper-story courts provide light and air to individual apartments within the block. The model illustrated only a typical block, however, and a variety of realizations would have been envisioned, including the possibility that, as Sert and Wiener indicated in additional drawings, some existing buildings within any given *cuadra* might remain, bonded into the overall block alongside new constructions. A similar possibility was envisioned for Habana Vieja; the plan shows a typical uniformity of the *cuadras*, as if they were all entirely new construction, but the indication that lot lines might be preserved and the logic of the normative system both demonstrate that considerably more variety could have resulted, with some blocks simply renovated or restored, others partially rehabilitated or modified, and others completely reconstructed.

FIGURE 6.9 Town Planning Associates, model of typical *cuadra* proposed for Bogotá plan, reproduced in *Plan Piloto de la Habana.* Courtesy of the Frances Loeb Library, Harvard Graduate School of Design.

The new *condicionales* would have regulated such modifications or reconstructions, limiting the variation in mass and scale between old and new buildings, although permitting clear stylistic and material differentiations. They defined the typical *cuadra* mass in relationship to street and to court with height and setback requirements, or, in other words, with bulk zoning. Sert was evidently preoccupied with the definition of these and other *condicionales* in the Plan Piloto. His notes, for example, included data on setbacks at several new subdivisions in the city, as well as dimensions from colonial buildings. Historic areas like the colonial city of Trinidad might, he conceded, have unique requirements, but he proposed that existing typical buildings could "be used as measuring units and help toward the determination of lot sizes, clearances between buildings, setbacks from street lines, and yard spaces." His intention was to define "standards that . . . fit as well as possible into the established customs of the country."[29] The relation between new *condicionales* and existing buildings was especially pointed in the cities that the JNP identified as historic centers that were to be preserved as touristic venues, but Havana Vieja was not in fact similarly categorized as a tourist site to be preserved in its entirety. In a 1956 memo, Wiener advised:

> For reasons of touristic interest as well as other considerations, cities like Trinidad, Nueva Gerona and others, should maintain their colonial patrimony. For the planning of such cities, studies should be undertaken for the design of *new architectural interpretations of buildings and new standards* for windows, roofs, colonnades, doors, marquees, and so on. The new interpretations should maintain the colonial proportions. The studies should not be approached from the archeological point of view which tries to copy the old patterns; a new modern architecture should be evolved that corresponds to the best of the colonial traditions in terms of utility and architectural proportions, human scale, building heights, and so on.[30]

In Habana Vieja, the balance was apparent, but normalization remained the unmistakable aim. For the *cuadra* configurations in the district, pedestrian streets maintained the narrow width of the original street while vehicular streets were dimensioned for their new traffic-flow requirements. The height of the *cuadra,* however, was actually set in proportion to the width of the street by an angle derived from Le Corbusier's Modulor; the complementary Modulor angle determined the dimensions of the interior *patio* openings.

An equally important dimension of the scheme in this regard was the proposed disposition of the historic monuments. By 1957, the staff of the JNP had completed its detailed surveys of Habana Vieja, and both Sert and Wiener had spent considerable time in the city over the preceding three years. Both were cognizant of the unique "character of Old Havana," and sought to preserve it in part. The potential touristic value of the district was understood, even though it was not emphasized as a criterion of the plan (possibly because the city of Havana as a whole was considered to be the touristic venue). Greater attention was paid to the district's role as a commercial center. Sert and Wiener cautioned that the commercial center of the city was not fixed, and that businesses could and would migrate to other areas of the city if its core were not rehabilitated. They claimed to seek a balance between these two concerns, for character and for function, as evidenced in the rationale for the strip of high-rise buildings at the center of the district: "Although this banking and office rehabilitation project should be limited in size, it is nonetheless necessary to develop such a project in Old Havana because office facilities are necessary in the proximity of the harbor. Higher buildings may be allowed in this area, while they should be strictly limited in the remaining sectors of Old Havana."[31] The real physical artifacts to be preserved (as distinct from qualities such as scale or character) consisted of specific monuments, such as the cathedral, and "several clusters of colonial houses which should be preserved as groups. They are not interesting enough as isolated buildings but form charming streets, beautiful in scale, recalling the origins of the city when it was peaceful and devoid of the congestion and noises that progress and mechanization have brought to the modern metropolis."[32] Most of these buildings of "archaeological interest" were situated in the northeast quadrant of the new plan, in the two clusters around the Plaza de la Catedral and the Plaza de Armas. The old convents in the southern part of Habana Vieja were also preserved as blocks, easily assimilated into the *cuadra* layout. The detailed drawing of the plan suggests how these monuments might have coexisted with the new *cuadras*. Rather than the blunt juxtapositions of the earlier scheme, in which the open space of the plazas was crudely equated with the open spaces of the superblock carpets, in the later scheme, historic buildings are set within *cuadras;* the remaining lots might be preserved buildings or new constructions, or perhaps a composite—the drawing indicates that building facades along two sides of the Plaza Vieja should be preserved even if the structures behind them are not. The striking aspect of these details is the suggestion of an almost seamless resolution or calibration of the singular and the typical. Both meet in a planned conjunction, with the singular—whether historic, like the cathedral, or new, like the financial sector—to be limited in its scope, and the typical to be expanded.

The Projection of the Civic Landscape

Publication of the Plan Piloto coincided with the republican period's concluding moments, and the text published in the folio volumes of the *Plan Piloto de La Habana* presciently cautioned that "a city is a living organism, subject to continuous changes and that a master plan can at best only guide those impending changes."[33] In the spring of 1959, Wiener and Sert did attempt to bring the Plan Piloto to the attention of the new revolutionary government, but the sudden political upheaval had transformed governmental and institutional intentions; their Cuban colleagues in the JNP all faced a pressing calculus of professional and personal decisions, and no clear means for advocating the Plan Piloto existed. The expectation that a pilot plan could "define the design-skeleton of the city" presumed circumstances of evolutionary, not revolutionary, change, in which the skeleton could remain flexible enough to be revised or adapted to changing conditions that exceeded foreseen eventualities, while its constituent parts and their attachments would remain the armature of future developments. Proceeding from the scale of the nation, with a diagram of Cuba's centrality to air routes in the region, to the scale of the region or province, to the scale of the city, the sector, and the neighborhood unit, the folio pages of the *Plan Piloto de la Habana* illustrated how instruments such as the sectors, the classified road system, the *cuadras,* and the linear parks and civic centers would produce the multiple dimensions of this skeleton. These typicalities might (in fact, almost certainly would) be embodied in idiosyncratic fashion, like El Reparto Santa Catalina, but they would still cohere through the skeleton of the plan.

The evolutionary presumption of a progressive historical process rather than a discontinuous one, and the skeletal metaphor, emphasized the organicist perspective declared by the depiction of the city as an organism. In an essay for the symposium volume *New Architecture and City Planning,* to which Sert and Wiener also contributed essays, the philosopher George Boas objected to the organic analogy:

> The analogy is tempting but misleading. In spite of the emotional force of such a term as "growth" or "vital" and their derivatives, there are certain important respects in which animals and plants differ from cities. The main difference is that what Aristotle called an *entelechy* is missing in cities. Maple keys left alone grow into maple trees, eggs turn into chicks. Cities, however, have no "natural" terminus but simply spread and sprawl, attaining neither a maximum size nor an inevitable shape. One of the functions of art is precisely to control nature, not to submit to it on all occasions.[34]

The illusory conception of a natural process at work in the growth of the city would prompt a misguided characterization of urban design as a corollary to that process, rather than as practice of artifice or in Boas's words, a work of art, a conscious act of intelligence applied to existing constraints. The distinctions between an artistic perspective and a scientific perspective—often a forced distinction but nevertheless one established decades earlier by Martínez Inclán as relevant to the question of the city—were apparent in Cuba, but in the end the mediation of those two perspectives was effected by the latent paradigm that both embraced, the paradigm of constitutionalism. Boas further argued that the central difficulty in addressing the city plan as a work of art was the city itself: "The most persistent and clearly unavoidable obstacle to perfect urbanism is the existence of the city for which one is making plans. It exists not only materially in a given location, but also culturally, impregnated with certain social prejudices and customs, and economically."[35] Such factors, however, could be discerned and evaluated, and thus subjected to the regulatory regime of city planning in manner similar to the use of material in any architectural object.

With its emphasis on system, classification, and typicality combined with its corresponding acceptance of a spectrum of realizations within those structures, the Plan Piloto de la Habana bears an affinity to a constitution, an affinity that would have been all the more apparent had the projected legislation of *condicionales* accompanied it, but which remains even in the absence of that explicitly juridical element, produced by the framework of norms that at once derived from existing reality and constituted it. The physical contextualism of its proposals should not be overstated—the Plan Piloto called for the wholesale alteration of Habana Vieja, and the linear financial sector would have stood as a radical contrast to the historic monuments a few hundred meters away—but its fuller potential as Haar's "impermanent constitution" should not be overlooked. The Plan Piloto attempted to reconcile the historical contingencies of the existing Habana Vieja (historic monuments, property, and typical character) and the normative order of an overall conceptual plan (the sectors, the classified road system, and *condicionales*). At the scale of the sector of Habana Vieja it became possible to represent these two elements quite factually as actual buildings and as real dimensions, so that the historical real contributed its existing patterns, and perhaps limitations, to the larger configurations of the normative order. The Plan Piloto was a representation not only of a future Havana, but of its present condition normalized and re-presented as an image of the city. Perhaps the concept of entelechy might be differently placed, not as the basis for the organic

FIGURE 6.10 Photograph of El Templete collected by Town Planning Associates as documentation of Habana Vieja. Courtesy of the Frances Loeb Library, Harvard Graduate School of Design.

fallacy, but as the corollary to constitutionalism; for what are the normative structures and organizations of the Plan Piloto but rules, codes, or laws of future development? And what is the aspiration of planning but the normative constraint of the future on behalf of the present? The task of urban design, then, was to produce or install a correlative entelechy in the physical dimension of the city and thereby regulate the transformation not only of that dimension, but its interaction with social, political, and economic spheres as well—in short, to prefigure a civic landscape.

It was a natural process of entelechy that produced the Árbol de la Fraternidad Americana from the seed of the ceiba tree planted at the founding of the Cuban Republic. The genealogy of national formation that accompanied the tree itself was fashioned in the documents of historical records. When Roig de Leuchsenring examined those records in 1957 to give a descriptive account of El Templete, the memorial building at the site of the original ceiba, he discerned sufficient discrepancies in the recorded events of the city's foundation to confidently declare that the conflation of the first mass, the first *cabildo,* and the site of El Templete was false (Figure 6.10). This determination would not undermine the significance of the foundational elements; it would only reveal the nature of their construction into a narrative of national development. Once revealed as an artifice, that narrative gained more, not less, resonance with similar artifices that participated in the constructions of constitutionalism. Despite the naturalizing effects of Forestier's plan and urban projects, the Parque de la Fraternidad Americana remained suspended as a symbol, a point in the city but incomplete as a civic object; its extension could be achieved with a broader confluence of law, planning, and architecture acting upon the political register of civil society through the projection of physical artifacts and normative orders projecting not what will be but what ought to be.

III

Monument

7 The Experience of Civic Conscience

Designs for the Monumento a Martí

THE enactment of civil society undertaken by citizens during the republican period included both affirmative and oppositional actions, the casting of ballots, for example, as well as participation in strikes. In the context of the revolutionary period that followed after 1959, the performances of civil society possessed a different valence entirely, bracketed by their political setting. As Fidel Castro would phrase it in a speech to intellectuals in the summer of 1961: "What are the rights of revolutionary or nonrevolutionary writers and artists? Within the Revolution: all; against the Revolution, none."[1] Immediately after Castro's coming to power, all of the institutions and mechanisms of civil society were scrutinized, challenged, manipulated, or abolished. The Junta Nacional de Planificación, for example, continued to operate, but with a new director, a changed mandate, and uncertain political sponsorship. Within such transformations, some considered and others capricious, the civic role of architecture was loosened from its prior foundations, yet it retained a relevance of civic connotation. One event might serve to illuminate the particular mutability of architecture's role: organized by the church and held in Havana in November 1959, the Primer Congreso Católico Nacional began as thousands of participants arriving from around Cuba assembled in the vast space of the Plaza de la República—which would now be known as Plaza de la Revolución—to celebrate mass at a temporary altar designed by the architect Eugenio Batista. Above the crowd towered the newly completed Monumento a Martí, with its sculpture of the national hero. Here, conjoined acts of congregation marked a civil declaration of identity, prerogative, and desire on the part of the citizens who participated. Indeed, their participation as citizens was the salient gesture in an urban space and in front of an architectural monument designed to commemorate the possibility of Cuban citizenship by soliciting a focused civic attention.

This monument was the belated result of Presidential Decree No. 1631 of June 2, 1937, which created the Comisión Central Pro-Monumento a Martí, an appointed body of government, military, and business leaders given responsibility for devising and executing a suitable national commemoration of José Martí. At its first meeting, the Comisión Pro-Monumento solicited and heard the opinions of prominent intellectuals and artists. Also in attendance was Colonel Batista, the authority behind the provisional government who was fawningly credited as the source of the idea and the key supporter of the process. Various proposals for commemoration were made, but it appears that the solution of a monument was preferred from the start, at least by Batista, whose opinion would have been decisive: "After an ample debate in which many speakers participated and presented diverse plans for said glorification, Colonel Batista . . . led the meeting to what was, really, in the minds of all present: the erection of a Monument, symbolic of the unique and polyfacetic personality of José Martí, a writer, poet, thinker, philosopher and orator, an Apostol and Martir of our struggle for Liberty, which culminated with Cuba's Independence."[2] In further meetings following that decision, the Comisión Pro-Monumento selected as the site for the monument the Loma de los Catalanes, the location of the civic center proposed by Forestier in his Plano del Proyecto de la Habana. The new Monumento a Martí would be the central focus of that civic square, taking advantage of the rise of the hill amplifying the monument's effect.

The ambition to erect a monument in Havana to the martyred leader of the Cuban independence movement arose as one aspect of the larger deification of José Martí (who was colloquially known as El Apóstol). Through his writings and political theories, as well as through recollections of his actions and demeanor and his death in battle, Martí served as a potent symbol of national consciousness during the early republican period. His written works, initially not widely read, were now rediscovered and republished; his image appeared in paintings and statues. The construction of a national monument was proposed and debated following the 1933 revolution, and authorized in December 1935, notwithstanding the opinion voiced by Gonzalo de Quesada y Miranda (an authority on Martí who was editing the writer's collected works) that only a living monument would suitably reflect the ideas and the example of El Apóstol. Schools, for example, or a professorship for the study of Martí's doctrines would be more appropriate than a lavish monument whose very grandeur would discord with the poet's ascetic life.[3] But monuments to honor national heroes and to commemorate historical events were being constructed in the expanding districts of the city and elsewhere in the country, and although one statue of Martí already stood in the Parque Central, Cuba did not possess a central national monument equivalent, for example, to any on the Mall in Washington, D.C. Moreover, the provisional governments of the period, and behind those governments Colonel Batista himself, regarded such physical symbols as means to consolidate support and assert legitimacy. The choice of a monument over other possible forms of commemoration was not remarkable. Its durability and visibility as an embodiment of national consciousness would have held considerably more appeal than a literary effort or a social program, whose greater compatibility with Martí's own sensibilities was nevertheless compromised by their intangibility. A large-scale building project promised a direct economic benefit, and therefore a political benefit as well. In that regard, the Monumento a Martí was no different from the construction of the Central Highway or the water infrastructure of the city. In the terms of planning, a monument lacking the pragmatic use of such projects might be categorized as an excessive expenditure or a nonfunctional object, but it could still produce functional effects in the economic sphere in a manner similar to such projects, and even to a degree that living memorials would not achieve. More crucially, though, the task of the monument, across the extended historical transition from the 1930s to the 1960s, was to prompt the civic recognition required to transmute the larger orders of planning into the realities of civic behavior. While a living memorial such as a school could participate in those realities, the aim of the Monumento a Martí would be to intercede in and alter them through the representational capacities of architecture.

Designs for the Monumento a Martí

The Comisión Pro-Monumento opened an architectural competition for the design of the Monumento a Martí in March 1938, publishing a volume containing the competition rules, topographic information about the site and Forestier's proposed civic center, a synoptic biography and photographic portraits of Martí, and excerpts from his works and an annotated bibliography, all printed in the four main languages of the Americas.[4] An introductory statement in the volume emphasized the influence of Martí's thought and deeds on the American continent as a whole, and his role as a successor to Simón Bolívar in producing an American consciousness for which he was to be honored by a competition open to citizens of any of the twenty-two American nations. In Cuba, which had been the focus of his political efforts and the site of his death, Martí's example would be preserved for future generations in the monument, "an altar of civic consecration where nationality feels itself glorified and strengthened."[5] Competitors—architects and sculptors paired in teams—were to design a fitting monument to José Martí at the Loma de los Catalanes, taking into account Forestier's arrangement, though not beholden to its formal composition in locating the position of their monument or in locating the surrounding buildings. Additional buildings at the site were to include the National Library and National Archives, the Academies of History and of Arts and Letters, the School of Fine Arts and the Conservatory of Music, and a large auditorium. Only the location, and not the specific form, of these structures had to be considered in the proposals, but somewhere in direct relation to the monument itself the submissions were to include space for a library and a museum dedicated to books and memorabilia associated with Martí. Finally, the brief pointedly imposed two further stipulations on the representational dimension of the monument: the designs were to be faithful symbolizations of Martí and his philosophy and at the same time to be completely original in form. The documentary photographs, the excerpted writings, and the biographical information had been provided in order to accomplish the first aim; by enabling competitors to understand the diversity of Martí's thought, these addenda might help them satisfy the requirement that his representation "express his moral greatness, his genius, and his simple life." With regard to the second stipulation, the brief called for the monument to be "a free architectural and sculptural conception," implying a creative solution unconstrained by prior example or notion.[6] Embedded within these requirements for both representational fidelity *and* novelty was the ambition to situate Martí, and through Martí the Cuban nation, in broader tendencies of modernity and freedom that the brief invoked unequivocally:

> Article 14.—MODERN EXPRESSION
> The Monument projects shall be original and unpublished and its lines shall constitute an expression of contemporaneous architecture and sculpture, with a careful study as to the effects of light.
> Article 15.—ALLEGORIES AND SYMBOLISM
> The Monument shall constitute a symbol of Martí's greatness and a representation of human freedom in a universal sense, as corresponds to the conception thereof always maintained by the Apostol. The Civic Square and the great buildings to be located thereon, shall complete the same.[7]

These two articles bound the meaning of the monument (as distinct from its understood commemorative function) and the surrounding civic plaza to a temporal emphasis placed on the present historical moment. It would have been clearly understood that the monument was to participate in the greater project of national development. To achieve this aim required an architectural conception that fashioned its relation to historical precedent as a narrative of progress and maturation, and consequently demanded that architecture both represent and supersede the past. This problematic underlay many variants of modernism; however, the required "Modern Expression" was not a call for stylistic modernism, as various entries would show. It did later provide an elastic standard for the stylistic assessment of the projects that would take on increasing importance as the debate over the monument developed, but it was at this moment a condensed articulation of the desire to constitute a present embodiment of a prior potential of civic aspiration.

Forty-seven entries were submitted to the competition, the majority from Cuba, several from the United States and from Brazil, and a handful from Mexico and Colombia. In reviewing these entries, the Comisión was assisted by a Comisión Técnica of four architects: Pedro Martínez Inclán, J. M. Bens Arrarte, Alberto Prieto, and José Menéndez. The architects advised the jury that none of the projects adequately fulfilled the intentions of the competition and that the first prize should not be awarded. The jury agreed with their suggestion, withheld the gold medal, and awarded the silver medal to a design submitted by Jean Labatut in collaboration with Enrique Varela, Raúl Otero, and two sculptors, Oliverio Waterland and J. Herrera. Ten other projects were premiated, including a design by Aquiles Maza, Raúl Macías, and Eugenio Batista with the prominent

Cuban sculptor Juan José Sicre, as well as a design by the young Mexican architect Mario Pani, then just beginning his career as one of the leading figures of the modern movement in Mexico. Some of the projected designs employed variations of classical style, with colonnaded atrium or temple configurations framing statues of Martí standing or seated. Others rendered the monument in the streamlined forms of modern deco, or the spare lines of an ascetic classicism.

In their design, Labatut, Varela, and Otero proposed a tall obelisk set at one edge of an enormous square plaza (Figures 7.1, 7.2). A ramp and stairs led down to a lower, formally landscaped area connected to a wide boulevard extending to the base of the Castillo del Príncipe. At the opposite, southern end of this proposed "Centro Cívico Martí," a semicircular ring of buildings provided a backdrop for the monument and a radial distribution of avenues opening toward the outskirts. Although it resembled somewhat Forestier's original schematic proposal—unsurprising given that Labatut and Otero had worked with the French urbanist a decade earlier—the scheme was considerably more refined and gave detailed consideration to connecting new boulevards and the required institutional buildings into the existing fabric of the city (Figure 7.3, 7.4). The monument itself was a composition in three parts: a plinth, the obelisk, and the statue. Both obelisk and plinth were articulated with five flanges in order to resemble in plan a five-pointed star—a representation, the designers explained, of the star upon the Cuban flag, itself a representation of liberty. At the base of the obelisk, inside the plinth, a visitor would find the library and museum, and at the top of the extruded obelisk would stand the statue of Martí, more than sixteen meters tall, overlooking the city of Havana.

Although this design received the highest prize, the jury had decided that no scheme was compelling enough to be selected and built as the winning design, and so, in the spring of 1939, the Comisión Pro-Monumento moved to hold a second, open competition, calling for the submission of ideas rendered in any form or medium for the monument. Many of the competitors from the first competition resubmitted their designs with some modifications. Having made small adjustments to their proposal, Labatut and his collaborators submitted a descriptive pamphlet to present the arguments in its favor, and the pamphlet's lengthy title—"Descripción sintética del proyecto basado en la simplicidad, dignidad y simbolismo de la planta en estrella y la cristalización de la Bandera Cubana" (Synthetic description of the project based on the simplicity, dignity, and symbolism

FIGURE 7.1 Jean Labatut, Raúl Otero, and Enrique Varela, perspective, Monumento a Martí (First Proposal), 1938. From *Pencil Points,* March 1939.

FIGURE 7.2 Jean Labatut, Raúl Otero, and Enrique Varela, plan, Monumento a Martí (First Proposal), 1938. Jean Labatut Papers, Department of Rare Books and Special Collections, Princeton University Library.

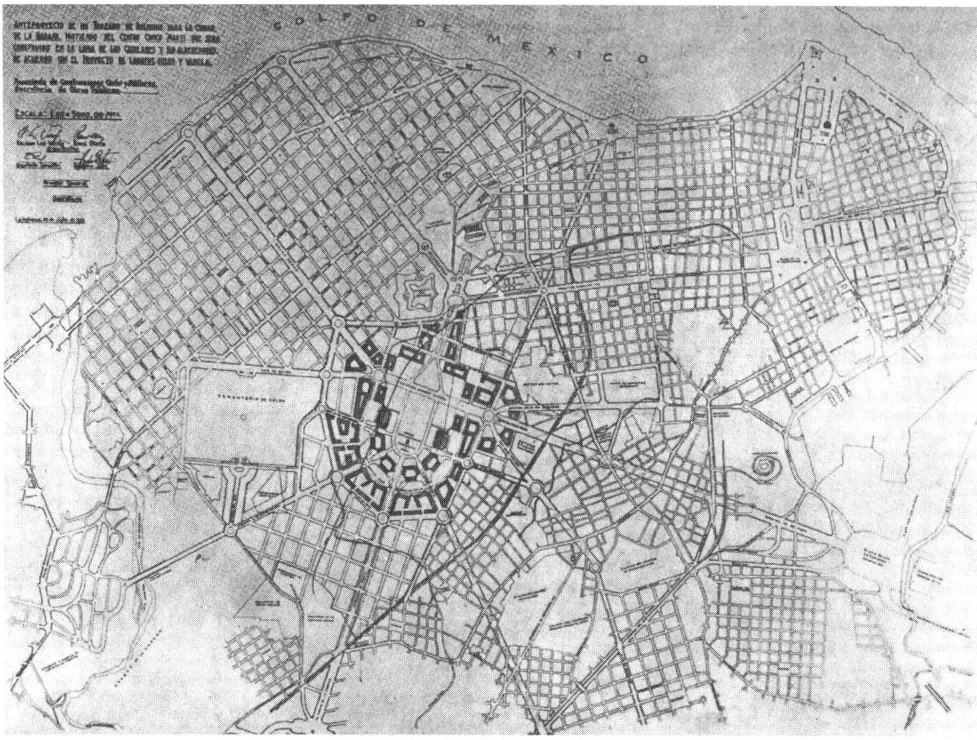

FIGURE 7.3 Jean Labatut, Raúl Otero, and Enrique Varela, site plan, Monumento a Martí (First Proposal), 1938. *Arquitectura,* March–April 1940.

FIGURE 7.4 Jean Labatut, Raúl Otero, and Enrique Varela, model, Monumento a Martí (First Proposal), 1938. From *Pencil Points,* March 1939.

of the star-plan and the crystallization of the Cuban Flag)—made clear that referentiality was the central element of these arguments. New entries added to the resubmissions made a total of seventy-eight proposals, but once again the jury declined to select any scheme as the winner. The jury did, however, propose that the overall design for the civic center proposed by Labatut, Varela, and Otero should be accepted as the basic plan for the site, so that whichever monument was eventually selected was to be set within their urban composition. Although the qualities of the specific proposals may have been the proximate cause of the jury's equivocation, its indecision reflected also the ambiguity prevailing in the national project as a whole. After all, this representation of the nation in monumental form was being judged not subsequent to but in parallel with the formulation of the nation being pursued in the constitutional debates.

Continuing its effort to obtain a fitting design for the monument, the jury reversed the open approach of the second stage, and instead selected ten of the proposals that appeared the most promising and requested those ten teams to submit new designs by the end of 1940. After meeting in April 1941 to review the new submissions, the Comisión approved subsidies of four thousand pesos for each of three teams to produce larger-scale maquettes for the jury to review. The three teams selected for this final stage were Labatut, Varela, and Otero, now joined by two other architects, Victor Morales and Manuel Tapia Ruano, and the sculptor Alexander Sambugnac; the team of Aquiles Maza and Juan José Sicre; and the team of Evelio Govantes and Félix Cabarrocas. These three teams submitted their proposals, refined and rendered in the detailed maquettes, in February 1942. Their designs were exhibited the following month in the hall of Los Pasos Perdidos of the Capitolio Nacional and reviewed by the jury for the final selection. The composition of the jury had changed over the preceding three years; no architects served as members, although Martínez Inclán, Bens Arrarte, and Menéndez still served as advisers on a technical commission that also included Gonzalo de Quesada y Miranda, the leading authority on Martí. Advisers submitted opinions to the jury, but did not vote or participate in deliberations; representatives of art and architecture were thus subordinated, and though three engineers served on the jury proper, it was dominated by representatives of the Cuban military. However, two important intellectual figures, Emilio Roig de Leuchsenring and Jorge Mañach, had been added to the jury, and its composition reflected the congruence of several motives, with the political consolidation sought by the government joined to the cultural and civic consciousness desired by intellectuals like Mañach and Roig de Leuchsenring, and supplemented in this instance by the disciplinary and discursive interests of architects like Martínez Inclán (who was simultaneously engaged in the advocacy efforts of the Patronato Pro-Urbanismo, which issued its manifesto and extensive publicity during this same year).

After deliberations, the jury announced its decision: the proposal by Maza and Sicre received nine votes; the design of Govantes and Cabarrocas, five; and the project by Labatut and his collaborators, three. Aquiles Maza and Juan José Sicre had won the competition and their design for the Monumento a Martí would be built on the Loma de los Catalanes.[8] Their scheme proposed a "templo martiano" (temple of Martí), a double colonnade, rectangular in plan, surrounding an open atrium to be called the Patio of Honor (Figures 7.5, 7.6). Within the atrium, rising up seventeen meters to the height of the columns, a statue of the seated figure of Martí would look down toward visitors to the monument. Behind the statue an enclosed space, also extended upward to the full height of the columns, would house the library and the museum. Spare details tempered somewhat the resolute classicism of the architectural design; cylindrical columns without base or capital supported a severe entablature without profiles or ornament (Figures 7.7, 7.8). The temple would thus appear more as a frame than a building, an effect to be reinforced by the drama of the visitor's approach. From the lower plaza, a visitor would first be confronted by an enormous bas-relief illustrated with historical scenes carved on the plinth of the monument above. Two flanking stairs rose gradually alongside these images to the perimeter of the colonnade above; a visitor might climb these stairs to stand within the enormous stoa and look across the sunken court within to view the statue. At the base of the two flanking stairs, between them and on axis with the figure of Martí, a door led directly into the interior of the temple. Entering through this door, the visitor would arrive at the Patio of Honor, an enclosed court a level below the statue and at the foot of a stair filling the breadth of the hall leading up past the statue to the museum and library beyond. These sectional contrivances exaggerated the sense of a building hollowed out, a void left open to shelter the icon within from the city around it. This seeming remove from the city, underscored by the overwhelming scale of the monument and the sculptural figure it contained, would take on a further emphasis at night when, presumably lit from within, the Patio

FIGURE 7.5 Aquiles Maza and Juan José Sicre, site model, Monumento a Martí (Third Competition), 1943. *Arquitectura,* October 1943.

FIGURE 7.6 Aquiles Maza and Juan José Sicre, front elevation view of model, Monumento a Martí (Third Competition), 1943. *Arquitectura,* October 1943.

FIGURE 7.7 Aquiles Maza and Juan José Sicre, view of statue maquette, Monumento a Martí (Third Competition), 1943. *Arquitectura,* October 1943.

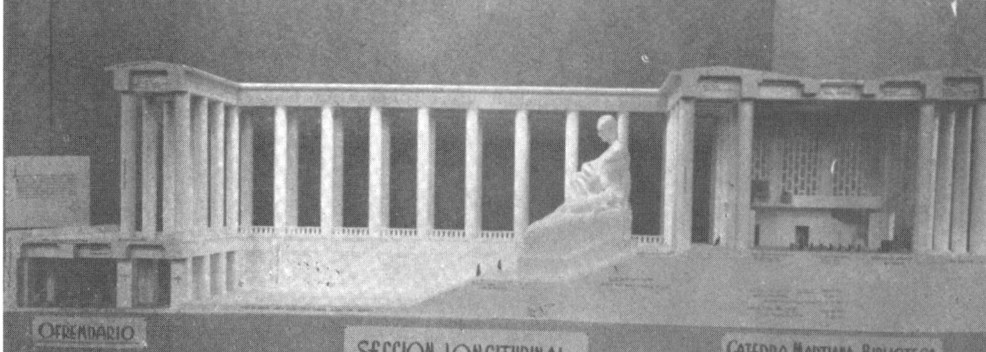

FIGURE 7.8 Aquiles Maza and Juan José Sicre, sectional model, Monumento a Martí (Third Competition), 1943. *Arquitectura,* October 1943.

of Honor and the seated figure of Martí would become an illuminated beacon in the city.

For some jurors the Maza and Sicre project may have offered a compromise of sorts between the solutions proposed by the other two teams. Govantes and Cabarrocas had presented a scheme for a monumental library with a slender vertical tower overlooking the civic center—as much an actual building as a monument. Labatut, Varela, and Otero submitted the obelisk, now refashioned into a pyramidal, tapering form but still topped by the statue of Martí, as one solution, and also presented a revised version in which the vertical element was split into two shafts separated a slight distance, with the statue set at ground level between them. All of the projects received some support from members of the jury, and although the Maza and Sicre design was selected, it did not garner overwhelming support. Some members of the jury abstained from voting. Gonzalo de Quesada y Miranda, submitting his opinion as a member of the technical committee, declined to endorse any of the schemes, and restated his conviction that Martí could be appropriately honored only by a functional or useful project, one that acknowledged Martí's disdain for the monumental and the grandiose. Another member of the technical committee, Bens Arrarte, gave close consideration to the relationship between architecture and sculpture in each proposal, seeking out what he felt was the necessary balance of force and equality of sophistication between the two. Mañach and Roig de Leuchsenring both supported Maza's and Sicre's design, and voted in its favor as members of the jury. Mañach offered particular support for the proposed sculpture, while other jurors voted for the scheme only on the condition that Sicre further refine the sculpture.

Consensus as to the purpose of the monument could be agreed upon. It is unlikely that anyone disputed Bens Arrarte's summary of three functions—"*to honor,* perpetuating in memory; *to inspire,* lifting the qualities of the spirit; and *to teach,* that is to say, opening perspectives to understanding"—but the fulfillment of those requirements in architecture and in sculpture provoked disagreement.[9] The form of the architectonic elements, the associations they provoked, and the precedents they invoked; the expressive character of the sculpture, the human qualities that it emphasized, or the symbolic attributions that it attempted—these elements produced the points of interpretation and dispute. The original competition brief had called for "modern expression" and originality, but also for the "symbolic or stylized" representation of Martí's attributes, while cautioning against the "arbitrary" association of representational form and content. In attempting to reconcile these demands in the first stage of the competition, several of the competitors seized upon one particular excerpt from Martí's writings included in the competition volume. "Liberty," Martí declared, "ought already to have its architecture. Not having it, it suffers." He called for "an architecture never before seen, where the redemption of thought will be consecrated," to replace the existing forms that signified and perpetuated existing hegemonies.[10] Fifty years on, in the context of realizing a monument to Cuba's independence, this phrase was construed to legitimate several disparate approaches that each staked a claim of originality. In the descriptive text appended to their first submission, Labatut, Varela, and Otero identified "Liberty" as the core of Martí's thought and life and so claimed, "that is what our project represents: The Architecture of Liberty, of that Liberty of which he said 'it suffered for not yet having its architecture.'" Martí's phrase "was precisely the phrase that served as inspiration for us during the entire process of development of our Project: something never before seen, unprecedented, absolutely original."[11] From this inspiration came their decision to employ the star of the Cuban flag as the plan of the monument, and to extrude its form vertically as the physical embodiment of that star, which linked the historical person of José Martí, the "universal concept" of Liberty, and the nation of Cuba.

This instantiation of the image of the star as a physical form aimed to achieve the referentiality required by the competition brief, and a literal form that established a reference between the monument and the flag also abided the stricture against "arbitrary" associations of form and content. The effort to define an appropriate "symbolic and stylized" representation of Martí, his person, and his intellectual contributions through a referential construction necessarily defined a historical position as well because the formulation of the nation from which reference would be established was a historicizing process. The Convención Constituyente in 1940 included a lengthy discussion between the delegates over the wording of article 5 of the new charter, which defined three national symbols: the flag, the seal, and the anthem of Cuba. The draft of the constitutional text written by preliminary committees defined the national flag with an exacting description of its proportion, its geometric figures, and its colors. The star was to be white, with five points, one oriented upward, proportioned to sit within a circumference one-third the breadth of the flag. As debate on article 5 began, Jorge

Mañach proposed that the text be amended to read: "The flag of the Republic is that which was raised in the fort of El Morro in Havana on the 20th of May, 1902, upon the transfer of public power to the people of Cuba."[12] To designate the national flag, Mañach was proposing that rather than provide a description of the flag's actual appearance, the constitutional text should identify a historical moment—the first day of Cuban independence—in which the flag attained a national significance. This concise designation, Mañach argued, would not only be more appropriate to a constitutional text, it would also secure an "unequivocal" reference that would put the definition of the national flag beyond doubt through its attachment to a historical event. Another delegate proposed a further elaboration of the historicity of the flag, moving that article 5 commence with the words "The flag of the Republic is that of Narciso López." López was the originator of the flag's design, which he commissioned prior to two incursions into Cuba in 1850 and 1851 that he hoped would initiate a rebellion against Spanish rule; when the independence wars began in 1869, the declared independence movement adopted his flag as its banner. A third delegate proposed an even more detailed text to include the poet Miguel Teurbe Tolón and his wife, who designed and sewed the flag for López. This last amendment was not adopted, but Mañach's amendment with the addition of López's name was accepted, effectively replacing the conventional abstraction of the draft text with the grain of historical reality.

Similar transactional efforts were evident in the competition for the Monumento a Martí, in which the necessarily historicizing representations incorporated imitative strategies and techniques. Quesada y Miranda, in offering his view of the final three selected projects, argued that a monument intended to honor Martí should begin by "respecting as much as possible his original 'American' architectonic vision, and accord with the style conceived by his always brilliant mind."[13] Quesada y Miranda was referring to Martí's sketched proposal for an American order of architecture to join the five classical orders. This new order, which Martí associated with his declaration of a new American consciousness, would use the palm tree as its referent. The new monument, Quesada y Miranda suggested, should "to the greatest degree possible correspond to the architectonic order that Martí devised for Our America, which in itself already brought an extraordinary Martían message to all those who contemplated it and would give unquestionable originality and historic value."[14] In advocating this homage to Martí, Quesada y Miranda effectively prescribed a historicist approach, or a reflection of historical situation in architectural form. Jorge Mañach, by contrast, supported the design by Maza and Sicre precisely for its aspiration to be atemporal and universal:

> The correct symbolism of the Maza–Sicre project is accentuated by the fact that the temple that serves as the core of the evocation is conceived in the eternity of classical lines. It does not adapt itself, however, to any of the Hellenic styles, which would have given it an excessive archaeological flavor, with an evident loss of originality; but it adopts from the Greek classical that admirable coordination of the vertical with the horizontal in which resides principally the impression of immutable equilibrium, of absolute and permanent serenity, of that which is not subject to vicissitude or anything temporary.[15]

Mañach wished to see Martí commemorated in a definitive architecture, not an architecture immersed within history but one removed from its vicissitudes. Furthermore, he regarded the temple form as a suitable representation that "also corresponds to the contemplative influence of the Martían mind, to his open character, and to the sense of universality, accessible to all, of his human and democratic creed." The almost diaphanous screen of the peristyle, the open roof, the seeming lightness of the stone structure, would together fashion an intimate, even mystical environment for the statue that would encourage "the spiritual attitude of almost religious veneration peculiar to the Martían cult."[16]

Bens Arrarte also had the impression that the Maza and Sicre design would represent Martí as "a lay god" (un dios laico) accepting the tribute of the nation. Such explicit veneration was, as Mañach pointed out, already invoked by Martí's characterization as El Apóstol. Descriptions of the proposed monuments included frequent recourse to the overtones of religious language, often citing Martí's own references to consecration and redemption. Labatut, Varela, and Otero quoted one of his famous aphorisms—"The Nation is an Altar, not a pedestal"—to suggest that their design be regarded as "a gigantic Altar."[17] Mañach turned the same phrase against their proposal, however, with disbelief that one could honor its author "with a statue on an obelisk."[18] The rendering of nationalism as a secular religion occurred in other settings as well in the twentieth century, particularly in periods of decolonization, and the elevation of a national hero to transcendent status was certainly not unique to Cuba. The persistence of the metaphorical language of religion in the instance of the Monumento a Martí, however, clearly imposed upon architecture an appeal outside of or beyond historical contingency. Mañach's descriptions of the proposed *templo martiano* suggested that the significance of the architecture would derive hardly, or not at all, from the association with the origins of democracy in classical Greece. Rather, its meaning would depend on the invocation of timeless ideals and a sense of equilibrium and repose through an environment of spiritual contemplation. The dirt and violence of history would not intrude—their semblance would appear only in the bas-relief below the temple, and even then, one imagines, in highly refined form. Mañach's later elaboration of *quijotismo*—the intercession of idealism within the provinces of lived experience—might be seen retrospectively to justify his insistent advocacy for a space suspended from the temporality of history, an architecture that preserved the possibility of the unattainable.

The sculptures themselves—the images of Martí—focused debate on the differing potentials of the representation of the ideal and the representation of the real. The competition brief had included photographs and portraits of Martí, thirteen in all, to provide the competitors with a basis for his realistic portrayal (Figure 7.9). But although his head and face would therefore be reproduced as a close likeness, a wide array of interpretive options remained, for the brief specified only that there would be a representation of Martí, and allowed that this could be "physical or symbolic." Would the sculpture be a bust, or a full body? Should he be standing or seated? What kind of clothing should be portrayed? Quesada y Miranda sharply criticized Sicre's proposed sculpture because of its reply to these questions. Sicre represented Martí seated on the ground, one elbow resting on a raised knee. His upper body was nude but for the cloth of a toga draped from one shoulder and gathered in folds over his legs. "In an age of the humanization of men," Quesada y Miranda protested, "Sicre wants to give to the Cuban people nothing less than an almost unclothed Martí, a Martí utterly different from how every Cuban conceives him." The sculpture should, Quesada y Miranda believed, portray Martí in "his poor suit," which would serve as a better and more familiar "symbol of his great austerity and true simplicity."[19] Furthermore, representing "a Greek Martí" forced Sicre into a second error, that of portraying an imagined "strong athletic body" instead of "his weak and skinny body." And finally, what Quesada y Miranda considered the fatal error,

> that of presenting a pensive, philosophical, static Martí; and in the architectonic object, its predominantly horizontal lines. Martí was above all rebellious, nervous, entirely a man of action, an ascending figure. And that impression can only be given with a statue of a living Martí, and with architectonic lines where height and verticality predominate.[20]

He illustrated these criticisms with three apposite images: the statue of Abraham Lincoln, in contemporary dress, seated in the comparable temple at the Lincoln Memorial; a statue of Walt Whitman striding vigorously, hat in hand; and the statue of Martí erected in the Parque Central in 1899, realistically rendered in a period suit, standing with arm outstretched.[21]

Mañach disagreed, and defended precisely the aspects that Quesada y Miranda decried. While the latter believed that the public imagined Martí as a simple man, and therefore in his modest suits, Mañach claimed that the Cuban people

FIGURE 7.9 Photographic portrait of José Martí included with the published competition brief. From Comisión Central Pro-Monumento a Martí, *En memoria de José Martí* (Havana: P. Fernández y Cía, 1938).

conceived of him as an ethereal figure. For this reason, "to excessively materialize his representation, to 'naturalize' it, to give it an emphatic 'likeness' or a quotidian air, betrays, in my judgment, that popular and national conception." The posture of the seated figure and the draped toga contributed the impression of contemplative serenity that Mañach thought reinforced the transcendent image. Sicre's attempt to avoid "excessive literalness" in his portrait suitably placed an emphasis on the "spiritual" instead of the material.[22] Mañach endorsed the resulting harmony between the architectonic form, equally serene and contemplative, and the sculpture, in particular because the architecture placed such a decisive focus on the statue, on the figure of Martí as the symbol of the nation. This relation contrasted sharply with that obtained in the design of Labatut, Varela, and Otero, where the sculpture succumbed to vertiginous effect. Their pyramidal obelisk crowned by the statue of Martí did indeed propose a different relation of architecture and sculpture, not only physically, but in terms of representational style. Working in the first stage of the competition with the sculptor Alexander Sambugnac, Labatut and his colleagues strove to synthesize the architectural and sculptural form. The standing figure of Martí wore a toga in their proposal as well, with its folds draped vertically to echo the lines of the extruded vertices of the star. Responding perhaps to criticisms or to their own concerns about the initial proposal, in the second stage of the competition the team introduced the tapered pyramidal form and also tried to better fuse the vertical obelisk with the statue it supported. In this proposal, the body of Martí now emerged from the star of the obelisk. "The interior ribbing—formed by a star with ten vertices—is perfectly tied to the vertical folds of the Flag, as different elements of a single architectonic Unity; and from these folds emerge, as from a toga, Martí's chest and his hands, one of which holds the Solitary Star against his heart." Both the figure and the obelisk would be of marble to reinforce the intended unity of the whole. Because the sculpture would be one hundred meters above the ground, rendering Martí's visage accurately required different techniques than those of Sicre's statue to produce the impression the architects sought to create: "The Head of Martí will have to be a magnificent portrait in which Sculpture expresses the grandeur, the calm, the serenity, and the stillness of the Architecture, as the Statue is more the 'crystalization' of the Flag than the physical and natural representation of the Maestro."[23]

Both sculptures eschewed tropes of realism in dress or posture in favor of the expression of intangible qualities and concepts, and both schemes, moreover, proposed a strong correspondence between architecture and sculpture. But where in Maza and Sicre's design the void of the architectural frame directed focus toward the statue and through the statue toward the personification of the nation in José Martí, in the proposal made by Labatut, Varela, and Otero, the condensed architectonic form predominated over the subordinate sculpture and directed focus toward the embodiment of the nation in the star of the Cuban flag. The two different styles of the respective proposals contrasted significantly not so much in the contrapuntal stylistic terms of classical and modern as through the distinctive associations of form and symbol in their respective structures of representation. One pointed through architectural form to the historical personage to the transcendence of ideals, and the other pointed through architectural form to the historical artifact to the aspirations of nationhood. The strategies and issues raised as contentions in debating the proposals—the discussion of literalism, for example, or Quesada y Miranda's dichotomy of static and living configurations—marked out distinctive relational positions toward historicity in the context of Cuban nationalism. In their design, Labatut, Varela, and Otero construed a link between the monument and a definitional element of nationhood that was itself simultaneously being defined as an inescapably historical artifact. In the Maza and Sicre design, the monument was intended to enact a separation from the temporally marked procession of history. The referential elements of their scheme engaged with tropes of permanence (or the permanence of repetition) with Martí himself extracted from the coarse confines of body, contemporaneity, and contingency, and transferred to a timeless, quasi-religious realm. In each case, the manipulation of architectural and sculptural form pivoted around mimetic techniques carefully calibrated for a precise engagement with, or a disengagement from, history. As evidenced by the pointed debates over the two proposals, architecture would participate in the process of civic consciousness not only in the overt terms of style and form, but also in the construction of modes of historical understanding, or, in other words, not only in representational objects but in modes of representation.

The Permanence of the Monument

Execution of the Maza and Sicre design was deferred for economic and political reasons. Its projected cost, which had risen from five hundred thousand dollars in 1938 to one million dollars at the time their proposal was selected in 1942, was an enormous expense that the government could not reasonably afford, particularly during the war.[24] Quesada y Miranda and others questioned the propriety of such a large expenditure on the grounds that it would be antithetical to Martí's own example and a disservice to the nation. Political concerns appear to have intruded as well, in the form of President Batista's coolness toward the winning scheme. Mañach accompanied Batista on a visit to Sicre's studio shortly after the jury's decision was announced and, as he claimed in a later account, immediately realized from Batista's manner and questions that "the Maza–Sicre project was condemned."[25] Even if Mañach's recollection had been colored by his later antagonism toward Batista, the prediction was correct. The design of the Monumento a Martí was not taken up during Batista's presidency, nor by the administrations that followed. After the war's end, other developments in the city proceeded—the Grau administration's Plan de Obras del Gobierno included several new road intersections embellished with parks, for example, as well as numerous public buildings—but the Plaza Cívica was not among them. In 1946, the architect Honorato Colete, beginning his involvement with the planning movement, devised a highly contrived triangular layout for the plaza that appeared motivated by a desire to contain the proliferation of subdivision grids with a rigid geometry. Two years later, another architect, Manuel Carrerá, proposed nearly the opposite approach, with an asymmetrical arrangement of two large park areas that attempted a more natural topographical disposition. Neither scheme gained official sponsorship but they joined with other periodic references in the press to maintain an attention toward the long-delayed project. The government of Prío Socarrás did finally begin the necessary expropriation of land for the site and in 1951 raised a billboard at the site to announce the future Zona Cívica.

After Batista seized power in 1952, he created the Comisión Nacional Organizadora del Centenario, a committee charged with planning events and ceremonies to commemorate the hundredth anniversary of Martí's birth the following year.[26] The centenary was to be a prolonged celebration of the Cuban nation, with publications, festivities, and even physical constructions. It was dismaying, certainly, and an affront to nationalist pride, that the Centenario would arrive without having as its centerpiece the long-projected Monumento a Martí. Insufficient time remained to realize the project, but the approaching national remembrance prompted Batista's renewed desire to complete the project that he had initiated fifteen years earlier. The design for the Plaza Cívica (which at this point became known as the Plaza de la República) that Labatut and his collaborators had proposed ten years earlier remained the template for the overall site and responsibility for commencing its construction fell, formally at least, to the Comisión Nacional del Centenario. One of Labatut's collaborators, Enrique Luis Varela, was now a member of the Comisión; having served as minister for public works during one year of Batista's elected presidency, he presumably had a strong relationship to the present administration as well. The precise sequence of instigations remains unclear, but after seizing power in 1952 and having decided to press for the rapid execution of the Plaza de la República, General Batista chose not to build the design proposed by Maza and Sicre, and substituted instead the monument proposed by Labatut, Varela, and Otero.

Replacing the first-place design with the third-prize winner provoked outspoken statements of professional concern as well as discreet denunciations of the dictatorship's heavy hand. Professional concern prompted the Colegio de Arquitectos to organize the "Fórum sobre la Plaza de la República y el Monumento al Martí," held in the Colegio building and in the Capitolio Nacional over several sessions in May and June 1953. Agustín Sorhegui, as president of the Colegio, directed the event, which included discussion of three dimensions of the plaza project. The first topic was the design of the Plaza de la República itself, with criticisms made both of the formal composition and of the deleterious effects resulting from the lack of national and urban planning efforts in relation to the project. The second topic was the proposed design of the Palacio de Justicia to house the Supreme Tribunal, the judicial branch of government, a project for which the architect José Pérez Benitoa (who was related by marriage to Batista) had received the commission a decade earlier. The building was to be located at the southwestern end of the plaza, behind the monument, and its enormous scale and classicized composition were quickly denigrated by members of the modernist camp and by proponents of the Monumento a Martí. The monument itself was the third topic, with the unendorsed substitution of the obelisk for the *templo martiano* selected by the competition jury the subject of searching debate.

The Colegio de Arquitectos expressed institutional concern as a professional body that the results of sponsored competitions not be undermined by political caprice, or influenced by political interest; the competition for the Monumento a Martí in particular had been a prolonged affair, with several stages, so that its final result should be regarded as a deeply considered judgment, not to be overthrown without satisfactory cause. It fell to Varela, as one of the designers of the newly elevated scheme and as the official coordinator of the works of the Plaza de la República, to explain the decision and defend his own design. Another speaker, Vicente Sallés, had already recounted to the Fórum a brief history of the laws and decrees related to the site of the Loma de los Catalanes, and presented a diagram showing the marked decrease in size of the projected civic center, from 2,300,000 square meters in Forestier's plan, to 1,049,000 square meters at the time of the final stage of the competition in 1942, and finally to only 600,000 square meters by 1953. That decreasing size reflected the increasing unavailability of the lands surrounding the site, which had attracted considerable attention from speculators. Rising costs of undeveloped land limited the government's ability to expropriate a larger area of terrain for the plaza and monument, the cost of which was also rising sharply. The reduction of the Plaza de la República, Varela explained, substantially altered the surrounding content of the monument. In addition, construction of some of the adjacent institutional buildings—the Palacio de Justicia, the Biblioteca Nacional, and the Tribunal de Cuentas—had already been initiated and works on the hill itself had lowered the topography several meters, creating further visual and contextual constraints. As a result, the "grandiose pergola of the Sicre–Maza monument would be seen as inadequate in the midst of very tall buildings, making it necessary to build the Varela monument, which is of a vertical type, whose height will be taller than anything else in Havana."[27]

The necessary conversion from a horizontal to a vertical orientation became the simple explanation for the substitution of projects, forestalling any open examination either of aesthetic judgment or of political motivation. The Colegio de Arquitectos offered two formal responses, one addressing the broad issue of planning and professional participation in political processes, and the other addressing the manner of restitution for Maza and Sicre. The original terms of the competition did specify that in the eventuality that the Comisión de Monumento or the government might decide not to realize the premiated design, the winning designers would receive a financial indemnity. With the support of the Colegio de Arquitectos, the government proposed an indemnity of thirty thousand pesos, with the terms of the agreement stipulating that the decision to abandon the temple design was based on one factor: "It is deemed only that the Monument should be of vertical lines, visible at great distances and with a powerful symbolism in its Plastic expression."[28] The newly commissioned architects were involved in these negotiations and in what they characterized as an "elevated concept of justice and professional fellowship," but probably also in an effort to deflect future antagonism that might threaten their own project, they suggested that twenty thousand pesos should be contributed from their own fees to raise the indemnity to fifty thousand pesos. Furthermore, the agreement represented that the new architects had offered to Maza and Sicre collaborative roles in the new design. Varela had suggested as much to the Fórum, pointing out that their proposal for the Monumento a Martí lacked a sculptural figure, which Sicre could provide, and required further elaboration of its landscaping, which he described as Maza's specialty. Sicre agreed to join the collaboration and Maza declined.[29]

This resolution mitigated the consequences of the manipulation of the competition process, but the larger concern of authoritarian influence remained and was addressed, obliquely, by the Fórum discussion of the demonstrable necessity of planning. Eduardo Cañas Abril attributed the disjunction of the plaza, monument, and surrounding context to the project's overall conception as an isolated endeavor and affirmed as an essential principle that an integrated process of planning should precede any such design or construction.[30] More forthrightly, Miguel Gastón "stated that the so-called Plaza de la República is corrupt in origin and concurred with the majority regarding the urgent establishment of National Planning and called upon the Colegio for the creation of an Instituto de Planificación and the intelligent dissemination of its principles."[31] Eduardo Montoulieu went even further, questioning the very idea of the monument: "To give to the people flowers of Martí, busts of Martí, is not to be patriotic nor to honor a man who would have been revolted that so many millions of pesos have been spent on something completely useless, uneconomic, and out of step with the epoch."[32] Such criticism bore a sharp edge because the plaza and the monument represented the nation, its history, and its aspirations—more than any other architectural or urban project up to that point, it offered an architectural correlate to the 1940 constitution—and yet the project was now fraught with political intrigue, patronage, financial waste, and disorganization.

After the conclusion of the Fórum, the editors of the student journal *Espacio* interpreted the significance of the meeting in elevated terms as a sign that the Colegio de Arquitectos was "extending the limits of its function in national life" and, rather than acting as defender of professional interests, was now assuming the profound task of binding architecture to the "material and spiritual environment *[ambiente]*" of the nation.[33] In a similar vein, but with a more pointed historical view, commentators unrelated to the profession praised the Colegio for attempting to perform what they regarded as an explicitly civic role. José Manuel Cortina, a member of the prewar provisional governments and a signatory of the 1940 constitution, in an essay in *Arquitectura* declaring his support for the Maza–Sicre design as the preferable commemoration of Martí, began by applauding the Fórum participants for their assumption of an active role in airing advice and criticism of government decisions. Democracy, Cortina wrote, consisted of more than elections and ballots, and he advised other cultural and professional groups to follow the example set by architects and to increase their consultations with political administrations so that government policies would not come to contradict the ideas and desires of the citizenry.[34] In a column in *Diario de la Marina,* Jorge Mañach expressed similar support for the civic participation of technicians, but with his optimism tempered by his concern with the likelihood that flawed decisions would still lead to irreparable consequences:

> We see that the architects think about all of it. It is hoped that their judgment does not see itself sequestered by excessively pro-government considerations, and, above all, that it is presided over by a strict awareness, not only of the just and of the beautiful, but also of the prudent. Because with the Plaza de la República and with the Monumento, something is being made *definitive* in its eminence; something, therefore, that should not be subject to momentary or circumstantial considerations. Tragedy in such matters is to commit the *irremediable [incurrir en lo irremediable];* only those crimes that are going to be *constant* cannot be pardoned. If such a ruin occurs, at least it would not be the architects who would have to carry the responsibility.[35]

Mañach seemed to advocate participation as a way to secure insurance against culpability as much as a demonstration of civic virtue, a calibration that reflects the measured view toward political transformation he voiced at the time. It reflected also an underlying tension between the idealism he sanctioned through his vote in favor of the *templo martiano* and the realistic evaluation of circumstances he evinced in assessing the Fórum. Mañach's opposition to Batista and his authoritarianism would have reinforced his support for the Maza and Sicre design, but as the intellectual author of the concept of *quijotismo* he also believed that any attempted transcendence of the realities of a prevailing situation carried risks greater than mere ineffectuality. Tragedy would not be the consequence of a simple error, but of an irremediable error, one that introduced a permanent flaw into the civic development of the nation. So, in considering the role that architecture might perform in the process of historical change, Mañach had two fears: one this newly expressed fear of the irremediable, the other the persistent fear of a distorted idealism. Better than either of these would be an architecture that sustained a further deferral of history, a further expression of an unfulfilled destiny.

Much was at stake in the Plaza de la República and the Monumento a Martí, and not only for professional interest. Mañach's statement made clear that the political valence of architecture extended from patronage, to production, and on to representation, and also that the monument would necessarily be assessed and experienced by different audiences—from Batista himself to the Cuban citizenry present and future. Architects like Varela and intellectuals like Mañach were united in their readiness to assign to architecture potent capacities of signification with the ability to construct civic consciousness. The section on Estética Urbana (urban aesthetics) of Martínez Inclán's *Código de Urbanismo* had described monuments as "educational ornaments of the city."[36] These writers agreed that the monument was ineluctably associated with the constitution of the civic, but their agreement only begged the further question of how, exactly, this constitution should be enacted through architectural representation. Sicre's decision to join with Labatut, Varela, and Otero settled, rather bluntly, one issue of the earlier debates. His seated figure of Martí, formerly enthroned in the *templo martiano,* was simply placed at the foot of the star-shaped obelisk between two vertices of the star-shaped base, so that the statue screened the entry doors to the museum and looked forward toward a speaker's rostrum that faced the large plaza (Figures 7.10, 7.11). This juxtaposition of sculpture and architecture obviously did not attain the physical synthesis that Labatut and his colleagues had previously described as their aim, nor did it promote the sense that the architecture served as a setting for the image of Martí, a quality that Mañach had praised in the Maza–Sicre design. The sculpture was, however, literally foregrounded so that while the obelisk focused attention from a distance the tall figure of El Apóstol

FIGURE 7.10 Cover of Esso road map showing obelisk with Sicre's statue of Martí, circa 1955. Author's collection.

FIGURE 7.11 Juan José Sicre, statue of José Martí at the base of the completed monument, 1953–59. Jean Labatut Papers, Department of Rare Books and Special Collections, Princeton University Library.

dominated a visitor's view as he or she approached the monument; and even draped in a classical toga the stylized character of the sculpture and its alternately faceted and rounded edges resonated with the treatment of stonework at the exterior of the base and shaft of the obelisk, where the softened points of the star contrasted with the sharp delineation of horizontal bands. Sculpture and monument were further harmonized by their material, marble quarried from the Isle of Pines to provide solid blocks for the sculpture and used as veneer on the pyramidal tower.

The pairing did not, however, explicitly reinforce the calculated symbolism of either original scheme. Martí's contemplative pose was no longer framed by the allusive forms of the classical temple. The statue no longer emerged as a kind of beacon of liberty from atop the tower. Instead, the sculpture now became one—albeit the most potent—of a larger inventory of symbolic elements that the architects believed would produce an allegorical representation of the Cuban nation. In the very first design they submitted to the competition, Labatut, Varela, and Otero had proposed a detailed iconographic program to accompany the physical form of their architectural design. The star supplied the primary component of this iconography as the "crystallization" of the Cuban flag and thus an embodiment of Liberty. Labatut was particularly concerned about the expression of the star-plan, which would, after all, never be viewed as such, and could only be perceived therefore through an additional interpretive gesture on the part of the viewer. To assist this interpretation, Labatut had proposed the stepped rise instead of the sheer extrusion of their first proposal, believing that the stepped horizontal bands suppressed the reading of an obelisk in favor of the reading of a pyramid, and revealed the star-plan somewhat more readily by exposing a series of layers, or stacked stars, that would have been invisible in an extruded shaft.

In 1953, Labatut expressed his concern to Varela and Otero that the model of their design presented at the time of the Fórum had not emphasized these horizontal bands. The resulting effect, he cautioned, caused them to be "criticized for doing an 'old fashion' *obelisque.*" The "obelisk line" distorted the vertical scale, and conjured an unfortunate resemblance to a chimney. Labatut warned that even the "use of the word 'obelisk' is a catastrophic interpretation of the original point of view" and recommended that the scheme be described as a "tall star-plan pyramid."[37] The terraced pyramid, he argued, was both more original in form and better suited to its context. Labatut's concern over possible misinterpretations of the form was likely exacerbated by a recurring, highly undesirable comparison between their first proposal submitted in 1938 and a pavilion design for the 1939 World's Fair by an architect retained by the Schenley Corporation, a liquor distillery. This comparison was evidently made almost immediately, for the descriptive memo accompanying the second submission in 1939 included a rather too emphatic disclaimer: "The Sanders project [for the Schenley pavilion] is the geometrically exact extrusion of a star, and furthermore, unpublished, because in Architecture to publish is to build; while our Monumento a Martí is the architectonic stylization of our *Estrella Solitaria,* treated with a freedom of conception to produce a sublime and grandiose effect of masses and volumes in an absolutely new and original form."[38] Shortly after Labatut wrote to his colleagues in 1953, the unwelcome comparison reappeared when the student journal *Espacio* published a rendering of the Schenley pavilion side-by-side with a rendering of the Monumento a Martí to denounce both the derivative nature of the design and the appalling association between El Apóstol and a whiskey distiller.

Labatut emphasized the criterion of originality in his letter, perhaps in part to deflect the insinuation of similarities to the pavilion, but more to insist on the adequacy of the monument to its physical and historical context. Accentuating the stepped terraces with horizontal reveals and moldings would "give a more original character belonging to a fertile-tropical land and climate . . . to Cuba." The only formal association Labatut acknowledged was to the form of a Mayan pyramid, although he made that comparison on the basis that the top of the monument should be "alive" and "express Life," rather than with explicit deference to a geographically proximate precedent. He wrote the letter while in Rome, which he noted was "full of obelisks," but stressed that "the Cuban solution should not be Egyptian, nor Yankee, nor Roman, nor Baroque . . . but Cuban 1953."[39] Uncoupling the monument from dependence on precedent—insisting on its originality and uniqueness, as Labatut repeatedly did—not only appealed to the stated terms of the competition, but attempted a deliberate editing of its referential associations. The repeated claim of originality, in other words, was an attempt to confine those primary associations to the three elements, the physical architecture, the symbol of the Cuban flag, and the concept of Liberty; and these elements were to be construed as simultaneously inhabiting the contemporary moment of "Cuba 1953," condensing the potentially historical field of referential association into a present experience.

The architectural form that was to produce this contemporary moment had, of course, been conceived two decades earlier, though the design of the monument now being readied for construction differed somewhat in its details. In their first descriptive memo written in 1938, the architects gave a detailed inventory of the images, sculptures, and engraved texts that would ornament the base of the monument, where they would be visible and legible to visitors as an extensive array of iconographic elements to supplement the central symbol of the star. The five *aletones,* or arms of the star, were to represent five of Martí's books, with a stylized figure standing above each vertice to symbolize one of five themes evocative of a nationalist sentiment: Republic, Liberty, Homeland, Work, and Peace.[40] The figures would be differentiated by objects they held and also by relevant inscriptions alluding to Martí's writings. The iconography would also incorporate Martí's writings directly, with dozens of his aphoristic phrases to be engraved on the walls of the *aletones,* separated by forty-five *escudos,* or shields, each carved with the crest of an American nation, a Cuban province, or a Cuban city. These shields were to invoke the Pan-American independence at the core of Martí's political philosophy and together with the aphorisms would create a scrim of Martían philosophy covering the marble surface of the monument. The exterior would thereby become "a promenade of Murals of Eloquence."[41] This elaborate surfacing suggested the degree to which the architects intended at least this first version of the monument to be encountered and interpreted as a text. (Of the essential element, the star, they wrote, "This symbolism speaks for itself, with an eloquence comparable only to the human word.")[42] In order to assemble the whole as a didactic civic instrument, they sought directness of meaning through the secondary images as well. Most of the aphorisms, for example, would be familiar to visitors, learned as schoolchildren or frequently encountered in essays, books, and even newspapers, which sometimes included them as daily inspirations; and the idea that the monument should be like a book, a textual surface, obviously resonated with the memory of a writer whose words helped define a particular consciousness in Latin America and in Cuba.

Following the 1953 Fórum, José Manuel Cortina criticized the decision not to pursue the Maza–Sicre proposal because he believed the obelisk design to be too mediated in comparison to the more familiar temple form; the monument, he protested, "Should not be a construction that needs difficult interpretations . . . It should be something that makes an impression from the first moment, and gives a direct idea of the Cuban Apóstol of Liberty."[43] The program of inscriptions had by this point been considerably reduced, so that quotations from Martí's writings were contained only on the walls inside the monument and the allegorical decorative elements on the exterior had been replaced by murals on the interior. These murals, mosaics by the artist Enrique Caravia, were abstract designs on themes not specifically tied to Martí. Most served as backgrounds for the inlaid letters of quoted phrases, while the one in the entrance lobby was, in Labatut's words, an "abstract design as contrast with the Cuban landscape and framing it."[44] That abstract modernist murals would be approved as representational elements in the Monumento a Martí would have seemed highly unlikely in 1938, when some exhibitions of modernism in Havana were still regarded as vulgar provocations, and so their later inclusion evidences the broader acceptance of modernism in Cuba in the postwar period. Still, in Cortina's terms, the modernist form of the monument and its iconography produced a difficulty of interpretation, because their modern style, at least when contrasted with the classicizing style of the proposed temple, offered an unfamiliar appearance. Labatut's intention, however, was quite the opposite of what Cortina judged an indirect exchange. Labatut employed these forms and symbols to increase the didactic efficacy of the monument by producing a vivid and immediate presentness in the monument and its referential associations—the star was not an abstract geometric figure but the rehearsal of a historical event endowed by the new constitution. The two contending designs, the temple and the obelisk, offered different modes of address to the nascent civil society. Once favored by Batista's patronage, the latter design was still thought by its authors to speak quite directly to and for the citizens of Cuba.

Designing a Civic Attention

From their first designs, Labatut and his colleagues considered the Monumento a Martí an element within a larger urban setting. Although the detailed prescriptions of their "Memoria Descriptiva" showed their concern for the architectural scale of the obelisk, several pages were devoted to describing their proposal for the overall composition of the site. "The Plaza," they wrote, "is the complement to the Monumento a Martí," and although the monument could exist independently its "extraordinary vitality will be manifest in its nobility and all its dignity when the Plaza and its surroundings, constructed, lend the ineffable charm of their designs and plans, of their volumes and spaces, to its coloring and profile."[45] While working on the third submission, Labatut suggested to his colleagues that they should use only the title "Centro Cívico," rather than referring to their project as the Monumento a Martí; Otero demurred, but Labatut's recommendation hinted at the role he was assigning to the larger site. Maza and Sicre had compressed the sculpture and its environment into the scale of the architectural frame, but Labatut saw the larger urban composition as the frame for the architectural representation. The jury of the second stage of the competition, while refraining from awarding the commission of the monument itself, did decide to adopt the site plan proposed by Labatut, Varela, and Otero as the plan for the future civic center. In the subsequent competition stages, therefore, their site plan served all the competitors and retained the status of an official plan during the decade that followed the competition. By the time their monument was selected by Batista for construction, the area of land that the government could realistically obtain had decreased significantly. This reduction in the scope of available land, along with the recent construction of buildings such as the Tribunal de Cuentas on the site and the allotment of land to imminent additional construction, forced a reconsideration of the urban frame.

A model presented publicly at the time of the 1953 Fórum showed the primary components of the scheme set within these new constraints (Figure 7.12). The southwestern limit of the site was still enclosed by an arc, but consisting now of

FIGURE 7.12 Model of Plaza de la República exhibited at the 1953 Fórum. The Tribunal de Justicia is at top center, behind the monument. The National Theater is at far right, and the National Library is at far left. *Arquitectura*, June 1953. Courtesy of Avery Library, Columbia University.

the enormous colonnaded front of the Palacio de Justicia instead of the facades of several individual buildings. The monument faced toward a reduced, though still very large plaza. From the center of the plaza a reflecting pool extended between the new Tribunal de Cuentas and the Ministry of Communications, both slab buildings that, despite rising asymmetrically above lower blocks, nevertheless balanced one another effectively within the explicit symmetrical intention of the site plan. Broad avenues extended northeast toward the Castillo del Príncipe so that a narrow landscaped area connected the base of that historical structure to the formal plaza of the Monumento a Martí. Locations for two other institutional buildings, the National Library on the eastern side of the plaza and the National Theater on the western side, had been selected and preliminary designs of those buildings were shown in the model. The National Theater by Arroyo & Menéndez would be realized in a modernist form indebted to the example of Le Corbusier, with volumetric expressions of its two auditoriums linked by a cubic tower containing fly space. The National Library, by Evelio Govantes and Félix Cabarrocas, shared the severe neoclassicism of the Tribunal de Justicia, with sharp vertical piers that gave the appearance of a colonnade to the entrance front and then continued up the high block containing the stacks.

Labatut and Varela had little or no influence over the designs of the buildings that were to surround the Plaza de la República. They did make recommendations regarding the positions of the buildings, requesting, for example, that the Palacio de Justicia be set back as far as possible from the Monumento a Martí so that it would not obscure the star-pyramid from view at close approach. But style, form, mass—all these architectural aspects of the immediate context were outside their direct control, constrained only to a limited degree by the original site plan. The surrounding buildings would therefore be as varied as their several architects chose to make them, which in turn made it possible to interpret the Plaza de la República as a contest of rival claims to a modern architecture. Labatut could not avoid this debate, but he refused to accept its customary terms. Shortly before the Fórum, as derogation of academic or beaux-arts composition began to be directed against their design by students and other critics, Labatut advised his Cuban colleagues that

> [t]hose people who are using the words "Beaux-Arts" are both right and wrong following the meaning given to them. In general, they do not know that they

> talk about what is bad in the "Beaux-Arts" type of architecture as anyone can talk about what is bad in the worst expression of modern architecture. Good modern is *very rare,* and a good part of the Gropius–Le Corbusier architecture is bad modern showing no scale, character, and meaning, corresponding to particular people, climate, and physical or psychological environment. Meaning, character, and scale are so difficult to express that instead to try they refuse to solve and deny the use of memorials and churches and they reject them as not being modern program. A way to escape their duty because they do not know how to do the work.[46]

Labatut did not oppose abstraction, either in art or in architectural form, and the reduction of sculptural and textual elements from the exterior of the monument in its later versions in fact demonstrated a more emphatic confidence in the signifying capacities of architectural form. Nor did he oppose figural referentiality, as was evident in the incorporation of the shape of the star into the body of the monument. These two formal attitudes were not the poles against which Labatut oriented his architecture. The more relevant dichotomy existed between meaning derived from the progress of history and meaning derived from experience in the present, and the Monumento a Martí demanded the synthesis of precisely these two sources.

In 1952, Labatut gave an account of his own theory of monumentality in a chapter titled "Monuments and Memorials" that he contributed to Talbot Hamlin's *Forms and Functions of Twentieth-Century Architecture.*[47] As an editor's note explained, the chapter appeared without illustrations so that the reader would not be distracted from its presentation of a basic philosophy on the composition of monuments and would be able to use its argument to project future, as yet unimagined, forms. The illuminating consequence of Labatut's decision was an emphasis on his general principles and an avoidance of the distortion of those principles by the antagonisms over style that underlay many other discussions of monumentality. In his chapter, Labatut proposed as a fundamental premise that a monument consisted in the relation between an expressive object and a receptive viewer through an intermediate context. Labatut called this intermediate context "architectural air space." It was the "frame" or the "environment" inhabited by the viewer, and the phrase could refer to space at a variety of scales—a part of a room, a garden, or a civic center. Its perimeter corresponded roughly with the range of vision of an experiencing subject, in physical terms, although its psychological scope might be far broader. Psychological qualities or values of the air space played a constructive role equal to the physical, according to Labatut's theory, and so both physical and psychological needs had to be accommodated in the design of a monument, the fundamental aim of which was to "organize" a space to fulfill them. Labatut described this process at length:

> Air space is invisible until light, traveling through it, reaches obstacles which act as modifiers of light—modifiers which create visible colored illumination or visible forms. Under the artist's control these forms within the spectator's range of visibility, these forms limiting man's immediate environment, create an architectural air space or small visible man-made world of which each individual is a center, an observer, and in the final analysis an approving or disapproving judge.
>
> The quality of man's judgment of this air space will depend on many factors, such as the type and condition of the wave lengths sent by the modifier and striking the observer's eyes; the size of the elements and their shape, texture, and relationship; the motion of the observer's eyes; the time spent looking; the motion of the observer's body in relation to the environment; the successive distances from the elements of the environment to the retina; the visual sensibility of the observer and his knowledge, feeling, and imagination; the influence of preceding visual experiences, immediate or old, direct or indirect; the difference between the emotional behavior of the author and that of the observer; and the state of mind of the observer.[48]

Labatut's prescription combined aspects of diverse concepts about perception, all of which reinforced the central thesis of an interpretive exchange between object and subject that was designable, that could be calculated and contrived by the designer in the pursuit of a meaningful architectonic form and its supporting air space.[49]

Even in the earliest version of the Monumento a Martí, while strongly emphasizing its textual and symbolic registers, Labatut and his colleagues carefully considered the visual experience of the monument. The vertical design was actually motivated by its peculiarly visual properties, its visibility, and the view afforded by its height. Visitors to the monument would, after registering the implications of the symbolic program and examining the exhibits of the museum, walk up a helicoidal stair to a *mirador,* an observation floor at the top of the obelisk (an elevator was added in the final design). Each arm of the star would be a room with windows looking out at a panoramic view of Havana. The *mirador* gave a new function to the Monumento a Martí, one not envisioned in the competition brief, as a platform for viewing the nation not only in symbolic terms but literally in views across the capital city that would encompass El Morro, the fortress at the mouth of the bay, the Capitolio Nacional, and the sweep of the Malecón (Figure 7.13). The conceptual centrality of the monument would be married to its physical centrality in the civic landscape of the city, with the view to be a reciprocal one because the prominent vertical obelisk could be seen at an enormous distance: "And what better and more meaningful symbol to announce from the horizon the presence of Cuba to ships of the air and sea than the immortal figure of Martí . . . ?"[50]

In their focus on approaches toward the monument, the architects considered also the contribution that landscaped areas would make to its symbolic and experiential dimensions. In their first proposal, claiming the complementarity of the monument and its approach, the architects described their use of royal palm trees: "These tropical palms we place in pairs in the gardens have a double meaning: they are the contribution that the picturesque landscape of our exuberant nature makes to the grandeur of the Apóstol, and, at the same time, are

FIGURE 7.13 Jean Labatut, sketch of First Proposal, showing panorama of city. Jean Labatut Papers, Department of Rare Books and Special Collections, Princeton University Library.

the elegant sentinels of his sanctuary; it is the queen of our countryside paying her tribute to the Hero for liberating our people."[51] Here again, a more literary attitude initially prevailed, but the later evolution of the design introduced a seemingly more scientific, and certainly more didactic, approach. With the larger area of open space now displaced from the formal square at the base of the monument to the avenue approaching from the Castillo, Labatut began to describe this area as a "park" that would be organized as a botanical garden and arboretum, with an inventory of indigenous flora capturing the image of the Cuban landscape and ordering it for didactic dissemination.[52] In 1955, Labatut, acting as he had throughout as the primary designer, began to revise the overall composition shown in the model in 1953. Underground parking areas were added to serve the Plaza de la República and the surrounding buildings, and the formal reflecting pool near the monument was removed. Labatut wished to avoid a resemblance to the National Mall in Washington, D.C., where an obelisk and pool were also paired, but he still considered the creation of reflected views of the monument to be especially important. They would, he asserted, accentuate the scale of the pyramid without an increase in height; "to reach greater scale with less dimension" was "the secret of greatness in monumentality."[53] By 1955, it was also clearer than it had been in 1938 that movement to and around the Plaza de la República would happen more often by car than on foot. Rancho Boyeros, the main avenue running through the length of the plaza, connected the city to the airport and was now heavily trafficked. The newly located cultural and institutional buildings would also attract visitors and employees arriving by car, who would encounter the Monumento a Martí only incidentally (Figure 7.14). In a site plan drawn in February 1956, Labatut indicated the sightlines of "vistas" from cars toward the monument, including reflections as well as direct views, to show how the Monumento a Martí would be perceived from a moving car.

Labatut clearly regarded the design of the "air space" between viewer and monument as a matter of quite precise calibration. He did not aim to approximate a general sense of experience, but rather to make available, or even unavoidable, a specific orientation and attention in the viewer toward the monument through the void that surrounded it. He therefore attended to the different directions of approach and their possible speeds in a car and on foot, choreographing the apparent rise of the monument from its own reflection as well as the progression of signifying marks from the labeled trees of the park to the inscriptions of Martí's

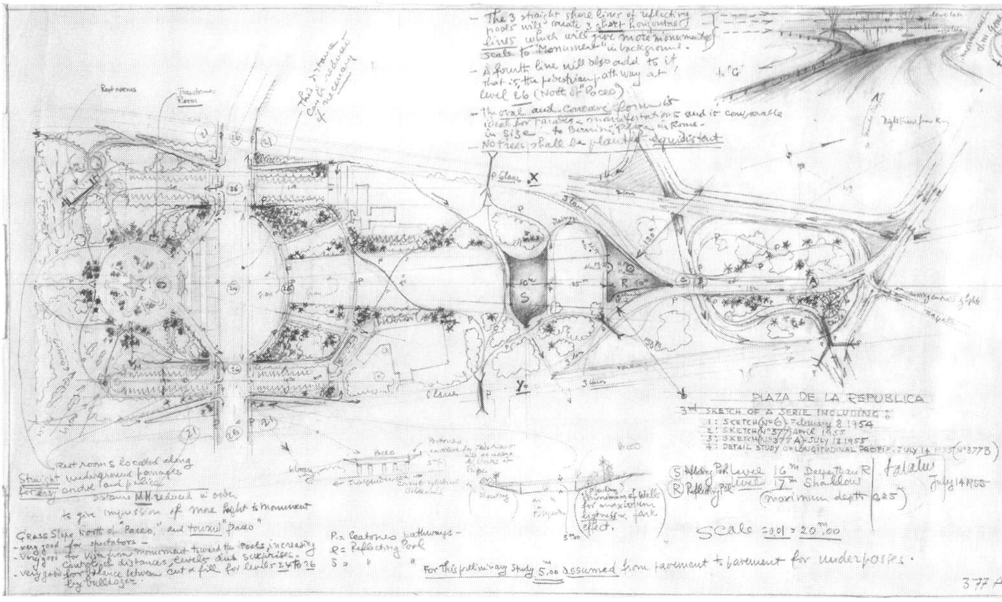

FIGURE 7.14 Jean Labatut, sketch site plan, Plaza de la República, Havana. Jean Labatut Papers, Department of Rare Books and Special Collections, Princeton University Library.

aphorisms. For Labatut, the final critical element in this calibration of air space was light. He often described light as the active component, a substance that produced a catalytic reaction with form. His intense interest in firework displays, first those in the 1937 Paris Exposition, which he filmed, and then the display that he designed for the Lagoon of Nations in the New York Fair two years later, arose from his insight that illumination, and in particular artificial, controlled illumination, represented a signal change in the conditions of architecture.[54] He called for a "twenty-four-hour architecture" in which monuments would be designed to "express their function as modifiers of both nature and artificial light."[55] For the Monumento a Martí, Labatut developed elaborate lighting specifications, taking intensity and color into account, in order to control this architectural dimension. These specifications resembled a choreography, in which the character of light altered continuously, with the most powerful effect to occur in the transitional light of dusk. Labatut recorded the event with a series of color photographs, that showed how the artificial light cast onto the monument was calibrated exactly to the changing hue of the background sky (see Plate 9). This calibration gave the effect not only of precise architectural form, but also of the synthesis of the monument with the Cuban landscape in a state of vivid presentness.

The exchange between viewer and monument, according to Labatut, depended on the "radiating power of or quality of the work of art" and on the "quality of our power of reception."[56] With regard to the latter, the quality of a viewer's power of reception, Labatut frequently repeated that "we see forms in general—and memorials and monuments in particular—as *we* are rather than as *they* are."[57] Requisite judgment on the part of the viewer was therefore a necessary component to the adequate production of meaning, and in the case of the Monumento a Martí would have consisted of the particular quality identified by the constitutional debates: civic consciousness. Listing the factors that would influence the quality of judgment, Labatut had included, in addition to physical and immediate factors, the "knowledge, feeling, and imagination" of the viewer, his or her "preceding visual experiences," "emotional behavior," and "state of mind." None of these could be assumed universal; to the contrary, together they amounted to the historical conditioning of the viewer, and in the context of republican Cuba these factors would include evocations of the construction of civil society. For example, the monument depended on the prior familiarity with Martí's thought and with his historic role. Some of the aphorisms would be known by memory, others would be familiar and readily recalled, so that all of the symbols and the much-discussed statue of Martí would already be possessed as civic vocabulary by a visitor. The contrivance of the experiential consequences of the architecture also aimed toward familiarity. Precise gradations of artificial light would, if the exchange of object and subject was successful, appear as a natural transition in full accord with the landscape experienced visually from the *mirador* and intellectually from the didactic classifications in the landscape of the park, and then attached by the viewer to the concept of the nation itself. Reliant upon the pedagogical preparation of civic education—a process that Labatut thought to reinforce with ideas such as donating to Cuban schools worn pennants that had flown at the top of the monument, as relics of the memorial to Martí—the design of the Plaza de la República and the Monumento a Martí anticipated a civic subject, a visitor already cultured in the tools of aesthetic interpretation through his or her prior participation in the signifying regimes that proliferated outward from the constitutional project.

By viewing the monument, to paraphrase Labatut's words, as themselves rather than in itself, Cuban citizens would carry not only inculcated civic knowledge but also real awareness of the compromised condition of citizenship under Batista's regime. To see the monument as themselves would be to confront a disparity between the idealized civic consciousness of Martí and the straitened civic aspirations of lived experience. Indeed, the role and the aim of the architecture of the monument were to manifest and make effective this disparity. The first-prize proposal proposed by Maza and Sicre would have done this as well, contrasting the ideal equilibrium evoked by the hallowed precinct of the temple to the mutability and uncertainty of its surroundings. Where the architecture of the *templo martiano* sought constancy by distancing itself with its bulwark of stairs and its perimeter colonnade and the void within, the architecture of the obelisk sought constancy also, but through a conflation with its surroundings. The difference between the two rival proposals was not ultimately to be measured as a stylistic difference, but rather as two possible strategies to overcome the difficulty of permanence. The permanence of architecture was, in the context of dictatorship, as likely to be a flaw as a merit, and so the critical dimension of each of the two proposals was not appearance, but duration, or temporality. Maza's architecture and Sicre's sculpture posited a temporality of timelessness. Labatut with his colleagues recognized and conceded the ineluctable progression of history and denied as an illusion any timeless architecture. They sought to bring this progression to a moment of presentness that would not simply slip into the past but that would recur as a perceptible stasis. Each day, in the finely tuned air space of the civic center, the Monumento a Martí would merge into its surroundings as the historical associations it conveyed were held in a suspension with the designed cast of artificial light and the real light of the Cuban sky.

8 The Prospect of *cubanidad*

Figural Forms and the Palacio de las Palmas

Under a Havana dateline on July 18, 1957, Cuban newspapers reported General Batista's unveiling of the design for the Palacio de las Palmas (Palace of the Palms) (see Plate 10, Figure 8.1). This new presidential palace was to accommodate all of the components of the executive branch—the offices of the presidential ministry, facilities for the press, formal reception halls, and the private residence of the president and his family. It would, declared Batista, fulfill the executive's need for a building comparable to the Capitolio Nacional and the Palacio de Justicia occupied, respectively, by the legislative and judicial branches of government. It would also provide a unifying national monument; its use of suitably evocative "Cuban materials" and its site, positioned between two historic fortresses on the heights looking across the harbor entrance toward Old Havana, would suggest that the "new Republic is sitting upon this base of historic colonial tradition."[1] Called upon to contrive an expression of *cubanidad* worthy of this new national monument, the architects—José Luis Sert, working with Mario Romañach and Gabriela Menéndez—responded with an enormous canopy roof, formed by dozens of individual parasols. In their size and shape, these parasols were intended to resemble royal palm trees, elements that Batista called "most typical of Cuba."[2]

Although Batista had technically restored the Constitution of 1940 in 1955—it had been periodically suspended after the 1952 *golpe de estado*—few hesitated to describe him as a caudillo, and many were willing to declare outright that his regime was a dictatorship. His decision to build the third-place scheme for the Monumento a Martí instead of the winning design by Maza and Sicre certainly

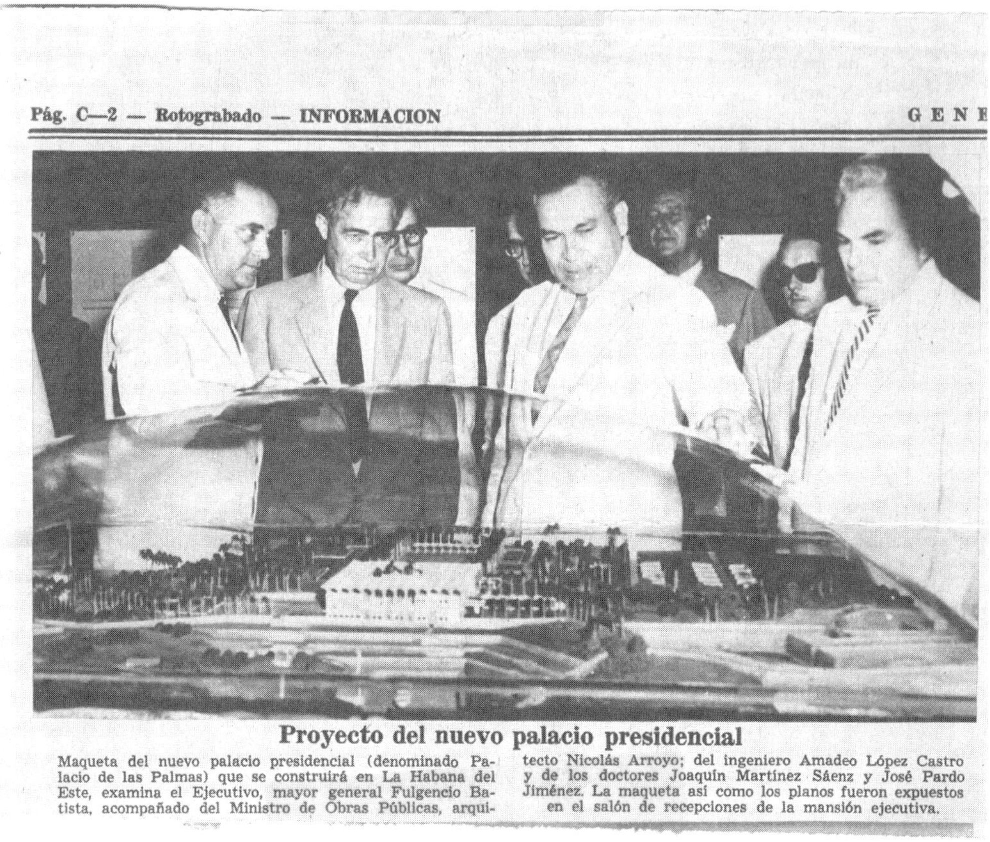
Pág. C—2 — Rotograbado — INFORMACION GENE

Proyecto del nuevo palacio presidencial

Maqueta del nuevo palacio presidencial (denominado Palacio de las Palmas) que se construirá en La Habana del Este, examina el Ejecutivo, mayor general Fulgencio Batista, acompañado del Ministro de Obras Públicas, arquitecto Nicolás Arroyo; del ingeniero Amadeo López Castro y de los doctores Joaquín Martínez Sáenz y José Pardo Jiménez. La maqueta así como los planos fueron expuestos en el salón de recepciones de la mansión ejecutiva.

FIGURE 8.1 General Fulgencio Batista viewing model of presidential palace. Nicolás Arroyo is at far left, and Paul Lester Wiener can be seen in the background to the right of Batista. Unidentified newspaper clipping, July 1958. Courtesy of the Frances Loeb Library, Harvard Graduate School of Design.

had the air of executive caprice, and the announcement of the Palace of the Palms must have been viewed in architectural circles in a similar light. The architects involved were not ignorant of the political significance that could attach to their participation—in 1957, Wiener would advise Sert that it seemed inadvisable to publicize the project in Cuba because of the political climate. Nicolás Arroyo, as a member of Batista's cabinet, had clearly tied his professional status to the government, but Romañach appears to have remained more detached from political affairs with his private practice flourishing during the 1950s and consuming much of the professional attention. He did not have any formal political association with Batista, though he participated extensively in the tasks of the

JNP and specifically requested to join the palace project. Sert and Wiener both held progressive political views, yet nevertheless eagerly pursued the palace commission. Unlike their work with the JNP, which all the protagonists probably saw as technical and therefore almost apolitical in nature, this commission was quite directly tied to Batista and his personal patronage. Given their respective relations to and understandings of the political situation of Cuba, different motivations might be surmised. They might have been complacently unconcerned with the connection between architectural work and political dimensions, content with the opportunity to work on significant and dramatic projects; or they might have supported Batista, tacitly or actively, accepting as compensation for diminished political freedom the potentially increased possibility of realizing projects under a central authority; or they may have been motivated by a belief in transformative change, seeing Batista's government as only the latest among several that had risen and fallen over the previous twenty years, soon to be superseded; or they may even have regarded architecture and planning as the actual instruments of progressive reform. Most likely, a mixture of these motivations were present, and though the evidence that remains from this unbuilt project—a detailed model, drawings, a few sketches, and fragmentary correspondence—provides no decisive answer, the protagonists were unquestionably fully cognizant of the political dimension of the proposed Palace of the Palms.[3]

Indeed, the summary compulsion to construct a representation of *cubanidad* produced a representational crisis in both the political and aesthetic registers of the project. In the first of these registers, the intention was that architecture not only symbolize nationhood and citizenship but contribute to the production of civic behavior. The architecture, that is, should contribute to the overall structure of civil society, as Martínez Inclán and others had repeatedly suggested. Yet the presentness attained by Labatut's conceptualization of the Monumento a Martí could not simply be reenacted here, for it would be utterly compromised by the inescapable purpose of the commission: a *palacio* for General Batista. The severe restraint imposed on civil society by the overarching authority of Batista's dictatorship would thus have left a choice, a choice between an architecture that supplied a fiction of participatory citizenship or an architecture that aspired to an ideal of citizenship as yet unfilled. The architecture, in other words, might aspire to represent the executive power defined in the 1940 constitution rather than Batista's usurpation of that power, abdicating its efficacy in the present in order to sustain such a possibility for the future. This dilemma cast in the political register was mirrored in the aesthetic register of the project by the startling appearance of figuration in the roof parasols. The parasols' forced analogy between nature and architecture proposed a verisimilitude unusual in the context of modernist discourse at that time and certainly unprecedented and unrepeated in Sert's abstract architectural idiom. The tension between modernist tenets of abstraction and the symbolic potency of figuration produced a representational equivocation comparable to the ambiguity of the political implications. In the terms of modernist architectural discourse, the turn to mimesis in an avowedly modern architecture circa 1955 would risk appearing a regressive capitulation toward a shallow expression of regionalism, for the imitation of a palm tree by a roof parasol was certainly mimetic in the classical sense. However, in the postwar period, as a range of architectural debates turned upon questions of expression, the concept of mimesis had already expanded well beyond its classical definitions to incorporate theoretical, philosophical, and anthropological facets, and the most suspect characteristic of mimesis—the imitation of some form prior and external to the representational object—was no longer inherently disqualifying.

The Aesthetic Politics of Regionalism

Since his 1943 proclamation of the "Nine Points on Monumentality" with Sigfried Giedion and Fernand Léger, Sert had been calling for modernism to fulfill the symbolic and emotional demands of its subjects. Entering the developing debate on the problem of monumentality and modern architecture, Sert and his colleagues made clear that the currency of monumental expression had been debased by its association with political repression at both totalitarian extremes and with political compliance in the liberal valorization of existing social configurations. It had been debased as well by its aesthetic cognate: the imitative practices of historicism. This condemnation of imitation captured a range of targets, from the conventions of academicism, to the promiscuity of eclecticism, to the reactionary posture of antimodernism. In Giedion's writings in particular, loathing of imitation assumed an intensity that recalled Plato's denunciation of mimesis as an inauthentic representation of an already untrue reality. Giedion portrayed historicist imitation as a similarly disruptive process—a degeneracy equal to robbery or poisoning—in which indiscriminate proliferation had impoverished the representational capacities of architectural form to the point of crisis, prompting the rupture and emergence of modernism. But although modernism initially eschewed imitation, it also quickly succumbed to academicism, according to the teleology described by Giedion and Sert. Sert unknowingly echoed Labatut's earlier appraisal of the growing tendency of the "bad modern" when, in a 1953 interview with the student editors of *Espacio,* he cautioned against "the production of modern clichés by repetition and copying of hallowed models."[4] Sert now elaborated the earlier calls for authentic emotional content by identifying the constrained idiom of functionalism as a disabling limitation. The consummate metaphor of functionalism, the machine, embedded the idea of repetition at the core of modernism, and the pursuit of the reproductive standards of mass production further compelled functionalism toward ceaseless iteration and toward dehumanizing consequences. "Functionalism has been widely accepted as the guiding principle of all architectural work," he argued in 1954, "but it has produced clichés of an appalling poverty. These clichés have replaced the old academic architectural vocabularies. Today we need a new vocabulary, rich and flexible . . . which need not conflict with the functional but should add other elements to it."[5]

In that same year, a variety of formal experiments might have served as potential examples: Carlos Raúl Villanueva's Área Central at the Ciudad Universitaria in Caracas, Edward Durrell Stone's United States Embassy in New Delhi, and Le Corbusier's Chapel of Notre-Dame-du-Haut at Ronchamp. In different ways, each of these buildings offered an expanded license of architectural expression, and certainly each was received, and not without interrogation, as a proposition for liberating architecture from functionalist dogma. According to Sert, human aspirations as much as physical necessities had to be accommodated, and "the superfluous, or 'that which is more than strictly needed,'" had to be incorporated into modern architecture.[6] Sert's category of the superfluous could include ornamental elements or lavish materials, but his recurrent use of the term made clear that he intended a broader definition as well, in which the superfluous was simply the expressive capacities of architecture. In 1955, coincident with the start of the palace design, Sert himself developed examples if not of superfluity then at least of elaborated function in contoured roofs for Joan Miró's studio on Mallorca and for the U.S. ambassador's residence in Baghdad (Figure 8.2). The broadening of the emotional and symbolic address of architecture evidently did

FIGURE 8.2 José Luis Sert, sketch for ambassador's residence, U.S. Embassy, Baghdad, 1955–61. Courtesy of the Frances Loeb Library, Harvard University.

not entail an abandonment of modernism's resistance to formal recapitulation, nor did it signal a weakening of modernism's predisposition for abstraction, for while these forms were evocative, they avoided *explicit* references or associations. In a 1956 house for Ana Carolina Font and in other residences designed at this time, Romañach employed similarly elaborated roofs and highly complex fenestration staged in deep relief against walls, signaling his own departure from the imposed constraints of structural or functional rationalism and toward the potentials of formal expression.

A set of parallel concerns appeared in debates on modernist regionalism, which increased in vigor and relevance after the war as the economic and cultural influence of the United States converged with the ambitions of decolonizing nations and international organizations, enabling a more extensive propagation of modernist architecture. In 1941, Lewis Mumford had helped recast prewar conceptions of regionalism by exposing the contemporary political implications of any architecture unwritten by essentialist claims, now inescapably associated with the Nazi valorization of *Heimatsarchitektur*. Mumford argued that the necessary response to the nativist regionalism propounded by the Nazis was not a deracinated universalism, but a calibrated balance of "regional characteristics" and "universal principles." "It would be useful," he advised, "if we formed the habit of never using the word regional without mentally adding to it the idea of the universal—remembering the constant contact and interchange between the local scene and the wide world that lies beyond it."[7] Sert, who met Mumford for the first time in 1941, had begun his own conceptualization of regionalism before the war while analyzing and publishing examples of vernacular architecture on Ibiza with his colleagues in the GATEPAC group in Barcelona. He was similarly concerned with establishing a relation between the universal and the regional, to the point of positing the spare vernacular forms of the Mediterranean islands as the source of the modern architecture emerging throughout Europe. More subtle was his translation of essentialist categories into "constants" such as climate and landscape, which permitted and even compelled the recapitulation of prior forms that had been refined over centuries in response to those elements. In a distinct difference from nativist strains of regionalism, however, Sert regarded culture as entirely historical, and therefore not demanding of imitative expression from one period to the next.

Sert met the group of young architects who would become his collaborators in the Pilot Plan for Havana and the presidential palace during his stay in Cuba in 1939, at a moment when these architects too were consumed with the search for a reconciliation of modernism and local tradition, drawing upon elements of colonial architecture such as louvered screens and walls, *patios,* and colonnades but deploying them in spare geometric forms influenced by European modernism. Against the political backdrop of this period in Cuba—in which a self-conscious nationalism emerged from the abrogation of the Platt Amendment and continued through the Constitution of 1940 and the decade of democratic rule in the 1940s—regionalism was a natural predisposition through which architecture could support the endeavor of national self-definition.[8] In 1943, ATEC opened an exhibition that presented a study of the colonial city of Trinidad (Figure 8.3). Directed by Nicolás Arroyo, the exhibition, "Trinidad: Lo que fué, es y será" (Trinidad: What it was, is, and will be), aimed to recuperate the historic artifact of the city not as a monument but as a vital and contemporary fabric: "Trinidad, in addition to its great archaeological value, is a city that lives . . . it is potentially a city that can and should revive its splendid glorious past in the

LA A.T.E.C. Y LA ULTIMA EXPOSICION de TRINIDAD

LA Exposición que con el lema "Trinidad; lo que fué, es y será" se celebró últimamente organizada por el Patronato Pro-Urbanismo de Cuba, con la valiosa cooperación del Patronato del Turismo, la Sociedad de Estudios Históricos y el Patronato Pro-Trinidad y que tuvo efecto en los salones del Club Fotográfico, cedidos amablemente por sus altos dirigentes, constituyó un acto de gran valor artístico e histórico, y, por lo tanto, un completo éxito para sus organizadores.

Tuvo a su cargo la difícil labor de montar la Exposición, la Sección de Exposiciones del Patronato Pro-Urbanismo, que preside el arq. Eduardo Montoulieu, que cuenta también con un valioso grupo de jóvenes, que trabajó incansablemente para lograr, como al final se obtuvo, un éxito grandes y definitivo. Este grupo de jóvenes, integra en su mayoría la nueva agrupación A.T.E.C.

Algunas de las personas que lean estos comentarios, ignorarán, seguramente, el significado de esas cuatro letras que constituyen el lema de dicha agrupación. Nosotros vamos a decírselo y también a exponerles los fundamentos básicos de su funcionamiento.

Su nombre es "Agrupación Tectónica de Expresión Contemporánea" y los fines que persigue son los siguientes:

A.T.E.C. se compone de un núcleo central de arquitectos, ingenieros y técnicos asociados al C.I.A.M. (Congresos Internacionales de Arquitectura Moderna) y hace un llamamiento a profesionales, científicos, artistas, industriales, comerciantes, obreros y estudiantes para cooperar al progreso artístico, científico, industrial internacional, estudiando y resolviendo el problema arquitectónico urbanístico cubano, siempre en presente y hacia el futuro.

A.T.E.C. entiende que es Arquitectura toda aquella técnica de construir que utiliza los materiales y métodos más apropiados a la obra de

Historia gráfica de la ciudad de Trinidad ♦ Entrada a la Exposición ♦ Estudio demostrando la necesidad de planear científicamente la nueva zona fabril.

FIGURE 8.3 Nicolás Arroyo, photographs and article on the ATEC Exhibition on Trinidad. *Arquitectura,* May 1943.

twentieth century, with the physiognomy of the twentieth century."[9] This interest in traditional colonial architecture, the ATEC members insisted, was not a romantic view; on the contrary, they wanted to draw from these examples the principles for contemporary adaptation to local physical and experiential conditions.

In the widespread architectural debates of the postwar period, definitions of regionalism varied in their intention and their opposed emphases on essentialism and idealism, but proponents in Cuba and elsewhere agreed largely on the techniques of regionalism—an attention to local architectural precedent, use of local materials and methods, scrupulous study of specific climatic effects, and accommodation of local customs and traditions. This catalog of techniques emphasized what could be called the specular aspect of regionalism, its capacity to reflect the disparate real elements of locality. Two important attempts to refine a conceptual rather than descriptive definition, Harwell Hamilton Harris's 1954 lecture "Regionalism and Nationalism" and Pietro Belluschi's 1955 essay "The Meaning of Regionalism in Architecture," emphasized instead its projective potential.[10] Following Lewis Mumford, both authors warned against succumbing to either romantic primitivism or nostalgic historicism, and both recommended the enthusiastic embrace of new technology regardless of its cultural attachments. Belluschi flatly declared that it was impossible to ignore scientific and technological advance. The embrace of novelty and change could be manifest even in the processes of imitative practices, as Harris made clear in praising the work of Bernard Maybeck: "He did not reconstruct the past; he made something altogether new under the sun out of these relics and reminiscences of the past. As a result, any previous incarnation of these forms appears as mere preparation for their present role."[11] Harris here allowed the architect to reverse the temporal pattern of imitation, so that the past would refer to the present rather than the present to the past. Belluschi also stressed the importance of an architect's perceptive imagination, and praised Sert's Baghdad embassy project for demonstrating "how a great modern artist can use his gifts toward a sensitive version of a regional architecture which is both creative and appropriate."[12] The concluding words, "creative and appropriate," conveyed a temporal implication, with appropriateness confirming a connection to the past while creativity asserts the prerogative of the future; their conjunction showed that regionalism, like the new monumentality of the "Nine Points on Monumentality," sought to balance continuity with the historical past against a necessary orientation toward the future.

Both essays suggested a significant displacement of the reflective action of regionalism. Harris juxtaposed what he called a "regionalism of restriction," which sought only to preserve a local architectural idiom, to a "regionalism of liberation," which developed new possibilities out of a region's resources. Those resources, Harris made clear, possessed a specific hierarchy: "A region's most important resources are its free minds, its imagination, its stake in the future, its energy, and last of all, its climate, its topography, and the particular kind of sticks and stones it has to build with." In other words, the physical elements were less important than experiential ones, and by also describing regionalism as the manifestation of "a located state of mind," Harris indeed confirmed that regionalism did not seek to reflect reality but rather to represent the subjective experience of a region.[13] Belluschi added that the task of representing experience fell to the architect, who now acted as surrogate for the prior activity of a people "acting under a community of experience" that had produced the autochthonous regional architecture of the past.[14] Regionalism, in the face of steadily increasing transformative effects of modernity, might permit what Belluschi called "a larger and more difficult order" to evolve out of the "enormous variety of situations which our age has created."[15] If architecture merely reflected the physical realities of different regions, or worse, if it adopted a nostalgic posture toward those features and artifacts, it placed the regional in opposition to the universalizing tendencies of modernity. But if, instead of the regions themselves, it was the *experience* of those regions that was represented, then regionalism could provide an epistemic mode through which the localized experiences of individuals or groups could be spliced into a larger whole, the "difficult order" of modernity.

Even though it subordinated the reflection of the physical reality of a region, the representation of experience still required the primary techniques of regionalism—in Cuba as elsewhere, the adoption of local materials and methods and the accommodation of local precedents and customs—which prompted imitative practices. As in the debates on monumentality, imitation was denigrated, and because imitation implied copying, mimesis specifically was condemned even as it became a crucial instrument. (As Belluschi admonished, "there is never real Beauty in the lie, in the fake, or in the blind copying.")[16] With the emerging politicization of modernism and social realism in Cold War alignments providing renewed motivation for tendencies toward abstraction, practitioners of modernist regionalism like Sert and Romañach faced a dilemma: the choice between the political and aesthetic legitimacy of abstraction and the cultural and aesthetic legibility supplied by mimesis. This dilemma was not dissimilar to the complexities confronted in the drafting of the 1940 constitution, in which the doctrines of pure law were balanced against the particularities of the Cuban situation. Political circumstances in Cuba in the mid-1950s, however, made the dilemma that much keener than it had been in 1940, for those circumstances were now sufficiently untenable that the present itself could no longer stand as a desired object of representation. One possible answer to the dilemma (in both regionalist representation and the constitution of norms) lay in the transformation of mimesis from a specular technique into a projective one; that is, rather than only reflecting the past in order to convey meaning through appropriation, could mimesis reorient the past toward the future? If so, the architectural problematic revealed by the Palace of the Palms, with its liabilities of political affiliation and its risks of aesthetic regression, could perhaps be differently construed.

Representation and the Civic Sphere

During the summer of 1955, Arroyo advised Wiener that a competition would be held for the design of a new presidential palace on the eastern side of the Havana harbor. Le Corbusier and Oscar Niemeyer would be invited to participate, and other potential candidates included Wells Coates, Franco Albini, and the firm of Welton Beckett and Associates. Town Planning Associates was added to the list and after Romañach indicated to Wiener his desire to collaborate, the firm had the advantage of close connections to Arroyo. Soon afterward, with the idea of a competition discarded, Town Planning Associates was given the commission directly in conjunction with Romañach and Gabriela Menéndez. The Cuban government already owned the selected site, a large, open piece of land lying between two historic fortresses, El Castillo del Morro and La Cabaña, which overlooked Havana from the east side of the bay. Designated a military zone, the land did not require expropriation and had the additional advantages of historic relevance and prominent topography. Its isolation from the city and its consequent defensibility may have been a further consideration.[17] Contemporaneous accounts also emphasized that the placement of the palace on the undeveloped east side of the bay in tandem with the construction of a new tunnel under the bay would encourage the incipient development of the city toward the east, maintaining Habana Vieja as a vital center and discouraging westward decentralizing sprawl.

With the commission secured, Sert and Romañach became the primary designers of the project, albeit with crucial contributions from two consultants they later retained for the project: Félix Candela as structural engineer and Hideo Sasaki as landscape architect. Given the collaboration between Sert and Romañach at the JNP, they presumably exchanged ideas from the start, but they appear not to have commenced the design until the following year, developing the scheme almost entirely between the fall of 1956 and the summer of 1957 when detailed plans and an elaborate model were exhibited for General Batista and his cabinet in the Salón de los Espejos of the existing presidential palace (Figures 8.4, 8.5, 8.6). The model revealed the considerable scale of the proposal, a building as large as the adjacent Castillo del Morro. Three ranges, each one hundred meters long, enclosed a large central *patio* and set the edges of a square defined by the

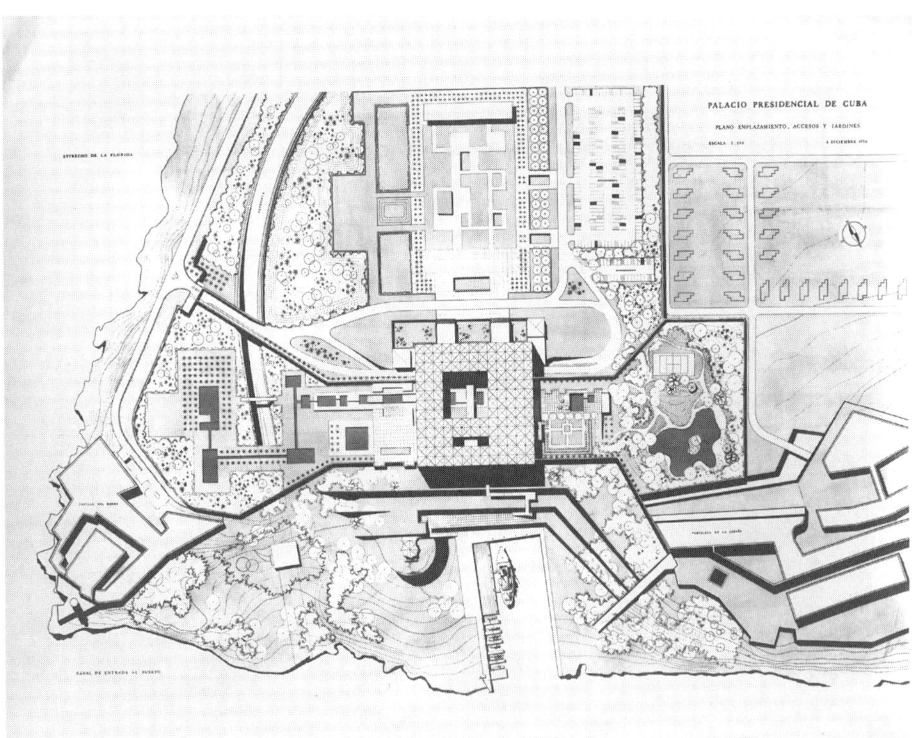

FIGURE 8.4 José Luis Sert et al., site plan, presidential palace, Havana, 1955–58. Courtesy of the Frances Loeb Library, Harvard Graduate School of Design.

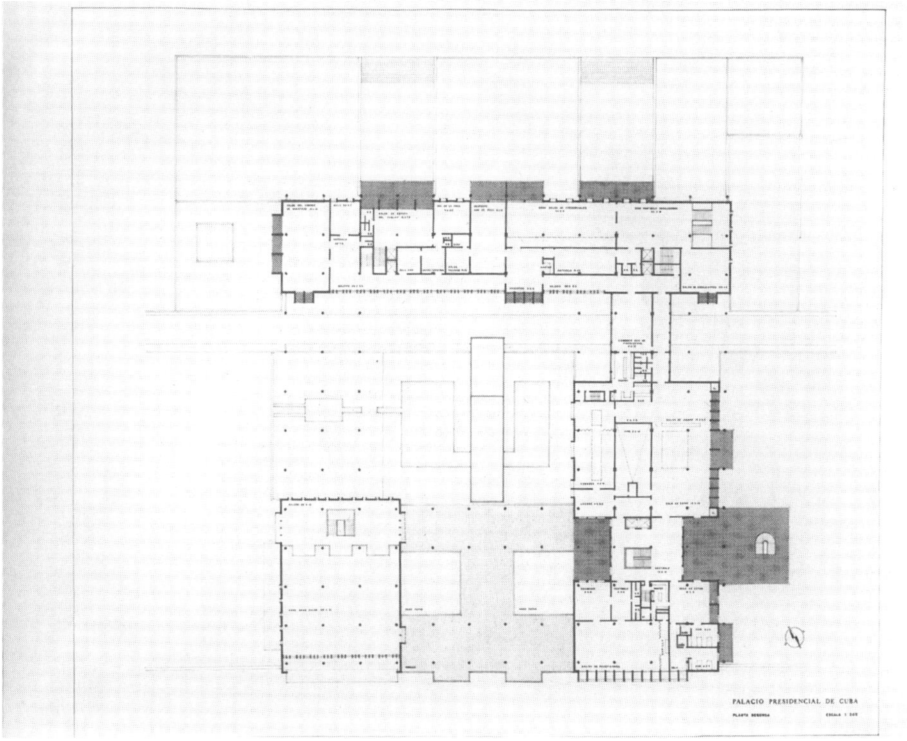

FIGURE 8.5 José Luis Sert et al., second floor plan, presidential palace, Havana, 1955–58. Courtesy of the Frances Loeb Library, Harvard Graduate School of Design.

FIGURE 8.6 José Luis Sert et al., model, view of east elevation and plaza, presidential palace, Havana, 1955–58. Courtesy of the Frances Loeb Library, Harvard Graduate School of Design.

perimeter of the parasol roof hovering above. The volume, enclosure, and fenestration of the ranges varied throughout to accommodate the mix of program; openings, frames, projections, and screens responded to interior elements and modulated the perceived relationship between interior and exterior *patios*. The eastern, primary facade incorporated two entrances, one for the public and one for official visits by ambassadors, leading into the presidential ministry and the executive offices on the second floor. To the south, the range containing the private residence overlooked an informal garden, while on the opposite side of the building, reception halls opened onto an outdoor network of paths, terraces, and pools. On the fourth facade, facing the city, the single volume of the reception hall balanced the aggregate pieces of the residential quarters and an elevated terrace provided an opening into the central *patio*. Exterior terraces dropped down to a dock and basin in the harbor.

Once the Palace of the Palms was linked to the Pilot Plan for Havana, its anticipated cost of eight million dollars might have been justified in terms of the broader program of national development. But the project would equally have been perceived as aggrandizing, a perception reinforced by its typological affiliation with grand historic structures. In the presentation drawings, the architects ingratiatingly illustrated this affiliation with a panel comparing the Palace of the Palms to the Palacio Real in Madrid, the Doge's Palace in Venice, and a number of other residences of heads of state (Figure 8.7). The panel was intended to demonstrate the appropriateness of the scale of the proposal, which was in fact similar to its typological predecessors, and emphasized as well the immense symbolic significance of the building regardless of its patron. The inclusion of the White House among the comparisons—in spite of its marked difference as a formal type—points not only to the continuing influence of the United States in Cuban culture but also to the plausibility of Batista's explanation that the executive branch required a symbolic presence equal to those of the two other branches of government. The legislature had, since 1929, been housed in the Capitolio and the judiciary had just occupied the new Palacio de Justicia. Both of these buildings had a more emphatic urban presence than the existing presidential palace and were certainly better accommodations functionally. No doubt anticipating criticism that the project was a personal glorification, Batista attempted to recast it as a symbol of the presidency, and made a point of assuring journalists that he himself would never occupy the building, but he would press for its

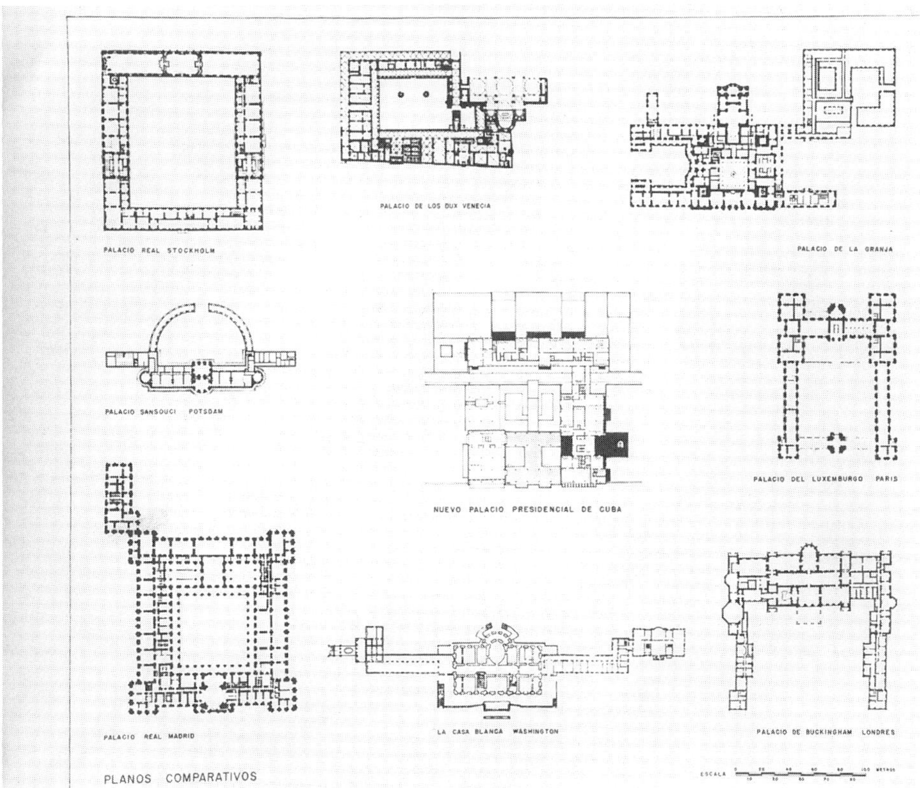

FIGURE 8.7 José Luis Sert et al., comparison of the plan of the presidential palace in Havana (center) to plans of other executive residences and palaces at the same scale. Courtesy of the Frances Loeb Library, Harvard Graduate School of Design.

quick completion in order that his immediate successor might inaugurate it. The typological perspective suggested by the comparative panel would obviously assume an inseparability of form and content, so that the courtyard organization of the proposed building would place it within a specific architectural lineage that would in turn conjure a genealogy of regimes of power. Yet Sert, recalling earlier positions taken in regard to the issue of monumentality, would certainly have rejected the direct imitation of earlier monumental buildings, while Romañach might additionally have resisted the implication that suitable forms were necessarily to be explicitly derived from European culture. Both architects could only have abided the typological affiliation in terms of function—symbolic function as well as programmatic—or if that affiliation occurred through an extended mediation that pursued what might be called an indirect rather than direct mimesis.

The formal resolution was to be singular and by distinctly deflecting referentiality, even to defy expectation—Sert wrote to Arroyo that "the Palace is a true Palace very different from what the majority of people imagine when they talk of a modern Palace."[18]

The project revealed its representational difficulties in tensions that emerged from the attempt to maintain a distance from typological lineage without severing that relation completely. The main facade provided the most obvious indications: two entrances symmetrically frame the central balcony at the second floor; the columns descending from the parasols stand in front of the surface of the wall, creating a colonnade that holds the secondary elements of the facade and masks the difference between the balconies above the two entrances. The symmetry and the static configuration of the facade contrast sharply with the highly differentiated organization of the rooms behind it. Moreover, the neoclassical composition of the facade was an unusual choice for Sert to make. Neoclassicism had provided the compositional and symbolic order of Stone's embassy in New Delhi, and was to do so also in the U.S. embassy in Athens, which Walter Gropius began to design in 1956.[19] But Sert, in his own recent proposal for the U.S. embassy in London, had set varied volumes and projections into differentiated relief against a pattern of fenestration, even though the context of London's Grosvenor Square had a strong neoclassical consistency to which many other entrants directly responded. Earlier sketched versions of the facade of the Palace of the Palms showed an idiosyncratic disposition of parts, with the balcony offset from the center. Sert's penciled revisions (and perhaps the desires of Batista himself) gradually drew the elements into their final more static arrangement (Figure 8.8). Given the discrepancy between the exterior order and the interior organization, the entrance facade clearly aimed to fulfill a symbolic purpose. It produced an obvious resemblance to the existing presidential palace, and also would have united symbolically the three branches of government insofar as all three would have been housed in buildings expressing neoclassical influence.

The neoclassicism of the facade of the Palace of the Palms, though, would bring the design perilously close to the imitative process denounced by Giedion as pseudo-monumentality, and so was unlikely to have been the basis for Sert's claim of the design's novelty and expressive truth. Regionalism would have provided a basis for that distinction, and in written descriptions of the project Sert emphasized the use of regionalist techniques, including those that Romañach and other Cuban architects had already established as links to Cuba's colonial tradition. These techniques would bind the new building to the physical historical residue of its regional context. On the site overlooking Havana, the two historic fortresses of El Morro and La Cabaña were, Sert wrote, "linked by an old stone wall [and] the new palace was placed so that this wall would become part of the new building."[20] When viewed from the city, the triptych formed by the three structures would represent the historical progression from colonial past to modern future (see Plate 10). Sert also referred to the materials and the wall components of the new building as evidence of enduring regional influence. Marble facing for the walls was to be quarried at the Isle of Pines off the southern coast, and the facades "composed of varied fenestration elements and glazed tile grills. The glazes are of different bright colors. Some of the windows make use of bright-colored glass . . . Many of these elements are to be found in the traditional architecture of Cuba."[21] Two other elements in the design recapitulated particular adaptations to climate that had assumed cultural significance: the arrangement of the three functions of the building around a central courtyard recalled the configuration of the colonial *palacios* of Habana Vieja, while the colonnade of the entrance facade, created by columns descending from the overhanging roof, evoked the *portales,* or arcades, that lined many of the streets and interior courtyards in the city. This primary facade was to overlook what Sert described as a "large public square laid out like the traditional Plaza de Armas."[22]

The arrangement of balcony, colonnade, and plaza offered the most direct invocation of the civic realm, particularly if considered in relation to the Capitolio Nacional and the Palacio de Justicia. Like those buildings, however, it evoked equally the pseudo-monumentality that Sert and Giedion excoriated as the manifestation of a weakened civil society. If the facade prompted reference to other

FIGURE 8.8 José Luis Sert et al., preliminary sketch for east elevation with revisions, presidential palace, Havana, 1955–58. Courtesy of the Frances Loeb Library, Harvard Graduate School of Design.

monarchical and imperial artifacts while lacking an equivalent association to its own historical and regional immediacies, it would produce only an illustration of the constraints of the present political situation. A more directed referential potential for the Palace of the Palms existed in the mimetic process prompted by another of its architectural figures, the recurring element of the *patio*. In addition to the central *patio* of the proposed building, which set the project within the typological set of monumental courtyard buildings, the architects incorporated various other *patios* into the palace: the large public plaza in front of the building, the elevated terrace connecting the reception halls and the residential wing, and the small courtyards inserted among the rooms of the private quarters. The courtyard and the courtyard building were invoked frequently in the architectural discourse of the time as archetypal forms common to almost every known culture, but the *patio* did have an especially strong local currency in Cuba (Figure 8.9). It was, first of all, the seminal element of the colonial Latin American cities, inscribed as their foundational gesture by the Laws of the Indies. In his detailed studies of the Plaza de Armas and the Plaza de la Catedral, Emilio Roig de Leuchsenring drew attention to the importance of the plazas located in Habana

FIGURE 8.9 Engraving of Plaza San Francisco in Habana Vieja published in *Plan Piloto de la Habana*. Courtesy of the Frances Loeb Library, Harvard Graduate School of Design.

Vieja, describing the several Plazas de Armas established in Havana prior to the one that survived, and documenting the enduring inseparability of the plaza from its surrounding colonial buildings as part of his larger advocacy of the preservation of Habana Vieja.[23] At a less monumental scale, the *patio* was also recognized as the distinctive feature of several historical structures in the city, such as the Palacio de Aldama, the Captain-General's Palace, and the existing presidential palace.[24] By the 1950s, the *patio* had been assimilated across all scales as a constitutive element of Cuban architecture.

Like his Cuban colleagues, Sert also placed great emphasis on the *patio* as a figure that recurred in architectural and urban contexts as any bounded space of social interaction, such as a courtyard in a house or *palacio* or a public square in a city. In earlier work that had prompted him and Wiener to discuss the *patio* as a figure—that is, as the deliberate weaving together of a discrete formal configuration and a figurative meaning—Sert undertook to demonstrate its correlation of form and content in order to argue its powerful and necessary social function. He had long been concerned with social function in different aspects and scales of architecture and beginning with the "Nine Points on Monumentality" had identified the monument or monumental ensemble as the site of collective expression. These two arguments converged when Sert and other CIAM members decided that the theme for the eighth CIAM congress would be the core, the physical center that symbolically expressed and directly fostered the collective life and the shared endeavors of a community. Addressing the congress in 1951 on that theme, Sert stipulated the original relationship between the *patio* form and the public square by quoting at length from José Ortega y Gasset's book *The Revolt of the Masses*.[25]

Ortega y Gasset had claimed that the creation of the public square was the foundational act of civilization—man's secession from the undifferentiated "amorphous" space of nature through an act of "innovation":

> The square, thanks to the walls which enclose it, is a portion of the countryside which turns its back on the rest, eliminates the rest and sets up in opposition to it. This lesser rebellious field, which secedes from the limitless one, and keeps to itself, is a space *sui generis*, of the most novel kind, in which man frees himself from the community of the plant and the animal, leaves them outside, and creates an enclosure apart which is purely human, a civil space.[26]

From this first enclosure, Sert traced out the lineage of myriad places of civic assembly: the agora, the piazza, and the Plaza de Armas of a colonial Latin American city, all of which provided the vital centers of the cities—and civil societies—in which they stood. The *patio* in front of the Palace of the Palms could certainly be understood as the adoption of an architectural precedent, an imitation of form parallel to the typological repetitions of the palace itself; as Sert stated in his descriptions, the large *patio* would suggest "traditional Plazas de Armas" such as those found in colonial cities and in Habana Vieja. But the *patio* assumed a significance beyond this initial connotation of *formal* precedent by being also a mimesis of the *effective* precedent, the founding act of the polis, extending spatially and temporally the scope of that earlier civic manifestation. The walling out of "limitless, amorphous space" in the original example posited by Ortega y Gasset became the imposition of metaphysical order upon aboriginal societies in the instances sponsored by the Laws of the Indies, which became—in Sert's writings—the arrest of the entropic chaos that consumed the modern city. Repetition of the form catalyzed the patterns that could reproduce the constitution of civilization: "Many cities of the past," wrote Sert, "had definite shapes or patterns, and were built around a Core that very often was the determining factor of those shapes. It was the cities that made the cores, but they in turn made the city a city, 'and not merely an aggregate of individuals.'"[27]

The core shaped the city not, or not only, through the bold gesture of civic unity, but by fostering the pedestrian transactions of public life. It wove together the coarse and the fine threads of civic fabric. At the congress, Sert described the social function of the core as "primarily that of uniting the people and facilitating direct contacts and exchanges of ideas that will stimulate free discussion" and claimed that new cores "could establish a frame where a new civic life and a healthy civic spirit could develop."[28] Although Sert's arguments, with their rhetoric of loss, bore a trace of longing for the sharper contours that may have characterized earlier civil societies, he avoided nostalgia in favor of a fixed attention on the future. The core, for example, might take advantage of "revolutionary means" of communication such as television to encourage public gatherings.[29] Along with such collective rituals of political and social life, the quotidian recurrence of individual encounters that relied on the "café table" and the "spoken word" would also foster civic life. "Through the centuries," Sert argued, "people have been getting together in the village greens, market places, promenades and piazzas . . .

People go there to see and to be seen, to meet friends and sweethearts, to make new acquaintances, to discuss politics, and sports, to tell of their lives, loves and adventures, or to comment [on] those of others."[30] To reinforce this point in *The Heart of the City,* Sert chose photographs of exemplary public squares in various states of human occupation. For the endpapers of the book, Sert selected a drawing of the Piazza San Marco by his friend the artist Saul Steinberg (Figure 8.10). Steinberg's drawing shows the two arcades of the piazza framing the activities of citizens and tourists. Waiters bring drinks to café tables, musicians play, the *cicerone* recites an abbreviated history. The impassioned conversation depicted along the bottom of the scene, illustrating the Italians' presumed propensity for gesticulation, calls attention to the literal mimetic dimension of the social interactions in the square—the speakers' hands trace out the content of each disputation as

FIGURE 8.10 Saul Steinberg, *Piazza San Marco,* 1951, published as endpaper in *The Heart of the City.* Ink and colored inks on paper, 23 × 29 inches. Private collection. Copyright The Saul Steinberg Foundation/Artists Rights Society (ARS), New York.

the participants mime their conversations. The architectural frame, according to Sert, acted as the "catalyzing element" that sponsored exactly this type of exchange, which should be understood more generally as the mimetic reproduction of social behaviors through human interaction.

Sert and Wiener had already in their earlier work proposed the synchronic dimension of the *patio*—its possible extension through the city as a module at a full spectrum of scales. The palace design depended on an additional diachronic dimension, with the reproduction of both the frame of the core and the activities it contained sustained by the mimetic figure of the *patio,* which had appeared historically not only as the monumental plaza, but also as the grand or modest residential courtyard that Eugenio Batista had described without qualification as "an indispensable element of our architecture" and that Sert saw as the space that permitted the family to enact daily life "in a different world—the world that each family can build for itself."[31] While the activities of the domestic and civic spheres were qualitatively different, they were still commensurable; the world building sponsored by the enclosure of the family house reflected the world building fostered by the enclosure of the core. Complementing the synchronic resonance of the form of the *patio,* the diachronic recapitulation of the content of the *patio* figure—the ritual foundation of the polis, the recall of architectural precedent, and the reproduction of social behavior—would enable the performative mimesis of the public square to percolate throughout the city and society.

In its manifest formal attributes the Palace of the Palms would have participated in this sequence of affiliations. The insistent repetition of the *patio* at all scales within the project itself was a mimicry of the distribution of those *patios* across the city. Moreover, the formal Plaza de Armas in front of the palace would serve to symbolize and also to accommodate the enactment of civic life, to reveal but also compel the performance of the rituals of civic order. Yet Sert himself offered a distinctly qualified assessment of the political capacities of architecture:

> Naturally, the character and the conditions of such awakened civic life do not depend entirely on the existence of a favourable [architectural] frame, but are tied to the political, social and economic structure of every community. If this political, social, and economic structure is one that permits a free exchange of ideas leading towards the government of the majority, such civic centers would consolidate those governments; for the lack of them and the dependence of the

> people on controlled means of information makes them more easily governable by the rule of the few.[32]

This view, by no means unconventional, stipulated a clear limit to the transformative capacity of architecture, and so changes the question of the representational status of the palace. If it cannot be assigned a reformist intention, to what it extent did it actually propose to sustain the existing political configuration? In its situated context, that compulsion of civic rituals has a very particular cast, reminiscent, of course, of infamous staged rallies. The activities suggested for the plaza, in Sert's descriptions at least, were not the myriad chance encounters and spoken exchanges vividly illustrated in the Piazza San Marco. It would be a public square "where vast crowds can assemble," facing the broad facade of the palace and its central projecting balcony, which Batista himself wanted extended further to be closer to the crowd.[33] Although this gathered crowd would not in itself signify the problematic nature of the figure—after all, such a crowd gathered in front of the Capitolio Nacional to hear the proclamation of the Constitution of 1940—the isolation and segregation of such a congregation from other spontaneous activities in the physical geography of the city and in the political register of citizenship would sharply divide the ceremonial and quotidian functions of the plaza, compromising the mimetic potential of the figure by failing to sustain the plenary performance of civic life.

Constructing *cubanidad*

The *patio,* facade, and other aspects of the building's architecture were subordinate to its dominant feature, the enormous, hovering roof, which "gives the Palace of the Palms its architectural character and monumental scale"[34] (Figure 8.11). The roof also gave the project its romantic name: the form of each of its parasols, curved concrete shells springing from an octagonal column, "recalls in scale, shape and size, the royal palm . . . the symbol of Cuba and a characteristic element in the landscape of the island."[35] Uniquely in Sert's work and in Romañach's as well, the form made a claim to mimetic naturalism. The architects insisted in preliminary plans and presentation drawings on the natural analogy, reinforcing it by juxtaposing parasols and palm trees in drawings. On the margin of a memorandum, Sert even sketched out a correction to show his model makers a

FIGURE 8.11 José Luis Sert et al., perspective of west elevation, presidential palace, Havana, 1955–58. Courtesy of the Frances Loeb Library, Harvard Graduate School of Design.

more faithful representation of the fan of palm leaves (Figure 8.12). Sert's statement that the parasols gave to the design both its "architectural character and monumental scale" indicates that they carried the full burden of the debates on regionalism and monumentality, and were to contribute decisively to the representation of *cubanidad.* In a group of preliminary sketches, Sert had first rendered the palace roof as a continuous folded plate raised above the building. He had devised this solution previously for the ambassador's residence in Baghdad, describing it as a climatic response that drew upon the local example of double roofs used to dissipate solar heat. But as the palace design evolved, the roof's representational dimension extended considerably beyond its compensatory environmental function. In the fall of 1956, Sert hastily recruited the engineer Félix Candela (who, like Sert, had been exiled from Spain for his republican activities and whom Sert had brought to lecture at Harvard the previous year).[36] Candela

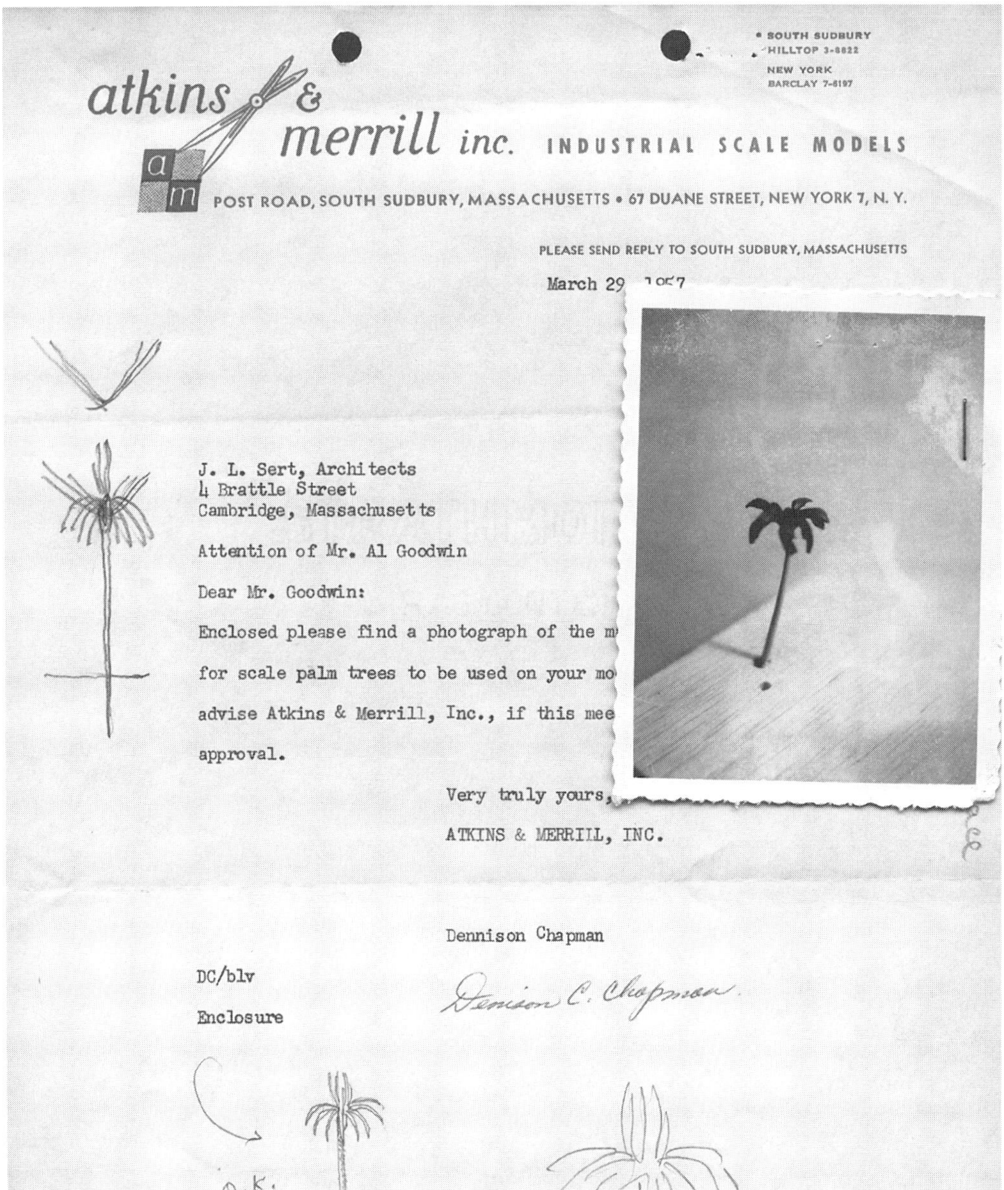

atkins & merrill inc. INDUSTRIAL SCALE MODELS

• SOUTH SUDBURY
HILLTOP 3-8822
NEW YORK
BARCLAY 7-8197

POST ROAD, SOUTH SUDBURY, MASSACHUSETTS • 67 DUANE STREET, NEW YORK 7, N. Y.

PLEASE SEND REPLY TO SOUTH SUDBURY, MASSACHUSETTS

March 29, 1957

J. L. Sert, Architects
4 Brattle Street
Cambridge, Massachusetts

Attention of Mr. Al Goodwin

Dear Mr. Goodwin:

Enclosed please find a photograph of the m
for scale palm trees to be used on your mo
advise Atkins & Merrill, Inc., if this mee
approval.

Very truly yours,

ATKINS & MERRILL, INC.

Dennison Chapman

Denison C. Chapman

DC/blv

Enclosure

O.K.

FIGURE 8.12 Memo with sketches of palm trees drawn by Sert, 1957. Courtesy of the Frances Loeb Library, Harvard Graduate School of Design.

met with Sert and Romañach in Cuba, and a new solution for the roof emerged from their discussions; shortly after returning to Mexico City, Candela supplied structural drawings and photographs of a model—the roof was transformed into independent parasols, each a hyberbolic paraboloid with an unusually articulated recurved form to create a steep arc rising up from the columns and descending in the manner of the fronds of a palm tree (Figure 8.13).

Félix Candela's innovations in thin concrete shells had begun to attract considerable attention in the United States, where the experimental deployment of concrete forms was often associated with Latin America. Its capacity for plastic expression prompted critics to see a ready affiliation between the technology and what they regarded as typically Latin American formal expression. Henry-Russell Hitchcock, for example, remarked on an "innate sympathy for the vault-like shapes of shell concrete construction" and the "appeal to the Iberian temperament" of "lyrical" forms.[37] For Candela, however, such immoderate regard for formal

FIGURE 8.13 Félix Candela, plaster model of parasol for presidential palace, 1956. Courtesy of the Frances Loeb Library, Harvard Graduate School of Design.

expression had led to a "sensationalism" that disregarded the true value of hyperbolic paraboloid structural forms. He noted that the technology's formal capacities had been seized upon in a "move to humanize the arid, primitive idiom left to us by the pioneers," but in his view, the minimal use of steel and simplicity of fabrication—its basis in "purely functional and economic reasoning"—particularly suited thin shell structures to the labor and manufacturing conditions of Latin America.[38] At the time he traveled to Cuba to meet Sert and Romañach, Candela could boast that his office was "casting twenty umbrellas *[paraguas]* a week."[39] Sert was familiar with Candela's prototypical structures—he had likely seen the single-umbrella roof that the engineer designed for a small flower shop in the Vedado district of Havana in 1955—and with the novelty of their forms. In a later recollection of Candela's first lecture at Harvard, Sert described the engineer's work as a product of the spirit and the limitations of his context, and the catalog of shell structures he presented as unprecedented.

But even if the forms were, in Sert's view, without precedent, they were nevertheless based on an imitative process. Sert would have been equally familiar with Candela's claim that his thin shells deliberately imitated the compound curve of natural shells, deriving from them the basic principle of their strength.[40] Both Spaniards were conscious of the influence of Antoni Gaudí. Candela recognized and admired how Gaudí extracted from natural forms complex principles of structure, and while Candela surpassed Gaudí in comprehension of the structural economy of these principles, he acknowledged the singular inspiration of the Catalonian works. At the time he met Candela, Sert had recently completed a manuscript of a book on Gaudí, written together with James Johnson Sweeney.[41] One of the first of several books that would rediscover and redeem Gaudí's work for modernism, the manuscript was organized around the thesis of Gaudí's relevance to the contemporary period. In Sert and Sweeney's account, Gaudí's derivation of form from natural models depended on imitation, but imitation of inherent principles rather than external appearances. His careful study of natural elements, they argued, revealed to him the "natural forces" that lay beneath "surface expressions" and these provided the inspiration and the model for angled columns and flexing walls. Mimesis of nature, then, could be manifested by means other than the reproduction of outer appearances. A mimesis of inherent principles of structural forces, of growth, or of extension, might avoid the relegation of architectural form to the inferior position of reference, drawing instead an equation of similarity. This interpretation would apply as well to Candela's shell vaults, rendering them as both signs and instances of a universal, intrinsic nature revealed as mathematical and geometric principle.

Yet the parasols of the palace also meant explicitly to evoke palm trees in their outer appearance, a specificity of reference not previously apparent in Candela's work, and one, moreover, that gave priority to particularity over universality insofar as its local affiliation also emphasized the conditions of Latin American modernization. Here too the text on Gaudí hinted at the significance of this double representation, as Sert and Sweeney's defense of Gaudí's relevance included an opening toward the potentials of overt referentiality with a hedging but deliberate paragraph on contemporary debates:

> There is today a feeling among certain architects that of late years the expressive or associative aspects of architecture have been neglected in favour of an undue emphasis on its technical side. Whether or not we subscribe to this view, we cannot deny that it is current, as we hear in such phrases as "the need for a new monumentality," "the humanisation of modern architecture" and "putting content back into art."[42]

Sert did, of course, subscribe to this view, having been its proponent from the earliest discussions on modern monumentality, but notable in the Gaudí manuscript was the opening toward not only expression but association as well. In their introduction, the authors stressed that Gaudí had in his own time "brought back an interest in the associational and imaginative factors of architectural expression."[43] In presenting the familiar evolutionary account of modern architecture from the restorative "stripping of architecture to its bare bones" to the contemporary necessity of a new vocabulary of expression, Sert and Sweeney outlined the parallel in modern art, arguing that Surrealists—such as Miró, one of Sert's closest friends—"were seeking a new imaginative expression in their own medium, but were not embarrassed if their work set up extra-plastic musings in the observer as many of their puritan predecessors had been."[44] License was therefore granted not only to plastic expression, but to the accommodation, or even perhaps cultivation, of "extra-plastic musings," the interpretive relationships fashioned by the observer between a work of architecture and other cultural, social, or physical experiences. With this expansion of the terms of modernism, the equation of the parasol and the palm tree would have taken on a more nuanced complexion. It was indeed a mimesis of nature, but its first literal order was seemingly subordinate to a second order of nature envisioned as abstract principles described by mathematical formulas and geometric diagrams.

The architects' very deliberate fidelity to the natural form of the palm tree was not only a prompt from the superficial aspect of nature to its underlying orders, but also, and profoundly, an associational element, a device to prompt extra-plastic musings in the minds of its Cuban audience, and there were in fact specifically Cuban resonances in the image of the royal palm tree, resonances beyond its familiar occurrence in the landscape of the island. The first of these resonances related to José Martí, who had come to be regarded as not only a historical agent of Cuban independence but as the author of an ideal of Cuban identity. In 1953, as numerous events and publications in Cuba marked the centennial of his birth and brought renewed depictions of his role in the nation's history, work commenced on the Monumento a Martí that would physically manifest Martí's central position in Cuban culture. Sert, who by 1955 had spent significant time in Cuba and had formed close friendships with younger colleagues there, would have been aware of Martí's significance, but it was the Cuban architects, Romañach in particular, but Menéndez, Arroyo, and others as well, who would have fully recognized his associative resonance. Martí's famous 1891 essay "Nuestra América" (Our America) declared the emergence in Latin America of an autochthonous consciousness with a mestizo, or hybrid, point of view forged from Indian and Spanish sources, from indigenous and colonial knowledge. Capable of resisting the overt hegemony of North American materialism and the covert hegemony of European culture, the new foundational culture of mestizo America would be grounded upon the "obvious realities [and] the natural constitution" of the Latin American continent.[45] But Martí's mimetic account, in which culture and political structure would reflect the conditions in which they were immersed, was neither primitivist nor parochial. North America and Europe would remain influential, but at the periphery rather than the center of the mestizo point of view. "Let the world be grafted onto our republics," Martí declared, "but the trunk must be our own."[46] The tree provided not only a literary metaphor but potentially a metonymic expression of naturalized hybridity. In his notebook, Martí drew a sketch of a new columnar order based on the palm tree, with the fronds transformed into an ornamental screen, arches, and the capital of a column (Figure 8.14). "Imagine this order for America," he wrote as a caption, "palms, as columns, in a precise representation of the palms in nature."[47]

Martí's regional metaphor soon became a national emblem—the royal palm tree appeared on the shield of the new Cuban Republic in 1902, and that heraldic device was given legal sanction by the Constitution of 1940—but his sketches were not published until 1943, when they appeared in the Cuban journal *Arquitectura* along with articles on the future monument to Martí. By that time, observation

FIGURE 8.14 José Martí, sketch for a palm tree order, circa 1891. *Arquitectura*, October 1943.

and expression of *cubanidad* was the deeply embedded preoccupation of the Cuban avant-garde, of writers and artists as well as the circle of modernist architects. Overlapping exchanges between architecture, art, and literature had introduced into architectural explorations an attention to factors beyond physical elements, beyond the elements contained in Harris's subordinate category of "climate, topography, and sticks and stones." The architect Eugenio Batista, whose Bonet House had demonstrated how colonial architecture might be married to new techniques and forms, would later note the resemblance between the typical pairing of strong horizontal roofs with vertical accents of columns and the low landscape "sprinkled with the vertical elements of our royal palm trees."[48] Inside the house, he painted a mural that transformed an interior corner into a dense grove of palms. Batista further argued that architecture could only be "faithfully expressive of what is ours if we follow the tradition of *patios, portales,* and *persianas* in the material realm, and of rhythm, gaiety, and cleanliness in the spiritual"—a claim that encouraged not only the pursuit of the physical elements of *lo cubano* but the pursuit of the experiential qualities of *la cubanidad.* The palm tree was employed as the basis of architectonic ornamentation in other instances during the prewar period, in which the search for modes of nationalist expression was under way in a number of cultural disciplines. In 1931, the Colegio de Arquitectos sponsored a competition for "La Estilización de un orden de Palma Real" (Design of an Royal Palm order), thus taking up Martí's suggestion; first place was awarded to the architect Aquiles Maza. In 1939, Pedro Martínez Inclán designed his own version of an "orden de Palma Real" for the columns and pilasters of the Escuela de Ciencias (School of the Sciences) at the University of Havana. The architects working on the design of the Capitolio in 1931 proposed a different ornamental incorporation of the royal palm in sketches of the cupola that showed the dome with a large, individual palm frond applied to its surface in the space between each rib[49] (Figure 8.15). Here the association between architecture, the royal palm, and civil society was made explicit, with the palm tree becoming an image of the legislative sphere of the state and thus joining the natural constitution of Cuba to the nation's civic structure.

Many of these architects, and certainly Eugenio Batista, shared with the modernist writers of *Revista de Avance* and the Vanguardia painters the common influence of anthropologist Fernando Ortiz, who was for most the intellectual source of the pairing of the physical and the experiential dimensions of *cubanidad.*[50] With

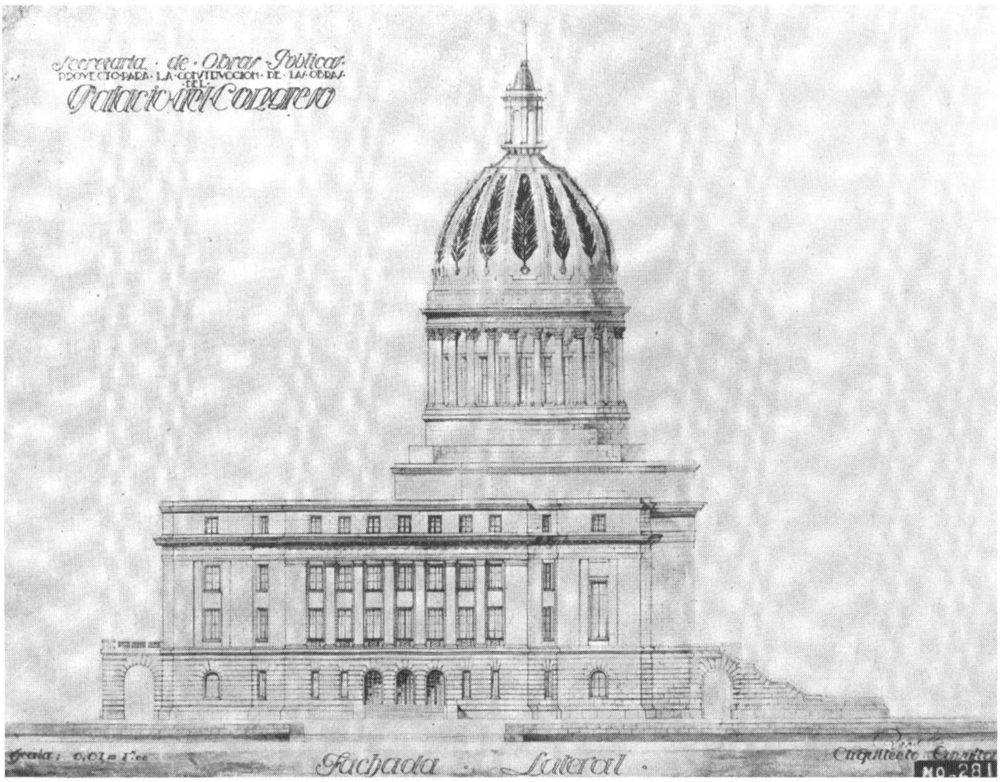

FIGURE 8.15 Elevation of Capitolio Nacional showing proposed cupola with palm frond ornamentation. From *El Libro del Capitolio* (Havana: P. Fernández y Cía, 1933).

his pioneering studies of Afro-Cuban culture, Ortiz had by the 1930s helped establish as the broad outlines of *cubanidad* its unique mixture of Spanish colonial and Afro-Cuban habits and practices staged within the occupation and cultivation of the Cuban landscape. His conception of the hybridity of Cuban culture became a fundamental conceit of avant-garde discourse. In 1940, Ortiz published his influential polemical study *Contrapunteo cubano del tabaco y el azúcar (Cuban Counterpoint: Tobacco and Sugar),* which described in precise detail the peculiar contrasting character of Cuba's two cultivated crops: the indigenous hand-worked tobacco and the mechanically produced sugar transplanted by colonists. Their characteristics, he claimed, underlay Cuban society and culture: "the amazing differences between the two products are reflected in the history of the Cuban nation from its very ethnological formation to its social structure, its political fortunes, and its international relations."[51] Economic relations and customs of behavior, class organizations and artistic productions, all mirrored these two natural ecologies. The concept of landscape was here far deeper than the pictorial, becoming at once the cause and the representation of social formations and the behavior of subjects.

The Palace of the Palms and Ortiz's conception of landscape can be drawn together retrospectively by one particular avant-garde artwork, *Paisaje con caballos salvajes* (Landscape with wild horses) painted in 1941 by the prominent representational artist Carlos Enríquez (see Plate 11). Enríquez was one of a group of artists related not only to Ortiz but also to architects in the JNP, including Romañach, Arroyo, and Quintana.[52] All of these architects carried on a continuing dialogue with artists, informally, collegially, and also professionally, with commissions for murals and sculptures in their residential and commercial work. In fact, in one of the earliest of these collaborations, a mural for the Edificio Esso painted in 1951, Enríquez employed the palm tree again as the central motif. But *Paisaje con caballos salvajes* has an additional importance because Sert himself would have seen this painting in 1943 when it was exhibited with the Latin American Collection at the Museum of Modern Art in New York. With the interwoven fronds of a dense cluster of royal palms forming an overarching roof above the converging rivers, the composition endowed the landscape with an architectonic aspect. At the same time, the erotic imagery of the painting tied the landscape to the female body and to what Enríquez believed was the inherent sensuality of *cubanidad*. Trying, therefore, to attain an almost physical sensation of the environment, he used a technique of blurred, transparent colors as a way to render the "tropical light [that] erases the distances, sometimes turns solid objects into liquid, fuses the colors."[53] Enríquez was describing here not the light itself, but the experience of that light. By drawing together the physical environment and the self-consciousness of subjectivity, Enríquez's figurative landscape represented the experiential point of view of *cubanidad*. It did so, notably, through a combination of explicitly associative elements (showing the influence of Surrealism on Enríquez) and formal technique (the blurred transparency of his paint as the reenactment of physical experience).

Enríquez drew the representation of experience from a conjunction of nature and the body, but the subsequent appropriation of the architectonic canopy of royal palms suggests its susceptibility, its capacity to represent constructed social manifestations as well. The semblance between Enríquez's image and the design of the presidential palace orients the question of mimesis differently (Figure 8.16). The imitation of actual palm trees was only the prefatory claim of the concrete parasols. Their requisite mimetic binding of imitative form and iterative content reproduced a broader rendering of reality, reality of situation as much as physical reality—the two were in fact inseparable. The parasols fulfill the basic functional criteria of a roof sheltering the building from its tropical climate, and thus abide by the core belief of modern functionalism; by their fidelity to the abstract principles of structural form, the parasols satisfy a second predilection of modernism; they also manifest the technological potentials of their context, with Candela's shell vault a metonymy of the modernizing technology applied to the cultures and climate of Latin America; and finally, they refer also to José Martí's invocation of the hybrid "natural constitution" of America, and to the experience of *cubanidad* conjured out of the landscape by Carlos Enríquez. The parasols could embrace literal and symbolic connotations but without thereby claiming essential authenticity or universal signification, and while also incorporating corollary figural referents. Aggregated to form the sheltering second roof of the palace, the parasols do perform a functional and arguably necessary role in the design. But the steep curve of the shell, the line chosen from infinite

FIGURE 8.16 José Luis Sert et al., model, view from north with proposed sculpture by Constantino Nivola in foreground, presidential palace, Havana, 1955–58. Courtesy of the Frances Loeb Library, Harvard Graduate School of Design.

possible arcs drawn by Romañach and tested by Candela as the two sat on the *patio* of the architect's house, possesses an indisputably ornamental character.[54] Although this ornamental element risked seeming a shallow imitation of nature anachronistically conceived in 1957, it in fact proposed an expansive mimesis of nature, culture, and technology collapsed into a single architectonic figure, one that could, through its historical affiliations, achieve a figural mimesis by recognition of its affinity to the prior figures of Martí's columnar order and Enríquez's landscape that precede or anticipate the parasols, which would themselves anticipate in turn some future recurrence.

This latter anticipation responds to the initial dilemma, aesthetic and political, provoked by the compulsion to produce a representation of *cubanidad*. How could architecture sustain civic consciousness in a civil society utterly compromised by Batista's dictatorship? In the instance of the *patio,* the insertion of the architectural figure within a genealogy of the performance of civic foundation revealed its potential dissonance within the representational terms of the project. Considered in conjunction with the parasols, that dissonance might be understood as a temporal one, corresponding to the tendency in figural mimesis toward anticipation rather than satisfaction, the tendency toward deferral. Through figural mimesis, the parasols announced the fulfillment of Martí's goal of an independent Cuba engaged with international currents as a nation, but they evoked also the deficient development of the civil society Martí had envisioned for a republican Cuba. The *patio* and the parasols did not close the figural sequence; they prefigured its future continuation, producing through the accretion of analogical figures a regionalist representation in the present while deferring representational resolution. The potential of the mimetic figures of the Palace of the Palms to sustain civil society lay not in their performance within that sphere, but in their prefiguration of the future possibility of its restoration.

Epilogue

Futures of Constitutional Modernism

In the final version, printed at the very end of 1958, the Plan Piloto de la Habana included an alternative organization of the space surrounding the Monumento a Martí on the Loma de los Catalanes. It would have been clear when Wiener, Sert, and Romañach commenced the Plan Piloto in 1955 that the monument designed by Labatut and his colleagues would be realized—its works were already under way—but the normative conception proposed by the Plan Piloto required that this important civic element be somehow assimilated into its encompassing order. Three changes to the actual site configuration were to accomplish this assimilation. First, some ministry buildings originally located as constituent elements of the Plaza de la República might be relocated across the bay to the area adjacent to the new Palace of the Palms. Second, the plaza itself could be connected to the proposed system of linear parks in order to incorporate its distinctive open space into the larger structure of open spaces. Third, most improbable but for the architects perhaps most necessary, the plaza itself could be transformed from an open plaza to a *patio* plaza in the formal idiom that the Plan Piloto would install in other civic centers at the neighborhood scale. There is no evidence that this assimilation was ever seriously considered, even by the partners of Town Planning Associates, but Sert and Romañach did insert their alternative plan for the Plaza de la República into the final drawings of the Plan Piloto de la Habana instead of using the Labatut, Varela, and Otero plan that was by then actually under construction, and this alternative scheme was plausibly rendered with some degree of precision (Figure E.1). It included the star-plan monument and the Palacio de Justicia correctly positioned, and the buildings for

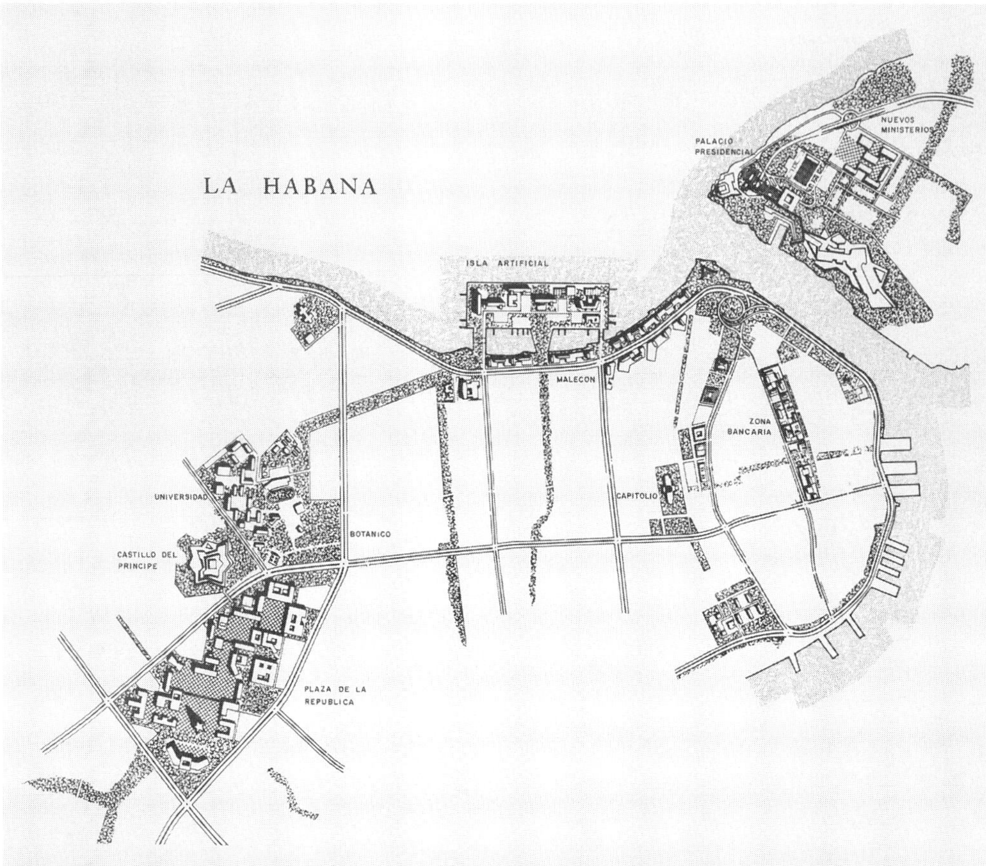

FIGURE E.1 Town Planning Associates and Junta Nacional de Planificación, Plan de Enlaces de Núcleos Cívicos, *Plan Piloto de la Habana*, 1955–58. Courtesy of the Frances Loeb Library, Harvard Graduate School of Design.

the National Theater, the Tribunal de Cuentas, the Ministry of Communications, and the Library were also shown, although with their position not conforming to the axis of the implemented design. In this version, the main axis from the monument does not bisect the space between the tribunal and the ministry; instead, a secondary axis leads between those two buildings into a secondary plaza space; at the corner of that plaza, an opening leads to a tertiary plaza to the east. The roadway is shown as a high-speed road running to the east of the site (in an area where some buildings already existed) and segregated entirely from the plaza. The enormous and cohesive environment of Labatut's site plan is rendered in this alternative version as discrete smaller spaces. A large space for public gatherings would still remain in front of the monument, but other areas would be of a different scale, distinctly urban, designed as hardscape and as buildings rather than as parks. The complex would connect directly to the quadrangles and new landscaped areas of the university and from there to a green boulevard running from Vedado to the waterfront in Centro Habana, completing one of the linear bands of green space to be woven into the city.

Drawn in 1957 and 1958, this alternative proposal was merely speculative; though perhaps designed with an optimistic awareness of the transience of public works projects typical in Cuban politics, it was more likely intended to illustrate the conceptual framework of the Plan Piloto and also to evade endorsement of Labatut's design. It ignores the complexity of Labatut's conception, which would preclude any such segregation of the design of the monument from the design of its context; an integral connection of the two was necessary to create the "air space" that would in turn produce the desired civic attention. Sert and his colleagues intended to confirm the cohesion of the urban whole by bringing the monument into conformity with their superimposed normative order, but Labatut's monument was already tightly bound to the broad urban context that surrounded it, by means of a quite different conception. With the *mirador* and the radiating pattern of streets below it, but also with the careful construction of the encounter with the monument by pedestrians and by people in cars, Labatut and his colleagues designed the manner in which the Monumento a Martí would participate in the city, in the lived experience of urbanity.

In one sketch of his later site plan, Labatut referred to the open area of the Plaza de la República as a concave oval suitable for public congregations and similar in scale to the Piazza San Pietro (St. Peter's Square) in Rome.[1] (The flanking wings of the Palacio de Justicia embracing the Monumento a Martí would have reinforced, albeit in utterly degraded fashion, the historical relationship.) It would indeed fulfill such a ceremonial role at times, but its function as an urban architecture required that it also engage reciprocally with the individual citizen in other moments and in other attitudes. The Monumento a Martí did so at several scales, from the close proximity solicited by its architecture and the sculpture of Martí, to the wider perspective of the plaza, landscape, and the city itself, in events and public gatherings as well as in the daily passages of *habaneros*. More difficult was the relation between the Monumento a Martí and historical context. From the outset, the aim of the competition had been the design and realization of a historical object that effected a connection between the nation's past and its present and also denoted an originary moment representative of the fulfillment of Cuban independence; hence the injunction that competition entrants produce an object both symbolically effective *and* original in form. Labatut, Varela, and Otero sought to resolve this potential contradiction through an architectural process of abstraction that Labatut understood as a means to free architecture from the confines of precedent by drawing out and distilling the significant experience of a work of architecture. Once loosed from the historical armature from which it developed, the Monumento a Martí could manifest the ideality of the Cuban nation in the singular contemporaneity of its citizen subjects.

Despite its seeming distance from the historical past, the monument did not assume an ahistorical posture. Not only was the object itself symbolic of an overwhelming historical circumstance—the progressive and therefore temporal process of independence—but it encouraged its audience to identify itself as a collective of historical subjects endowed with civic consciousness. When Labatut insisted to his colleagues that the monument would be "Cuban 1953," he both denied any historicist patrimony for the tapered form and asserted the contemporaneity of the experience it would produce. Yet the tapered form itself embodied the symbolic figure of the star from the Cuban flag, which the discourse of constitutionalism had rendered inescapably historical by altering the text of the constitutional article to fix the image of the flag to the event of Cuban independence. The national flag was thereby established not as an abstract symbol, but as an index of the recurrence of a historical event, of which the Monumento a Martí might now serve as a further repetition. The historicity of the monument was, however, of a particular kind, a historical consciousness condensed into an experience not merely of temporality, but of presentness.

Against the presentness of the Monumento a Martí, the deferrals located within the architecture of the Palacio de las Palmas might assume a dialectical perspective. As two architectural monuments that aimed to achieve the representation of the Cuban nation with the backdrop of Batista's dictatorship, the monument and the palace both revealed the dilemmas of modernism within this political context and offered different terms of resolution. When considered retrospectively in the context of the constitutionalism that projected the civic society to which they were to contribute, those terms function together as a dialectical pair. Recall that in 1938, in the initiatory moments of the constitutional project,

Gustavo Gutiérrez had argued that every nation has two constitutions, "one *theoretical* or *literary* that lives in the formalities of the Fundamental Charter, and another *real* or *practical* formed by life itself in the development of national institutions . . . While the constitutions separate themselves more, the more difficult is constitutional life and more disposed to disturbances and revolutions. While they draw closer and mix more, the life of a nation is made easier, and social welfare more likely and more lasting."[2] Architecture and the disciplines with which it was entangled assumed the responsibility to induce this proximity, but with the consequent complexities of a representational medium that is also an economic and material practice. Architecture, in other words, was, in any given instance, bound to both constitutions, the real and the theoretical. Even as an architectural object such as a monument or palace responds to the real circumstances in which it is conceived, it alters and changes those circumstances as a material and social fact in itself. By thus occupying and acting upon the real and theoretical registers simultaneously, architectural objects such as the Monumento a Martí and the Palacio de las Palmas could offer as their civic projections both actual and unattained historical possibilities.

In such projections, the potential enabled by the negotiation with constitutionalism that Sert and Romañach proposed could be described as prefiguring a future state of civil society, while that of the negotiation proposed by Labatut, Varela, and Otero was its direct engagement with "Cuba 1953." With these potentials, though, came corresponding limitations. For the Palace of the Palms, its remove from real social or economic structures limited the likelihood of effective agency in the development of those structures, whereas for the Monumento a Martí, its nearness to the realities of those same structures virtually assured some degree of political complicity. Complicity here would refer not to the collaboration of individuals with political structures (although that was certainly one consequence) but rather to the susceptibility of these respective modes of architecture to becoming concrete representations of those political structures, becoming the symbols of Batista's dictatorship rather than the effective institutions of civil society. The work of Sert, Wiener, Romañach, Arroyo, Montoulieu, and their several colleagues could not, of course, be directly appropriated because it was left unrealized after the revolution. But Wiener's subsequent reflection (quoted earlier in part) made following that pivotal turn suggested the consequences: "You can imagine our awkward situation with respect to the Cuban

Revolution. Here we are good liberals and democrats and are probably identified in the minds of some people as Batista men. Of course, I lose no sleep over it, and am fortunate in having come out of the situation fairly well."[3] Wiener was referring, very likely, to the not inconsiderable financial gain Town Planning Associates had accrued from its work in Cuba, but was surely contrasting his situation with that of his Cuban colleagues who were placed into far more precarious positions professionally and personally. An additional gloss on Wiener's comment, though not one he himself intended, would be that the project in which he participated, the formulation of civil society through the mode of constitutionalism, had been advanced even though its realization had not been achieved. As for the Monumento a Martí, one of its more remarkable aspects has been its ready conversion, at the moment of the Cuban Revolution in 1959, from a signifier of Batista's dictatorship to a signifier of the historical legitimacy of his successor, Fidel Castro, whose lengthy speeches from a rostrum at the base of the Monumento a Martí soon became iconic in themselves.

This conversion depended on more than the physical theatricality of the monument and its surroundings. Those surroundings were, in any case, completed with a number of changes to Labatut's design, so that the statue of Martí looked out across a vast plaza largely empty of trees and without his carefully studied approaches. The two buildings opposite, the Tribunal de Cuentas and the Ministry of Communications, closed the plaza without a graduated connection to the city; the blank stone face of the circulation tower of the tribunal building was then used to mount a bas-relief outline of the famous Alberto Korda image of Che Guevara, a supplement of revolutionary iconography to create a backdrop for the mass public demonstrations of revolutionary fidelity. While the spare armature of this opening in the urban fabric and the visibility of the monument as a marker certainly enabled the substitution of revolutionary performance for civic performance, the architecture itself was a willing participant, so to speak, in the process. The architectural conception advanced by Labatut and his colleagues, an architecture of presentness and vivid experience, functioned as a persistent and periodic appraisal of the conditions of civil society. The monument maintained Martí's civic significance, but not as a steady or conclusive verity; rather, it produced the expressions of the changing significance that was determined through the didactic formation of the citizens who approached it, and then collapsed that significance with the present physical reality of environment and form.

Thus the revolutionary ideology, far from encountering resistance in the architecture of the monument, was readily absorbed into it. This is not to say, however, that the monument was appropriated by the revolution. It might in fact be more accurate to say that the revolution was appropriated by the architecture of the Monumento a Martí.

The insistent repetition to be enacted by the monument's periodic synthesis was one mode of recurrence. The palm tree parasols of the unrealized Palace of the Palms introduced another mode of recurrence into the set of circulating architectural potentials at this concluding moment of the Cuban republic. By introducing figuration into the modernist form of the Palace of the Palms, the parasols introduced also the possibility that mimesis would incorporate a temporal dimension and so produce not only a direct representation but also a narrative of its referent. While the palm tree might first be taken as an unmediated embodiment of the physical geographic place, both it and the parasols that mimetically reproduced it were properly metaphors for not only the island but also the nation of Cuba, metaphors, that is, not only for the place of society but also for the space of civil society as rendered in historical time. Envisioned as a structure of reference layered upon a synchronic axis, the royal palm tree would be the bottom level, the parasols the next, and the nation of Cuba the top. The parasols would mediate between the actual (a royal palm tree) and the conceptual (Cuba), supporting and also taking advantage of the metaphorical sequence, because the palm tree as an environmental reality serves as a metonym for the concept of Cuba. The parasols are similarly metaphors for the concept of Cuba, connected indirectly rather than immanently. This synchronic axis of metaphorical relation contains as well the central essentialist presumptions of regionalism. Even though the parasols introduce, through their material and their fabrication, technological tropes of universalism, the dependence on the actuality of the palm tree would reduce the proliferated references to one local, presumptively authentic constant.

Mimesis, however, if manifest also as a temporal dimension, would introduce a marked change in orientation, setting the parasols within a different referential set of figures. Arrayed along a diachronic axis, the prior figures of Martí's columns and Enríquez's landscape precede or anticipate the parasols, which would themselves then anticipate a future figure. This diachronic axis marks out historical time, so that the rhythm of figure and fulfillment stands out clearly and the historicity of each figure can be affirmed.[4] The synchronic axis retains a crucial importance, providing for each figure the poles of metaphoric association—reality and concept. But these poles too remain historical as they bracket the figures developed from the paired referential extents of nature and nation. Within these brackets, the task of representation is performed through the specific actions of figural mimesis. One mechanism of metaphorical language substitutes another, but with important implications, for in place of the essentialist foundation of the synchronic axis, the diachronic or figural axis introduces assertions of agency: first in the specifically historical manifestation of context through specular mimesis in any one figure, second in the retroactive stipulation of prefiguration that occurs in figural mimesis, and third in the anticipation of future figures, inevitable yet undetermined, to ameliorate or supplement the insufficient practices of the present. Furthermore, the process of mimetic figuration allows for the production of meaning within its perpetual sequence of deferrals, meaning held provisionally so that, following Mañach, it may possess a positive rather than negative valence. Through the historical affiliations described in the preceding chapter, the parasols would become figurally mimetic with the recognition of their affinity to the earlier palm tree figures, with the recognition that the parasol is a mimesis of its context, *and* the mimesis of another figure, *and* the anticipation of a future recurrence.

Two modes of recurrence, one a repeated summons to presence and the other a repeated deferral, distinguished the modernism of the palace and the monument from each other. What they contributed in common to the political context they inhabited was the manifest appearance of the temporalities of civil society. The importance of their expressive capacities was not limited to their symbolic registers, to illustrations of civic value and national patrimony. It consisted also of the manner in which the architecture could reinforce a structured relation of the past, present, and future. For the obvious progression of lived time, these two architectural objects substituted temporalities better described as contemporaneous, in the case of the monument, and retrospective, in the case of the palace. Within the constrained, compromised circumstances of the final years of the Cuban republic under the Batista dictatorship, these temporalities, as different elaborations of the meaning and the instrumentality of history, entered into and helped define the broader formulation of constitutionalism.

Romantic Constitutionalism

Writing at the end of the 1940s, Jorge Mañach identified "romantic constitutionalism" as a disposition to which the Cuban nation might be predisposed. "Romantic constitutionalism," he wrote, "with its fundamental confusion between what is and what one desires, prepared the way for the barbarous rule by caudillo, which identified political right with personal choice."[5] Mañach suggested that the characteristic trait had emerged in Latin America following the independence wars of the early nineteenth century as the new nations began to define their political and social structures. Their inheritance from Spain met with the American environment, forging that combination of a contemplative idealism and a determined sense of action, a paradoxical equation that Mañach called *quijotismo*. The tendency of romantic constitutionalism arose from *quijotismo* precisely as the confusion of norm and reality, or as the conflation of the "ought" and the "is." The will to forcefully compel their reconciliation, characterized by "arrogant particularisms *[particularismos arrogantes]*," was the will of the caudillo, the dictator.[6] Mañach described romantic constitutionalism as a general dimension of Latin American thought, but the setting in which, and for which, he was writing was the political sphere of postwar Cuba. His audience consisted of those intellectuals, professionals, and politicians engaged in the formulation of the civic environment under the Constitution of 1940, the protagonists of the discursive entanglements deciphered throughout the preceding chapters. Offering this caution, Mañach undoubtedly had in mind the prewar dictatorship of Gerardo Machado—the revolutionary opposition to whom Mañach himself had helped lead—but also the undiminished potential for the rise of another caudillo even out of a period of constitutional rule. Events justified Mañach's concern when Batista, who by his restraint had played a central role in the creation of the 1940 constitution, later supplanted that charter with his authoritarian rule.

In the seven years of Batista's dictatorship, many architects, planners, and intellectuals did continue to press for the maturation of Cuba's governmental and civic institutions, but in their efforts they had to contend with the caudillo's mistaken identification of "political right with personal choice." In fact, personal caprice was less the obstacle than the extension of corruption and illicit political motivation into most structures of government and of civil life. In these circumstances, how could architecture make its appearance in civil society other than as a comprised reflection of those circumstances, or as a fiction to conceal them? Constitutionalism projected civil society as the sphere of reciprocal exchange between citizen and state, both of which were themselves to be constituted as normative figures of the Cuban nation and as the actual people and activities of Cuban society. Architecture—in the form of monuments, master plans, and texts—sought to be the agent of this reciprocation by embodying normative principles, standards, and patterns, on the one hand, and by shaping the streets and blocks of the city and fashioning the habits of daily life, on the other. However, the pressures of real-estate speculation, the emphasis on tourism in the considerations of urban development, and the volatility of political patronage could and did readily undermine the progression of architectural projects, so that the architectural remains—buildings, projects, plans, and texts—can seem as much the detritus of a venal dictatorship as the traces of an appearance of a modernist formulation of civil society.

Whether signs or remains, they became artifacts of republican Cuba in January 1959, when Castro's guerrilla forces entered Havana and Batista fled into exile. Although it might briefly have been regarded as one more in the sequence of violent transitions of power, the Cuban Revolution of 1959 soon proved to be the concluding event of the turbulent period inaugurated by the 1933 revolution. It proved also to be a historical break, a decisive forestalling of the project that emerged from the earlier revolution to establish in Cuba a durable and democratic civil society. In the aftermath of the Cuban Revolution, some of the protagonists of that project left Cuba almost immediately. Nicolás Arroyo, who had been appointed ambassador to the United States not long before, simply stayed in Washington, D.C. Several of his colleagues soon became exiles as well; Eduardo Montoulieu, Mario Romañach, Nicolás Quintana, and Eugenio Batista all emigrated to the United States within the first years of the revolution. Jorge Mañach, for whom the revolution might have offered an opportunity of vindication and more settled residence in Cuba, returned to the island but soon left again disillusioned.

Central to his disillusionment was the course of nationalism in the early years of the revolution. What had been an effort to formulate the basis of civil society now became an effort to forge a collective society. An idealized project of the nation still existed, but in response to internal political conceits as well as the international pressures of Cold War geopolitics, Fidel Castro adopted the posture of a marxist revolutionary leader and channeled the desires and energy of nationalism into collective projects: first national defense, then later the crucial sugar harvest and the construction of housing, were each organized as participatory projects in which citizens were arranged into groups to accomplish specific tasks of national urgency. From militias in the early years to "micro-brigades" to build housing in subsequent decades, the role of citizen was no longer performed in reciprocal engagement with state. Rather, the citizen was now to be conceived as identical to the state. Architecture, in this new equation, no longer performed a mediating role but was instead appropriated for explicitly instrumentalized roles. Inside Ciudad Deportiva, a concrete stadium designed by Arroyo & Menéndez, thousands of spectators in the banked seats watched the revolutionary government conduct a series of show trials of Batista's former officers; the Banco Nacional de Cuba, with Che Guevara as its newly appointed president, was to occupy a new tower designed by Nicolás Quintana and overlooking the Malecón in Centro Habana, but under revised revolutionary priorities the building was instead converted into a hospital. And the open space facing the Monumento a Martí, completed in 1959 as a vast hardscaped plaza instead of Labatut's design for a differentiated plaza of the reflecting pool and large areas of landscaping, served as the setting for mass rallies organized to demonstrate and to assert the singular focus of the revolution. The architectural spaces of civic participation and civic institutions were stripped of their figurative registers and, though still manifestly public spaces, recast in only instrumental form.

Modernism continued as a formal idiom and as a discourse in the initial years of the revolution. The searching inquiry into a truthful expression that had been a foundation of modernist argument was still pursued in essays such as Nicolás Quintana's "Arquitectura cubana . . . una búsqueda de la verdad" (Cuban architecture . . . a search for the truth). Fertile experimentation in architecture, prompted by both an intense optimism and material shortages, was evident in housing proposals such as those of Martín Domínguez and Ernesto Gómez Sampera, the design of urban spaces, and in the designs for institutions such as the new Escuelas Nacionales de Arte in the western suburb of Cubanacán.[7] This modernism, though, was not a constitutional modernism; it did not assist or extend constitutionalism as an object or effect in Cuban society. With the Cuban Revolution to be seen as a sheer break, a rupture in the historical continuity that preceded it, the constitutionalist presumption of a deferred fulfillment no longer held significance. While Castro's famous claim that "history will absolve me," spoken in his own defense at his trial in 1953, contains the grammatical structure of a future retrospection, it exemplifies the tendency that Mañach branded romantic constitutionalism in its identification of political right with personal choice. Constitutionalism, however, should ultimately be assessed only according to its greater or lesser actualization, not its instantiation or completion. Its component processes—representation, performance, and prefiguration—are all disposed toward postponement, to defer fulfillment to a future moment. With the Cuban Revolution, the mode of constitutionalism became, like the Laws of the Indies before it, a historical relic, but even so it remains the concept necessary to decipher in the pre- and postwar decades in Cuba the critical entanglement of law, planning, and architecture. Furthermore, and more prospectively, constitutionalism remains as the visible evidence of the intricate and reaching possibilities of the *quijotismo* that Mañach explained as a peculiar but compelling realism: "[T]he realism to which Cervantes aspired when he wished for Don Quixote and Sancho to live together and not to part except to disappear into their respective destinies of the oblivion of death and the oblivion of the village. And our America," Mañach continued, "wishes neither to die from tradition nor to be reduced to a province. It still has its whole future ahead of it, large as the world itself."[8]

Acknowledgments

Conducting research on twentieth-century Cuba as an *estadounidense* scholar can be a complex endeavor, so I express my gratitude to several institutions and the many individuals in Cuba and elsewhere who made available to me their time, expertise, archival materials, and personal recollections, and who, in general, made possible the research on which this book is based.

Archivists, librarians, and staff at the Archivo Nacional de Cuba; the Biblioteca of the Ministerio de la Construcción de Cuba; the Cuban Heritage Collection at the University of Miami Libraries; the Department of Rare Books and Special Collections at Princeton University Library; and the Avery Library at Columbia University all provided generous assistance. Special thanks are owed to Bruce Tabb and Linda Long at the Special Collections of the University of Oregon Libraries and to Mary Daniels and Inés Zalduendo of Special Collections at Frances Loeb Library at Harvard University for their expertise and patience.

I was very fortunate to have had the opportunity to speak with several of the protagonists of the events discussed in this book. The late Eduardo Montoulieu, with incomparable hospitality, shared his recollections and his papers; I regret that he died before this book was completed. The late Nicolás Quintana also shared with me his recollections, papers, and publications, and Gabriela Menéndez and the late Nicolás Arroyo spoke with me about their work in Cuba. Maria Romañach provided her memories of her father and his work in Cuba, and several former employees of Town Planning Associates gave me the benefit of their recollections of working in that firm.

This book is based on research begun with my dissertation and owes an intellectual debt to a number of scholars who provided in various combinations and degrees invaluable insight, advice, mentorship, and inspiration. My graduate advisers, Neil Levine and Michael Hays, set the initial challenges that led me into this research and provided the intellectual tools to pursue it, and I am immensely grateful to them both. Other scholars whose influence and assistance I acknowledge with thanks include Tom Cummins, Jorge Domínguez, Jean-François Lejeune, Jorge Francisco Liernur, Eric Mumford, and Hashim Sarkis.

I was fortunate to participate in conference sessions and seminars in which the ideas and arguments of this book were helpfully critiqued by many individuals. I extend my thanks to them all and mention in particular Alan Colquhoun for comments given at the Buell Dissertation Colloquium at Columbia University; and Karen Knop, David Schneiderman, and Simon Stern, whose invitation to participate in the Critical Analysis of Law Workshop at the Faculty of Law at the University of Toronto helped me assess my work in a transdisciplinary perspective.

For some years now I have been surrounded by an exceptional cohort of colleagues. My particular thanks go to Daniel Abramson, Lucia Allais, John McMorrough, and Ana Miljacki, as well as to all of the members of the Aggregate Architectural History Collective for both the challenges and the support they have given to my work.

This book received financial support most recently from the Graham Foundation for Advanced Studies in the Fine Arts. The MacDowell Colony provided the essentials of time and space for writing. At earlier stages my research was assisted by a Harvard University Sheldon Fellowship and by the David Rockefeller Center for Latin American Studies at Harvard University.

The publication of this book with the University of Minnesota Press is possible only because Edward Dimendberg was kind enough to inquire about the project and to suggest its suitability to the Press; because my research assistant, Elizabeth Bacon, offered vital assistance in preparing the manuscript; and because the patient efforts of Pieter Martin and the staff at the Press shepherded it through the editorial and production processes.

My final and most profound thanks go to the members of my family. I am fortunate indeed to have parents who offer only unqualified encouragement for my every endeavor; a sister and brother-in-law who set an example of the challenges and satisfactions of intellectual life; two children, India and Elias, to show me the pleasures of insatiable curiosity; and, most of all, Sarah, with whom to share it all.

Notes

Introduction

1. For condensed surveys of modern architecture in Havana, see Gómez Díaz, *De Forestier a Sert,* and Rodríguez, *The Havana Guide.*

2. The first instructions given by Ferdinand and his council of advisers to the conquistador Pedrarias Dávila in 1513 were further elaborated by Charles V in 1523 and supplemented by ordinances issued by Felipe II in 1573. The official publication of these laws is Consejo de Indias, *Recopilación de leyes de los reynos de las Indias.*

3. Rama, *The Lettered City.* The text was first published in 1984, a year after Rama's death. For an interpretation of Rama's position in the cultural discourse of Latin America, see Campa, *Latin Americanism.* For a rich theorization of the significance of law and *letrados* in Latin America, see González Echevarría, *Myth and Archive.*

4. Rama, *The Lettered City,* 5–6; emphasis in original.

5. Ibid., 6; emphasis in original.

6. For accounts of the first decades following Cuban independence, see Whitney, *State and Revolution in Cuba,* and Pérez, *Cuba,* both of which examine the events of the 1930s in depth. This period is also addressed in Argote-Freyre, *Fulgencio Batista,* and Pérez, *Cuba and the United States.* A very evocative account of subsequent events from the firsthand perspective of a journalist can be found in Phillips, *Cuba, Island of Paradox.* In general, though with important exceptions, historical accounts of Cuba in the twentieth century tend to orient themselves in relation to the Cuban Revolution of 1959. The marxist historiography of Cuban scholarship in the latter half of the century is only the most forthright instance, and this tendency has resulted in a noticeably flattened rendering of parts of the nation's history, to which greater depth and definition are more recently being restored. For historical surveys of Cuba, including the colonial period, see Thomas, *Cuba,* or Gott, *Cuba.*

7. For the text of the manifesto and its list of signatories, see Larrazabal, ed., *Manifiestos de Cuba,* 85–97. The morphology of history proposed by Oswald Spengler in *Decline of the West* had a strong influence in Cuba and in Latin America. A Spanish translation of 1923, *La decadencia de Occidente,* was widely disseminated, contributing to theories that sought to define the relationship between global and local tendencies and to assert that

Latin American nations were the vanguard of a new cultural formation. Several authors in Cuba appropriated Spengler's trope of decline and decadence, using it as a rhetorical impetus for reform. On Spengler's influence, see González Echevarría, *Alejo Carpentier,* 52–57.

8. *Carteles* (May 22, 1927): 16, 25. That same year, members of the Grupo Minorista also founded the *Revista de Avance,* a journal committed to *vanguardismo,* political reform, and the cultivation of national civic conscience. See Masiello, "Rethinking Neocolonial Esthetics." The political dimensions of modernist art movements in Cuba are discussed in Martínez, *Cuban Art and National Identity.* (Here and throughout, translations are by the author unless noted otherwise.)

9. Cf. chapters 5–8 in Argote-Freyre, *Fulgencio Batista,* and chapter 9 of Pérez, *Cuba.*

10. Quoted in Argote-Freyre, *Fulgencio Batista,* 247.

11. Mañach, *Indagación del choteo.* Mañach published many of his prewar essays as a book, *Pasado vigente.* For Mañach's intellectual and literary influence, see Díaz Infante, *Mañach o la república,* and Torre, *Jorge Mañach.*

12. Ortiz, *Contrapunteo cubano del tabaco y el azúcar.* The book was first published in English translation in 1947 and most recently reprinted as *Cuban Counterpoint.* The significance of Ortiz's argument and the more general intellectual milieu of the period is examined in Rojas, *Essays in Cuban Intellectual History.*

13. The term "modernism" as it will be used throughout this book references not the sum of projects realized in modern style, nor the calculated actions of certain individuals, but rather a compound of institutional intentions, aesthetic modes, and instrumental techniques produced and proposed in response to the contemporaneous situations of Cuba. Intentions, modes, and techniques were modern in that they were construed as appropriate to their contemporary moment and that insofar as they maintained traditional forms or practices, did so through deliberate choice; modern also because they were intended to accommodate the transformative modernization under way in material and immaterial registers—in the construction of urban infrastructures of transportation and sanitation, for example, but also in the installation of new legal organizations or the creation of new aesthetic movements. In these latter movements, the modern tendencies were also visibly modernist tendencies, meaning that they adopted and extended the principles and practices of the modernist movements in art and architecture available from their European sources and in their North American variations.

14. The chronological period between 1933 and 1959 will be identified as the Cuban Republic, in keeping with the language of the protagonists of the political transformations of the 1930s. Cuban history between 1902 and 1959 is also sometimes periodized as a sequence of three republics, with the period covered in this book referred to as the third republic. Fulgencio Batista had several titles. Here he will be referred to as Colonel Batista before 1940, as President Batista during his elected term of 1940–44, and as General Batista during his subsequent dictatorship.

1. The Idealized Republic

1. Gutiérrez y Sánchez, "La convención constituyente y la constitución de 1940," 155. *Guajiros,* the rural peasants of Cuba, were iconic figures in folklore and art; *polainas* were

short chaps worn over boots and the guayabera is the traditional collared shirt worn by Cuban men.

2. Ibid., 158.

3. Ibid., 159. The president of the Constitutional Convention was Carlos Márquez Sterling.

4. Ibid., 157.

5. Ibid., 158.

6. The constitutional law issued by Mendieta's government on June 11, 1935, pleaded that prior suspensions of constitutional laws had been necessary "to save the nation from anarchy." It restored the 1901 constitution, adding such modifications as were required to inscribe the gains of the revolution, but announced the necessity for a firmer and more complete restoration of political legitimacy—an "estado de derecho" (rule of law)—through a comprehensive reconstruction of legal authority: "Our nation is armed by this Charter to provide itself another, more extensive one, in agreement with its manifest aspirations for renewal and with the unstoppable ideological current of the times" (Lazcano y Mazón, *Las constituciones de Cuba*, 719–20).

7. See Gutiérrez y Sánchez, *Proyecto de nueva constitución para la República de Cuba (con el proyecto del congreso de 1936)*. Gutiérrez's several publications on Cuban constitutional history also included *Historia del derecho constitucional cubano*, the preface of which acknowledged Emilio Roig de Leuchsenring as "mi fraternal amigo."

8. Gutiérrez y Sánchez, "La convención constituyente y la constitución de 1940," 122.

9. Gutiérrez y Sánchez, *Proyecto de nueva constitución para la República de Cuba*, 81.

10. A number of these documents are listed in the bibliography of Gutiérrez's essay "La convención constituyente y la constitución de 1940."

11. Abalo, *La forma técnico-funcional de gobierno*, 47.

12. Ibid., 12.

13. Ibid., 13.

14. Abalo's rendering of what he called the "fundamental norms" of the constitution was more ornate than his technocratic proposal. The preamble of his text elucidated six principles—concepts of God and of Nature or Life, a philosophy of Will, a theory of Knowledge, a socioeconomic morphology, and a political technique—from which the structure of the constitution was deduced. Abalo's faith seemed to lie in the political technique, with the work of the expert specialists at the core of his "technico-functional" government responsible for negotiating between principles and events. But the detailed expositions of each principle that he supplied in an accompanying glossary reveal an extensive if idiosyncratic working of philosophical and scientific concepts.

15. Gutiérrez y Sánchez, *Proyecto de nueva constitución para la República de Cuba*, 21; Gutiérrez y Sánchez, "La convención constituyente y la constitución de 1940," 122.

16. Professor Josef Kunz of the University of Toledo, in a historiographical and critical assessment of modern Latin American philosophy of law compiled during the 1940s, asserted that Kelsen was at that time "the greatest influence" on legal theory in Latin America in general and in Cuba in particular. Kelsen's writings were available in several Spanish translations by the early 1930s. His thematic concerns were widely discussed in Cuban literature on legal philosophy, and some Cuban figures had direct contact with

Kelsen himself. Kelsen provided a preface to *Filosofía juridical contemporánea* (1932), written by Emilio Fernández Camus, professor at the University of Havana. Another professor, Antonio Sánchez de Bustamente y Montoro, studied with Kelsen in Geneva and published a comprehensive account of Kelsen's theories in *Teoría general del derecho* (1940). See Kunz, "Latin American Philosophy of Law in the Twentieth Century."

17. Kelsen, *General Theory of Law and State,* 111.

18. Ibid., 36, 111.

19. Sánchez de Bustamente y Montoro, *Teoría general del derecho,* 21.

20. Ibid., 22.

21. According to Josef Kunz, an enthusiastic yet analytic acceptance of Kelsen was typical in Latin America, where several schools of legal thought sought to embrace Kelsen's ideas and to move beyond them. Kunz provides an account of the early emergence of phenomenology in legal philosophy in Latin America and in Cuba. Bustamente y Montoro, to give but one example, published a lecture titled "La Fenomenología: De Husserl a Heidegger" in 1933. See Kunz, "Latin American Philosophy of Law in the Twentieth Century."

22. Jorrín, "La fenomenología y el derecho [I]"; Jorrín, "La fenomenología y el derecho [II]." The possible circulation of ideas through adjacent disciplines, and the intimacy of the discursive circle examined here, are both suggested by the editorial board of the *Universidad de la Habana Publicación Bimestral;* its members in 1939 included Antonio Sánchez de Bustamente y Montoro and Emilio Fernández Camus, from the field of jurisprudence, and Luis de Soto, Joaquín E. Weiss, and Luis A. Baralt from the field of history of art and architecture.

23. Jorrín, "La fenomenología y el derecho [II]," 215.

24. Bustamente y Montoro, *Teoría general del derecho,* 237.

25. "The basic norm of a national legal order is not the arbitrary product of juristic imagination. Its content is determined by facts. The function of the basic norm is to make possible the normative interpretation of certain facts, and that means, the interpretation of facts as the creation and application of valid norms" (Kelsen, *General Theory of Law and State,* 120).

26. Bustamente y Montoro, *Teoría general del derecho,* 243.

27. Gutiérrez y Sánchez, *Historia del derecho constitucional cubano,* xxviii.

28. Gutiérrez y Sánchez, "La convención constituyente y la constitución de 1940," 118.

29. Ibid.

30. The body of historiography on José Martí is enormous, varied, and has undergone periodic renovations in Cuba's changing political climates. Martí's bibliography is similarly varied, encompassing the genres of aphorism, poetry, journalism, and essay, and topics ranging across history, political theory, and aesthetics. But some suggestion of his particular significance in the prerevolutionary period can be given in outline. Martí lived much of his life in exile, studying and working in Spain and Central and North America as a journalist and essayist. His poetry became the foundation of the *modernismo* literary movement at the end of the nineteenth century, while his political efforts fostered the final, successful stage of the Cuban independence movement begun decades earlier. In 1895, Martí died in a battle against the Spanish at Dos Ríos, Cuba, an event that was soon understood as a martyr's death. Although Martí was immediately recognized as the central

figure of Cuban independence—his statue was erected in the Parque Central in Havana in 1899—the more deliberate formulation of an idea of Martí as the symbol of Cuba's civic conscience developed later, during the 1930s, when images of Martí proliferated in literature, art, and even quotidian settings. The first of the eventual seventy-four volumes of the *Obras completas de Martí* was published in 1936. In 1933, Jorge Mañach published *Martí, el apóstol,* a concise biography that defined the poet's significance for Cuba and that gives a portrait of Martí from the perspective of the period under discussion here. For a discussion of the evolution of the historical image of Martí through the mid-twentieth century, see Guerra, *The Myth of José Martí,* and Gray, *José Martí.*

31. Martí, *The America of José Martí,* 141. The translation by Juan de Onís is significant for having presented Martí to a wider readership in 1953, and will be used here. But significant phrases are clarified by referring to Martí's original text in Spanish. In the passage cited, where the translation refers to government as a "child," and to a "natural constitution," Martí writes that "el gobierno ha de nacer del país" and that its form should correspond to "la constitución propia" of the nation. The distinction is subtle, but suggests an emphasis on an internalized origin and on properties that are inseparable from the thing itself. It should be noted that Martí did not subscribe to the positivism so prevalent in Latin America at the time. His thought was influenced by romanticism and its preference for organicist formulations over formalist ones.

32. Gutiérrez y Sánchez, "La convención constituyente y la constitución de 1940," 118. This correspondence would be reiterated at the ceremony to promulgate the constitution, when the charter was described as a "faithful reproduction of an epoch."

33. Over a three-month period prior to the convention, the Club Atenas in Havana sponsored a series of lectures, "Conferencias de orientación ciudadana," in which representatives of these parties presented their arguments and manifestos on constitutional issues (see ibid., 185). The Club Atenas was the most prominent Afro-Cuban association, or "sociedad de color," in the city. For the intricacies of the political parties' respective dispositions and platforms, and the significance of Afro-Cuban participation, see Pérez, *Cuba.*

34. For the full text of the 1940 constitution, see Lazcano y Mazón, *Las constituciones de Cuba.* For the transcripts of the Convención Constituyente, in which the proposed articles of the charter were debated one by one, see Lazcano y Mazón, *Constitución de Cuba (con los debates sobre su articulado y transitorias en la convención constituyente).*

35. Gutiérrez was referring here specifically to his draft *Proyecto de reforma integral.* He claimed later that the delegates of the convention had chosen not to use the text approved by the Congress, owing to their "inconceivable urge for originality *[inconcebible purito de originalidad].*" Nevertheless, Gutiérrez's text ultimately supplied the lineaments of the final constitution and the insight still pertained. See Gutiérrez y Sánchez, *Proyecto de nueva constitución para la República de Cuba,* xxiii.

36. Gutiérrez y Sánchez, *Constitución de la República de Cuba, promulgada el día 5 de julio de 1940,* 9.

37. Ibid., 11. Gutiérrez adopted the descriptive term "invertebrate" from the philosophical writings of José Ortega y Gasset.

38. Gutiérrez, echoing other commentators, emphasized that the charter was a "multiple, radial plan for the constructive and organic needs of the Nation" (ibid., 40).

39. Alvarez Tabío, *Teoría general de la constitución cubana,* 19.
40. Gutiérrez y Sánchez, *Historia del derecho constitucional cubano,* xvii.
41. See Lazcano y Mazón, *Las constituciones de Cuba,* 849.
42. Ibid., 847.
43. Alvarez Tabío, *Teoría general de la constitución cubana,* 27.
44. Lazcano y Mazón, *Las constituciones de Cuba,* 847.
45. The Spanish word *constitución* maintains the equivocation of its Latin root to permit the simultaneous invocation of both inherent quality and productive action, and hence both descriptive and performative functions. The use of the verb *ser* (to be) in the first article confirms that the qualities described are part of an inherent constitution. The related concept of performative utterances as developed by J. L. Austin can be found in Austin, *How to Do Things with Words.*
46. Gutiérrez y Sánchez, "La convención constituyente y la constitución de 1940," 154.
47. Bustamente y Montoro, *Teoría general del derecho,* 179.
48. Kelsen, *General Theory of Law and State,* 115.
49. On revisionist historiography in Cuba, see Miller, "The Absolution of History," and Smith, "Twentieth-Century Cuban Historiography."
50. Not least of the evidence of the contemporaneous importance of the 1940 constitution is the large bibliography of analysis and critique it provoked. Gutiérrez compiled a bibliography of more than three dozen specific commentaries published between 1940 and 1952, along with an equal number of publications dealing more generally with Cuban constitutional law. See Gutiérrez y Sánchez, "La convención constituyente y la constitución de 1940," 184–88.

2. Better Cities, Better Citizens

1. "Patronato Pro-Urbanismo," 187–89. The manifesto cited articles 79, 83, 91, 134, 211, 212, 213, 215, and 216 as evidence that the overall intention of the constitution was consistent with the concept of planning.
2. The Colegio Nacional de Arquitectos was the body that represented and regulated the profession of architecture, and the Lyceum y Lawn Tennis Club was a leading cultural institution in Havana that presented numerous exhibitions of modern art. By 1943, the Patronato claimed it had 135 members. Jorge Mañach and Francisco Ichaso were listed as part of the membership in a memorandum written by Eduardo Montoulieu in 1943, although it is unclear whether they played any formal role. Montoulieu recalled Mañach as being a constant participant during that period in debates about the civic sphere through his newspaper writings and his radio program *Universidad del Aire* (interview with Eduardo Montoulieu, June 8, 2005, Coral Gables, Florida).
3. "Estatutos del Patronato Pro-Urbanismo de Cuba."
4. Montoulieu, "Architect Explains Need of City Planning Body in Cuba."
5. Montoulieu, "Lo que es y lo que pudiera ser Varadero," 26.
6. This process is recognizably similar to the campaigns that accompanied proposals in the City Beautiful movement. In the text of Daniel Burnham's 1909 Plan of Chicago, the claim was made that "good citizenship is the prime object of good city planning." The

distinctions of the Cuban case included a clear specificity about the role of the citizen, the constitutional context, and the correlation to nationalism. For comparison, see Commercial Club of Chicago et al., *Plan of Chicago.*

7. Lazcano y Mazón, *Las constituciones de Cuba,* 849.

8. Lazcano y Mazón, *Constitución de Cuba (con los debates sobre su articulado y transitorias en la convención constituyente),* 1:142.

9. Mañach, *Pasado vigente,* 112.

10. Lazcano y Mazón, *Constitución de Cuba (con los debates sobre su articulado y transitorias en la convención constituyente),* 1:144.

11. Lazcano y Mazón, *Las constituciones de Cuba,* 864.

12. Montoulieu, "Enfoque sobre el urbanismo contemporáneo."

13. Montoulieu, "Architect Explains Need of City Planning Body in Cuba."

14. Montoulieu, "Lo que es y lo que pudiera ser Varadero," 26. Gustavo Gutiérrez described the purpose of a constitution similarly as creating a "conjunto metódico" out of the particulate elements of national life.

15. Montoulieu, "Enfoque sobre el urbanismo contemporáneo."

16. "Ha quedado inaugura la primera exposición cubana de urbanismo en el Lyceum y Lawn Tennis Club."

17. See Domínguez, "Urbanismo de sobremesa redonda (I)."

18. Eduardo Montoulieu, "Panel No. 1." This and the other original sketches are among the papers of the late Eduardo Montoulieu. Permission to examine and to publish them was generously granted to the author by Eduardo Montoulieu.

19. Eduardo Montoulieu, "Panel No. 7."

20. Montoulieu probably adopted the title for the agency from Puerto Rico, where a Junta Nacional de Planificación was created by legal decree in May 1942.

21. Montoulieu, "Enfoque sobre el urbanismo contemporáneo."

22. For an overview of architectural discourse during this period, including summations of the work of individual architects, see Part II of Gómez Díaz, *De Forestier a Sert.*

23. "Patronato Pro-Urbanismo," 187.

24. Hegemann, *City Planning, Housing,* 40, 42. Hegemann supported his assertion with the rather broad claim that the constitutional objective to promote the general welfare was in essence a programmatic conception. He was seeking to overturn the presumption of an American affinity for laissez-faire policies and attitudes and to defend the developing structure of the New Deal. The significance of his claim lies not in its questionable historical validity but in the meaning it would have held for Martínez Inclán or other Cuban readers. For Martínez Inclán's reading of Hegemann, see Collins, *Werner Hegemann and the Search for Universal Urbanism,* 359.

25. Montoulieu's father, who later served as secretary of state in one of the provisional governments of the prewar period, had attended Columbia University. His uncle Enrique Montoulieu, an engineer who would receive belated credit for having envisioned a comprehensive infrastructural plan of Havana in 1923, had attended Harvard University. Montoulieu attended the University of Havana until it was closed by the government in response to the widespread unrest during the final years of the Machado regime; he then

chose to continue his studies in the United States, where he had previously attended high school. He entered Columbia with special standing in 1933 or 1934.

26. For the context and overall themes of CIAM discourse on planning, see Mumford, *The CIAM Discourse on Urbanism, 1928–1960.*

27. See Rodríguez, *The Havana Guide,* xvi–xxxiv. Eugenio Batista was not related to Fulgencio Batista. Montoulieu did not formally complete the thesis requirements at the Graduate School of Design until after his return to Cuba. He received his Master in Architecture degree in 1940. He returned to the school in 1954 to pursue additional studies for a Master in City Planning degree under Reginald Issacs. José Luis Sert was the dean at that time and provided Montoulieu with teaching fellowships in architecture.

28. Sert, already in exile from his native Spain following the Republican defeat in the Spanish civil war, left France in 1939. He lived in Cuba while awaiting a visa to enter the United States as a refugee. Gabriela Menéndez recalled that Sert met frequently with her, Arroyo, and other students during this stay in Havana (interview with Gabriela Menéndez, June 29, 2005, Washington, D.C.). Gómez Díaz also discusses ATEC and its individual members in *De Forestier a Sert,* 257–63, 424–33.

29. Giedion, *A Decade of New Architecture,* 16. Giedion included three projects from Cuba in this survey: one by Montoulieu, one by Arroyo and Menéndez, and one by Emilio del Junco and Miguel Gastón.

30. *Can Our Cities Survive?* had been distributed by the end of 1942, but it is not clear when it first arrived in Cuba. Sert did have preliminary materials for the book with him when he resided in Cuba in 1939, and his writings were certainly known to the architectural profession in Cuba by October 1946 when his essay was published. *Arquitectura,* the monthly journal of the Colegio de Arquitectos, published a wide range of articles, including projects and essays by European, North American, and South American architects, alongside those of Cuban architects. On Cuban architectural periodicals, see Gómez Díaz, *De Forestier a Sert,* 263–75.

31. Neutra described individual projects as typical components of larger developments produced in consultation with other technical disciplines. See Neutra, "Puerto Rico."

32. Secretaría de Obras Públicas, *Memoria del plan de obras del gobierno del Dr. Ramón Grau San Martín.*

33. Hudnut, "The Political Art of Planning," 45.

34. The Junta de Economía de Guerra formed in 1943 was transformed into the Junta Nacional de Economía (JNE) in 1949 without a substantial change in its composition. In 1952, the mandate of the JNE was altered to establish it as an autonomous technical organization with the objective "of guiding and coordinating the economic policy of the State." In 1955, it was renamed Consejo Nacional de Economía and charged with the "study of plans for economic development." See Consejo Nacional de Economía, *El programa económico de Cuba,* 10.

35. Gutiérrez concluded his 1952 recollection of the Convención Constituyente with the following appeal: "Power changes hands and parties, the opposition rises up and overthrows the Palace, the armed forces can leave or remain in their barracks, anything can happen. The only truly permanent thing is nationality, *la Patria.* We must make her

stronger, more pure, more welcoming for all" (Gutiérrez y Sánchez, "La convención constituyente y la constitución de 1940," 176; emphasis in original).

36. The JNE was not the only agency involved in economic development in Cuba; similar institutions proliferated, in some instances as devices of political patronage or as representations of specific interests, in other cases as analogues of institutions established in other nations. Other institutions that played a role in development and in economic management include the Banco Nacional (created in 1948 and opened in 1950), the Banco de Fomento Agrícola e Industrial de Cuba (BANFAIC), and the Banco de Desarrollo Económico y Social (BANDES); and in 1950, a mission from the International Bank for Reconstruction and Development traveled to Cuba at the request of President Prío, and the following year published its findings and recommendations in a one-thousand-page *Report on Cuba*.

37. Jorge Mañach, "Introducción," in Gutiérrez y Sánchez, *Presente y futuro de la economía cubana*, viii–ix.

38. Martínez Inclán, "Urbanismo," 136.

39. *The Road to Serfdom* was first published in 1944; a Spanish translation appeared in 1946.

40. Martínez Sáenz, "La economía," 63.

41. Mañach, *El pensamiento de Dewey y su sentido americano*. Mañach attended Harvard University just after the first world war, at a time when the influence of William James was still strong. Mañach's later career as professor of philosophy also prompted his detailed study of pragmatism, but it was a political potential in Dewey's thought that seems to have attracted Mañach's attention in the 1950s, when his criticisms of Fulgencio Batista became increasingly pronounced.

42. Ibid., 23; emphasis in original.

43. See Bugeda Lanzas, *La propiedad horizontal*. Rafael Picó, chairman of the JNP in Puerto Rico, had recently argued that the origins of *propiedad horizontal* could be traced to Roman law (Picó, "New Uses for a Roman Law").

44. "Información general sobre la conveniencia de una ley de planificación."

45. Colete was an architect and an engineer and in 1953 was president of the Sociedad Cubana de Ingenieros. He had a particular interest in the concept of *plusvalía* (unearned increment) and its effects on the development of physical infrastructure. He had studied the—in his view—ambiguous treatment of the concept in the 1940 constitution and it was this work that led Gutiérrez to solicit Colete's participation in the work of the JNE.

46. "Información general sobre la conveniencia de una ley de planificación," 183.

47. "[W]ith the aim of organizing this enormous conglomerate into which the contemporary city developed, simple elements of aesthetic ordering integrated those of circulation, zoning, the anticipation of elements of recreation and hygiene, and the coordination of housing and business centers, into the efficient and total organization of the great metropolis by means of urban planning; and to integrate the enormous tributary spaces of the metropolitan city and from the need for efficient coordination between cities and the countryside arrived at Regional Planning" (ibid., 191).

48. Ibid., 192.

49. Ibid., 184.

50. Letter, Eugenio Batista to José Luis Sert, May 28, 1953 (folder C13, CIAM Collection, Special Collections, Frances Loeb Library, Graduate School of Design, Harvard University).

51. Estévez, "El Fórum del Colegio de Arquitectos sobre la Plaza Cívica y Monumento a Martí," 44.

52. Telegram, Eugenio Batista to José Luis Sert, June 2, 1953 (folder E58, José Luis Sert Collection [JLS], Special Collections, Frances Loeb Library, Graduate School of Design, Harvard University).

53. Estévez, "El Fórum del Colegio de Arquitectos sobre la Plaza Cívica y Monumento a Martí," 44; emphasis in original.

54. Reports of Rafael Picó's visit and the texts of his lectures were published in *Arquitectura* in issues 242 (September 1953) and 243 (November 1953). Accounts of Sert's visit written by Armando Maribona were also published in the November 1953 issue. For Sert's interview with the editors of *Espacio* during this visit, see Estévez and Biniakonski, "Habla José Luis Sert para *Espacio*."

55. On the company letterhead of Town Planning Associates, the name of José Luis Sert appeared between those of his partners Paul Lester Wiener and Paul Schulz, who were, respectively, identified as "Director of Design" and "Architect." Sert's title was "Town Planner." These denominations appeared in publicity for the firm as well. The *New York Times* of March 26, 1945, in an article on the firm's proposal for prefabricated housing, referred to Wiener as "designer," Schulz as "architect," and Sert as "city planner." But all three partners had been trained as architects, and although there was a division of responsibilities within the firm, it did not necessarily correspond to their official titles. Wiener, while maintaining an interest in industrial and exhibition design from his prewar activities, collaborated with Sert in the design and supervision of the firm's planning projects. Sert maintained the primary design responsibility for most of the firm's architectural projects. Schulz played primarily an administrative role for the firm. The three partners formed Town Planning Associates in 1942, although Sert and Wiener had been affiliated the previous year in a group called Planning Associates, composed of Sert, Wiener, and the architectural firm Morris & O'Connor. Sert and Wiener also worked independently for individual clients during the period of their partnership.

56. See Sert and Wiener, "The Work of Town Planning Associates in Latin America 1945–1956," 213.

57. According to Nicolás Quintana, Arroyo and his partner and spouse, Gabriela Menéndez, had attracted the attention of Fulgencio Batista's wife—their firm Arroyo & Menéndez had designed community projects, such as schools and clinics, of which she was the patron. Arroyo was aware of the advantages that government patronage would provide professionally, for himself but also for the group of architects he represented (interview with Nicolás Quintana, June 9, 2005, Miami, Florida).

58. See "Memorandum to Dr. Arroyo from Town Planning Associates," September 22, 1953 (box 5, folder 7, Paul Lester Wiener Collection [PLW], Special Collections, Knight Library, University of Oregon).

59. Letter, Rita Gutiérrez to Paul Wiener, July 31, 1954 (box 5, folder 30, PLW). Rita Gutiérrez was an architect employed in the firm of Arroyo & Menéndez.

60. Letter, Paul Wiener to José Luis Sert, November 31, 1954 (box 5, folder 30, PLW).

61. Memo, Paul Wiener to Paul Schulz, December 6, 1954 (box 5, folder 30, PLW).

62. The law took effect when it was published in the *Gaceta Oficial* on February 5, 1955. See "Obras Públicas," 2119–21. Haar's draft, deemed by Batista to be the creation of a "super-government," was revised, but seems still to have provided a framework for the final decree.

63. The actual constitution in effect at the time was the Constitutional Law imposed by Batista in 1952, but references to its articles were almost invariably accompanied by a reference to the corresponding article of the 1940 constitution, conceding and indeed depending on the legitimacy of the latter.

64. "Obras Públicas," 2119.

65. It seems very likely that Luis José Abalo was the same person who had written the "técnico-funcional" proposal for the constitution in 1938, although that work was signed J. L. Abalo. The apparent inversion of forenames cannot be accounted for, but there are distinctive similarities to books and essays published by Luis José Abalo after 1950.

66. A sum equivalent to nearly one million dollars today (Folder Addenda/Cuba, Letters, JLS).

67. "Comentarios sobre la Ley de Planificación Nacional," 110.

68. Ibid., 107.

3. A Perfect Structuring

1. By 1573, several of the major colonial cities of the New World had already been established. Those in the Caribbean—including Havana, founded in 1514 and moved to its present location in 1519—had been among the first points of settlement at the beginning of the sixteenth century, and by 1559 the conquistadores had destroyed and rebuilt the imposing Aztec city of Tenochtitlán as the viceregal seat Mexico City. Las Leyes de Indias, therefore, did not regulate the founding of these earliest urban settlements, and some elements of the ordinances may actually have been codifications of existing examples.

2. Solá, *Historia del arte hispano-americano* (this volume was published in Spain and Latin America); Kubler, "Mexican Urbanism in the Sixteenth Century"; and Kubler, *Mexican Architecture of the Sixteenth Century*. Also see Stanislawski, "The Origin and Spread of the Grid-Pattern Town" and "Early Spanish Town Planning in the New World."

3. The enduring investigation appears to have been initiated by Zelia Nutall, an American archaeologist who worked in Mexico. Nutall located the ordinances in the archives in Madrid in 1912 and made available a partial text with English translation that was published ten years later (Nuttall, "Royal Ordinances concerning the Laying Out of Towns" and "Royal Ordinances concerning the Laying Out of New Towns"). Additional research was introduced by historians in Mexico in the 1930s (see note 9 below). Contributions adding to the work of Kubler and Stanislawski were made by Robert C. Smith and Ralph Gakenheimer in Smith, "Colonial Towns of Spanish and Portuguese America," and Gakenheimer, "Determinants of Physical Structure in the Peruvian Town of the 16th Century." A second period of research was later initiated by Dora Crouch, who gave significantly more attention to the social formations implied by the ordinances. See Crouch and Mundigo, "The City Planning Ordinances of the Laws of the Indies Revisited," and Crouch,

Garr, and Mundigo, *Spanish City Planning in North America.* For examples of current research, see Gasparini, "The Spanish-American Grid Plan, an Urban Bureaucratic Form," and Lejeune, ed., *Cruelty and Utopia.*

4. More recent research has broadened the study of the ordinances to consider what type of social forms they implied and to fix precisely the urban forms they stipulated, but even these examinations elide whole groups of articles that do not directly address urban morphology. The reprint of the ordinances that appears in *Cruelty and Utopia* uses the translation published in 1977 by Dora Crouch, who had elected to exclude articles that "dictate the legislative, legal, and fiduciary regulations." Kubler may have used a more complete version, as he cites the official text of the Laws published in Madrid in the eighteenth and nineteenth centuries, but he made no references to specific articles. González Echevarría has elaborated the literary influence of the ordinances in *Myth and Archive.*

5. Gutiérrez y Sánchez, *Historia del derecho constitucional cubano,* xxiv–xxv; emphasis in original.

6. Ibid., xxv.

7. Gutiérrez y Sánchez, "La convención constituyente y la constitución de 1940," 175.

8. The other Cuban attendees were José María Bens Arrarte, Adrían Carmona Romay, José Luciano Franco, Aquiles Maza y Santos, and Carlos Morán Valdés.

9. Justino Fernández was a consulting urbanist for Mexico City, while Federico Gómez de Orozco, who was acquainted with Zelia Nuttall, compiled a bibliography of the Laws of the Indies in 1939. (George Kubler cited both Orozco's notes and the congress publication.) See Orozco, "Las Leyes de Indias," and Fernández, Gómez de Orozco, and Toussaint, *Planos de la ciudad de México, siglos XVI y XVII, estudio histórico, urbanístico y bibliográfico.*

10. Carrera y Jústiz, *Breves notas sobre la constitución de Cuba de 1940 y el régimen municipal;* Carrera y Jústiz, *Urbanismo;* Carrera y Jústiz, *Preliminares de ciencia municipal urbanismo. Primera parte.*

11. Domínguez Compañy, *El urbanismo en las Leyes de Indias (estudio histórico y jurídico-social).* The pamphlet was published by the School of Social Science and Public Law at the University of Havana, from which the author had graduated. He introduced the concept of urbanism by quoting a definition coined by Francisco Carrera y Jústiz.

12. Ibid., 6.

13. Mañach first presented his idea of *quijotismo* in lectures that were published in Cuba as Mañach, *Filosofía del quijotismo,* and then in a longer essay, *Examen del quijotismo.*

14. Mañach, *El pensamiento de Dewey y su sentido americano,* 29.

15. Mañach, *Examen del quijotismo,* 156. *Quijotismo* would refer to an active tendency, in contrast to *quijotidad,* which would refer to a state of being.

16. Ibid., 161–62.

17. Sert had carried with him an annotated manuscript of the official CIAM version in 1939, during the months he lived in Havana, and would certainly have familiarized the young architects with whom he associated with the principles of the Athens Charter. Le Corbusier had a version of the text published in France in 1943, under the authorship of "Le Groupe CIAM-France." See Le Corbusier and Giraudoux, *La charte d'Athènes.* By 1957, the planner Francis Violich was able to condemn the influence of the Athens

Charter for having firmly established a too-limited conception of physical planning: "The CIAM Charter of Athens has been a major factor in holding back a natural evolution of planning concepts and in the maintenance of the monopolistic architectural emphasis" (Violich, "Planning in South America," 123).

18. Le Corbusier and Giraudoux, *The Athens Charter,* 86–88. Sert's annotation on a manuscript copy titled this section an "Appendix," and he used a footnote in *Can Our Cities Survive?* to clarify that the section was not part of the "general text." The 1933 CIAM meeting and the drafting of the Athens Charter are dicussed in chapter 2 of Mumford, *The CIAM Discourse on Urbanism, 1928–1960,* 73–91.

19. Le Corbusier and Giraudoux, *The Athens Charter,* 100.

20. Martínez Inclán, *Código de Urbanismo.* Martínez Inclán gave a copy of his book to Walter Gropius during the latter's visit to Cuba in 1949. Gropius forwarded it to Sert as an example of the dissemination of CIAM doctrine: "I send you enclosed a branch which has blossomed off our chart of Athens. It was given to me by Professor Inclán in Havana. I thought it might interest you to see his interpretation" (letter, Walter Gropius to José Luis Sert, June 14, 1949 [folder C2, CIAM]).

21. Ibid., 3. (The full italics in this and other cited passages below were used in the original to signify additions made to the Athens Charter text.)

22. Martínez Inclán's article 145 reads: "The two classical principles, 'salus populi suprema lex,' and 'utere tuo ut alienum non laedas,' will have to be strongly taken into account in all legislation related to planning, whether local or national: all of this, without losing sight of the inherent right of property, is based on social 'status.'"

23. Martínez Inclán, *Código de Urbanismo,* 31; emphasis in original.

24. Ibid., 26; emphasis in original.

25. A parallel appeared in Lewis Mumford's critique of the Athens Charter, which he offered to Sert in comments on the latter's text for *Can Our Cities Survive?* The city, Mumford argued, not only consisted of the four functions, but was a "civic nucleus" of "political, educational, and cultural functions." He made these comments in a letter to Sert, but the general theme of the civic (and the aesthetic) took hold in CIAM discussions beginning with the 1947 meeting in Bridgwater, which Martínez Inclán's younger colleagues, Batista and Arroyo, attended and no doubt reported on. See letter, Lewis Mumford to José Luis Sert, December 28, 1940 (folder E1, JLS). Also see chapter 3 of Mumford, *The CIAM Discourse on Urbanism, 1928–1960.* At the same time, the well-known "Debate on Monumentality" was taking place in symposia and in the pages of architectural journals. See Zucker, ed., *New Architecture and City Planning, a Symposium;* and "In Search of a New Monumentality."

26. Martínez Inclán, *Código de Urbanismo,* 20.

27. Ibid., 21.

28. Ibid., 22.

29. See Rovira, *José Luis Sert,* and Rovira, ed., *Sert, 1928–1979.* For a study of the relationship between the plans for Bogotá (a collaboration between Town Planning Associates and Le Corbusier), see Schnitter, "José Luis Sert y Colombia."

30. Letter, E. Mangucci (on behalf of Paul Wiener) to Katherine McNamara, September 3, 1947 (box 12, folder 63, PLW).

31. See Sert and Wiener, "Conditions générales de l'urbanisme en Amérique Latine." Also see the draft version of their text in box 11, folder 1, PLW.

32. Box 11, folder 60, PLW. The essay is undated, but its contents and phrasing suggest that it is one of the numerous lectures Wiener drafted in the early 1950s.

33. Ibid.; emphasis and capitalizations in original. All quotations are presented exactly as they appear in the original, including the errors.

34. Team 10 (or Team X), a group of younger members of CIAM who began to challenge many of the congress's presumptions in the early 1950s, directed the initial strokes of its critique at the astringent functionalism of the Athens Charter, calling for an analytic format capable of less rigid categorizations. The text of the "Urban Reidentification Grid" that Alison and Peter Smithson presented at CIAM 9 included the following statement: "We are of the opinion that such a hierarchy of human associations should replace the functional hierarchy of the 'Charte d'Athènes.'" For the emergence of Team 10 and its associated critique, see Mumford, *The CIAM Discourse on Urbanism, 1928–1960,* 225–58.

35. Wiener did not attend CIAM 9, but submitted his paper to be read at the meeting. Wiener's participation in CIAM was likely initiated by his partnership with Sert, but consisted of quite individual contributions on his part. It began in 1944, when he joined the CIAM Chapter for Relief and Postwar Planning, and continued with his attendance at the sixth and seventh CIAM congresses; his essay "New Trends Will Affect the Core" was published as part of the proceedings of the eighth CIAM congress. Wiener's concepts of planning and the environment, laid out in the context of CIAM, were components of the discourse that he and Sert jointly articulated in the work of Town Planning Associates.

36. Le Corbusier and Girardoux, *The Athens Charter,* 100.

37. Box 11, folder 31, PLW.

38. Wiener, "El ambiente humano y el urbanismo," 21.

39. Ibid.

40. Sert, "The Human Scale in City Planning," 398. Sert did not invent these conceptual categories—the idea of the neighborhood unit can be traced back to Clarence Perry's contribution to the Regional Plan of New York, and Patrick Geddes elaborated the significance of the region in his earliest writings—but the crucial point here is Sert's reliance on the sequence as contiguous formal categories. At CIAM 9 in 1953, Alison and Peter Smithson presented their "Urban Reidentification Grid"—with its categories of house, street, district, city—as a continuous "hierarchy of associations." While the Smithsons did reconceptualize the categorical contents, the essential concept of sequence and connection was undisturbed.

41. Sert, "The Architect and the City," 21.

42. Tyrwhitt, "Cores within the Urban Constellation," 105. Sert's close involvement with this publication is documented in his extensive correspondence with Tyrwhitt regarding the format, texts, and illustrations for the volume.

43. Sert, who as president of CIAM was involved in the preparations for the meeting, likely participated in the development of the presentation format.

44. Tyrwhitt, "Cores within the Urban Constellation," 105. The thematic focus of CIAM 8 placed an emphasis on the representation of the core as a formal object in relation to a context, which permitted the distillation reflected in the format of the MARS Grid.

45. Le Corbusier, "Grille CIAM d'urbanisme," 12; Le Corbusier, "Description of the CIAM Grid, Bergamo 1949," 172–74; Le Corbusier, "Tools of Universality," 42.

46. Le Corbusier, "Description of the CIAM Grid, Bergamo 1949," 174; Le Corbusier, "Tools of Universality," 42; Le Corbusier, "Description of the CIAM Grid, Bergamo 1949," 172. For an examination of the epistemological claims of the CIAM Grid in relation to those of the "scales of association" proposed by Team 10, see Pedret, "Dismantling the CIAM Grid." A different study of the relationship between diagram and planning in the pre- and postwar periods in the United States can be found in Shanken, "The Uncharted Kahn."

47. Sert, *Can Our Cities Survive?*, 10.

48. "Comentarios sobre la Ley de Planificación Nacional," 110.

49. Junta Nacional de Planificación, *La ley sobre planificación, la JNP,* n.p.

50. "I understand planning as 'a thought process . . .' We could also say that Planning is: 'a coordination of conscious forces and the rational adaptation of methods to obtain results—which implies, to look to the future to establish objectives and then—after having analyzed the past—and with a fair evaluation of the resources available at the moment and in the future *set ourselves to achieve them*" (Montoulieu, *Planificación,* n.p.; emphasis in original).

51. Text of a manuscript prepared by Montoulieu in 1957 for the JNP. Eduardo Montoulieu, "La planificación, el Plan Nacional y los Planes Regionales. Las funciones y estructura de una junta nacional de planificación. Lo que deben y pueden ser en Cuba" (folder SA321, JLS).

52. Junta Nacional de Planificación, *JNP Primera Exposición,* 9.

53. Montoulieu, *Planificación.*

54. Ibid. The citation here uses the original English text. See Association for Planning and Regional Reconstruction, *Town and Country Planning Textbook.*

55. Tugwell, *The Place of Planning in Society,* 38. Montoulieu quoted this passage in full in *Planificación,* and its appearance in that text makes visible a certain change of emphasis from planning understood independently of the specificities of its physical manifestation in Tugwell's writings, to a predisposition toward physical planning in Montoulieu's examples. Other relevant publications by Tugwell include "The Fourth Power," in which he hypothesizes that planning could be elevated as a fourth, coequal branch of government, and "The Utility of the Future for the Present."

56. Tugwell, *The Place of Planning in Society,* 38.

57. Montoulieu, *Planificación.* The word *plasmación* can mean either an embodiment or a reflection. Both senses are in play in this instance, but Montoulieu's emphasis on the efficacy of *planes* over *planos* suggests that the former is more appropriate.

58. Memo, Paul Lester Wiener to José Luis Sert and Paul Shultz, September 29, 1955 (box 5, folder 9, PLW).

59. See Paul Wiener's journal of his stay in Havana during the summer of 1955 (box 11, folder 80, PLW).

60. Letter, Paul Lester Wiener to José Luis Sert, November 28, 1955 (box 13, folder 15, PLW).

61. Letter, Paul Wiener to Charles Haar, February 13, 1959 (box 13, folder 15, PLW). It is difficult to fix retrospectively the political positions of the various protagonists, as these have been irremediably colored by the Cuban Revolution; the assessments here are based in part on participants' later recollections (interviews with Nicolás Quintana; Maria Romañach).

62. See box 4, folder 28, PLW.

63. From an unpublished manuscript written in 1958: Eduardo Montoulieu, "The Recent Symposium and Exhibition on Cuban Natural Resources" (papers of Eduardo Montoulieu).

64. Ortega y Gasset, *España invertebrada,* 33. Ortega y Gasset was widely read in Latin America prior to the second world war, and his writings were well known and influential in Cuba.

65. Town Planning Associates, "Review of Consultations and Future Programs" (box 4, folder 28, PLW).

66. Eugenio Batista, who had not played a role in the JNP, served in the Department of Physical Planning until he left Cuba. Felipe Préstamo's account of the department is found in Préstamo, "City Planning in a Revolution."

67. Batista y Zaldívar, *Piedras y leyes.*

68. Rama, *The Lettered City,* 25.

69. Ichaso, "La nueva conciencia cubana y la constituyente de 1940," 87.

70. Ibid.

4. Public Works

1. Bernaldo de Quirós, *La picota en América,* 37. *Cabildo* refers to the administrative council of a town.

2. Ibid., 38. In 1957, Roig de Leuchsenring published a description of the significance of El Templete with several illustrations in a volume documenting the historical significance of the Plaza de Armas in Habana Vieja. This publication is discussed in chapter 6. See Roig de Leuchsenring, *Los monumentos nacionales de la República de Cuba,* vol. 1.

3. Martínez Inclán, *La Habana actual,* 7. Martínez Inclán wrote the book after he had worked as Jefe de la Sección de Arquitectura in the Departamento de Fomento of the Ayuntamiento de la Habana, the public works division of the municipality of Havana.

4. Ibid., 211.

5. Forestier had begun his professional career as a graduate of the École Polytechnique and the École Forestière at Nancy. Work as an administrator in the Service Autonome des Promenades et des Plantations in Paris prompted the concern for boulevards and parks, or the landscape of the city, that became the focus of his practical and theoretical work. In 1911, he founded the Société française des urbanistes with a roster of architectural colleagues that included Henri Prost, Ernest Hébrard, Donat-Alfred Agache, and Tony Garnier. Like those colleagues, he received numerous invitations from outside France to apply his expert knowledge of urbanism. In 1915, at the recommendation of José María Sert, the uncle of José Luis Sert, he received a commission in Barcelona for

the design at Montjuïc that would serve as the stage of the 1929 International Exposition. In 1924, he submitted plans for parks and avenues in Buenos Aires. He had been commissioned by the Cuban government once before, in 1918, to design a small park between the Palacio Presidencial and the Punta, but he did not visit Havana until 1925. See Leclerc, ed., *Jean-Claude Nicolas Forestier 1861–1930*.

6. See chapter 1 of Wright, *The Politics of Design in French Colonial Urbanism*.

7. For more detailed examinations of Forestier's Plano del Proyecto de la Habana, see Lejeune, "The City as Landscape"; Duverger, "El maestro francés del urbanismo criollo para la Habana"; and Segre, "La Habana de Forestier." On Martínez Inclán's acquaintance with the Forestier circle, see Segre, "Pedro Martínez Inclán (1883–1957)."

8. Martínez Inclán probably had in mind traffic systems such as those proposed by members of the Société française des urbanistes. See, for example, the "carrefour à giration" illustrated by Eugène Hénard in *Études sur les transformations de Paris* (Wright, *The Politics of Design in French Colonial Urbanism*, 25, Figure 8).

9. Jean-François Lejeune has pointed out that these elements conjure up the physical landscape of Cuba, providing what he calls "a memory of the geological origins of the island" (Lejeune, "The City as Landscape," 152).

10. Robinson, *Modern Civic Art, or, the City Made Beautiful*. Forestier, too, was well acquainted with the City Beautiful movement. In Paris in 1901, he met with the members of the MacMillan Commission, the group headed by Daniel Burnham charged with developing plans for the center of Washington, D.C. For the influence of American city planning movements on Forestier, see Lejeune, "La Ville et le Paysage."

11. Hegemann had used that term in his first widely read book, *The American Vitruvius: An Architect's Handbook of Civic Art*, published in 1922. Martínez Inclán submitted a brief review of volume 3 of Hegemann's posthumously published *City Planning, Housing* to the book's publisher. He praised it and the first volume as "didactic and documental," saying that together they constituted "one of the best works published." I am grateful to Christiane Crasemann Collins for providing me with a copy of the review from her archival collection related to Werner Hegemann.

12. Quoted in Collins, *Werner Hegemann and the Search for Universal Urbanism*, 113. Collins also provides a detailed differentiation between Hegemann's theories and the City Beautiful movement.

13. Because Hegemann's final book was posthumously edited, its contents cannot be conclusively assigned to his arguments, but they do correspond substantially. See chapter 6 in ibid.

14. Joseph Hudnut worked with Hegemann between 1917 and 1921. When he became dean of the School of Architecture at Columbia University in 1934, Hudnut was in a position to hire Hegemann to teach a new Town Planning Studio, one of the many curricular reforms that he imposed in an effort to modernize architectural education. The concern for city planning also motivated Hudnut's reforms at Harvard University shortly afterward, when the separate departments of Architecture, Landscape Architecture, and City Planning were, at his recommendation, merged into the Graduate School of Design under his deanship. These reforms and the theoretical positions that sponsored them provided the context of Eduardo Montoulieu's professional education; even without attending

a course taught by Hegemann, who died in 1936, Montoulieu would have been immersed in the articulation of city planning that Hegemann promoted. For an account of Hudnut's role in architectural education, see Pearlman, *Inventing American Modernism.*

15. Hudnut, "The Political Art of Planning," 48; emphasis in original.

16. Hudnut, "The Political Art of Architecture," 296–97. The characteristic terms of John Dewey's pragmatism suffused Hudnut's writings in turns of phrase such as "habit of collective thought and action" and "patterns of thought and conduct." Hudnut had subscribed to Dewey's pedagogical theories since the beginning of his teaching career at Columbia University, and such phrases suggest a broader adoption of Dewey's philosophy.

17. Hegemann, *City Planning, Housing,* 1:vii. The two passages in full read as follows: "City planning is also an art of expression and strives repeatedly to attain an aesthetic excellence through the creation of patterns—geometric or free—whose elements are streets and squares, planted areas, and structures"; "[Aristotle] could have meant no existing city but rather that city which men in all ages have built out of their aspirations: the planned city, the city made consonant with an exalted pattern of life inwardly apprehended."

18. Hudnut, foreword to Sert, *Can Our Cities Survive?,* iv. Rexford Tugwell cited the 1936 foreword in his essay "The Fourth Power," confirming the continuation of common exchanges of these discourses (1).

19. Hudnut, foreword to Sert, *Can Our Cities Survive?,* iv.

20. Ibid.

21. Bens Arrarte, "La grande Habana de 1950," 19.

22. Secretaría de Obras Públicas, *Memoria del plan de obras del gobierno del Dr. Ramón Grau San Martín,* n.p.

23. Sert, "Urban Design" (folder D91, JLS).

24. Sert, "The Architect and the City" (folder D45, JLS).

25. Unmentioned but surely obvious to participants, the substitution also implicitly rejected the earlier practices that had organized under the banner of civic design or civic art, from the City Beautiful movement to Werner Hegemann. José Luis Sert had taken over from Joseph Hudnut as dean of the GSD in 1953 and, while sympathetic to many aspects of Hudnut's position, he began to assert the primacy of a new formulation of the architecture of cities that traced its lineage (albeit impurely) back to prewar CIAM discourse. See "Urban Design," 97.

26. Sert, "Urban Design" (folder D91, JLS). The title of the conference, "The Architect and Urban Design and Urban Redevelopment," also employed the term although it is not clear who was responsible for its inclusion. During the next few years, Sert did continue to use the term "civic design" in referring to architectural practice at an urban scale. On the postwar emergence of "urban design" as a discipline, see Mumford, *Defining Urban Design.*

27. Sert, "Urban Design" (folder D91, JLS); emphasis in original.

28. Sert, "The Architect and the City" (folder D45, JLS).

29. Wiener, "Los problemas de la Arquitectura y del Urbanismo" (box 11, folder 45, PLW).

30. Wiener, "Future World's Fairs," 120.

31. Wiener, "New Trends Will Affect the Core," 82.

32. Letter, Paul Lester Wiener to Sylvinha, April 28, 1947 (box 12, folder 63, PLW).

33. Sert, "The Architect and the City" (folder D45, JLS).

34. Wiener derived this definition from a passage in the 1945 Report of the Chicago Plan Commission. Town Planning Associates also used the passage as one of the citations in its general bibliography of planning, in a section titled "What Is a Master Plan?" See box 11, folder 40, PLW, and box 4, folder 32, PLW.

35. Haar traveled to England in 1948 to study the workings of the Town and Country Planning Act, and declared, in the publication of his findings, that the act held out great promise for a democratic planning to improve the physical framework of human life (Haar, *Land Planning Law in a Free Society*). The first edition of the casebook on City Planning Law was published in 1959, but drafts were available to Harvard Law School students in 1955, and one of these drafts was contained in the library of the Graduate School of Design.

36. Haar, "In Accordance with a Comprehensive Plan," 1156.

37. Ibid., 1175.

38. Standard City Planning Act (1928) as quoted in Haar, "The Master Plan," 353.

39. The first position, regarding the master plan as technique, was advocated by Edward Bassett, who had proposed one of the earliest definitions of the master plan, but whose thesis Haar rejected. The second position, regarding the master plan as legislation, could be exemplified by the Fourth Power doctrine advocated by Rexford Tugwell, in which both the plan and the agency that produced it were to be sustained by statutory or constitutional means.

40. Haar, "The Master Plan," 356.

41. Ibid., 370.

42. Ibid., 375.

43. Ibid.

44. Ibid.

45. See letter, Charles Haar to Paul Wiener, June 24, 1955 (box 14, folder 27, PLW): "I am enclosing herewith a reprint of an article I wrote dealing with the comprehensive plan. I know that the whole notion of a master plan is one which you consider highly significant, and I would appreciate getting the benefit of your criticism and your experience in evaluating this article. I am at work on some other aspects of the master plan, and so would welcome your suggestions."

46. Haar, "The Master Plan," 376.

5. Master Plans

1. Between 1955 and 1956, Sert relocated his professional activities from New York City to Cambridge, Massachusetts, where his appointment at the GSD compelled his regular residency. Work on the Cuban projects was thus divided even within Town Planning Associates, with some design work undertaken in the New York office and some in Sert's new Cambridge office. Arroyo and Romañach visited both places for consultations. Arthur Wrubel and Constantine Michaelides, who worked in the New York and

Cambridge offices, respectively, recall the frequency of telephone consultations and also the relative independence of the various projects undertaken. According to the recollections of Eduardo Montoulieu and Nicolás Quintana, the office of the JNP in Cuba was similarly segregated, with the separate divisions advancing design work independently and at times in separate locations (telephone conversations with Alison Goodwin, February 1, 2005; Arthur Wrubel, July 19, 2005; Constantine Michaelides, June 2, 2005; interviews with Eduardo Montoulieu, June 8, 2005, Coral Gables, Florida; Nicolás Quintana, June 9, 2005, Miami, Florida).

2. Sketch dated July 13, 1955 (box 5, folder 13, PLW).

3. See memo, José Luis Sert to Paul Lester Wiener, November 18, 1955 (box 13, folder 10, PLW). Little or no formal coordination appears to have occurred between the JNP and the municipal government of Havana, which independently carried out planning projects and public works during this time period.

4. Box 5, folder 13, PLW.

5. The authorship of the Rule of the 7V seems rightly credited to Le Corbusier, but it is likely that the collaboration of the Bogotá project extended to some extent to the road system as well. Not only Sert and Wiener would have been involved, but also the New York engineering firm Seeyle, Stevenson, Value and Knecht that was responsible for traffic studies and roadway design in the project. Seeyle, Stevenson, Value and Knecht worked in a similar capacity on the Plan Piloto de la Habana. Certainly, Sert saw the classified road network as a crucial dimension of the plan; in Sigfried Giedion's 1958 Urban Design seminar at Harvard titled "Human Scale in Design," Sert was scheduled to present the Cuba plan and discuss specifically the role of the road system in restoring harmony to the civic realm of the city.

6. Le Corbusier, *Œuvre complète, 1946–1952,* 110.

7. Town Planning Associates, *Plan Piloto de la Habana,* 14. Quotations are from the English text that was included with folio.

8. Memo, José Luis Sert to Paul Lester Wiener, November 18, 1955 (box 13, folder 10, PLW).

9. Memo, Paul Schulz to José Luis Sert, September 1, 1956 (box 13, folder 8, PLW).

10. Memo, José Luis Sert to Paul Lester Wiener, November 18, 1955 (box 13, folder 10, PLW).

11. See box 11, folder 70, PLW. Wiener was naturally quite self-conscious in addressing the readers of his report—the state department officials who had underwritten his tour. He continued by arguing that public knowledge of planning would increase the promotion of democracy: "The idea of going to grass roots in obtaining public support for the planning process hardly exists in Central and Latin America. The public should be made aware of the benefit of planning and be taught the spirit of civic-mindedness so that they may democratically and effectively participate in the planning process. Physical, social and economic Regional and City Planning contribute greatly to the *promotion of* the healthy development of *democracy* and lead to greater productivity through efficient utilization of natural resources, thereby producing higher living standards. Therefore, this is one field that deserves our government's special consideration" (emphasis in original).

12. In the original text, the word *patterns* is included in English as a translation of the Spanish word *lineamientos* (Mañach, *El pensamiento de Dewey y su sentido americano,* 23).

13. Memorandum, September 27, 1957 (box 5, folder 8, PLW).

14. José Luis Sert, "The Neighborhood Unit: A Human Measure in City Planning," 1 (folder D100, JLS).

15. In his text, Sert quoted the definition proposed in 1939 by Clarence Perry: "that area which embraces all the public facilities and conditions required by the average family for its comfort and proper development within the vicinity of the dwelling." The school was usually identified as the element that determined "vicinity" or the scale of the neighborhood unit.

16. José Luis Sert, "The Neighborhood Unit: A Human Measure in City Planning," 29 (folder D100, JLS).

17. This private firm appears to have had some prior contact with the Cuban government. Sert and Wiener saw the opportunity to cultivate future work in Cuba and renewed their contact with Sert's friends in the ATEC chapter of CIAM. The housing proposal was exhibited in Havana, and the Town Planning Associates project received mention in the Cuban press, but no further contact between Town Planning Associates and the government occurred at that time.

18. "A Proposal for Community Planning and Housing for Cuba" (box 5, folder 6, PLW).

19. Ibid., 1.

20. Ibid. Wiener made this point again in a lecture, given in either 1953 or 1954, when describing the Cuban proposal: "The beauty of the neighborhood unit is obtained by the grouping of houses; the simplicity of their architecture, the landscaping, the pedestrian paths, and so on, rather than by diversity of individual buildings. The housing is for low to medium income groups, and it corresponds to the Latin way of living—built around patios. Where the American house is open to the street, the Latin Americans prefer to be seduced from the street. The lawn and garden of the North American house are become the patios of the L.A. [Latin American] house" (box 11, folder 42, PLW).

21. As a member of the Spanish CIAM Group GATEPAC (Grup d'Arquitectes i Tècnics Españoles per al Progrés de l'Arquitectura Contemporània), Sert traveled to Ibiza and published several articles on the typical architecture of the island, which he regarded as an exemplary "Mediterranean architecture." His articles on the topic are republished in Pizza, ed., *J. Ll. Sert y el Mediterráneo.* Parallel design studies of the courtyard house type were undertaken just before and after the war by Bernard Rudofsky in Brazil, and Mies van der Rohe in Germany and the United States.

22. Sert and Wiener, "Can Patios Make Cities?" 124. The text of this article combines passages from writings by Sert and Wiener with unattributed text by the editors. The word *module* in reference to the patio comes from Sert and Wiener, who used the same phrasing elsewhere. The illustration (Figure 5.9) was most likely produced by the magazine.

23. Sert and Wiener, "The Work of Town Planning Associates in Latin America 1945–1956," 191; emphasis in original.

24. See Sert, "The Rebirth of the Patio," 135.

25. Town Planning Associates, "Housing, Cuba," 83.

26. Sert, "The Rebirth of the Patio," 135.

27. Sert, "Centres of Community Life," 6. In this passage, Sert was quoting the congress invitation, which he undoubtedly helped draft.

28. Eduardo Montoulieu, text from sketches for La Exposición sobre Urbanismo, 1942 (papers of Eduardo Montoulieu).

29. See "Una obra del Arq. Emilio del Junco."

30. Letter, José Luis Sert and Paul Lester Wiener to Nicolás Arroyo and Rita Gutiérrez, March 12, 1954 (box 13, folder 8, PLW).

31. Letter, Rita Gutiérrez to José Luis Sert, October 25, 1954 (box 5, folder 30, PLW).

32. Undated report on Quinta Palatino (box 5, folder 29, PLW). In one sketch of a possible layout, Sert's note suggests that he was considering how the *cuadra* could be employed in other Cuban cities, such as Trinidad, where the historical fabric was to be substantially conserved.

33. The sketch indicates a dimension from floor to ceiling of 2.25 meters. The height of the Modulor figure is 2.26 meters. Such minor adjustments reconciled the Modulor proportions with potential contingencies such as material dimensions, construction practices, and drafting conventions; Le Corbusier himself pointed out the inherent tolerance of the Modulor system. The full range of Modulor dimensions is given in Le Corbusier, *The Modulor*.

34. Ibid., 210. Wiener probably saw Le Corbusier's presentation of the Modulor at the 1947 convention of the American Designers Institute in New York, at which Wiener was also a featured speaker, and Wiener had been with Le Corbusier when he met with Albert Einstein and received the scientist's approbation of the system. "I had the pleasure of discussing the 'Modulor' at some length with Professor Albert Einstein at Princeton University. I was then passing through a period of great uncertainty and stress; I expressed myself badly, I explained the 'Modulor' badly, I got bogged down in the morass of 'cause and effect' . . . At one point, Einstein took a pencil and began to calculate. Stupidly, I interrupted him, the conversation turned to other things, the calculation remained unfinished. The friend [Paul Lester Wiener] who had brought me was in the depths of despair" (ibid., 58). By 1953, Town Planning Associates was using the Modulor in architectural projects in Venezuela, in Sert's unbuilt design for the church in Puerto Ordaz, and in their design for the hospital at Maracaibo. One of the local architects working on revisions to the hospital design assured Sert in a letter that "You will see that we have tried to preserve the original spirit as far as possible and that we have even used the Modulor in accordance with your wishes" (letter, Miguel Casas Armengol to José Luis Sert, August 24, 1953 [box 8, folder 16, PLW]).

35. Paul Lester Wiener diary entry for July 20, 1955 (box 11, folder 80, PLW). The Modular proportion was also used to define bulk zoning limits for new *cuadras*.

36. Le Corbusier derived the numerical series of the Modulor from a sequence of geometric diagrams, in which a right-angle triangle fixed the positions of two contiguous squares. These diagrams were inaccurate, in that only one of the resulting squares was in fact a square, while the other was almost imperceptibly rectangular. For Le Corbusier, such a minute discrepancy had no practical implication. However, "in philosophy . . . I

suspect that these six thousandths of a value have an infinitely precious importance: the thing is not open and shut, it is not sealed; there is a chink to let in the air; life is there, awakened by the recurrence of a fateful equality which is not exactly, not strictly equal . . . and that is what creates movement" (Le Corbusier, *The Modulor,* 235). For an analysis of the specifically juridical aspects of the Modulor, see Pottage, "Architectural Authorship."

37. Le Corbusier, *The Modulor,* 84.

38. José Luis Sert, "The Neighborhood Unit: A Human Measure in City Planning," 3 (folder D100, JLS).

39. José Luis Sert, untitled address to the symposium De Divine Proportione, March 11, 1953 (folder D56, JLS).

40. Ibid.

41. Ibid.

42. See "Una obra del Arq. Emilio del Junco." A brief entry on the realized houses of the Santa Catalina development can be found in Rodríguez, *The Havana Guide,* 226.

6. Historic Districts

1. Since its addition in 1982 to the UNESCO World Heritage List, it has been common to regard Habana Vieja as a single, integral historic monument. The analysis that follows reveals that this presumption was not in fact prevalent during the 1950s, and should instead be understood as only one among several possible conceptions of the historic district that were held at that time.

2. Weiss, *Arquitectura cubana colonial;* Castro, *Contribución al estudio de la arquitectura cubana.*

3. Weiss, "Ventanas y balcones coloniales," 46.

4. Roig de Leuchsenring, *Los monumentos nacionales de la República de Cuba,* vols. 1 and 2.

5. Quoted in ibid., 1:127.

6. One article of Martínez Inclán's *Código de Urbanismo* was certainly prompted by concern about the restoration efforts: "111: Restorations of historic monuments will not be undertaken under any pretext, when sufficient authentic documents do not exist that show their primitive state" (Martínez Inclán, *Código de Urbanismo,* 19). Martínez Inclán also spoke against efforts to prevent the intrusion of new architectural styles into the precincts of Habana Vieja: "To believe that it is an artistic sacrilege to construct absolutely modern buildings in places near an *architectural jewel* (few jewels we have in Havana) seems to me an idea more suited to poets around the middle of the last century than to intellectuals of our time" (Martínez Inclán, "Arqueología versus arquitectura," 9).

7. Ley de Julio 24, 1928, reprinted in Roig de Leuchsenring, *Los monumentos nacionales de la República de Cuba,* 1:11.

8. Decreto-Ley No. 613, reprinted in ibid., 2:141.

9. The initial roster of appointees to the commission included Luis Bay Sevilla and Joaquín Weiss. Decreto No. 3057, reprinted in ibid., 1:12.

10. Ibid., 7–8.

11. Cordovi, "El primer Congreso Nacional de Planificación," 9.

12. Ibid., 11.

13. "Rehabilitación de la Habana Antigua," 55. Ley-Decreto 1996 was signed by Gustavo Gutiérrez, who was then serving as minister of housing.

14. La Financiera Nacional de Cuba was an autonomous agency established by General Batista in August 1953 as an instrument for financing public works projects. It was responsible, for example, for the concession for building the tunnel under the harbor. It was intended to provide capital for projects that would generate income, effectively liquidating their own debt. Because the Financiera Nacional could award concessions for these income-generating projects, it was also a crucial instrument for Batista's government patronage and its inevitable corruption. For Batista's own description of the agency, see Batista y Zaldívar, *The Growth and Decline of the Cuban Republic,* 145–46.

15. The members of the JNP themselves were not necessarily in a position to benefit from speculation in the area of Habana Vieja, but the structure of rehabilitation, combined with the JNP proposals for extensive modifications to the colonial quarter in order to maintain or even increase its commercial value to the city, would certainly have given incentive to financial speculation. There is some suggestion that both the Cuban architects working in the JNP and the firm of Town Planning Associates considered investing in a corporation that would have been responsible for new development projects in the city of Trinidad, but this does not seem to have been carried out, and there are no further indications of direct involvement in other financial dealings.

16. See Keith and Feiss, "A Report on the Renewal Possibilities of the Historic Triangle of the City of San Juan." For the relevant legislation, see Junta de Planificación de Puerto Rico, *Reglamento de zonas antiguas e históricas.*

17. Jordana Mendelson has traced this technique back to Sert's early career in Barcelona and photographs published in the architecture journal *AC* (see Mendelson, *Documenting Spain*).

18. These survey drawings, compiled in two bound volumes, contradict the claim that Sert and Wiener lacked a detailed view of Havana and its districts. Similarly, during the preparatory work for the Plan Piloto, Town Planning Associates built a large-scale model of the metropolitan area to provide a better understanding of the relation between sectors and the potential course of roadways. The surveys of Habana Vieja are now among the papers of Mario Romañach. I am grateful to Maria Romañach for allowing me to examine them.

19. Box 11, folder 80, PLW. The location for the new Banco Nacional had been debated for some time, with the finance industry preferring a site in Habana Vieja where the banking industry had long been located; advocates of the protection of monuments in the district argued for sites elsewhere in the city in order to avoid increasing the scale of buildings and the congestion of traffic in the Habana Vieja. One site, occupying a block near the Plaza de Armas, had been rejected by the mayor of Havana, Justo Luis del Pozo, after the Junta Nacional de Arqueología had voiced its opposition. A site overlooking the Malecón in Centro Habana was subsequently selected and Nicolás Quintana commissioned to design a tower to house the Banco Nacional. See Sorhegui, "La ubicación del Banco Nacional."

20. Box 11, folder 80, PLW.

21. Ibid.

22. The provenance of this composite drawing cannot be definitively determined, but it seems most likely that it was produced under the auspices of the JNP, although it may have combined fragments of proposals devised by other sources. The drawing shows the newly constructed Palacio de Bellas Artes, trapezoidal in plan, but proposes a surrounding area of new construction that may not derive directly from the work of the JNP. The composite plan must have been produced by the end of 1955 because the photographs of the plan reproduced here are contained among Paul Lester Wiener's papers, which also include overlaid sketches drawn and dated by Wiener in that year, as well as drawings in which several of the elements shown are drawn independently in more detail.

23. Much of the drafting work fell to Constantine Michaelides, a GSD student who worked for Sert and who received direction from Sert and Zalewski in preparing the design. He recalls that Sert was in contact, often by phone, with Arroyo or Romañach. Alison Goodwin also worked in the Cambridge office during this time, but worked primarily on the presidential palace project and the design of the U.S. embassy in Baghdad, the other major project occupying Sert's attention. At a late stage in the design of the Plan Piloto de la Habana, François Vigier, also a GSD graduate, worked in the office, and prepared the final rendered plates for the folio publication (telephone conversations with the author: Alison Goodwin, February 1, 2005; Constantine Michaelides, June 2, 2005.)

24. On this transition, see Mumford, *Defining Urban Design.*

25. Town Planning Associates, *Plan Piloto de la Habana,* 32. Quotations are from the English text published with the folio volume. The English translation differs in minor respects from the Spanish text.

26. Ibid., 32–33.

27. See, for example, *Can Our Cities Survive?* and also the illustrations included in *The Heart of the City.* Sert does not, however, seem to have responded in particular to the advancement of such rhetorical representational techniques presented by the Smithsons at CIAM 9 and subsequently.

28. Town Planning Associates, *Plan Piloto de la Habana,* 36.

29. Folder Addenda/TPA/Havana Master Plan, JLS.

30. Memorandum, Paul Lester Wiener to JNP, January 3, 1956 (folder Addenda/TPA/Junta, Havana, JLS); emphasis in original.

31. Town Planning Associates, *Plan Piloto de la Habana,* 35.

32. Ibid., 34–35.

33. Ibid., 4.

34. Boas, "The City as a Work of Art," 362.

35. Ibid., 356. Sert later participated in a panel discussion moderated by Boas on the topic "Present Issues in Design," held in 1956 at the Southeastern Regional Conference of the Association of Collegiate Schools of Architecture.

7. The Experience of Civic Conscience

1. Castro, *Palabras a los intelectuales,* 11.

2. Comisión Central Pro-monumento a Martí, *En memoria de José Martí,* 43–44. This and subsequent quotations are in English in the original. Errors are not corrected.

3. Quesada y Miranda, "Martí y los monumentos." Debate over the vitality of living memorials was not taken up more fully until the postwar period, when commemoration of the tragic recent past became a widespread issue. In 1937, questions about monumentality were only just beginning to dislocate presumptions that had held sway since the beginning of the nineteenth century. The Paris Exposition held that year took as a theme the unification of art and technology, and several of the national pavilions were designed to achieve through art and architecture a monumental expression as a prerequisite of national expression. The German and Soviet pavilions in particular were received as aggressive rival postures of monumentality. Other pavilions also took advantage of the effects of scale—for the U.S. pavilion Paul Lester Wiener designed a small skyscraper—but without the rhetoric of monumentality. In the Spanish pavilion, designed by José Luis Sert, art contributed that rhetorical dimension through narrative and expression, allowing the frankly modernist architecture to at least purport an absence of rhetoric altogether. Cuba did not participate in the Paris Exposition of 1937, but the fair was reported in the Cuban press and the exemplary pavilions were certainly known to architects in Cuba.

4. See chapters 5–10 in Comisión Central Pro-Monumento a Martí, *En memoria de José Martí*.

5. Ibid., 15.

6. Ibid., 51.

7. Ibid., 52.

8. Juan José Sicre was at this time a member of the Patronato Pro-Urbanismo.

9. "Dos informes sobre el Monumento a Martí," 401; emphasis in original.

10. The excerpt was from a letter Martí wrote to a newspaper in 1887. Comisión Central Pro-Monumento a Martí, *En memoria de José Martí*, 162.

11. "Memoria descriptiva: El Monumento" (box 28, folder 9, Jean Labatut Papers [JL]).

12. Lazcano y Mazón, *Constitución de Cuba (con los debates sobre su articulado y transitorias en la convención constituyente)*, 59. (The transcribed debate on article 5 is found on pages 58–102.)

13. "Dos informes sobre el Monumento a Martí," 397.

14. Ibid. The sketches Martí had made to illustrate the idea of an American order were in Quesada y Miranda's own archive of Martí documents and were published in the October 1943 issue of *Arquitectura*. It is uncertain whether he presented or discussed them publicly prior to that publication. In 1931, a competition had been held on the theme "La estilización de un orden de Palma Real" (The stylization of a royal palm order), and their existence might have become known at that point.

15. Mañach, "El Monumento a Martí (historia de un lauro frustrado)," 98. Mañach was quoting unpublished comments he had written ten years earlier as a juror in the final stage of the competition.

16. Ibid., 64.

17. "Monumento a José Martí," pamphlet dated June 14, 1939 (box 30, folder 2, JL).

18. Mañach, "El Monumento a Martí (historia de un lauro frustrado)," 64, 98.

19. Quesada y Miranda, "El Monumento a Martí," 386–88.

20. Ibid., 390.

21. Apart from Quesada y Miranda's reference to its statue, the Lincoln Memorial does not appear to have been discussed as a precedent. The omission is curious given the clear resemblance of the Maza and Sicre proposal, though the probable explanation is a desire to avoid overt association with the cultural influence of the United States. But the critique posed by Quesada y Miranda does suggest how significant a representational issue the clothing was. Lincoln's portrayal in period clothing sets the grit of history against the timelessness of the temple.

22. Mañach, "El Monumento a Martí (historia de un lauro frustrado)," 98.

23. "Monumento a José Martí" (box 30, folder 2, JL). Sambugnac did not participate in this second proposal, and the architects suggested that the absence of a sculptor from their team occurred because the sculptural was inseparable from the architectural, and that a later competition could be held to select a sculptor should their scheme be preferred.

24. From the late nineteenth century until 1960, the Cuban peso was valued as the equivalent of the U.S. dollar.

25. Mañach, "El Monumento a Martí (historia de un lauro frustrado)," 64.

26. The membership of the committee included government and military officials and was not meaningfully independent from the administration, but among the members were several figures who played roles in other events recounted here: Emilio Roig de Leuchsenring, Gonzalo de Quesada y Miranda, Enrique Luis Varela, Fernando Ortiz, and Francisco Ichaso. The full legal name of the committee was La Comisión Nacional Organizadora de los Actos y Ediciones del Centenario y del Monumento de Martí (National Organizing Committee for Centenary Acts and Editions and the Martí Monument).

27. "Pérez Benitoa habló en el Fórum sobre la Plaza de la República." See also "Iniciado del Fórum sobre el Monumento al Apóstol Martí y la Plaza de la República."

28. "Convenio de Indemnización" labeled "copy No. 5" (box 28, folder 3, JL).

29. Ibid. In a handwritten note to Varela, dated December 23, 1954, and appended to the draft agreements, Labatut suggested that it was important to include a description of the "change from horizontal to vertical composition" as a "'historical' fact." He concluded, "I hope that all documents will be signed soon for the good of the monument and for our reputation as architects. Hoping to have the opportunity to talk about *architecture* with you soon"; emphasis in original.

30. Estévez, "El Fórum del Colegio de Arquitectos sobre la Plaza Cívica y Monumento a Martí," 42.

31. Ibid., 43.

32. Ibid., 42.

33. Ibid., 36.

34. Cortina, "La Plaza de la República," 331.

35. Mañach, "El santo temor a lo irremediable"; emphasis in original.

36. Martínez Inclán, *Código de Urbanismo*, 22.

37. Letter, Jean Labatut to Enrique Luis Varela and Raúl Otero, March 28, 1953 (box 28, folder 4, JL).

38. "Monumento a José Martí" (box 30, folder 2, JL). The Schenley pavilion designed by architect Morris Sanders was published over several pages of the March 1938 issue of *Pencil Points*, so the scheme was probably relatively well known.

39. Letter, Jean Labatut to Enrique Luis Varela and Raúl Otero, March 28, 1953 (box 28, folder 4, JL); ellipses in original.

40. See "Memoria Descriptiva—El Monumento" (box 28, folder 9, JL).

41. Ibid.

42. Ibid.

43. Cortina, "La Plaza de la República," 332.

44. See inscription on verso of photograph of Caravia (box 29, folder 3, JL).

45. Ibid.

46. Letter, Jean Labatut to Enrique Luis Varela and Raúl Otero, March 28, 1953 (box 28, folder 4, JL); emphasis in original.

47. See Labatut, "Monuments and Memorials." Labatut did not participate directly in the exchange of essays that constituted the architectural debate on monumentality in the mid-1940s, but he was nevertheless tangentially involved. He had been asked but declined to submit an essay to the symposium volume *New Architecture and City Planning.* Sigfried Giedion, in his own essay in that volume, "The Need for a New Monumentality," cited Labatut's proposed fireworks display for the 1939 World's Fair as an example of a possible new monumentality. Labatut did attend the 1947 symposium "Building for Modern Man" at Princeton University, where one of the topics was philosophy of form. Also in attendance were Giedion and Hudnut, who gave presentations, and Sert, who, like Labatut, did not. See Creighton, *Building for Modern Man.*

48. Labatut, "Monuments and Memorials," 524.

49. Labatut's role in postwar architectural discourse has long been overlooked. For an examination of Labatut's work, including his intellectual sources and contributions, see chapter 2, "Eucharistic Architecture," in Otero-Pailos, *Architecture's Historical Turn.*

50. "Memoria Descriptiva—El Monumento" (box 28, folder 9, JL).

51. Ibid.

52. See box 28, folder 10, JL.

53. Letter, Jean Labatut to Enrique Luis Varela and Raúl Otero, March 28, 1953 (box 28, folder 4, JL).

54. See Otero-Pailos, *Architecture's Historical Turn,* 40–57. On the relation between architecture and artificial illumination, see Neumann, *Architecture of the Night.*

55. Labatut, "Monuments and Memorials," 531.

56. Ibid., 522.

57. Ibid., 524; emphasis in original.

8. The Prospect of *Cubanidad*

1. Undated newspaper clipping (folder F004, JLS).

2. Ibid.

3. Only fragmentary evidence remains to document views held at the time by the various participants, and those views are in any case now recast by the history of the 1959 Cuban Revolution. Nicolás Arroyo was, as minister of public works, actually a member of Batista's government; the others, however, were not so closely aligned. Maria Romañach, Mario Romañach's daughter, recalls her father's distaste for Batista and suggests that the

political sphere was, in Havana at least, distinctly separate from the professional activities and artistic endeavors that preoccupied him. Nicolás Quintana makes the same claim, which is corroborated to some degree by the fact that both were allowed to practice in Cuba for at least a year following the revolution, a permission that would not have been granted to anyone perceived as a close supporter of Batista. In a letter to Gabriela Menéndez written following the public presentation of the project to Batista, Wiener noted Romañach's unexpected absence from the presentation, and added, "This attitude reflects the general tenor of Mario in connection with this project. I am afraid he is 'lukewarm' and . . . is not taking any of the risks involved and has spent very little time so far in the designing." Wiener goes on to attribute this lack of full commitment to "attitude and temperament" and though there is no evidence that Romañach's distancing was motivated by political or ethical reservations, it is possibly part of the explanation (letter, Paul Lester Wiener to Gabriela Menéndez, July 23, 1953 [box 13, folder 13, PLW]). Richard Bender, who worked with Wiener after the dissolution of Town Planning Associates, recalls that he delayed joining Wiener earlier because of his own distaste for the implications of the palace project, which Wiener likely understood (interviews: Maria Romañach, June 30, 2005, Philadelphia, Pennsylvania; Nicolás Quintana, June 9, 2005, Miami, Florida; telephone conversation: Richard Bender, September 1, 2005).

4. Estévez and Biniakonski, "Habla José Luis Sert para *Espacio*," 18.

5. José Luis Sert, "The Changing Philosophy of Architecture" (folder D54, JLS).

6. José Luis Sert, "The Scope of Architecture" (folder D87, JLS).

7. Mumford, *The South in Architecture*, 132, 31.

8. In this respect, the motivations of Cuban regionalism were similar to those of the GATEPAC group, which supported the republican movement in Catalonia during the 1930s. The political situations were different, of course, but there are clear parallels to the Catalonian movements during those years, which were also founded on demands for self-determination. See Rovira, *José Luis Sert*, 23–91.

9. Arroyo, "La A.T.E.C. y la última exposición de Trinidad," 192. In subsequent years, members of the ATEC group, and Sert as well, continued to regard Trinidad as an exemplary specimen for architectural and urbanistic thought. During the late 1950s, Nicolás Quintana led an effort to establish a foundation that would manage the preservation and development of the city of Trinidad, and he solicited the collaboration of the anthropologist Lydia Cabrera, among others, to formulate a historical understanding of the city.

10. Pietro Belluschi's essay, because it was published in *Architectural Record*, would have had a wider circulation within and outside of the United States than Harris's lecture, which was presented to a regional meeting of the AIA and not published until 1965. But Harris was well known and had been a friend of Sert's since participating in the formation of the American chapter of CIAM in 1944. In 1954, Harris was the director of the School of Architecture at the University of Texas. Following his early apprenticeships in California with Richard Neutra and Rudolph Schindler, he had developed a strong interest in the work of Frank Lloyd Wright, an attachment that was central to his ideas of regionalism, in which the regional was understood as the source for any broader perceptions or effects architecture might attain. Belluschi, at the time of writing his article on regionalism, was dean of the School of Architecture at MIT and also a close acquaintance

of Sert's. Belluschi's work in the Pacific Northwest of the United States was recognized as a distinctive contribution to regionalism, marked by an attentiveness to materials, construction techniques, and, significantly, a perception of architecture as a fundamentally humanist endeavor.

11. Harris, "Regionalism and Nationalism," 28.

12. Belluschi, "The Meaning of Regionalism in Architecture," 138. Sandy Isenstadt has elaborated the importance of concepts of time and temporality in Sert's Baghdad project (Isenstadt, "US Embassy in Baghdad").

13. Harris, "Regionalism and Nationalism," 29.

14. Belluschi, "The Meaning of Regionalism in Architecture," 132.

15. Ibid., 136–37.

16. Ibid., 136.

17. Although the rebellion against Batista was under way in 1955, with Castro still in exile and the notorious guerrilla attack on the existing presidential palace two years in the future, the resistance to Batista was at an ebb and security may not have been as immediate a motivation as it would seem in retrospect.

18. Undated memorandum, José Luis Sert to Nicolás Arroyo (folder SA320, JLS).

19. Strong formal similarities exist between the designs of the presidential palace and the U.S. embassy in Athens. The embassy project was first published in *Casabella* in 1958, but given their friendship and the proximity of their offices, Sert and Gropius might well have discussed the project before then. In elevational view, the presidential palace also resembled Le Corbusier's design for the High Court at Chandigarh, begun in 1951. The High Court facade, asymmetrically disposed and enclosed in a "box" formed by sheer side walls joined flush to a flat roof of equal thickness, was not neoclassical; its vaulting and piers, though, created a elevational profile on which Sert unmistakably drew in the design of the palace. Another precedent of which Sert and Romañach would have been aware was Le Corbusier's 1936 proposal for a University City in Rio de Janeiro, which included a ceremonial Plaza of Ten Thousand Palms, a dense grove of royal palm trees planted in a grid at the center of the campus. A subsequent version was proposed by the Brazilian architect Lúcio Costa, who had worked with Le Corbusier on the plan and who incorporated the plaza element into an initial sketch for Brasília as the Forum de Palmieras Imperiaes. That sketch was published in the summer of 1957.

20. Typescript, "Palace of the Palms, the Presidential Palace of Cuba: Havana" (folder SA317, JLS).

21. Ibid.

22. Ibid.

23. See Roig de Leuchsenring, *Los monumentos nacionales de la República de Cuba*, vols. 1 and 2.

24. The Palacio de Aldama was one of the grand colonial residences in Havana, and Sert's notes indicate that he visited it and recognized its *patio* as a precedent. The Palacio de Aldama was owned by the family of Emilio del Junco's wife, and del Junco was one of the circle of architects professionally and personally acquainted with Sert and Romañach.

25. "I have finished with my introduction and started with Ortega's *Revolt of the Masses* that defines the core. It is the best definition I have found so far" (letter, José Luis Sert to Walter Gropius, June 27, 1951 [folder C8, CIAM]).

26. Ortega y Gasset, quoted by Sert (folder D14, JLS).
27. Sert, "Centres of Community Life," 6.
28. Folder D14, JLS.
29. Sert, "Centres of Community Life," 8.
30. Folder D14, JLS.
31. Sert, "The Rebirth of the Patio," 135.
32. Sert, "Centres of Community Life," 8–11.
33. "The Palace of the Palms" (folder SA317, JLS); memorandum, Paul Lester Wiener to José Luis Sert (folder SA321, JLS).
34. Ibid.
35. Ibid.
36. Sert's first choice had been Pier Luigi Nervi, who replied that he was unavailable. Candela recounted in a letter to Max Borges Jr. how he received an unexpected call from Sert, who "invited me to come to Havana to take charge of the structural design of a very important government building." Romañach had sent a simultaneous summons by telegram, and Candela made plans to go the following week (letter, Félix Candela to Max Borges, September 6, 1956 [box 36, folder 4, Félix Candela Papers (FC), Drawings and Archives Collection, Avery Library, Columbia University]).
37. Hitchcock, *Latin American Architecture since 1945*, 26.
38. Candela, "Understanding the Hyperbolic Paraboloid," 191.
39. Letter, Félix Candela to Max Borges, September 6, 1956 (box 36, folder 4, FC).
40. "Shells are as old as nature, and it was from nature that Félix Candela learned his first lesson: all shells have compound curves, and their strength is derived from their shape rather than their thickness." These are the opening sentences of Esther McCoy's catalog essay for the exhibition "Félix Candela: Shell Forms" held at the University of Southern California in 1957. See Candela and McCoy, *Félix Candela*.
41. Although the book was not published until 1960, correspondence between the authors suggests that the text must have been drafted by 1954; Sert published excerpts in *Casabella* in 1954 and in *L'Œil* in 1955. See Sert and Sweeney, *Antoni Gaudí*.
42. Ibid., 136.
43. Ibid., 8. Sert and Sweeney cautioned that the interpretive attributions of the Surrealist Salvador Dalí were excessive, but admitted that Dalí recognized that Gaudí's work offered more than lessons in "structural integrity."
44. Ibid., 9.
45. Martí, *The America of José Martí*, 141. (See chapter 1, note 31 regarding the English translation.)
46. Ibid., 143.
47. Quoted in Quesada y Miranda, "El Monumento a Martí," 387. Martí's palm tree symbolized not only his America, but also its engagement with a world culture—if one recalls Marc-Antoine Laugier's suggestion in his *Observations on Architecture* that a new French order might include "small branches of palm," then one recognizes Martí's columnar order as a regional variant of the classical orders.
48. Batista, "Herencia, patios, portales y persianas." It is unclear exactly when Batista wrote this essay, but it was several years prior its publication.

49. The architects of the Capitolio Nacional at that time included Emilio Govantes, Félix Cabarrocas, Raúl Otero, and J. M. Bens Arrarte, all of whom had also been associated with Forestier during his time in Cuba.

50. Architectural regionalism was pursued with considerable rigor and success in Cuba during the 1940s and 1950s. Its central theme was the adaptation to climate (a common aspect of regionalism that Richard Neutra would have reinforced when he visited Cuba in 1944 and met with the ATEC group), but some prominent works incorporated cultural dimensions as well, often influenced by Ortiz and other intellectuals. In 1949, only ten years after Eugenio Batista had provided the early prototype, the Cueto House by Mario Romañach announced the maturation of sophisticated regional modernism in Cuba.

51. Ortiz, *Cuban Counterpoint, Tobacco and Sugar,* 4. In this book, Ortiz also coined his term *transculturación* to describe the formation of new cultures from the uprooting and re-rooting of existing ones, establishing the sociological and anthropological foundations for his argument that *cubanidad* was an experience of hybridity.

52. Nicolás Quintana was a member of Ortiz's circle from 1948 onward, dining regularly at his house and participating in discussions with other guests, who included Jorge Mañach. Eduardo Montoulieu recalls attending Ortiz's lectures, and Maria Romañach recalls her father's close acquaintance with several modernist artists of this circle (interviews with: Nicolás Quintana, June 9, 2005, Miami, Florida; Eduardo Montoulieu, June 8, 2005, Coral Gables, Florida; Maria Romañach, June 30, 2005, Philadelphia, Pennsylvania). Also see chapter 11, "La vanguardia integrada," in Rodríguez, *La Habana, arquitectura del siglo XX.*

53. Quoted in Martínez, *Cuban Art and National Identity,* 122.

54. Interview with Maria Romañach, June 30, 2005, Philadelphia, Pennsylvania.

Epilogue

1. In 1953, in a letter from Rome, Labatut told Varela and Otero that he was spending time carrying out a "survey" of the plazas in that city, attempting to "look at [them] in modern terms" and analyzing factors such as "height, proportions and angles of line of vision." He was particularly intrigued with Bernini's works—the oval piazza in front of St. Peter's and the Piazza Navona—and considered carefully the relation of form, space, and sculpture in both designs. By 1959, he had prepared a lecture on Piazza Navona, titled "Bernini's Message to Modern Architects," that included diagrams of the visual perception of the piazza's enclosing buildings and its sculptures (letter, Jean Labatut to Enrique Luis Varela and Raúl Otero, March 28, 1953 [box 28, folder 4, JL]).

2. Gutiérrez y Sánchez, *Historia del derecho constitucional cubano,* xxiv–xxv; emphasis in original.

3. Letter, Paul Lester Wiener to Charles Haar, February 13, 1959 (box 13, folder 15, PLW).

4. Erich Auerbach, philologist and literary critic, described the mode of figural interpretation that "establishes a connection between two events or persons in such a way that the first signifies not only itself but also the second, while the second involves or fulfills

the first. The two poles of a figure are separated in time, but both, being real events or persons, are within temporality. They are both contained in the flowing stream which is historical life, and only the comprehension, the *intellectus spiritualis,* of their interdependence is a spiritual act." In this narrative structure, the "connection between occurrences is not regarded as primarily a chronological or causal development" but the reflexive relation of figure and fulfillment. See Auerbach, *Mimesis,* 73, 555. For the elaboration of the relevance of Auerbach's figural interpretation to historiography, see White, *Figural Realism.*

5. Mañach, *Examen del quijotismo,* 156.

6. Ibid.

7. See Loomis, *Revolution of Forms.*

8. Mañach, *Examen del quijotismo,* 162.

Bibliography

Archives

Archivo Nacional de Cuba, Havana, Cuba
Centro de Información de la Construcción, Ministerio de la Construcción, Havana, Cuba
CIAM Collection, Special Collections, Frances Loeb Library, Graduate School of Design, Harvard University, Cambridge, Massachusetts
Cuban Heritage Collection, University of Miami Libraries, University of Miami, Miami, Florida
Félix Candela Collection, Department of Drawings and Archives, Avery Architectural and Fine Arts Library, Columbia University, New York, New York
Jean Labatut Papers, Department of Rare Books and Special Collections, Princeton University Library, Princeton University, Princeton, New Jersey
Josep Lluís (José Luis) Sert Collection, Special Collections, Frances Loeb Library, Graduate School of Design, Harvard University, Cambridge, Massachusetts
Papers of Eduardo Montoulieu, private collection
Papers of Mario Romañach, private collection
Paul Lester Wiener Collection, Special Collections, Knight Library, University of Oregon, Eugene, Oregon

Interviews

Alison Goodwin, February 1, 2005, telephone conversation with author
Constantine Michaelides, June 2, 2005, telephone conversation with author
Eduardo Montoulieu, June 8, 2005, interview with author, Coral Gables, Florida (digital recording); December 1, 2005, telephone conversation with author
Nicolás Quintana, June 9, 2005, interview with author, Miami, Florida (digital recording)
Nicolás Arroyo, June 29, 2005, interview with author, Washington, D.C. (digital recording)
Gabriela Menéndez, June 29, 2005, interview with author, Washington, D.C. (digital recording)

Maria Romañach, June 30, 2005, interview with author, Philadelphia, Pennsylvania (digital recording); March 3, 2003, telephone conversation with author

Arthur Wrubel, July 19, 2005, telephone conversation with author

Ingebord TenHaeff, July 25, 2005, interview with author, New York, New York (digital recording)

Richard Bender, September 1, 2005, telephone conversation with author

Periodicals

Arquitectura (Havana, Cuba)

Bohemia (Havana, Cuba)

Carteles (Havana, Cuba)

Diario de la Marina (Havana, Cuba)

Books and Articles

Abalo, José Luis. *La forma técnico-funcional de gobierno.* Havana: Jesús Montero, 1939.

Alvarez Tabío, Fernando. *Teoría general de la constitución cubana.* Havana: Jesús Montero, 1946.

Álvarez y Martínez, José Manuel. *Sentido actual del urbanismo.* Havana: Editorial de Libros y Folletos, 1945.

Argote-Freyre, Frank. *Fulgencio Batista: From Revolutionary to Strongman.* New Brunswick, N.J.: Rutgers University Press, 2006.

Arroyo, Nicolás. "La A.T.E.C. y la última exposición de Trinidad." *Arquitectura* 11, no. 118 (May 1943): 190–95.

Association for Planning and Regional Reconstruction. *Town and Country Planning Textbook.* London: Architectural Press, 1950.

Auerbach, Erich. *Mimesis: The Representation of Reality in Western Literature.* Princeton, N.J.: Princeton University Press, 2003.

Austin, J. L. *How to Do Things with Words.* Cambridge: Harvard University Press, 1962.

Barr, Alfred. "Modern Cuban Painters." *Bulletin of the Museum of Modern Art* 2 (April 1944): 2–14.

Bastlund, Knud. *José Luis Sert: Architecture, City Planning, Urban Design.* Zurich: Les Éditions d'Architecture, 1967.

Batista, Eugenio. "Herencia, patios, portales y persianas: La casa cubana." *Artes Plásticas* 2 (1960).

Batista, Víctor. "Mañach y los inicios insulares de la nacionalidad cubana." *Encuentro,* no. 8/9 (spring/summer 1998): 205–13.

Batista y Zaldívar, Fulgencio. *The Growth and Decline of the Cuban Republic.* New York: Devin-Adair, 1964.

———. *Piedras y leyes.* Mexico City: Ediciones Botas, 1961.

Belluschi, Pietro. "The Meaning of Regionalism in Architecture." *Architectural Record* (December 1955): 131–39.

Benítez-Rojo, Antonio. "Fernando Ortiz and Cubanness: A Postmodern Perspective." *Cuban Studies,* no. 18 (1988): 125–32.

Bens Arrarte, J. M. "El Malecón será urbanizado y ampliado con terrenos ganados al mar." *Arquitectura* 26, no. 296 (March 1958): 124–31.

———. "La grande Habana de 1950." *Revista del Colegio de Arquitectos de la Habana* (May 1931): 18–25.

Bernaldo de Quirós, Constancio. *La picota en América.* Havana: Jesús Montero, 1948.

———. *Nuevas noticias de picotas americanas.* Havana: Jesús Montero, 1952.

Biniakonski, Samuel. "La ley sobre planificación." *Espacio* 3 no. 16 (November/December 1954).

———. "Más sobre la Junta Nacional de Planificación." *Espacio* 4, no. 17 (January/April 1955).

Boas, George. "The City as a Work of Art." In *New Architecture and City Planning,* edited by Paul Zucker, 353–65. New York: Philosophical Library, 1944.

Bugeda Lanzas, Jesús. *La propiedad horizontal: Estudio de la Ley-decreto 407 de 16 de septiembre 1952.* Havana: Cultural, 1954.

Bullrich, Francisco. *New Directions in Latin American Architecture.* New York: G. Braziller, 1969.

Bustamente y Montoro, Antonio Sánchez de. "Kelsenism." In *Paul Sayre,* 43–51. New York: Oxford University Press, 1947.

———. *Teoría general del derecho.* Havana: Editorial "Alfa," 1940.

Campa, Román de la. *Latin Americanism.* Minneapolis: University of Minnesota Press, 1999.

Candela, Félix. "Understanding the Hyperbolic Paraboloid." *Architectural Record* (July 1958): 191–95.

Candela, Félix, and Esther McCoy. *Félix Candela: Shell Forms.* Los Angeles: University of Southern California Press, 1957.

Capablanca, Enrique, and Carlos Venegas Fornias. *La Habana vieja.* Havana: Letras Cubanas, 1998.

Carbonell Cortina, Néstor. *El espíritu de la constitución cubana de 1940: Principios y doctrina.* Madrid: Playor, 1974.

———. *Grandes debates de la Constituyente cubana de 1940.* Miami: Ediciones Universal, 2001.

Cárdenas, Eliana. *En la busqueda de una arquitectura nacional.* Havana: Editorial Letras Cubanas, 1991.

———. *José Martí: Arquitectura y Paisaje Urbano.* Havana: Editorial Letras Cubanas, 1988.

Carpentier, Alejo. *Tientos y diferencias.* Buenos Aires: Calicanto Editorial, 1976.

Carrera y Jústiz, Francisco. *Breves notas sobre la constitución de Cuba de 1940 y el regimen municipal.* Havana, 1940.

———. *Preliminares de ciencia municipal urbanismo. Primera parte: El urbanismo como ciencia.* Havana: Cultural, 1935.

———. *Urbanismo: El distrito central de la Habana es un caso científico de urbanismo regional.* Havana: Carasa y Cía, 1929.

Castro, Fidel. *Palabras a los intelectuales.* Havana: Ediciones del Consejo Nacional de Cultura, 1961.

Castro, Martha de. *Contribución al estudio de la arquitectura cubana: Algunas ideas acerca de nuestro barroco colonial.* Havana: Imprenta "La Verónica," 1940.
Cespedes, Pedro G. de. "Nación y planificación." *Arquitectura* 26, no. 298 (May 1958): 208–9.
Chailloux Cardona, Juan M. *Síntesis histórica de la vivienda popular, los horrores del solar habanero.* Havana: Jesús Montero, 1945.
"The Changing Philosophy of Architecture." *Architectural Record* (August 1954): 180–83.
"City Plan Projects for Latin America." *Architectural Record* (January 1954): 162–63.
Collins, Christiane Crasemann. *Werner Hegemann and the Search for Universal Urbanism.* New York: W. W. Norton, 2005.
"Comentarios sobre la Ley de Planificación Nacional." *Arquitectura* 23, no. 260 (March 1955): 104–25.
Comisión Central Pro-monumento a Martí. *En memoria de José Martí.* Havana: P. Fernández y Cía, 1938.
Commercial Club of Chicago, Daniel Hudson Burnham, Edward H. Bennett, Charles Moore, and Jules Vallée Guérin. *Plan of Chicago.* Chicago: Commercial Club, 1909.
Congreso Internacional de Planificación y de la Habitación. *Papers.* Mexico City: Congreso Internacional de Planificación y de la Habitación, 1938.
Consejo de Indias. *Recopilación de leyes de los reynos de las Indias.* Madrid: A. Ortega, 1774.
Consejo Nacional de Economía. *El programa económico de Cuba.* Havana, 1955.
Cortina, José Manuel. "La Plaza de la República: Misión spiritual del Monumento a Martí." *Arquitectura* 21, no. 124 (1953): 331–34.
Costa, Xavier, and Guido Hartray. *Sert, arquitecto en Nueva York.* Barcelona: Museu d'Art Contemporani de Barcelona/ACTAR, 1997.
Creighton, Thomas H. *Building for Modern Man.* Princeton, N.J.: Princeton University Press, 1949.
Crouch, Dora P., Daniel J. Garr, and Axel I. Mundigo. *Spanish City Planning in North America.* Cambridge: MIT Press, 1982.
Crouch, Dora P., and Axel I. Mundigo. "The City Planning Ordinances of the Laws of the Indies Revisited." *Town Planning Review* 48, no. 3 (July 1977): 247–68.
Díaz Infante, Duanel. *Mañach o la república.* Havana: Letras Cubanas, 2003.
Domínguez, Martín. "Diversión hacia Varadero." *Diario de la Marina,* September 20, 1942.
———. "Urbanismo de sobremesa redonda (I)." *Diario de la Marina,* October 4, 1942.
Domínguez Compañy, Francisco. *El urbanismo en las Leyes de Indias (estudio histórico y jurídico-social).* Havana: González y Cía, 1945.
"Dos informes sobre el Monumento a Martí." *Arquitectura* 11, no. 123 (October 1943): 395–401.
Duverger, Hériberto. "El maestro francés del urbanismo criollo para la Habana." In *Jean-Claude Nicolas Forestier 1861–1930: Du jardin au paysage urbain,* edited by Bénédicte Leclerc, 221–40. Paris: Picard, 1990.
"Estatutos del Patronato Pro-Urbanismo de Cuba." Havana: Patronato Pro-Urbanismo, 1942.
Estévez, Reynaldo. "El Fórum del Colegio de Arquitectos sobre la Plaza Cívica y Monumento a Martí." *Espacio* 2, no. 9 (May/June 1953): 36–44.

Estévez, Reynaldo, and Samuel Biniakonski. "Habla José Luis Sert para *Espacio*." *Espacio* 2, no. 10/11 (July/October 1953): 18–20.
Faber, Colin. *Candela: The Shell Builder.* New York: Reinhold Publishing Corporation, 1963.
Fernández, Justino, Federico Gómez de Orozco, and Manuel Toussaint. *Planos de la ciudad de México, siglos XVI y XVII, estudio histórico, urbanístico y bibliográfico.* Vol. 2. Mexico City: Congreso Internacional de Planificación y de la Habitación, 1938.
"Five Civic Centers in South America." *Architectural Record* (August 1953): 121–36.
Freixa, Jaume. *Josep Ll. Sert.* Barcelona: G. Gili, 1989.
Gakenheimer, Ralph. "Determinants of Physical Structure in the Peruvian Town of the 16th Century." Ph.D. dissertation, University of Pennsylvania, 1964.
Gasparini, Graziano. "The Spanish-American Grid Plan, an Urban Bureaucratic Form." *New City,* no. 1 (fall 1991): 6–17.
Giedion, Sigfried. *A Decade of New Architecture.* Zurich: Girsberger, 1951.
———. "The Need for a New Monumentality." In *New Architecture and City Planning,* edited by Paul Zucker, 549–68. New York: Philosophical Library, 1944.
———. "The State of Contemporary Architecture 1. The Regional Approach." *Architectural Record* (January 1954): 132–37.
Giedion, Sigfried, Fernand Léger, and José Luis Sert. "Nine Points on Monumentality." In *Architecture Culture 1943–1968: A Documentary Anthology,* edited by Joan Ockman and Edward Eigen, 27–30. New York: Rizzoli, 1993.
Gómez Díaz, Francisco. *De Forestier a Sert: Ciudad y arquitectura en la Habana (1925–1960).* Barcelona: Abada Editores, 2008.
González Echevarría, Roberto. *Alejo Carpentier: The Pilgrim at Home.* Ithaca, N.Y.: Cornell University Press, 1977.
———. *Myth and Archive: A Theory of Latin American Narrative.* Cambridge: Cambridge University Press, 1990.
Gott, Richard. *Cuba: A New History.* New Haven: Yale University Press, 2004.
Gray, Richard Butler. *José Martí, Cuban Patriot.* Gainesville: University Press of Florida, 1962.
Guerra, Lillian. *The Myth of José Martí: Conflicting Nationalisms in Early Twentieth-Century Cuba.* Chapel Hill: University of North Carolina Press, 2005.
Gutiérrez Cordovi, Ángel. "El primer congreso nacional de planificación." *Arquitectura* 25, no. 282 (January 1957): 8–19.
Gutiérrez y Sánchez, Gustavo. *Constitución de la República de Cuba, promulgada el día 5 de julio de 1940. Sus antecedentes históricos. Su espíritu. Estudio crítico sobre sus más fundamentales principios.* Havana: Editorial Lex, 1941.
———. *El desarrollo económico de Cuba; homenaje a la República en el cincuentenario de su independencia.* Havana: Junta Nacional de Economía, 1952.
———. *Historia del derecho constitucional cubano.* Havana: Cultural, 1938.
———. "La convención constituyente y la constitución de 1940." In *Historia de la nación cubana,* edited by Ramiro Guerra y Sánchez, vol. 8, 97–188. Havana: Editorial Historia de la Nación Cubana, 1952.
———. *La orientación de la economía nacional.* Havana: Junta Nacional de Economía, 1947.

———. *Presente y futuro de la economía cubana*. Havana: Junta Nacional de Economía, 1950.

———. *Proyecto de nueva constitución para la República de Cuba (con el proyecto del congreso de 1936)*. Havana, 1940.

"Ha quedado inaugura la primera exposición cubana de urbanismo en el Lyceum y Lawn Tennis Club." *Diario de la Marina*, September 17, 1942.

Haar, Charles Monroe. "The Content of the General Plan: A Glance at History." *Journal of the American Institute of Planners* 21, no. 2–3 (spring–summer 1955): 66–70.

———. "In Accordance with a Comprehensive Plan." *Harvard Law Review* 68, no. 7 (1955): 1154–75.

———. *Land Planning Law in a Free Society: A Study of the British Town and Country Planning Act*. Cambridge: Harvard University Press, 1951.

———. "The Master Plan: An Impermanent Constitution." *Law and Contemporary Problems* 20, no. 3 (summer 1955): 353–418.

Harris, Harwell Hamilton. "Regionalism and Nationalism." *Student Publication of the School of Design North Carolina State* 14, no. 5 (1965): 25–33.

Hegemann, Werner. *City Planning, Housing*. 3 vols. New York: Architectural Book Publishing Co., 1936.

Hegemann, Werner, and Elbert Peets. *The American Vitruvius: An Architect's Handbook of Civic Art*. New York: Architectural Book Publishing Co., 1922.

Hitchcock, Henry-Russell. *Latin American Architecture since 1945*. New York: Museum of Modern Art, 1955.

Hoover, Robert C. "On Master Plans and Constitutions." *Journal of the American Institute of Planners* 26, no. 1 (February 1960): 5–24.

Hudnut, Joseph. "The Political Art of Architecture." *Journal of the American Institute of Architects* (June 1946): 289–98.

———. "The Political Art of Planning." *Architectural Record* (October 1944): 45–48.

Ichaso, Francisco. "La nueva conciencia cubana y la constituyente de 1940." *Bohemia* 44 (1952): 35, 87.

"In Search of a New Monumentality." *Architectural Review* 104 (September 1948): 117–29.

"Información general sobre la conveniencia de una ley de planificación." *Arquitectura* 21, no. 238 (May 1953): 182–94.

"Iniciado del Fórum sobre el Monumento al Apóstol Martí y la Plaza de la República." *Diario de la Marina*, May 12, 1953, 1, 22.

Isenstadt, Sandy. "US Embassy in Baghdad." In *Sert, 1928–1979: Half a Century of Architecture*, edited by Josep M. Rovira, 207–17. Barcelona: Fundació Joan Miró, 2005.

Jorrín, Miguel. "La fenomenología y el derecho [I]." *Universidad de la Habana Publicación Bimestral*, no. 23 (March/April 1939): 165–89.

———. "La fenomenología y el derecho [II]." *Universidad de la Habana Publicación Bimestral*, no. 24–25 (May/June/July/August 1939): 183–216.

"José Luis Sert." *Architectural Record* (January 1958): 125–40.

Junta de Planificación de Puerto Rico. *Ley de Planificación*. Santurce: Departamento de Hacienda, 1955.

———. *Reglamento de zonas antiguas e históricas.* San Juan: Junta de Planificación de Puerto Rico, 1955.

Junta Nacional de Planificación. *JNP Primera Exposición.* Havana: Junta Nacional de Planificación, 1957.

———. *La ley sobre planificación, la JNP.* Havana: Junta Nacional de Planificación, 1955.

Keith, Nathaniel S., and Carl Feiss. "A Report on the Renewal Possibilities of the Historic Triangle of the City of San Juan." Washington, D.C., 1955.

Kelsen, Hans. *General Theory of Law and State.* Cambridge: Harvard University Press, 1945.

Kirstein, Lincoln. *The Latin-American Collection of the Museum of Modern Art.* New York, 1943.

Kubler, George. *Mexican Architecture of the Sixteenth Century.* New Haven: Yale University Press, 1948.

———. "Mexican Urbanism in the Sixteenth Century." *Art Bulletin* 24, no. 2 (June 1942): 160–71.

Kunz, Josef L. "An Introduction to Latin-American Philosophy of Law." *University of Toronto Law Journal* 15, no. 2 (1964): 259–82.

———. "Latin American Philosophy of Law in the Twentieth Century." *New York University Law Quarterly Review* 24, nos. 2, 3, 4 (April, July, October 1949): 283–318, 473–513, 801–44.

———. "Teoría general del derecho [Book Review]." *Harvard Law Review* 55, no. 7 (May 1942): 1240–42.

"La conferencia del Prof. Paul Lester Wiener." *Arquitectura* (June 1954): 259–61.

"La Havane." *L'Architecture d'aujourd'hui* (February–March 1960): 62–71.

Labatut, Jean. "Monuments and Memorials." In *Forms and Functions of Twentieth-Century Architecture,* edited by Talbot Hamlin, vol. 3, 521–33. New York: Columbia University Press, 1952.

Larrazabal, Padrón, ed. *Manifiestos de Cuba.* Seville: Universidad de Sevilla, 1975.

Lazcano y Mazón, Andrés María. *Constitución de Cuba (con los debates sobre su articulado y transitorias en la convención constituyente).* 3 vols. Havana: Cultural, 1941.

———. *Las constituciones de Cuba.* Madrid: Ediciones Cultura Hispánica, 1952.

Lazo, Raimundo. *Martí y la Política.* Havana: Universidad de la Habana, 1946.

Le Corbusier. "Description of the CIAM Grid, Bergamo 1949." In *The Heart of the City,* edited by Jaqueline Tyrwhitt, 171–76. New York: Pellegrini and Cudahy, 1952.

———. "Grille CIAM d'urbanisme." *L'Architecture d'aujourd'hui* (January 1949): 1–27.

———. *The Modulor.* Cambridge: Harvard University Press, 1954.

———. *Modulor 2.* Cambridge: Harvard University Press, 1958.

———. *Œuvre complète, 1946–1952.* Zurich: W. Boesiger, 1953.

———. "Tools of Universality." *Transformations,* no. 1 (1950): 40–42.

Le Corbusier and Jean Giraudoux. *La charte d'Athènes, avec un discours liminaire de Jean Giraudoux.* Paris: Plon, 1943. Translated by Anthony Eardley as *The Athens Charter.* New York: Grossman Publishers, 1973.

Leclerc, Bénédicte, ed. *Jean-Claude Nicolas Forestier 1861–1930: Du jardin au paysage urbain.* Paris: Picard, 1990.

Lejeune, Jean-François. "The City as Landscape: Jean-Claude Nicolas Forestier and the Great Urban Works of Havana, 1925–1930." *Journal of Decorative and Propaganda Arts*, no. 22 (1996): 150–85.

———. "La Ville et le Paysage: Influences et projets américains." In *Jean-Claude Nicolas Forestier 1861–1930: Du jardin au paysage urbain*, edited by Bénédicte Leclerc. Paris: Picard, 1990.

———, ed. *Cruelty and Utopia: Cities and Landscapes of Latin America*. New York: Princeton Architectural Press, 2005.

Loomis, John A. *Revolution of Forms: Cuba's Forgotten Art Schools*. New York: Princeton Architectural Press, 1999.

Mañach, Jorge. "El Monumento a Martí (historia de un lauro frustrado)." *Bohemia*, May 24, 1953, 64, 98.

———. *El pensamiento de Dewey y su sentido americano*. Havana: Comisión Nacional Cubana de la UNESCO, 1953.

———. "El santo temor a lo irremediable." *Diario de la Marina*, May 13, 1953.

———. *Examen del quijotismo*. Buenos Aires: Editorial Sudamericana, 1950.

———. *Filosofía del quijotismo*. Havana: Universidad de la Habana, 1947.

———. *Indagación del choteo*. Havana: La Verónica, 1940.

———. *Martí, el apóstol*. Madrid: Espasa-Calpe, 1933.

———. *Pasado vigente*. Havana: Editorial Trópico, 1939.

Manuel de Céspedes, Carlos. "Aproximación a la constitución de 1940." *Encuentro*, no. 24 (spring 2002): 171–89.

Maribona, Armando. "Ha quedado inaugurada la primera Exposición cubana de Urbanismo en el Lyceum Lawn Tennis Club." *Diario de la Marina*, September 17, 1942.

———. "Tiende al desarrollo económico la Ley de Planificación Nacional." *Arquitectura* 23, no. 260 (March 1955): 128–30.

Martí, José. *The America of José Martí*. Translated by Juan de Onís. New York: Noonday Press, 1953.

———. *Obras completas de Martí*. Edited by Gonzalo de Quesada y Miranda. 74 vols. La Havana: Editorial Trópico, 1936–53.

Martínez, Juan A. *Cuban Art and National Identity: The Vanguardia Painters, 1927–1950*. Gainesville: University Press of Florida, 1994.

Martínez Inclán, Pedro. "Arqueología versus arquitectura." *Arquitectura* 14, no. 150 (1946): 6–13.

———. *Código de Urbanismo: Carta de Atenas, Carta de la Habana*. Havana: P. Fernández y Cía, 1949.

———. *La Habana actual: Estudio de la capital de Cuba desde el punto de vista de la arquitectura de ciudades*. Havana: P. Fernández y Cía, 1925.

———. "Urbanismo." *Arquitectura*, no. 190 (1949): 133–40.

Martínez Sáenz, Joaquín. "La economía: Liberalismo y planificación." *Cuadernos de la Universidad del Aire del Circuito CMQ*, no. 1 (1949): 57–63.

Masiello, Francine. "Rethinking Neocolonial Esthetics: Literature, Politics, and Intellectual Community in Cuba's *Revista de Avance*," *Latin American Research Review* 28, no. 2 (1993): 3–31.

McCoy, Esther. "Concrete Shell Forms—Félix Candela." *Arts and Architecture* (1957): 16–19, 32.
Mendelson, Jordana. *Documenting Spain: Artists, Exhibition Culture, and the Modern Nation, 1929–1939*. University Park: Pennsylvania State University Press, 2005.
Menocal, Narciso G. "Lo cubano in Cuban Architecture, 1924–1964." *Herencia* 7, no. 1 (summer 2001): 38–43.
Mesa Rodríguez, Manuel I. *La casa natal de Martí*. Havana: Comisión Nacional Organizadora de los Actos y Ediciones del Centenario y del Monumento de Martí, 1954.
Miller, Nicola. "The Absolution of History: Uses of the Past in Castro's Cuba." *Journal of Contemporary History* 38, no. 1 (2003): 147–62.
Montoulieu, Eduardo. "Architect Explains Need of City Planning Body in Cuba." *Havana Post*, September 6, 1942.
———. "El verdadero urbanismo se basa en estadísticas." *Arquitectura* 13, no. 139 (February 1945): 55–58.
———. "Enfoque sobre el urbanismo contemporáneo." *El Cusol*, June 17, 1942.
———. "La enseñaza de la planificación." *Arquitectura* 26, no. 294 (January 1958): 21–28.
———. "Lo que es y lo que pudiera ser Varadero." *Carteles*, January 17, 1943, 26–27.
———. *Planificación: Contribución al mejor conocimiento de su posible función en Cuba ordenando el medio social, económico, físico, político y administrativo; el mejor instrumento de buen gobierno*. Havana, 1956.
———. "Relación entre los planos regionales y el nacional, importancia de este último y sus objetivos." *Arquitectura* 26, no. 301 (August 1958): 353–58.
Mumford, Eric. "CIAM and Latin America." In *Sert, arquitecto en Nueva York*, edited by Xavier Costa and Guido Hartray, 48–75. Barcelona: ACTAR, 1997.
———. *The CIAM Discourse on Urbanism, 1928–1960*. Cambridge: MIT Press, 2000.
———. *Defining Urban Design: CIAM Architects and the Formation of a Discipline, 1937–1969*. New Haven: Yale University Press, 2009.
Mumford, Lewis. *The South in Architecture*. New York: Harcourt Brace, 1941.
Neumann, Dietrich, ed. *Architecture of the Night: The Illuminated Building*. Munich: Prestel, 2002.
Neutra, Richard. "Puerto Rico: Island of Promise." *Survey Graphic* 33, no. 6 (June 1944): 293–95.
Nuttall, Zelia. "Royal Ordinances concerning the Laying Out of New Towns." *Hispanic American Historical Review* 4, no. 4 (November 1921): 743–49.
———. "Royal Ordinances concerning the Laying Out of Towns." *Hispanic American Historical Review* 5, no. 2 (May 1922): 249–54.
"Obras Públicas." *Guceta Oficial de la República de Cuba* 53, no. 30 (February 5, 1955): 2119–21.
Orozco, Gómez de. "Las Leyes de Indias." *Investigaciones históricas* 1, no. 2 (January 1939): 134–39.
Ortega y Gasset, José. *España invertebrada*. Madrid: Revista de Occidente, 1946.
———. *Meditations on Quixote*. New York: W. W. Norton, 1961.
———. *The Revolt of the Masses*. New York: W. W. Norton, 1957.

Ortiz, Fernando. *Contrapunteo cubano del tabaco y el azúcar.* Havana: Jesús Montoro, 1940. Reprinted with translation by Harriet de Onís as *Cuban Counterpoint, Tobacco and Sugar.* Durham, N.C.: Duke University Press, 1995.

Otero-Pailos, Jorge. *Architecture's Historical Turn: Phenomenology and the Rise of the Postmodern.* Minneapolis: University of Minnesota Press, 2010.

Padilla, Bartolomé S. "La importancia que tiene para la Habana el Centro Cívico con el Monumento al Apóstol Martí." *Arquitectura* 20 (1950): 542–45.

"Patronato Pro-Urbanismo." *Arquitectura,* no. 106 (May 1942): 187–89.

Pearlman, Jill. *Inventing American Modernism: Joseph Hudnut, Walter Gropius, and the Bauhaus Legacy at Harvard.* Charlottesville: University of Virginia Press, 2007.

Pedret, Annie. "Dismantling the CIAM Grid: New Values for Modern Architecture." In *Team 10, 1953–81: In Search of a Utopia of the Present,* edited by Max Risselada and Dirk van den Heuvel, 252–57. Rotterdam: NAi, 2005.

"Pérez Benitoa habló en el Fórum sobre la Plaza de la República." *Diario de la Marina,* May 14, 1953, 1, 15.

Pérez, Louis A. *Cuba: Between Reform and Revolution.* New York: Oxford University Press, 1988.

———. *Cuba and the United States: Ties of Singular Intimacy.* Athens: University of Georgia Press, 1990.

———. *Cuba under the Platt Amendment, 1902–1934.* Pittsburgh: University of Pittsburgh Press, 1986.

Phillips, R. Hart. *Cuba, Island of Paradox.* New York: McDowell Obolensky, 1959.

Picó, Rafael. "New Uses for a Roman Law." *Housing Yearbook* (1950): 39–40.

Pizza, Antonio, ed. *J. Ll. Sert y el Mediterráneo.* Barcelona: Ministerio de Fomento, 1997.

Pottage, Alain. "Architectural Authorship: The Normative Ambitions of Le Corbusier's Modulor." *AA Files,* no. 31 (1996): 64–70.

Préstamo, Felipe J. "City Planning in a Revolution: Cuba, 1959–61." *Planning Perspectives* 8, no. 2 (1993): 188–212.

Préstamo y Hernández, Felipe, and Marcos Antonio Ramos. *Cuba: Arquitectura y urbanismo.* Miami: Universal, 1995.

Quesada y Miranda, Gonzalo de. "El Monumento a Martí." *Arquitectura* 11, no. 123 (October 1943): 386–88.

———. "Martí y los monumentos." *Bohemia,* November 24, 1935.

Quintana, Nicolás. "Arquitectura cubana . . . una búsqueda de la verdad." *Arquitectura,* no. 309/310 (1959): 166–73.

———. "Cuba en su arquitectura y urbanismo." *Encuentro,* no. 18 (fall 2000): 9–22.

———. "Cuba en su arquitectura y urbanismo, los años 50: Pasado, presente y futuro." *Herencia* 7, no. 1 (summer 2001): 14–23.

Rama, Ángel. "La dialéctica de la modernidad en José Martí." In *Estudios Martianos,* 129–97. San Juan: Editorial Universitaria, Universidad de Puerto Rico, 1974.

———. *The Lettered City.* Durham, N.C.: Duke University Press, 1996.

"Rehabilitación de la Habana Antigua." *Boletín Informativo* 4 no. 2 (February 1955): 55–56.

Robinson, Charles Mulford. *Modern Civic Art, or, the City Made Beautiful.* New York: G. P. Putnam's Sons, 1903.

Rodó, José Enrique. *Ariel.* Translated by Margaret Sayers Peden. Austin: University of Texas Press, 1988.

Rodríguez, Eduardo Luis. *La Habana, arquitectura del siglo XX.* Barcelona: Blume, 1998.

———. *The Havana Guide: Modern Architecture 1925–1965.* New York: Princeton Architectural Press, 1999.

Roig de Leuchsenring, Emilio. *Los monumentos nacionales de la República de Cuba.* 2 vols. Havana: Junta Nacional de Arqueología y Etnología, 1957 and 1959.

Rojas, Rafael. *Essays in Cuban Intellectual History.* New York: Palgrave Macmillan, 2008.

Roldán Oliarte, Esteban. *Cuba en la mano: Enciclopedia popular ilustrada.* Havana: Imprenta Ucar García y Cía, 1940.

Rovira, Josep M. *José Luis Sert: 1901–1983.* Milan: Electa, 2003.

———, ed. *Sert, 1928–1979: Half a Century of Architecture.* Barcelona: Fundació Joan Miró, 2005.

Sánchez-Roca, Mariano. *Leyes civiles de Cuba y su jurisprudencia.* Havana: Editorial Lex, 1951.

———. *Legislación sobre edificación, urbanismo e hygiene.* Havana: Editorial Lex, 1943.

Sánchez-Roca, Mariano, Rafael Pérez Lobo, and Calixto Ruiz-Sierra. *Leyes civiles de la república de Cuba. Constitución de la república de 1940.* Havana: Editorial Lex, 1940.

Scarpaci, Joseph L., Roberto Segre, and Mario Coyula. *Havana: Two Faces of the Antillean Metropolis.* Chapel Hill: University of North Carolina Press, 2002.

Schnitter, Patricia. "José Luis Sert y Colombia: De la Carta de Atenas a una carta del hábitat." Ph.D. dissertation, Universitat Politécnica de Catalunya, 2002.

Secretaría de Obras Públicas. *Memoria del plan de obras del gobierno del Dr. Ramón Grau San Martín.* Havana: Ministerio de Obras Públicas, 1947.

Segre, Roberto. "La Habana de Forestier: Los epígones del modelo Haussmaniano en América Latina." *Quaderns,* no. 151 (March–April 1982): 19–26.

———. "La Habana de Sert: CIAM, ron y cha cha cha." *DANA,* no. 37/38 (1995): 120–24.

———. *Lectura crítica del entorno cubano.* Havana: Editorial Letras Cubanas, 1990.

———. "The Pearl of the Antilles: Havana's Tropical Shadows and Utopias." In *Cruelty and Utopia: Cities and Landscapes of Latin America,* edited by Jean-François Lejeune, 134–45. New York: Princeton Architectural Press, 2005.

———. "Pedro Martínez Inclán (1883–1957): Primero urbanista cubano." *Ciudad y Territorio* 32, no. 123 (spring 2000): 122–26.

Sert, José Luis. "The Architect and the City." In *The City in Mid-Century,* edited by H. Warren Dunham, 13–32. Detroit: Wayne State University Press, 1957.

———. *Can Our Cities Survive? An ABC of Urban Problems, Their Analysis, Their Solutions.* Cambridge: Harvard University Press, 1942.

———. "Centres of Community Life." In *The Heart of the City,* edited by Jaqueline Tyrwhitt, 3–16. New York: Pellegrini and Cudahy, 1952.

———. "CIAM 8: The Core of the City." *Transformation* 1, no. 2 (1951): 114–16.

———. "The Human Scale in City Planning." In *New Architecture and City Planning,* edited by Paul Zucker, 392–412. New York: Philosophical Library, 1944.

———. "Les plans régulateurs de Medellín et Bogotá." *L'Architecture d'aujourd'hui* 80 (October–November 1958): 73–75.

———. "The Rebirth of the Patio." In *José Luis Sert,* edited by Knud Bastlund, 134–35. Zurich: Les Éditions d'Architecture, 1967.

Sert, José Luis, and James Johnson Sweeney. *Antoni Gaudí.* London: Architectural Press, 1960.

Sert, José Luis, and Paul Lester Wiener. "Can Patios Make Cities?" *Architectural Forum* 99, no. 2 (August 1953): 124–31.

———. "Conditions générales de l'urbanisme en Amérique Latine." *L'Architecture d'aujourd'hui* 21, no. 33 (December–January 1950–51): 4–9.

———. "Urbanisme en Amérique du Sud; town planning in South America." *L'Architecture d'aujourd'hui* 21, no. 33 (December–January 1950–51): 1–55.

———. "The Work of Town Planning Associates in Latin America 1945–1956." *Architectural Design* 27, no. 6 (June 1957): 190–213.

Shanken, Andrew M. "The Uncharted Kahn: The Visuality of Planning and Promotion in the 1930s and 1940s." *Art Bulletin* 88, no. 2 (June 2006): 310–27.

Smith, Robert C. "Colonial Towns of Spanish and Portuguese America." *Journal of the Society of Architectural Historians* 14, no. 4 (December 1955): 3–12.

Smith, Robert Freeman. "Twentieth-Century Cuban Historiography." *Hispanic American Historical Review* 44, no. 1 (1964): 44–73.

Solá, Miguel. *Historia del arte hispano-americano: Arquitectura, escultura, pintura y artes menores en la América espãnola durante los siglos XVI, XVII y XVIII.* Barcelona: Editorial Labor, 1935.

Sorhegui, Agustín. "La ubicación del Banco Nacional." *Arquitectura* 22, no. 253 (1954): 325–29.

Stanislawski, Dan. "Early Spanish Town Planning in the New World." *Geographical Review* 37, no. 1 (January 1947): 94–105.

———. "The Origin and Spread of the Grid-Pattern Town." *Geographical Review* 36, no. 1 (January 1946): 105–20.

Sweig, Julia. *Inside the Cuban Revolution: Fidel Castro and the Urban Underground.* Cambridge: Harvard University Press, 2002.

Thomas, Hugh. *Cuba: The Pursuit of Freedom.* New York: Harper & Row, 1971.

Torre, Amalia V. de la. *Jorge Mañach, maestro del ensayo.* Miami: Ediciones Universal, 1978.

Town Planning Associates. "Housing, Cuba: A Proposal for Community Planning." *Architects Yearbook,* no. 6 (1955): 83–88.

———. *Plan Piloto de la Habana.* New York: Wittenborn Art Books, 1959.

Tugwell, Rexford G. "The Fourth Power." Cambridge: American Institute of Planners, 1939.

———. *The Place of Planning in Society.* San Juan: Puerto Rico Planning Board, 1954.

———. "The Utility of the Future for the Present." *Public Administration Review* 8, no. 1 (winter 1948): 49–59.

Tyrwhitt, Jaqueline. "Cores within the Urban Constellation." In *The Heart of the City,* edited by Jaqueline Tyrwhitt, 103–8. New York: Pellegrini and Cudahy, 1952.

———, ed. *The Heart of the City.* New York: Pellegrini and Cudahy, 1952.

"Una obra del Arq. Emilio del Junco: El reparto Santa Catalina." *Arquitectura* 26, no. 305 (December 1958): 552–58.
"Urban Design." *Progressive Architecture* (August 1956): 97–112.
Venegas Fornias, Carlos. *La urbanización de las murallas: Dependencia y modernidad.* Havana: Letras Cubanas, 1990.
Violich, Francis. "Planning in South America." *Journal of the American Institute of Planners* 23, no. 3 (1957): 112–25.
Weiss, Joaquín E. *Arquitectura cubana colonial.* Havana: Cultural, 1936.
———. "La nueva morfología de la historia aplicada a la arquitectura." *Universidad de la Habana Publicación Bimestral,* nos. 73–75 (July–December 1947): 248–61.
———. "Ventanas y balcones coloniales." *Arquitectura* X, no. 103 (February 1942): 42–46.
White, Hayden. *Figural Realism: Studies in the Mimesis Effect.* Baltimore: Johns Hopkins University Press, 1999.
Whitney, Robert. *State and Revolution in Cuba: Mass Mobilization and Political Change, 1920–1940.* Chapel Hill: University of North Carolina Press, 2001.
Wiener, Paul Lester. "El ambiente humano y el urbanismo." *Nuestra Arquitectura,* no. 320 (1956): 20–23.
———. "Future World's Fairs." In *New Architecture and City Planning,* edited by Paul Zucker, 108–24. New York: Philosophical Library, 1944.
———. "New Trends Will Affect the Core." In *The Heart of the City,* edited by Jaqueline Tyrwhitt, 81–86. New York: Pellegrini and Cudahy, 1952.
Wright, Gwendolyn. *The Politics of Design in French Colonial Urbanism.* Chicago: University of Chicago Press, 1991.
Zucker, Paul, ed. *New Architecture and City Planning, a Symposium.* New York: Philosophical Library, 1944.

Index

TIMOTHY HYDE is associate professor of architecture at the Graduate School of Design, Harvard University.